TEXAS RISING

ALSO BY STEPHEN L. MOORE

Pacific Payback: The Carrier Aviators Who Avenged Pearl Harbor at the Battle of Midway

Battle Surface! Lawson P. "Red" Ramage and the War Patrols of the USS Parche

Presumed Lost: The Incredible Ordeal of America's Submarine POWs During the Pacific War

Relic Quest: A Guide to Responsible Relic Recovery Techniques with Metal Detectors

Savage Frontier: Rangers, Riflemen, and Indian Wars in Texas. Volume IV: 1842–1845

European Metal Detecting Guide: Techniques, Tips and Treasures

Last Stand of the Texas Cherokees: Chief Bowles and the 1839 Cherokee War in Texas

War of the Wolf: Texas' Memorial Submarine, World War II's Famous USS Seawolf

Savage Frontier: Rangers, Riflemen, and Indian Wars in Texas. Volume III: 1840–1841

Spadefish: On Patrol with a Top-Scoring World War II Submarine

Savage Frontier: Rangers, Riflemen, and Indian Wars in Texas. Volume II: 1838–1839

Eighteen Minutes: The Battle of San Jacinto and the Texas Independence Campaign

Savage Frontier: Rangers, Riflemen, and Indian Wars in Texas. Volume I: 1835–1837

Taming Texas: Captain William T. Sadler's Lone Star Service

The Buzzard Brigade: Torpedo Squadron Ten at War (with William J. Shinneman and Robert W. Gruebel)

TEXAS RISING

The Epic True Story of the Lone Star Republic and the Rise of the Texas Rangers, 1836–1846

★

STEPHEN L. MOORE

WILLIAM MORROW
An Imprint of HarperCollinsPublishers

TEXAS RISING. Copyright © 2015 A&E Television Networks, LLC and ITVS Studios, Inc. All rights reserved. Printed in the United States of America. No part of this book may be used or reproduced in any manner whatsoever without written permission except in the case of brief quotations embodied in critical articles and reviews. For information address HarperCollins Publishers, 195 Broadway, New York, NY 10007.

HarperCollins books may be purchased for educational, business, or sales promotional use. For information please e-mail the Special Markets Department at SPsales@harpercollins.com.

A hardcover edition of this book was published in 2015 by William Morrow, an imprint of HarperCollins Publishers.

FIRST WILLIAM MORROW PAPERBACK EDITION PUBLISHED 2016.

Designed by Jamie Lynn Kerner

Map of Texas, 1836, by Nick Springer
Map of San Jacinto by Gary Zaboly, illustrator, from Texian Iliad: A Military History of the Texas Revolution, courtesy of Stephen L. Hardin

Library of Congress Cataloging-in-Publication Data has been applied for.

ISBN 978-0-06-239431-6

16 17 18 19 20   DIX/RRD   10 9 8 7 6 5 4 3 2 1

CONTENTS

Map of Texas, 1836   vii
Map of the Battle of San Jacinto   viii
Prologue   1

1   Ranger Life   5
2   Seeds of Rebellion   19
3   "Come and Take It"   33
4   "The Day Was Soon Ours"   45
5   The Raven   55
6   Revolutionary Rangers   76
7   "You May All Go to Hell and I Will Go to Texas"   84
8   "I Shall Never Surrender or Retreat"   98
9   The Fall of the Alamo   119
10   Fannin's Battle at Coleto Creek   134
11   "Damned Anxious to Fight"   149
12   The Fork in the Road   166
13   "Daring Chivalry": The First Duel   183
14   Slaughter at San Jacinto   204
15   Texas Rising   223
16   New Challenges for a New Nation   230
17   Lamar's Cherokee War of Extinction   255
18   War with the Comanches   288
19   Captain Devil Jack   302
20   Triumph at Walker's Creek   326

Epilogue   337
Acknowledgments   341
Notes   343
Bibliography   367
Index   379

REPUBLIC OF TEXAS

UNITED STATES

Natchitoches

Sabine R

Red R

[Fort Kickapoo]

Nacogdoches

San Augustine

[Fort Houston]

Houston

Parker's Fort (Fort Sterling)

El Camino Real

Angelina R

Jasper

Neches R

Trinity R

Neches R

Brazos R

Trinity R

San Jacinto R

Colorado R

[Fort Fisher (Waco)]

Fort Milam (Fort Viesca)

Leon R

San Saba R

[Little River Fort]

San Gabriel R

Nashville

Llano R

San Gabriel R

Brushy Cr

Tumlinson's Blockhouse

Washington

Liberty

Pedernales R

[Austin]

Bastrop

Groce's Landing

Buffalo Bayou

San Jacinto

Anahuac

Medina R

Burnham's Crossing

San Felipe

New Washington

[Seguin]

Beason's Ferry

Gonzales

Harrisburg

Guadalupe R

Lavaca R

Colorado R

Navidad R

Fort Bend

San Antonio de Béxar

Frio R

San Antonio R

Columbia

Brazoria

SEE DETAILED MAP BELOW

COAHUILA

CLAIMED BY TEXAS AND MEXICO

Presidio del Rio Grande

Nueces R

Goliad (La Bahía)

Camp Coleto

Victoria

Matagorda

Gulf of Mexico

Guerrero

Refugio

Copano

Lipantitlán

San Patricio

El Camino Real

Laredo

Rio Grande

MEXICO

Revilla

Atascosito Trace

Monclova

Camargo

Reynosa

Saltillo

Monterrey

NUEVO LEÓN

Matamoros

TAMAULIPAS

Texas, 1836

- ▬▪▬ National boundary
- ▬ ▬ ▬ State boundary
- ▬▬▬ Major road
- ○ Named place
- [Name] Places and names after April 1836

0   50   100 miles

Maps by Nat Case, ©Springer Cartographics LLC

Troop Movements March–April, 1836

March 31

April 16 "The Fork in the Road"

San Jacinto R

Liberty

Burnham's Crossing

Groce's Landing

(Texans) March 24

San Felipe

April 18

April 21

March 20

March 18

March

(Mexicans) April 7

Buffalo Bayou

San Jacinto

LA BAHÍA ROAD

Beason's Ferry

Brazos R

Fort Bend

Harrisburg

New Washington

April 20

March 15

March 14

March 15

San Bernard R

April 15

April 12

Colorado R

Gonzales

▬▬▬ Mexican Forces
▬▬▬ Texan Forces

Battle of San Jacinto

Texian Army
Mexican Army
Attempted escape routes of Mexicans

San Jacinto River

Lynch's Ferry

Peggy's Lake

Marsh

Buffalo Bayou

TEXIAN CAMP

ARTILLERY

2ND REGIMENT

1ST REGIMENT

Road to New Washington

CAVALRY Col. Lamar

Gary Zaboly, illustrator, from *Texian Iliad: A Military History of the Texas Revolution*, courtesy of Stephen L. Hardin

TEXAS RISING

PROLOGUE

STEPHEN SPARKS COCKED THE hammer on his rifle as he moved stealthily forward.

The seventeen-year-old had left his schooling months earlier to join an uprising that had consumed his homeland. Sparks's Irish great-grandfather had perished in the Revolutionary War when America secured its independence from Great Britain. Now young Stephen Franklin Sparks was participating in his own war of rebellion—the efforts of Texas settlers (known as Texans or Texians) to secure their freedom from the reign of Mexico and its tyrannical leader, General Santa Anna.

It was just after 4 P.M. on April 21, 1836, and the moment of truth was at hand. Sparks and a little more than nine hundred Texians and *tejanos* (Hispanic residents of Texas) were advancing on the campground of the formidable Mexican Army. The Texans had endured six weeks of great hardships, mostly retreating before another army that had everything they did not: true uniforms, government-issued weapons, formalized training, and superior numbers.

But revolutionaries like Sparks possessed a unifying desire for vengeance that could scarcely be contained. The Mexican Army in recent weeks had overrun and slaughtered all the defenders of the Alamo presidio in San Antonio and had proceeded to capture more than four hundred Texans near Goliad.

Instead of holding these men prisoner until the raging Texas Revolution could be decided, Santa Anna had ordered them marched out from the fort to be shot down like wild dogs.

The self-equipped and largely non-uniformed Texas Army was led into battle on April 21 by General Sam Houston. This hard-drinking and quick-tempered officer was more prone to foul language and long marches away from the enemy than he was to instilling any confidence in his troops. Houston had been unable to contain the bloodthirsty desires of many under his command. Colonel Sidney Sherman, the fiery Kentuckian who now led a regiment of infantry, had very nearly stirred up a full-scale battle the previous afternoon—in defiance of Houston's orders. At the head of the Texas cavalry was a valiant Georgia poet named Mirabeau Lamar. A day ago, Colonel Lamar was a mere buck private but he knew how to work a crowd to make his wishes known. This afternoon, he held senior command of more than five dozen of the ablest gunslingers and scouts who had ever graced the wild frontiers of Texas.

Captain Juan Seguín, commander of a company of *tejanos* who had been performing mounted frontier defense duty in Texas for generations, was equally driven for revenge. His Mexican Texans wore playing cards in their hats and sombreros to help prevent them from being mistaken as enemy Mexican soldiers by their fellow Texians. Noble scout Deaf Smith, the cavalryman considered to be the eyes of the army, raced across the plains to announce that his men had successfully destroyed the only bridge over the nearby bayou. No more Mexican troops would be able to join the fight. Conversely, there would be no quick escape from the battlefield for either army's combatants. The stage was set.

Stephen Sparks noted an odd quiet over the Mexican Army's campground as his company advanced. He would be stunned to soon learn that many of the enemy's *soldados* were taking siestas, recovering from a forced overnight march. Other infantrymen lounged about, munching tortillas, while the cavalry had turned their horses loose to graze. Even General Santa Anna showed little concern for his guard detail. He was last seen retiring to his command tent in company with a beautiful captured mulatto servant girl.

Sparks's infantry company pushed through waist-high coastal prairie grass that helped conceal their advancement. They eased into a little thicket of moss-draped live oaks, striding silently but quickly forward. Their captain had ordered the men to hold their fire until they could see the whites of their enemies' eyes. Three hundred yards from the Mexican Army camp, they approached a gulley. In plain view beyond it was a tightly packed defensive breastworks, built by Mexican soldiers with crates, saddles, and brush to afford them some protection.

Colonel Sherman turned toward his Second Regiment of Infantry and barked the long-awaited order: "Charge!"

Sparks dashed toward the mounded barrier. Beyond it, stunned soldiers were leaping to their feet. He raised his Kentucky rifle, and touched his trigger. Flames and sparks erupted from the barrel and flintlock pan with a healthy roar and a swift kick to his shoulder. Only one other man of the Texan army had gotten off a shot ahead of him. Stephen grabbed his powder horn and ramrod to prepare his next shot, and snatched another molded lead ball from his shot pouch.

In the twenty seconds it took him to prime his weapon to fire another round, the world around him had erupted into chaos. Acrid black smoke climbed above the mossy trees. A cacophony of screams, shouts, curses, and the rippling cracks of black powder muskets, rifles, and pistols filled the air. To the right, the throaty roar of cannon fire shook the earth as the artillery came into play. All hell had broken loose. There would be no quarter.

"Remember Goliad!" shouted one Texian.

Another hoarse voice bellowed, "Remember the Alamo!"

Ramón Caro, personal assistant to General Santa Anna, found that his army had been taken by "complete surprise. The rest of the engagement developed with lightning rapidity."

The intense action erupting near the banks of the San Jacinto River, too close for the proper reloading of rifles and muskets, turned to hand-to-hand combat in many cases. To the victor would go proper claim to the newly proclaimed Republic of Texas.

Victory or death was the only order of the day.

1

RANGER LIFE

THIS WAS NOT WHAT George Erath had signed up for.

Since childhood, the twenty-two-year-old had dreamed of participating in a real military campaign. He had once marveled at the spectacle of passing masses of soldiers, properly uniformed and equipped with the finest firearms, trailing behind powerful cannons as they marched in step with martial music. He fancied it as "military glory"—regular meals, steady pay, and the enterprising life of an army on a dangerous expedition against a treacherous opponent. Erath's first opportunity to partake in such an armed expedition was playing out in late July 1835 at a frontier fortification in the eastern extremes of the Mexican territory called Texas.

The scene was less than majestic. Erath and his fellow men wore no formal uniforms with glittering epaulets and shiny brass buttons with gilded finish. They were instead adorned with primitive frontiersmen garb—homespun cotton shirts, buckskin pants, moccasins, and caps made from the furs of various mammals. His company had no imposing iron cannon nor had they been issued the latest quality percussion cap musket rifles. Each man carried his own hunting knife, long rifle or flintlock musket, smaller-caliber belt pistol, and shot pouch filled with molded lead musket balls.

Erath's company was not regular army but instead composed entirely of volunteer rangers. Such units operated in the fashion of early English colonial rangers, groups of self-armed men who served for short periods of time with no formal attachment to any organized military command. His company had been hurriedly assembled two weeks earlier in response to a call to help defend the frontier against Indian depredations. When Erath's company and three other volunteer units moved out, they had not marched in disciplined, picturesque columns. They instead rode some eighty miles north toward a remote frontier fort on their own farm horses or mules or on steeds borrowed from neighbors. There were but few promises that had enticed most to join the campaign: adventure, revenge against marauding foes deemed to be "savages," and healthy wages.

Erath and his fellow volunteers had been offered $1.25 per day served. He did not think to question whether anyone truly had the bankroll to compensate him for time served. The promised per diem was more than twice what the young man had been earning per month as a common laborer in the Mexican-ruled territory of Texas. The frontier on which he served was part of the Mexican state called Coahuila y Tejas (Coahuila and Texas)—one of the nineteen states and four territories that had been formed fourteen years earlier when the republic of Mexico fought for and won its independence from Spain in 1821.

Militia companies had operated in Texas since the first Anglo colonists had begun to settle but longer-term ranger companies had rarely served in Coahuila y Tejas. Erath was actually participating in the first-ever organized *battalion* of Texas Rangers to go on campaign against the Indians. None of the volunteer gunmen of his company—farmers, merchants, land speculators, men from all walks of life—were native to this region. All had been born in the United States or overseas. The company commander, Captain George Washington Barnett, was a forty-one-year-old doctor who had moved his practice from Tennessee to Texas only a year before. Twenty-eight-year-old First Lieutenant William Warner Hill, who made his living trading horses and mules, had only been in Texas for seven months. Private Isham G. Belcher, originally from Missouri, had settled ten years earlier, making him one of the oldest "Texians" of the unit.

Such was the mixed bag of settlers serving with Private Erath on the first of August 1835 when they rode into the little stockade and blockhouse fort recently constructed by the Parker family. Brothers James and Silas Parker had overseen the project and their results were impressive. The four-acre complex was surrounded by twelve-foot-high log walls, with the tops hewn to sharp points. On two corners, wooden blockhouses were built both as lookout posts and as bastions for firing upon attacking Indians. Six tiny cabins were attached to the inside walls of the fort. Each cramped cabin had a fireplace, a bed, a homemade meal table, and bare dirt floors. Thousands of acres of fertile croplands sprawled in the prairies surrounding Fort Parker. Their land lay in Robertson's Colony, and three of the married men—James Parker, Silas Parker, and their brother-in-law, Luther Thomas Martin Plummer—had each received a league and labor of land, amounting to forty-six hundred acres.

They built the fort near present Groesbeck near the headwaters of the Navasota River.[1]

George Erath noted the recuperating members of the volunteer ranger company of Captain Robert Morris Coleman, who had been at the Parker compound for several weeks. The young children of the outpost had become accustomed to the sights, sounds, and smells of dirty, rugged frontiersmen who now used the family's settlement as their temporary staging area. Nine-year-old Cynthia Ann Parker scurried about, trying to keep her younger siblings John, Silas Jr., and Orlena out of the way of the rangers. Tragedy had already fallen on her brother James, who was killed en route to Texas when the family's wagon lost a wheel and he was impaled through the chest by splintered wood. Erath was more captivated by his first sight of victims of Indian attack—three members of Coleman's company whose arrow and musket ball wounds were still being tended to by the Parker family.

It was a strange and deadly new world—being called forth on expedition against Indians—for George Bernard Erath. He had been born on January 1, 1813, in Vienna, Austria. His father, a tanner by trade, wanted more for his son than to be a hidesman. George studied both English and Spanish in his early school years, languages that he hoped would serve him well if he was to carry out his early dream of sailing to America one day. Erath had little desire to be pressed into the Austrian army for a lengthy service period. The Eraths had friends of influence who helped smuggle young George into the Polytechnic Institute at age twelve, two years before legal enrollment could occur.[2]

Erath managed only two years at the university before his father died, leaving him to return to help work with his mother and younger sisters to maintain the family business. His mother sent him to live with his uncle Jacob Erath in Rottenburg, Germany. His uncle died in April 1831, and with the help of relatives, he worked out his passage to America in 1832. He sailed on a U.S. brig bound for New Orleans. It was a perilous voyage plagued with a cholera epidemic and a hurricane that turned the seas into towering mountains. "The ship was dismantled to her lower joints, and the rigging, falling overboard on the leeward side, dragged the ship nearly on her side," recalled Erath.[3]

He arrived in New Orleans on June 22, 1832. Erath traveled via riverboat to Cincinnati in search of employment and was there forced to return to his hated family profession of tanning, making seventy-five cents per day. He worked long enough to save the money needed to reach Florence, Alabama, where he went to work for another tanner he had met in New Orleans. His pay was better and he liked Alabama but Erath had no intention of making a career out of tanning animal hides to produce leather. "By this time I had heard much of Texas, a land barely known in Europe," he wrote.[4]

He made his way to New Orleans in 1833 and secured passage on the schooner *Sabine* to Texas. He arrived at Velasco and then sailed on up the Brazos River. Erath moved toward Cole's Settlement, the highest settlement of any note on the Brazos, with the family of John W. Porter. When he arrived at the little settlement of Tenoxtitlan, only about a half dozen Mexican families occupied the area, along with another half dozen American families. Porter's family settled on a stream crossing the San Antonio Road, and Erath helped them build pens and shelters at their new place.

During the fall of 1834, Erath went to work for an elderly surveyor named Alexander Thomson. He was to be the chain carrier as they surveyed into leagues a section of the country twenty-file miles square, west of the Brazos and north of the

San Antonio Road. Surveying work was scarce during the winter so Erath earned income on Thomson's farm at the rate of seventeen dollars a month. He also located his own headright of one-quarter league of land from the Mexican government. On July 20, 1835, he gathered with sixteen other men in the town of Tenoxtitlan in Robertson's Colony and enrolled in the volunteer ranging company of Captain George Barnett.[5]

Their mission: to ride into Indian territory and help chastise a band of Indians who had recently fought a battle with another frontier company.

THE VOLUNTEERS AT PARKER'S Fort needed a leader.

Five ad hoc companies had rendezvoused by August 5, and there were even more opinions among the assembled farm boys, merchants, lawyers, and entrepreneurs as to who should properly lead their expedition. In the true spirit of rangers, a popular vote was cast and the men elected Colonel John Henry Moore into command. The thirty-five-year-old farmer and stock raiser from Tennessee had been among the Old Three Hundred original settlers of Texas. Moore made his home on the Colorado River, laying out the town of La Grange in 1831, where he owned a twin blockhouse known as Moore's Fort. He was a natural leader of men who had made a previous expedition against Huaco (Waco) and Tawakoni Indians on the upper Brazos River the previous year.

Moore turned command of his company over to a twenty-seven-year-old Michigan native, Captain Michael R. Goheen. The other three most recent ranging companies to reach Fort Parker were those of Captains Barnett, Philip Haddox Coe, and Robert McAlpin Williamson. Captain Coe, thirty-five, had been born in Georgia and later moved to Texas in 1831 from Alabama. Captain Williamson, known as "Three-Legged Willie," was a feisty lawyer and former editor of one of the first newspapers in Texas. He had been crippled by a bone infection known as white swelling at age fifteen that left his right leg drawn back at the knee and forced him to be fitted with a wooden leg from the knee to the ground. Known to friends simply as "Willie," Williamson was able to ride and fight with the ablest of men.

The fifth company gathered at Parker's Fort was commanded by the man who was the source of all the commotion, Captain Robert Coleman. The War of 1812 veteran had campaigned against the Indians during the past two months and was bloodthirsty for more action. The thirty-eight-year-old lawyer originally from Christian County, Kentucky, was known as a skilled horseman and marksman. Coleman had moved for a time to Alabama, married Elizabeth Bounds, and began raising his family. He returned to Kentucky in 1825 and began farming cotton. The following year, he listened to a stranger named Sterling Robertson, who had traveled from Texas with promises of a new life in a vast new territory.

Robertson said that he was recruiting settlers for his new colony, where each head of a farming family would receive 177 acres of rich bottomland and 4,428 acres of pastureland for their stock. The new residents were exempt from taxes, and the land was abundant with wild game, fruits, and a relatively mild climate. Coleman was likely interested in the pitch to settle in Texas, but another five years would pass before he made his move. During that time, he lost both his mother and his youngest daughter, Caroline, who passed away in 1830. Robert and Elizabeth Coleman arrived in Texas in May 1831 with their four surviving children and settled near the town of Mina (later renamed Bastrop). They established a homestead on the east side of the Colorado River, a mile or two from the river, on what was known as Webber's Prairie. Robert Coleman was well respected by his peers, and he became the first alcalde, or mayor, of Mina in 1834. The biggest trouble in the early days of his community was the occasional depredations carried out by various raiding Indian parties.[6]

Several violent encounters had transpired during the early months of 1835, and by May relations with the "wild Indians" reached a serious level. The Bastrop-area citizens were concerned enough to form a five-man safety committee, of which Edward Burleson was a member. The colonists employed Caddo Chief Canoma, long considered to be friendly to Anglo colonists, to go into the field to hold peace talks to attempt to secure the release of two small children who had been taken captive. Canoma returned with disturbing news: at least half of the Indians he had visited were opposed to making peace with white settlers who had moved into the upper areas of the Colorado River. Chief Canoma also reported that the most unsettled Indians were on the move toward the settlement at Bastrop where Coleman lived.[7]

The settlers at the Falls of the Brazos sent runner Samuel McFall to race ahead to warn the Bastrop citizens. Before he could arrive, a group of eight Indians attacked a party of Anglo wagoneers on the road from San Felipe to Bastrop on June 1, near Pin Oak Creek. Amos R. Alexander was killed outright and his son was gravely wounded. The younger Alexander had been shot through the body but he lived long enough to race his horse back toward Moore's Fort, in the closest town of La Grange. He met the second wagon being hauled by a pair of teamsters his father had hired. Alexander died from his wounds and the teamsters raced into La Grange to spread the alarm.[8]

John Henry Moore raised a party of men at his twin blockhouse to pursue the killers. As this was going on, two settlers had stopped at the home of frontiersman John Marlin near the Falls of the Brazos. When the ill travelers' horses wandered off, Marlin employed Chief Canoma and his companion Dorcha to bring the horses back. They were still in the field when Captain Moore led his La Grange volunteers out to seek justice for the Alexander murders. They found and buried the bodies of the dead wagoneers but lost the trail of the Indians near the three forks of the Little River. Moore's party was joined in the field by another hastily assembled mounted group led by Captain Edward Burleson of Mina. The united force numbered sixty-one men, Robert Coleman being among Burleson's Mina company.[9]

Burleson and Moore led their men to a spot about fifty miles above the Falls of the Brazos and made camp for two days. Several of the volunteers who were out hunting encountered the friendly chief Canoma and a few other Indians. Because the Indians were traveling with well-shod American-style horses, they were apprehended under the suspicion of being guilty of theft. Robert Coleman announced that the Indians should be put to death for the Alexander murders, although Canoma protested that they were merely returning runaway horses for John Marlin.[10]

Burleson hoped to take the Caddos and Cherokees back into Mina for a fair trial, but he was ignored by his volunteers two-to-one in a common vote. Coleman and eight others lashed Canoma and his son Dorcha to trees, shot them to death, and released Canoma's wife into the wilderness to spread the word about what would happen to horse thieves in Texas. Some of the white volunteers were appalled by the senseless murders and left their party. Settler Moses Cummins wrote in disgust, "Such men, in such a state of mind, are not apt to discriminate between guilt and innocence." George Erath added, "The pursuing settlers were indifferent as to whether they found Caddos or wild Indians." [11]

The two volunteer groups returned to their respective settlements, having taken two innocent lives as "revenge" for the murder of the Alexanders. The Mina safety committee decided to maintain an active armed presence of mounted riflemen to defend its citizens against any future Indian uprisings. Coleman was elected captain of the local ranging company of eighteen men on June 12, 1835. Captain Coleman wrote to the committee of his intentions, saying that he departed Bastrop on July 2 with his company "for the purpose of chastising those menaces to civilized men." [12]

Coleman's rangers crossed the Brazos River at Washington on July 4 and made a campaign against the Tawakoni Indians living near Tehuacana Springs in present Limestone County. During the early morning hours of July 11, his men crawled up to the edge of the village, which contained an estimated one hundred Tawkonis, mixed with a few Caddos and Ionies. Coleman's company attacked, killing a number of the Indians, but they suffered one ranger killed and three badly wounded, including Bastrop store owner Jesse Halderman. Coleman's company retreated, falling back on nearby Parker's Fort to seek medical attention for his wounded men.

Captain Coleman rode for Viesca, the capital of Robertson's Colony, where he called out for reinforcements. "Those Indians must be chastised or this flourishing country abandoned, and again become a wilderness," he wrote on July 20. The word spread through the Texas colonies and four more mounted companies under Coe, Barnett, Moore, and Williamson had ridden to Coleman's aid. Silas Parker and Samuel Frost, residents of the little Parker fortification, provided beef, corn, bacon, and medical attention to the rangers assembled in their compound. The blistering August sun had scorched the prairie grasses in recent days but now a heavy front was turning the prairies into quagmires. The nearby Navasota River swelled from its banks, forcing Colonel Moore's expedition to camp at the fort several nights before moving out during the second week of August.

The party reached the Tawakoni village only to find that it had been recently abandoned. They rested their horses for two days while stocking up on the available crops. "We found sixty acres in corn, which was just hard enough to be gritted, and by making holes in the bottom of the tin cups we carried we fashioned graters, and supplied ourselves with bread," Erath related. The rangers also found plentiful supplies of pumpkins, watermelons, muskmelons, peas, and other vegetables raised by Indians.[13]

Once Moore's battalion departed the Tawakoni village, they moved twenty miles over the prairie before advance scouts rode back with the excited call, "Indians!" They had reached a heavy belt of timber extending along Pin Oak Creek, which emptied into the Trinity River. Colonel Moore and his adjutant James Clinton Neill quickly formed their companies into a battle line. Erath felt they "took as much precaution as if we were about to fight such formidable foes as Creeks, Cherokees, and Seminoles—foes the two had faced in their younger days under Jackson."

Some fifteen minutes were spent parading and arranging the riflemen, precious minutes that allowed the Indians in the forest ahead to move out. When Moore finally gave the order to charge, the more eager volunteers spurred their mounts forward. Erath was riding a young horse that had been captured from a herd of wild mustangs. His horse and that of Samuel McFall darted forward ahead of all others, charging several hundred yards through post oak timber over boggy soil. Some of the rangers thought it funny enough to nickname McFall "the Flying Dutchman." Erath whipped and cursed his fiery beast to try to contain his energy as the battalion leaders cursed at the two Texans who refused to maintain their place in the battle line. "Our steeds had determined to give us a reputation for bravery which we did not deserve," wrote Erath.

In the timber line, the rangers were met by their advance scouts, who brought news that the Indians, only a half dozen in number, had fled. They had taken flight as the troops were being organized. Erath found the whole affair to be a joke: one hundred strong, they had managed to capture only a single pony. "In camping near the place that night there was much laughing over the adventure," he said. The expedition was unable to overtake the Indians they were pursuing during the next days. The Indians found it easy to stay ahead of such a large and ill-formed force that had to contend with mud bogs and swollen streams. Moore's battalion did encounter a small camp of Wacos, killing one of them and capturing five others. They learned from their prisoners that a larger body of Indians was camped shortly ahead of them. Pushing forward at daylight, Moore's men found an Indian encampment abandoned so quickly that the Indians had cut the stake ropes to their horses.[14]

This was the final straw for many of the Brazos-area volunteers. Their horses were worn down from weeks of chasing Indians, and many of the men grumbled aloud that they were finished. Colonel Moore found a great division amongst his companies, but he was determined to carry on if possible. Some of Captain Coleman's men turned for home, as did the entire companies of Captains Barnett and Coe. Coleman was later paid as a captain of rangers through August 28, 1835, and

Captain Coe's men were paid until they mustered out in their settlement on August 31.

John Henry Moore pushed on with the remaining rangers, largely the companies of Captains Michael Goheen and Willie Williamson. They moved through the countryside up to the forks of the Trinity River, where Dallas now stands. Along the way, they struggled with their unruly Waco captives. One of the Indian women somehow managed to steal a knife one night in camp. She murdered her own infant daughter before turning the blade on herself to commit suicide. Captain Burleson called for a volunteer to speed her suffering, to which Oliver Buckman of Williamson's company drew his large homemade knife and put the Waco out of her misery.

The ill-fated expedition finally turned for home in early September, and encountered two more Indians in a timber grove along the way. The men with the fastest horses chased them into the forest, killing one and continuing to hunt the other. In the thicket, William Magill raised his rifle to fire at a fleeting figure rushing from the brush. He mistakenly hit Moses Smith Hornsby of Captain Goheen's company and nearly severed his arm. Hornsby agonized in pain for nearly two days before he died and was buried along the return trail. To protect his body from being further mutilated by Indians, his fellow rangers kindled a campfire on the dirt above his grave and left it burning to conceal his corpse.[15]

Colonel Moore's battalion reached Mina on September 13, where they were drummed out of service to return to their respective home settlements. "This was my first experience of war in Texas," wrote George Erath. More than one hundred strong, the five ranging companies had covered a vast section of East Texas with only meager results to show for their suffering. The campaign did instill some discipline in its volunteers, preparing them for future military service, and it helped create many future leaders who would guide Texas through some of its turmoil that lay ahead.

Robert Morris Coleman, the vengeful company commander who had helped stir up much of the Indian aggression, had laid the groundwork for the system that would become known as the Texas Rangers. His desire to continually operate a multi-company ranger battalion would take another year to realize. Loosely organized ranger companies had operated in conjunction with the Texas Militia since 1822, but within two months of the 1835 Moore campaign, Captain Coleman was recognized as being the organizer of the first Texas Ranger company legally organized by the new provisional government of Texas.

Coleman was not only instrumental in helping to emphasize the need for rangers. He was a leader who would have a central role as the seeds of rebellion began to grow in Texas. His involvement with the Texas Rangers would continue but a more powerful opponent than Indians would first command his attention for the next year.

2

SEEDS OF REBELLION

THE ANGLO AND TEJANO settlers of Texas had far more to fear than random Indian depredations in their near future. The seeds of a larger rebellion had been planted on almost the very day that *empresario* (colonization agent) Stephen Fuller Austin realized his late father's dream of colonizing Texas.

By the time Austin began bringing in his first settlers in 1823, the Texas territory had been claimed by Spain, France, and finally Mexico. Spanish explorer Francisco Vázquez de Coronado had crossed the Texas panhandle in 1541 during his fruitless quest to find the fabled Seven Cities of Cíbola. The name of the future republic of Texas came from the word *tejas,* a term meaning "friend" that was widely used by the Indians of that area. Spain had been the first European nation to claim what is now Texas, beginning in 1519, but the first Spanish settlement—Ysleta Mission in present El Paso—was not established until 1681. During that time, France had planted its flag in eastern Texas near the Gulf Coast. Fort St. Louis was founded by French nobleman and explorer René-Robert Cavelier (known more popularly by his title, Sieur de La Salle), who had hoped to establish a colony near the mouth of the Mississippi River. La Salle missed his mark and instead landed his colonists at Matagorda Bay on the Texas coast in February 1685.

The French flag was planted in Tejas soil, but it would not fly long. La Salle was killed by one of his own people two years later and the remaining colonists of Fort St. Louis struggled greatly to survive due to poor diet, exposure, and disease. The remaining men and women were massacred by coastal Karankawa Indians around Christmas 1688. The first European birth of record in Tejas was an infant born to the wife of Lieutenant Gabriel Barbier. The Karankawas killed Madame Barbier, then held her baby by its heels and smashed its head against a tree. French claims on Tejas evaporated by 1690.

Spain continued to claim all territories of the lower North American region from the Pacific shores of present California to the Gulf of Mexico as far east as the Florida panhandle. Mexico City was the center of Spain's empire in the New World. Their rival nation France continued to claim only the areas of Canada, Louisiana, and the Mississippi Valley. Spanish authorities decided to establish missions near the Rio Grande River to Christianize the natives there and to help guard their borders. The first Spanish mission settlement to be established deep within Texas in 1716 was Nacogdoches, named for the Nacogdoche Indians, a Caddo group.[1]

Twenty-six Spanish missions would be established for varying lengths of time between 1682 and 1793 within the future boundaries of what would become the state of Texas. Five missions were created between 1718 and 1731 near the head of the San Antonio River and a thriving town began growing around the first, San Antonio de Béxar Presidio. San Antonio de Béxar, known commonly as Béxar, became the capital of Spanish Texas in 1773 and its population had surpassed two thousand souls within another five years.

The North American territories changed ownership through the great conflicts of the eighteenth century—the French and Indian War, the American Revolution, and the French Revolution. Louisiana passed from French control to Spain and back to France in 1800, although Napoleon soon sold this territory to the United States. The acquisition of the Louisiana Purchase only gave President Thomas Jefferson an appetite to properly claim Texas. War was avoided between Spain and the United States by a temporary Neutral Ground that was established between Texas and Louisiana. Spain finally resolved the issue in 1819 by selling the Neutral Ground to the United States for $5 million with the agreement by U.S. secretary of state John Quincy Adams that all claims to Texas were renounced.

Spanish authorities were aware that Texas remained attractive to future American growth, but Spain had enjoyed little success in persuading its own citizens to move to the remote and sparsely populated region. As of 1820, there were but three settlements in the province of Texas: Nacogdoches, San Antonio de Béxar, and La Bahía del Espíritu Santo (later known as Goliad). Spain thus began recruiting foreigners to help develop their northern frontier in Texas. It was in this window of opportunity that fifty-eight-year-old American entrepreneur Moses Austin paid a visit to San Antonio de Béxar, the capital of the province.

Austin had previously established a lead-mining operation and colony in northern Louisiana, but the War of 1812 had slowly driven him into financial ruin. He arrived in Béxar a penniless man with a big plan. He would bring three hundred

hardworking Catholic families from the former Spanish territory of Louisiana to settle. The Mexican governor was unimpressed with the proposal but Moses Austin found support in
another opportunist, a former Dutch nobleman and current
Béxar alcalde who went by the lofty name Baron de Bastrop.
With the help of Bastrop, Austin convinced the Spanish governor of the advantages of his proposal.

Austin returned home to Missouri and began planning his
Anglo colonization of Texas. He had developed pneumonia,
however, and the illness claimed his life in June 1821 before his
dreams could be fulfilled. To his wife, Maria, his last wish was
conveyed: his eldest son Stephen should take over the *empresario* business he had started. With great reluctance, Stephen
Austin decided to take over his father's venture even as Mexico
was fighting a war of independence with Spain. He arrived in
San Antonio in August 1821, just as a treaty granting Mexican
independence was being signed. He found his father's deal to
be null and void, necessitating an eleven-month stay in Mexico
City to win the new government's approval. Austin returned
to New Orleans and published the invitation terms for colonists
to join him in settling the Brazos and Colorado river areas.
He would take as compensation twelve and a half cents per
acre, this on top of the sixty-seven thousand acres of land an
empresario was to receive for each two hundred families he
introduced.

The terms were simple. Colonists were demanded to take
an oath of loyalty to the new Mexican government of Mexico
and profess to be a Christian, with the Catholic Church being
the established religion of the region. In return, each married
head of family would receive at least one labor (177 acres) of
land if they farmed, and one league (4,428 acres) if they raised
stock. Austin and his land commissioner, Baron de Bastrop,

issued 272 titles during 1823–24. In all, 307 titles were issued, with nine families receiving two titles each—bringing the total number of land grantees to 297 instead of three hundred. Still, the original settlers of Austin's first colony were long referred to as the "Old Three Hundred." [2]

One early settler described the opportunity of settling in Texas during the 1820s as being as yearned for as California would become during its 1849 Gold Rush period. He wrote that colonists were "to be exempt from taxation six years from date of settlement, with the privilege of importing, duty free, everything they might desire for themselves and families." He found "an abundance of game, wild horses, cattle, turkeys, buffalo, deer, and antelope by the drove. The woods abounded in bee trees, wild grapes, plums, cherries, persimmons, haws, and dewberries, while walnuts, hickorynuts, and pecans were abundant along the water courses." The winter climate was mild enough so that buckskin sufficed in the summer and heavier buffalo robes or bearskins afforded ample protection in the winter. "Corn in any quantity was to be had for the planting," he added. [3]

The people built dogtrot-style windowless cabins from logs, with chimneys for heat and cooking. Floors were either dirt or wood plank, which were sawed by hand from logs. Farmers began working the land, building new and better lives for themselves. The encroaching white men soon found resistance with the numerous Indians, whose ancestors had lived there for many generations. In 1821, some thirty-five hundred white settlers had inhabited Texas but they were outnumbered nearly six-to-one by approximately twenty thousand Indians. The Karankawas were the main threat to coastal settlers while Wacos, Tonkawas, and Tawakonis were tribes that had long inhabited the inner regions of the Texas area. Relations between both cultures were uneasy at best. Mexican authorities secretly hoped that the new immigrants would serve as a buffer against aggressive Indians. Instead a cultural and geographical divide was created in which the Anglo Texans were fairly subdivided from the Mexican Texans. Both communities still had to contend with Indians.[4]

Mexican citizens were concentrated in the region surrounding San Antonio. They also spread down the San Antonio River to La Bahía (Goliad) and beyond. Other Mexican rancheros herded cattle and sheep in the chaparral plains, with their towns stringing up the Rio Grande from Matamoros to Laredo. The Anglo settlements were virtually nonexistent west of the Guadalupe River. To the north, the Hill Country and the Edwards Plateau were ranged by Comanches, considered to be the finest horsemen of the continent.

The early Anglo settlers lived primarily in the coastal plains, prairies, and woodlands along the Trinity, Brazos, and Colorado rivers. The people took up planting crops of cotton and corn, and raising livestock. Not all of the Old Three Hundred were productive citizens, as Texas attracted its fair share of opportunists who sought refuge from past misfortunes or legal issues. Stephen Austin was granted civil and military power over his settlers by Mexican authorities. José Félix Trespalacios, the first Mexican governor of Texas, gave written orders for the colonists to create the Brazos and Colorado districts with mounted militia companies and to elect an alcalde, the equivalent of a justice of the peace, for each district. In December 1822, Josiah Bell was elected alcalde in the Brazos District and John Tumlinson Sr., alcalde in the Colorado District. Governor Trespalacios further advised the new alcaldes to administer justice and "to oppose the Karankawa or other intruders who might attack their persons or their property." Stephen Austin had been advised that detachments of Mexican troops might be deposited in the larger settlements but that he and his settlers were primarily responsible for their own defense.[5]

In early 1823, the two districts held popular elections for officers to lead local militia companies, electing Captain Robert Kuykendall for the Colorado District and Captain Andrew Robinson in the Brazos District. One of the first engagements between the Anglo settlers and Indians occurred that winter when three men paddling up the Colorado River were attacked by Karankawas near the mouth of Skull Creek. Two were killed but the third escaped badly wounded. A fourth man in a separate incident was also severely wounded by an arrow shot at him. Captain Kuykendall raised about twenty militiamen and found the Indian camp just after dawn. They killed between eight and twenty-five Indians, according to various accounts, and sustained no losses in the first organized Texas Militia action in Austin's colony.[6]

The roots of the Texas Rangers can be traced to both Spanish/Mexican and anglo influences. Alcalde John Tumlinson and Captain Kuykendall proposed to Governor Trespalacios in early spring 1823 that a more permanently manned company be stationed at the mouth of the Colorado River to construct blockhouses or fortifications to protect supplies and new colonists arriving by ship. They recommended for its commander Moses Morrison, an Old Three Hundred bachelor settler who had recently been elected as a lieutenant in the militia. On May 5, 1823, Lieutenant Morrison mustered in his first ten men, apparently unable to raise his allotted fifteen men even with the promise of pay. It was the first standing militia command of Austin's first colony and as such performed as had earlier rangers of English colonial groups, who "ranged" the frontier as partisan fighters separate from any regular army or militia unit.[7]

Morrison's men spent much of their time on the Colorado River trying to find enough food to sustain themselves. They returned to their settlement in August to find that alcalde John Tumlinson had been murdered by Karankawa and Waco Indians on July 6 while en route to San Antonio. His nineteen-year-old son, John Jackson Tumlinson Jr., raised a posse that tracked down a band of thirteen Wacos camped above the present town of Columbus. Captain Tumlinson's younger brother Joseph killed the first Indian and the remainder of the company dispatched all but one of the remainder.[8]

John Tumlinson Jr., no doubt feeling great anger for the murder of his father, would become one of the foremost ranger leaders and Indian fighters of the early years of Texas. Moses Morrison's original ranging unit, promised fifteen dollars per month in land from Stephen Austin's personal holdings, had disbanded by the fall. The militia system would continue for the colonists, aided by a new Mexican national law of April 1823 that made every male citizen between the ages of eighteen and fifty subject to such service. In the ensuing years, Austin's colony consisted of six militia districts. Representatives met in August 1826 and they drew up a plan for a Ranger company of twenty to thirty mounted men. Each landowner would serve for a month, or furnish a substitute, for every half league of land owned.[9]

Militia companies fought a number of small battles with Karankawas and other tribes during the first years of Austin's colonization. John Tumlinson took part in another Indian offensive in 1826 against a party of sixteen Tawakoni Indians who had stolen horses from the settlements. The riflemen caught the Tawakoni camp by surprise, killing or wounding most of the Indians. Aside from the brief forays into the wilderness to pursue marauding Indians, the colonists did not keep constantly manned ranging companies in service during this time. The next exception to this rule occurred in January 1827, when Colonel Austin marched his militia out to Nacogdoches to maintain order during the Fredonian Rebellion, a dispute between the Mexican government and local settlers regarding land grants. During his absence, Austin ordered Captain Abner Kuykendall and eight other men "to range the country" between the Brazos and Colorado rivers along the San Antonio Road. Kuykendall's rangers were short-lived as the rebels holed up in the Old Stone Fort in Nacogdoches fled when Colonel Austin's militia and Mexican soldiers arrived in town.[10]

The 1826 Fredonian Rebellion was but one of several sparks that would lead to rising tensions between the Mexican government and the new colonists, who were increasingly desirous of independence. Two other major events occurred in the coastal settlement of Anahuac, one in 1832 and one in 1835. The town was named by Colonel John (Juan) Davis Bradburn, a Virginia-born mercenary who had earned his commission while fighting for Mexican independence. Bradburn was ordered by Commandant General Manuel de Mier y Terán to erect a Mexican garrison and customs house on the northeastern edge of Galveston Bay.

Bradburn was placed at Anahuac to enforce the collection of duties and to help control the increased smuggling of slaves, goods, and illegal immigrants into Texas. He created great tensions among the local settlers by refusing to allow Mexican authorities to issue settlers' titles and by collecting the resented customs, even though the exemption from paying such tariffs granted to Austin's colonists had expired. Among the leaders opposing the actions of Bradburn in Anahuac were attorneys Patrick Jack and William Barret Travis, who were both arrested in 1832 for organizing a militia company and acting in such a manner as to incite a rebellion.

Colonel Bradburn announced that Jack and Travis would be given a military trial in Matamoros, three hundred miles away in the Mexican state of Tamaulipas. Some 160 enraged Anglo colonists from Austin's colony organized and marched toward Anahuac, led by Frank Johnson and "Three-Legged Willie" Williamson. The two prisoners were bound and staked to the ground as Johnson's party approached. Bradburn threatened to have Travis and Jack shot if the colonists opened fire. Travis, a twenty-three-year-old lawyer who had abandoned his wife, son, and unborn daughter to depart for Texas in 1830, was prepared to die. His hands bound over his knees, he shouted to Johnson's men to attack the fort and let him die like a man if need be.[11]

Johnson's men had captured nineteen of Bradburn's cavalrymen en route to Anahuac, planning to exchange them for the handful of men that Bradburn had arrested. Travis and Jack survived the tense face-off that day when both sides stood down, but Johnson's rebels clashed with Bradburn's forces over the next few days at Anahuac and at Velasco, seventy miles down the Gulf Coast. Colonel José de las Piedras, Bradburn's immediate supervisor, arrived from Nacogdoches and negotiated a settlement in which Bradburn was removed from command. Jack and Travis were released on July 2, seven weeks after being imprisoned.

Travis thereafter moved inland to San Felipe de Austin, using his new celebrity to build a healthy legal profession. He used his wealth to buy up great quantities of land and dress himself in fine clothes. He was a ladies' man, but he soon fell in love with a young woman named Rebecca Cummings, whom he told he would marry once he could properly divorce his wife in Alabama. Before any of this could be carried out, Travis became engaged in the second big disturbance at Anahuac in the spring of 1835.

Another company of Mexican troops sent to garrison the fort at Anahuac had incited inevitable clashes between citizens and soldiers. Merchant Andrew Briscoe, a friend of Travis, was jailed on suspicions of smuggling. A secret war party met in San Felipe, and they elected William Travis to lead a force to bust Briscoe from jail. He was joined by two dozen armed men who used the password slogan "victory or death." They sailed into Galveston Bay on a chartered sloop on which was mounted a six-pound cannon. Travis's rebels announced their arrival at Anahuac by firing a cannon shot on the late afternoon of June 27.

Travis and his company rowed ashore and demanded that Captain Antonio Tenorio and his forty-four men surrender. The Mexicans were paroled after pledging to leave Texas, and Travis returned to San Felipe to find that several Texian communities, fearful of reprisals, had condemned his actions. He used the local newspaper to communicate his defense, but instead was faced with orders issued in August by the Mexican president for the arrest of Frank Johnson, Robert Williamson, and Travis.

Travis avoided arrest for the time, spending his energy at whipping up rebellious sentiment among his influential friends. Upon hearing that two hundred *soldados* would be garrisoned in San Felipe within a few weeks, Travis wrote, "We shall give them hell if they come." [12]

THE PRESIDENT OF MEXICO was more than willing to give hell right back to Travis and any other colonial rebels.

The leader of the newly independent Mexican nation was

hailed as a patriot. Antonio López de Santa Anna Pérez de Lebrón, a master showman, was a thirty-eight-year-old hero of the revolution in which Mexico secured its independence from Spain in 1821. Santa Anna had been born into a *criollo* (persons born in the New World to Spanish-born parents) middle-class family and had received only limited schooling. He found his calling in the military, where he was cited for bravery and was promoted to brigadier general by 1821.

At five feet ten inches, Santa Anna was taller than the average Mexican of his time and he possessed the looks and confidence to impress women. His military record also impressed his countrymen, who appointed him military governor of Yucatán. Following the Mexican Revolution, Santa Anna retired to civilian life and became the civil governor of Veracruz. One of his great strengths was in his ability to pull an army together quickly in times of crisis, as evidenced by his defeat in 1829 of a 2,600-man Spanish invasion force in the coastal city of Tampico. Santa Anna emerged as a national hero, shifted his former allegiances to the liberals fighting for the establishment of a republic, and was elected president of Mexico in April 1833. He allowed his vice president to largely run the country during the next year but he seized control in April 1834 with a vengeance. President Santa Anna overthrew the constitutional government and replaced the Federal Constitution of 1824 with his own laws, upsetting Anglos and liberal Americans alike. Santa Anna called for greatly reducing the independent state militias in favor of his regular military, which backed his dictatorial style command.[13]

Almost half of Mexico's nineteen states expressed their outrage, including the state of Coahuila y Tejas, in which Austin's Colony had been established. Most notable of those opposing Santa Anna's new regime were the citizens of Zacatecas, who refused to disband their large, well-trained militia. In April 1835, President Santa Anna led a four-thousand-man army north from Mexico City to Zacatecas and fought a bloody battle. Santa Anna's centralists suffered only a hundred casualties, while the Zacatecan militarists incurred as many as twelve hundred killed.

Santa Anna returned to Mexico City a great hero, winding through several cities en route to celebrate his great victory over the rebels. When the alarming news of his butchery reached the colonists of Texas, some settlements began forming militia companies and Committees of Safety in fear of what this powerful leader might do to those born on foreign soil. Convention leaders meeting in October 1832 and in April 1833 drafted a constitution for statehood, electing *empresario* Stephen Austin to deliver the petitions to the Mexican government. Austin arrived in Mexico City in July, and eventually succeeded in persuading officials to repeal an April 1830 ban on immigration into Texas from the United States. Santa Anna, however, refused to approve state government for Texas. Austin was arrested on his way back home in January 1834, under suspicion of trying to incite insurrection in Texas.

Austin was imprisoned and shuffled from one jail to another until December 1834. He was released on bond but was not allowed to leave Mexico until July 1835. He met with President Santa Anna at his hacienda outside Veracruz before departing, whereupon the famed general helped clear up Austin's permission papers. Santa Anna promised to visit Texas the following March as a friend, but the "Father of Texas" had good reason to doubt the good intentions of the self-proclaimed "Napoleon of the West." [14]

Colonel Austin returned to Texas in late August 1835 after an absence of twenty-eight months. On September 8, he gave a notable speech at Brazoria to endorse a general convention, or consultation, that was to meet in October. The seeds of rebellion had taken strong root by this time, and events that would forever change the fate of Texas transpired before the convention could be seated.

3

"COME AND TAKE IT"

IT ONLY TAKES A spark to ignite a powder keg. For the already aroused Texan colonists, it took only a beating and a little bronze cannon to start a revolution.

The residents of Gonzales—the capital of *empresario* Green DeWitt's colony and the westernmost point of Anglo-American settlement—had shown loyalty to Mexico throughout the summer of 1835. This trust was shattered on September 10, when twenty-five Mexican soldiers appropriated the store of merchant Adam Zumwalt to quarter for the night. Thirty-two-year-old Jesse McCoy, recently appointed second lieutenant of the town militia, attempted to make his way into Zumwalt's storeroom. The son of a former Indian fighter from Missouri, McCoy had arrived in Texas and settled on the east side of the Guadalupe River south of Gonzales. Without provocation, one of the Mexican soldiers began beating the young militiaman with the butt of his Brown Bess musket.[1]

McCoy survived, bloodied and badly injured. News of the beating spread quickly through the settlements of the colony. Weeks later, the Mexican military commander at San Antonio, Colonel Domingo de Ugartechea, sent a Corporal DeLeon and several soldiers to request the town's cannon from alcalde Andrew Ponton. The old cannon was a bronze six-pounder, crudely mounted on a makeshift wooden caisson, presented to the town in 1831 by Mexico for local defense against Indians. Ponton found that his townspeople had no intentions of handing over the cannon to DeLeon upon his arrival on September 25. The small party of Mexican soldiers was disarmed and marched out of town. Gonzales citizens then moved their families together for safety, consolidated weapons, and dispatched messengers through the surrounding settlements.

Colonel Ugartechea responded to this act of defiance by sending Lieutenant Francisco Castaneda and his hundred-man Alamo Presidial Company to Gonzales to demand the brass weapon. They had orders to arrest alcalde Ponton and anyone else who resisted. The soldiers reached the west bank of the rain-swollen Guadalupe River on September 29, where they were met by a force of eighteen armed colonists. The Texians had removed the ferry and all the boats to the east side of the stream. This force of freedom fighters—which included such noteworthy names as George Washington Davis, William W. Bateman, Almeron Dickinson, and Captain Albert Martin—was later immortalized as the "Old Gonzales Eighteen."[2]

Castaneda yelled across the river, demanding the cannon. Captain Martin, leader of the eighteen rebels, shouted back that their alcalde was not available until the next day. The hundred Mexican soldiers therefore bivouacked three hundred yards from the fording site on the Guadalupe. The Gonzales colonists had no intentions of handing over their cannon. Martin then sent three of his men to haul the artillery piece to one of Davis's peach orchards to bury it. Express riders raced to spread the call for help in the settlements of Mina, San Felipe, Columbus, and Washington while Martin stalled.

Foremost of the armed Texians who headed for Gonzales to aid the effort were many of the rangers recently returned from Colonel John Henry Moore's Indian expedition. By September 30, more than a hundred men had gathered in Gonzales, including former ranger captains Edward Burleson and Robert Coleman. The assembled volunteers voted on leaders, electing Moore as colonel, Joseph Washington Elliott Wallace as lieutenant colonel, and Burleson as major. The settlers prepared for action while Dr. Launcelot Smither rode from Béxar to attempt to keep the peace with Lieutenant Castaneda. Moore's men held a council of war and decided to fight.[3]

A squad of men dug the Gonzales cannon from the Davis orchard, while townsmen gathered metal scraps to use as canister shot. A Methodist preacher, Reverend William P. Smith, delivered a sermon that night with references to the American Revolution. He told the determined volunteers that the blood "of our ancestors in '76 still flows in our veins." Castaneda's troops moved their camp about seven miles upriver by dusk on October 1 while Colonel Moore's 180 men began crossing the Guadalupe River, nearly one-third mounted on horseback. As dawn of October 2 approached, Moore ordered his men to take cover in a thicket along the riverbank.

Small rounds of sniping ensued during the early morning hours on the farm of Ezekiel Williams, one of the Old Gonzales Eighteen. Forty mounted Mexican cavalrymen charged. The Texians wounded one of their opponents before falling back into cover of a wooded riverbank. Castaneda sent Dr. Smither forward to request a parley, but Colonel Moore had him taken to the rear under arrest. Moore and Castaneda then met on neutral grounds between their forces to discuss the situation. After a brief but tense exchange, Castaneda announced that he was obliged to follow his orders to seize the rebels' cannon.

Moore returned and ordered artilleryman James Clinton Neill to fire their cannon toward the Mexicans clustered on the hill. The Texians then unfurled a defiant battle flag, sewn from the white wedding dress of Green DeWitt's daughter Naomi. It sported the outline of an unmounted cannon bearing the phrase COME AND TAKE IT in bold print. Neill's cannon boomed out its first shot of metal scrap as Moore's riflemen fired their first volley and charged. Lieutenant Castaneda's outnumbered troops turned and fled toward Béxar.[4]

The Texians suffered only one man slightly injured while the Mexican force had at least one *soldado* killed. The whole event, later dubbed the Battle of Gonzales, could scarcely be considered even a skirmish but it marked the beginning of the Texas Revolution. Lexington, Massachusetts, had been the first battle of the American Revolution in 1775, in which the "shot heard round the world" had been fired. The Gonzales skirmish was no comparable battle but the little Guadalupe River settlement was thereafter referred to by some newspapers as the "Lexington of Texas."

THE STAGE FOR REVOLUTION had been set. The next act against Santa Anna's regime took place in mere days as word spread through the colonies of the action at Gonzales.

The hero of Tampico had already determined that stronger measures were needed to maintain peace in Texas and had dispatched his brother-in-law, General Martín Perfecto de Cos, with five hundred soldiers into the troublesome area to disarm all colonists. The troops landed at Copano Bay and had reached Gonzales by October 2. Some three hundred colonists rallied in Gonzales during the next week, encouraged by the "victory" near the river and intent upon marching in force upon San Antonio.

The defiant spirit exercised by the Gonzales colonists was contagious. Settlers of the coastal town of Matagorda met on October 6 to elect officers for a provisional militia company. Captain George Morse Collinsworth of Mississippi was elected into command and the force marched that evening toward Goliad, known to many as La Bahía. Rumors had spread that General Cos had marched into the town with a military chest containing at least fifty thousand dollars. Collinsworth's militiamen intended to attack the Mexican garrison at the presidio of La Bahía outside Goliad. This fortress was crucial in that it guarded the principal supply line from the port of Copano on Aransas Bay to San Antonio. More than one hundred other volunteers joined them en route, many of them *tejanos* who felt the Mexican forces had stripped them of their rights. Another who joined the march was a well-known recent prisoner of Mexico, Benjamin Rush Milam.[5]

General Cos had departed already for Béxar with most of his soldiers and his war chest. The volunteers under Captain Collinsworth desired to defend the republican institutions of the Constitution of 1824 by driving out any Mexican soldiers remaining at the La Bahía fortress who might threaten their rights. They found only fifty-three officers and men holed up in the old Spanish fortress when they assaulted the presidio before dawn on October 10. The militiamen seized La Bahía in less than half an hour, suffering only one of their own—Samuel McCulloch, a free slave formerly owned by Collinsworth— wounded in the shoulder by a bullet.

The fort was found to contain lance heads, bayonets, and about two hundred muskets and carbines, although most of the latter were in almost useless condition. Other reinforcements soon arrived at Goliad, including volunteer companies led by captains John Alley and Ben Fort Smith. The combined troops proceeded to organize themselves, electing Smith as colonel, George Collinsworth as major, and Philip Dimitt as captain. *Empresario* Stephen F. Austin sent word that a force under Captain Dimitt should remain to hold the La Bahía fortress while the balance of the colonial troops marched toward Gonzales to join Austin. They brought with them two of the captive Mexican officers to meet with Austin as plans were laid for a follow-up siege.

THE CROWDS GATHERING IN Gonzales were energized by the easy victories both near their town and at the presidio La Bahía. Many, perhaps fueled by corn liquor, spoke out strongly that the fight should be carried to San Antonio de Béxar to put down the freshly landed military force under General Cos.

Numerically, the Texians had the upper hand. A full revolution with more than thirty thousand settlers could hardly be contained by less than seven hundred Mexican troops at Cos's service. The settlers could easily contain any supply shipments arriving at the coast, forcing Mexican reinforcements to San Antonio to travel overland more than four hundred miles from San Luis Potosí. By October 11, the swelling force of volunteers in Gonzales elected General Stephen Austin as their commander. His judgment and militia experience dealing with hostile Indians were respected by his peers, even if he held no formal military training.[6]

Austin knew that he had more men than guns and a critical

supply of gunpowder and lead. There was no uniformity to the ragtag little Texian army that would carry forth the revolution. Some men had shotguns, effective only for short-range action. The more precise weapons were the Kentucky long rifles carried by many settlers. The only attempt of a cavalry he had were novice lancers who carried cane poles topped with sharpened steel files. They rode slow mules or half-broken mustangs. The whole lot would be sorely outmatched by a first-rate Mexican cavalry company, but it was all that Texas had.

One of those arriving from Matagorda was blacksmith Noah Smithwick. His father had fought in the American Revolution, where one of his uncles was killed at Cowpens. As a boy, Noah watched his older brother march off to serve in the War of 1812. He dreamed of the day he could don a bright new uniform and march off with people cheering, drums beating, and flags flying. "I thought it was the grandest thing on earth," he recalled. Upon his arrival in Gonzales, Smithwick found neither glare nor glitter.[7]

Smithwick went to work in the blacksmith shop of Andrew Sowell, where the men scraped and scoured the old six-pound cannon before mounting it on old wooden trucks built from trees. "We had no ammunition for our artillery," he related, "so we cuts slugs of bar iron and hammered them into balls, ugly-looking missiles."

True, the rebels were poorly equipped with proper supplies, horses, arms, and training. They wore no uniforms. What they lacked in all of this, they made up in determined spirit. And Austin found key figures available at his disposal. One notable arrival was that of William Travis, who had already played a major role in the two disturbances at Anahuac. Noah Smithwick found that recruits arrived daily in town, "each squad being duly officered as if there were men enough to go round, and we soon had more officers than men." Austin reorganized the mass of volunteers into proper companies, wherein many of the smaller squads were absorbed.

The Texian force marched from Gonzales toward Béxar, seventy miles away, on October 12. Austin named Captain Ben Milam commander of a mounted spy company to help lead them through the unfamiliar country. The volunteer army of Texas did not come close to resembling the army Smithwick had dreamed of joining in his childhood. Most men wore buckskin pants, some soft and new with a yellowish color; others wore buckskins that were black and shiny, hardened with grease, dirt, and rain. Footwear ranged from moccasins to shoes to boots. The Texians had no common soldier's cap for their army, their heads instead being adorned with a wide variety of coonskin caps, broad-brimmed sombreros, and even tall, silk "beegum" hats. Austin's force marched with the "Come and Take It" flag at the head of his formation and two yokes of long-horned steers hauling the little brushed cannon in its center.

When the Texians made camp on the banks of Cibolo Creek, Milam's scouts discovered the trail of a hundred Mexican cavalrymen only ten miles away. Austin sent other scouting parties to locate this enemy force. On October 15, the patrol under Lieutenant Pleasant M. Bull fought a brief skirmish on the Cibolo with a ten-man Mexican cavalry patrol. Bull's men chased them for two miles as the cavalrymen retreated for Béxar. The minor skirmish was the first action since the little army had left Gonzales and it served to energize the Texians.[8]

General Austin's army marched to within five miles of San Antonio by October 20 and made camp on Salado Creek. The Mexicans appeared to be too well fortified for a full frontal assault. He hoped instead to surround Béxar with enough men to prevent General Cos from receiving any reinforcement or provisions until he opted to surrender himself. One of his greatest aids to Austin came in the form of support from *tejanos,* Mexican-born citizens who declared themselves loyal to the Mexican Constitution of 1824, which President Santa Anna had abolished.

Victoria alcalde Plácido Benavides reached the volunteer Texas Army with about thirty mounted rancheros on the day of the Cibolo skirmish. On October 22, twenty-eight-year-old Juan Nepomuceno Seguín rode into camp with news that many Mexican citizens of Béxar supported the revolt and were willing to fight. The following day, General Austin authorized him to "raise a company of patriots to operate against the centralists and military." [9]

Juan's father, Erasmo Seguín, was a former Béxar alcalde and a good friend of Austin. A devout federalist, Erasmo had built a fortified compound known as Casa Blanca on the nine-thousand-acre tract of land his family owned downriver from San Antonio. General Cos, upon learning that young Juan Seguín had sided with rebels skirmishing with Mexican troops near Monclova, Mexico, forced his father out of San Antonio on foot. Captain Juan Seguín was thus only too happy to recruit Mexican Texians from the ranches on the lower San Antonio River to join General Austin's troops gathering outside the city. During the next days, more than one hundred *tejanos* would be available to General Austin, including twenty-six under Seguín's brother-in-law, Salvador Flores. The *tejanos* were invaluable as skilled horsemen and were well acquainted with the Béxar countryside to lead foraging parties or to serve as couriers.

Stephen F. Austin's ragged army thus gained *tejano* advantages, to which was added another necessary ingredient: rugged, raw courage and fearless fighters. He found that in several men, one of the most notable being a forty-year-old Kentuckian named James Bowie, who had come into Texas in 1830. Bowie was a powerful man of six foot height and 180 pounds, with a fair complexion, gray eyes, and high cheekbones. Once his family had moved to Louisiana, Jim Bowie and his brothers bought and sold slaves, some captured in the Caribbean and Gulf of Mexico by the pirate Jean Lafitte. Bowie had an easy-going disposition but a vicious anger when he was aroused by insults. Family tales say that he trapped bears, rode alligators, and caught and rode wild horses in his early years.[10]

Some of Bowie's fights were legendary. On September 19, 1827, he participated in the Sandbar Fight, in which two opponents had proposed to settle their differences with a pistol duel on the Mississippi River in Louisiana. Neither man was able to fire accurately enough to wound the other but one of the observers drew his own pistol to settle the dispute. Jim Bowie tried to prevent bloodshed but he was shot twice in the process—one lead ball passed through his lung and another slammed into his thigh. Three opponents then fell on Bowie, stabbing him with their sword canes in his hand and his arm. Another blade was bent as it was plunged against his breastbone. Louisiana parish sheriff Norris Wright, a bitter rival of Bowie, then pulled the bloodied frontiersman to his feet. Bowie used his remaining strength to drive his large butcher-like hunting knife into Wright's chest, where he twisted the blade and caused Wright to collapse. The frightful river sandbar brawl only ended after Bowie severely slashed another of his opponents in the side with his blade.[11]

Bowie's superhuman strength was reported in newspapers across the country and his prowess with his lethal blade became legendary. He would recover from his dreadful wounds while men in many regions began asking blacksmiths to make them a large knife like that of Jim Bowie. Jim and his brothers lived for several more years in Louisiana, dealing in slave trade, land ventures, and even a steam-powered sugar mill. Bowie then moved on to Texas, married the daughter of wealthy Don Juan Martín de Veramendi, and became an official Mexican citizen after being baptized into the Catholic Church.

He became fluent in Spanish, and in fall 1831 went in search of fabled silver mines in the hills around the San Saba River. Accompanied by his brother Rezin and ten others, Bowie soon found that his party was being trailed by a large group of Indians. They were attacked, and from a grove of trees and behind a hastily assembled breastworks, Jim Bowie's party fought for their lives for thirteen hours. When it was over, three of Bowie's men were wounded and another lay dead. They estimated they had killed or wounded seventy of their opponents. Fighting such a battle, outnumbered perhaps by at least ten-to-one, only gave rise to the increasing fame of Bowie as a fearless fighter.

Bowie was a man of action. He led citizen soldiers on a scouting expedition in early 1832, and was asked by Stephen Austin that summer to help put down an insurrection in Nacogdoches. He arrived one day late to prevent a skirmish between two hundred Mexican soldiers and three hundred Texians, but he ambushed the Mexican troops as they marched from town and marched most of them back into town as prisoners.

That fall, his wife, Ursula, his mother-in-law, father-in-law, and other members of the Veramendi family died from an outbreak of cholera that had spread into the region. The only two children born to him by Ursula had also died soon after birth. Heartbroken, Bowie turned to shady landing dealings in 1834 that helped him amass more than a half million acres of Texas land. He hoped to make a fortune in land deals to incoming immigrants, but he and other speculators were rounded up and imprisoned in May 1835 by Santa Anna. Bowie and a companion managed to escape from their captors in Matamoros and made their way to Nacogdoches. Within days of his arrival in Nacogdoches, a hundred men gathered in the town square and elected Bowie to be their honorary "colonel" in command of their local militia. He and his men marched to a warehouse in San Antonio used by the Mexicans to store weapons and armed themselves with muskets.

When Jim Bowie heard the news of the outbreak of hostilities in Gonzales in October 1835, he and some companions saddled up and rode toward the Lexington of Texas to join the cause. Bowie was always good for a fight and President Santa Anna's brutal tactics were just the thing to take on.

4

"THE DAY WAS SOON OURS"

REVEREND DANIEL PARKER BELIEVED in the gun as much as he did the Bible in 1835. He was not a man prone to fight but he lived on a frontier where violence was likely to find him or his family.

Parker gazed at the scraggly collection of log cabins and stores nestled on the bank of the Brazos River. And yet this town was the economic and political hub of Stephen Austin's colony. San Felipe de Austin had been founded as the unofficial capital in 1824. Seven separate postal routes converged in San Felipe, as both the Old San Antonio and Atascosito roads were easily accessible. The town population was pushing six hundred, and four schools served the capital community. The colonial land office was located in town, as were general stores, two taverns, a hotel, a blacksmith shop, and even a brand-new printing press owned by Gail Borden Jr. His first issue of the *Telegraph and Texas Register* had just been published on October 10. An earlier paper, the *Texas Gazette,* had moved from San Felipe to Brazoria years earlier.

Fifty-four-year-old Reverend Parker, a former state senator in Illinois, was now representing the Municipality of Nacogdoches. His family had settled near present-day Groesbeck in eastern Texas and built Parker's Fort on their vast landholdings. The wily Baptist preacher, knowing that Mexican law forbade the creation of non-Catholic churches in Texas territory, had found these same laws could not prevent the immigration of an already organized Protestant church. So, on July 26, 1833, Daniel Parker and his family formed the Pilgrim Predestinarian Regular Baptist Church and prepared to move to Texas.

The subject of proper frontier protection was on Parker's mind when he arrived at the Brazos capital with his brother James Wilson Parker, who had been elected a delegate for the Municipality of Viesca. The provisional government had on September 19 called for a consultation, at which representatives from each Texas district would attend. Due to the state of the young revolution, two-thirds of those previously elected were in the field and unable to attend when the Consultation convened on October 15. Those who had gathered chose to proceed as a temporary "Permanent Council" until a proper quorum of the elected representatives could be gathered in the near future. They elected Richardson Royall of the Matagorda District as their president and commenced official business.

The delegates met in the grist mill of Joseph Urban. Martin Parmer, the delegate for the District of Tenaha, griped aloud about the meeting hall. The old stove smoked up the room badly and the crude grist mill made such an irritating grinding sound that it was hard for the delegates to hear. Daniel Parker served on many committees and made his feelings known that he opposed a war with Mexico. He felt that the land granted to the early settlers and tax exemptions were more than generous. He had a more pressing concern: how to deal with guarding the frontier settlements from Indian attacks. On October 17, he proposed an idea that had been suggested to him by Captain Robert Coleman, whose ranging company had retreated to Parker's Fort after fighting Tawakonis in July.[1]

Parker's resolution called for "creating a corps of Texas Rangers to consist of small detachments stationed on the Indian frontier." Three men were selected to be superintendents of the regional ranging units, two of them having close ties to Parker. Garrison Greenwood, an ordained minister in the Parker church, would oversee a ten-man ranger unit to serve in the east between the Trinity and Neches rivers. Silas Mercer Parker, a brother of Daniel, was picked to supervise twenty-five rangers between the Brazos and Trinity rivers. The third superintendent, Daniel Boone Friar, would oversee another thirty-five rangers who were to operate between the Brazos and Colorado rivers. These three men were authorized to draw on the council for money to defray personal expenses.[2]

Daniel Parker then served on a five-man committee formed to consider his resolution. On October 17, they agreed on specifics regarding the new Texas Rangers corps. Greenwood's men would be based out of the developing little East Texas settlement of Houston, located in present Anderson County. The companies under Friar and Silas Parker would both rendezvous at the Waco Indian village on the Brazos River. Each company was to elect its own officers and report to the regional superintendent every fifteen days. Individual rangers were to be paid $1.25 per day served.[3]

The ranger proposal passed on October 18, and several men were dispatched to spread the word. Among them was James Parker, who would alert his brother Silas that he was now authorized to serve as a ranger superintendent. The Permanent Council then authorized three commissioners—Jacob Garrett, Joseph L. Hood, and Peter J. Menard—to meet with various Indian tribes to advise them of their rights and privileges under the new Texas leadership. The Permanent Council continued in session through October 26. Still unable to achieve a proper quorum to conduct business, the members were adjourned until November 1.

Gail Borden's *Telegraph and Texas Register* printed in its October 26 edition the news that the council had "made arrangements for raising three companies of Rangers." Their services would be well utilized in the months to come on the Texas frontiers as the colonists pursued their war of rebellion against the Mexican forces of Santa Anna's government.

GENERAL STEPHEN AUSTIN NEEDED a few good men to achieve his goal.

His position near the Mission San Francisco de la Espada in late October was too far from Béxar to effectively serve as an operations base. He needed a search party willing to fight if necessary while they scouted out a new position closer to San Antonio. He thus ordered Jim Bowie, James Fannin, and Andrew Briscoe to head a ninety-man scouting party. The reputations of fabled fighters Bowie and Briscoe, who had been jailed during the most recent Anahuac uprising, were solid.[4]

The third leader selected by Austin had never commanded men in battle but he held great promise. James Walker Fannin Jr. had entered West Point in 1819 but dropped out after only two years. He returned to his home state of Georgia and later married Minerva Fort, with whom he had two daughters. In

1834, the Fannins moved to Texas and settled at Velasco, where he became a plantation owner and slave trader. Fannin believed in the Texas independence movement and was appointed by the Columbia Safety Committee in August 1835 to solicit financial aid and West Point officers to command the rising volunteer army in Texas.

Bowie was in tactical command of the companies under Fannin and Briscoe, although they were supported by additional volunteers led by Robert Coleman, Valentine Bennett, and Michael Goheen. They departed Mission Espada on October 27 in company with a small group of Captain Juan Seguín's mounted *tejanos*. They moved up the San Antonio River, examining first Mission San Juan Capistrano and then Mission San José y San Miguel de Aguayo. Neither appeared to be worthy as a solid, defensible base for operations. By nightfall, Bowie's forces reached Mission Purísima Concepción.

Some five hundred yards above the mission, Bowie located a perfect spot for defense within a U-shaped bend of the San Antonio River. Captain Seguín and his men "passed the night in making preparation to resist an attack which we considered imminent." Bowie sent a rider back to Mission Espada to inform General Austin of their decision to make camp near Mission Concepción. The general was outraged that Bowie would split his forces from the main body and potentially subject themselves in such small number to a strong attack from the troops under General Cos.[5]

The intelligence of the camping Texian scouting party did indeed make it to Cos. He moved for Concepción with one hundred infantrymen and three hundred Mexican dragoons to seek battle. Jim Bowie allowed some of his men to sleep by their weapons, while pickets were kept on lookout duty until dawn.

The lookout posted in the old Spanish mission's bell tower found little to see at dawn's first light: a heavy fog rolling off the river had reduced visibility to mere feet.

The first indication of trouble came when sentry Henry Karnes and rifleman Creed Taylor were fired upon by a Mexican soldier. They fell back on their command, who quickly prepared for battle. Bowie had his men secure their horses below the riverbank and then positioned his companies to achieve the best firing points. The Mexican force under Colonel Domingo de Ugartechea advanced with two cannon and proceeded to fire them toward the entrenched Texians at about eight in the morning.

"When the fog lifted, we found ourselves pretty well surrounded," recalled Noah Smithwick. The Texans lay below the riverbanks as grape and canister shot crashed through the ripe pecan trees above, raining nuts down upon them. "I saw men picking them up and eating them with as little concern as if they were being shaken down by a norther," said Smithwick.[6]

Bowie ordered his riflemen to remain cool and be deliberate with their shots. The Mexicans advanced but suffered many casualties in the process. The Texans particularly concentrated on killing anyone attempting to fire the cannon. The Mexican Brown Bess muskets were ineffective beyond seventy yards while Texan snipers with their long rifles could kill a soldier at two hundred yards. Several Texans were hit by musket balls fired from such a long range that their impact left only a heavy bruise without even breaking the skin. One Texan, Pen Jarvis, escaped injury when a musket ball struck the broad blade of his Bowie knife. The first Texan killed in the revolution was Richard Andrews of Captain Coleman's company. His unit was moving to give firing support to other Texians in the river bend when Andrews brazenly dashed across an open area above the river bluff. He was taken under fire by every *soldado* within range and even a round of cannon fire. Andrews crumpled with grapeshot that tore through his right side and lacerated his bowels.[7]

Smithwick watched the Mexican troops make three charges. Three times they were turned back by deadly fire, until he felt "a panic seized them, and they broke." Bowie then ordered a general charge and managed to capture one of the enemy's cannon. "The day was soon ours," recalled Juan Seguín. The Texans turned the artillery piece around and fired the Mexicans' own grapeshot into them as they fled. General Austin and the remainder of his Texas Army reached the field about a half hour after the Mexican troops had been broken. Lieutenant William Travis led some of his mounted cavalrymen in pursuit of the fleeing soldiers.[8]

Austin rode about, shouting for his men to prepare to chase the *soldados* right into Béxar. He was met with strong objections from Fannin, Bowie, and Briscoe, however. Their concentrated fire had been deadly against their foes. Their fortunes might not be so kind should they charge foolishly into a town that was well fortified by General Cos's men. The Mexicans had suffered fourteen killed and thirty-nine wounded, some of whom later died. The Texians lost only Dick Andrews of Coleman's company killed and one man wounded.

CAPTAIN PHILIP DIMITT, LEFT behind to command the rebel garrison of La Bahía at Goliad, was hoping for some action of his own.

He had been writing to General Austin for two weeks in hopes of getting approval to seize Fort Lipantitlán (meaning "Lipan land" in Apache), located on the west bank of the

Nueces River along the Atascosito Road about three miles up-stream from the old town of San Patricio. Two of Dimitt's men, sent to deliver dispatches to the town's federalist leaders, had been seized and were being held prisoners within the fortress. Austin was also informed that Fort Lipantitlán housed a can-non, a herd of horses, and much-needed arms and ammunition.[9]

Major George Sutherland departed Goliad on October 28 with twenty-five men and twelve teams of supplies to deliver to the main camp of the army. A small detachment was sent ahead to report to General Austin near Béxar but they were attacked by Indians the next morning. Lieutenant David M. Collinsworth, brother of Major George Collinsworth, was shot through the neck and killed instantly. Five survivors fled for La Bahía. They returned with more armed men on October 30 to retrieve the body of Collinsworth. He had been scalped and mutilated.[10]

Philip Dimitt also dispatched an expedition from Goliad on October 31 to seize Fort Lipantitlán. Adjutant Ira J. Westover headed out with thirty-five men under his command, plus an advisory committee—Consultation delegates John Linn, Major James Kerr, and Colonel James Power. They decided their leg-islative duties in San Felipe could wait a few days. There was a fort full of Mexican soldiers to overthrow first. As fate would have it, Captain Don Nicolás Rodriguez, the commander of the Lipantitlán post, marched his *soldados* for Goliad on the same day. He had orders from General Cos to harass Dimitt's rebels at the La Bahía fort.[11]

Westover's Texians did not travel the main road toward Lipantitlán, opting instead for a southeasterly course toward Refugio. They managed to slip into San Patricio on Novem-ber 3 unmolested while Captain Rodriguez was moving toward Goliad. They moved on to the fortress of Lipantitlán shortly before dark and found that only twenty-seven Mexican soldiers remained there. Westover arrested an Irishman named James O'Riley for sympathizing with the centralists. O'Riley convinced Westover to guarantee his personal safety if he could talk the *soldados* from the fort. He did just as he promised, and the Texians had control of the fortress before midnight without a shot being fired.

Westover's men remained at the fort only until midafternoon on November 4, when they began crossing back over the river to head for Goliad. Captain Rodriguez was informed by a spy that the Texians had seized his fort and captured his men. His force of about sixty Mexicans and ten Irish supporters rode hard for San Patricio and arrived in about an hour. The Texans took positions favorable to their long rifles and prepared for a fight. The Battle of Lipantitlán lasted only thirty-two minutes. Once again, the Mexicans' Pagent carbines and Brown Bess muskets were useless when they opened fire at two hundred yards.

Snipers made their Kentucky long rifles count. The Mexicans and Irishmen moved forward into firing range, but they were cut down as they did. Twenty-eight *soldados* were killed, including the second in command, Lieutenant Marcellino García. The judge, alcalde, and sheriff of San Patricio—Irishmen who had fought with the Mexicans—were all wounded in the battle. Westover's only injury on the Texan side was Sergeant William Bracken, who had three fingers cut off his right hand by a half-ounce lead rifle slug.[12]

Westover's plans to remove the cannon from the fort were ruined by a bitter cold rain that set in over the field. Feeling his men would be at risk of a Mexican counterattack while hauling heavy cannon down boggy roads, he opted to have the artillery dumped into the Nueces River. Many of the captured muskets and ammunition proved to be so useless that they were also dumped into the river.

The Texans moved downstream to San Patricio, where they were treated like heroes. Westover's men soon returned to Goliad, bringing with them only fourteen captured horses. The Battle of Lipantitlán was hailed as a Texian victory, even though the fort itself had been quickly abandoned due to a lack of men to man it. The defeated Captain Rodriguez vowed to return to San Patricio soon. He wrote to the town's leaders, promising their forgiveness if they would join with his ranks. Should they choose to side with the other Texian rebels, Rodriguez promised to unleash "the vengeance of the Mexican army" upon the town.[13]

5

THE RAVEN

SILAS PARKER WAS THE first of the three newly designated ranger superintendents to put a company into service.

His brother James Parker arrived fresh from the meeting of the Permanent Council with news that his sibling was authorized to oversee twenty-five rangers operating between the Brazos and Trinity rivers. He met with his brother at Parker's Fort—also known at the time as Fort Sterling in honor of empresario Sterling Robertson—to issue the council's orders. The rangers were designated to rendezvous and organize at the old Waco Indian village, but a recent act of violence on the frontier negated this possibility.[1]

About the time James Parker reached Fort Sterling, word reached the men of a recent Indian attack on frontier settlers. The first seven men to be employed as Texas Rangers under the new laws of the provisional government of Texas mustered into service on October 23, 1835, under Captain Eli Hillhouse. He took his company into the field and two days later dispatched forty-one-year-old Joseph Allen Parker—older brother to superintendent Silas—off to round up more men, ammunition, and guns. During the absence of this unit, the Parker's Fort settlers were temporarily guarded by Captain David Faulkenberry and several other armed men.[2]

Silas Parker sent his first report to the General Council, or provisional government, of Texas from "Fort Sterling" on November 2. He informed them that Captain Hillhouse's rangers were hot on the trail of recent Indian marauders. Joe Parker was successful in drumming up more recruits and supplies during late October. Hillhouse's company was bolstered by the addition of nine more rangers by November 2.

The second ranger company to be organized on November 1, under the new authority, was that of Captain Daniel Friar. He became the only ranger superintendent who doubled as the captain of his own company. Friar's sixteen-man company mustered into service in the settlement of Viesca, located in Robertson's Colony at the Falls of the Brazos on the west bank near present Marlin. His men elected Ennes Hardin as first lieutenant and Curtis A. Wilkinson as their sergeant. Daniel Friar furnished all provisions and ammunition for his company, and even some of the horses.[3]

Within two weeks of their formation, Captain Friar's rangers were greeted by colonist George W. Chapman. He brought news that Indians had attacked and burned down the home of Joseph Taylor, located near the Three Forks of the Little River about three miles from the Forks of the Brazos. The Taylor home had been attacked on the night of November 12 by a party of about eleven Kickapoos. They were alerted to trouble by the fierce barking of the family's dog, which the Indians quickly silenced with an arrow. The family fought back valiantly as the Kickapoos fired rifle balls and arrows into their dogtrot-style log home and tried to force their way in. Stepson Stephen Frazier fired through a window vent and killed one Indian who was advancing on the main door with an axe. Joseph Taylor then shot and killed another Kickapoo who rushed forward to drag away his comrade's body.

The Indians then tried to burn down the family's home. Wife Nancy Taylor fought the flames, extinguishing much of the blaze with the family's milk supply and a barrel of home-made vinegar. Taylor and his stepson Stephen wounded at least two other Kickapoos with their rifles, and the Indians finally retreated. An hour later, the family cautiously emerged from the charred remnants of their home, stashed their valuables in the nearby Leon River bottom, and raced for their nearest neighbor's cabin. Captain Friar's rangers visited the Taylor home but found no Indians to fight. According to one of Taylor's daughters, they found only that "the bodies of the two Indians were being eaten by the hogs." The rangers reportedly raised the heads of the two charred corpses on long poles, leaving them as a gruesome warning to any other marauders who should pass through the settlement.[4]

THE SERVICES OF THE early Texas Rangers were further addressed by the General Council of Texas when it reconvened at San Felipe. James Parker, returning from Fort Sterling to represent the Nacogdoches Municipality, asked for an increase to forty men from the twenty-five allocated to his brother Silas's Brazos-to-Trinity district.[5]

The state of conflict gripping the Texas region again made it impossible to round up all the delegates for the scheduled November 1 Consultation. Some were with Austin's army near

Béxar, while others were engaged in the battle for the Lipan-titlán fort. By November 3, only fifty-eight of the ninety-eight credentialed delegates had reached the Consultation in San Felipe, but it was enough for a quorum. They set to work forming a provisional government as a state within the Mexican federation.

The Consultation resolved on November 9 to add additional regional rangers and a fourth superintendent. George Davis, a representative of the Gonzales Municipality and one of the eighteen who had instigated the revolution with the "Come and Take It" cannon, was to supervise twenty more rangers who would cover the area from the Colorado River to Cibolo Creek, a tributary of the San Antonio River. The place of rendezvous for his company was to be the headwaters of the San Marcos River.[6]

The legislators then turned to the issue of providing for the men who were serving under General Stephen Austin near San Antonio. They decided these volunteer troops should be paid at the rate of twenty dollars per month, from the day they left their homes until the day they returned. On November 12, the Consultation elected Henry Smith (who had long advocated independence) as the provisional governor of Texas, James W. Robinson as his lieutenant governor, and Sam Houston as the major general of the Texas Army. The San Felipe lawmakers also appointed William Harris Wharton, Branch Tanner Archer, and Stephen Austin as commissioners to solicit aid from the United States for the current crisis. Austin's new appointment would require him to pass command of the Texas Army to Colonel Ed Burleson, now second in command under Major General Houston. Two days later, the Consultation broke up for a week's hiatus.[7]

The Consultation's selection of Sam Houston over Stephen

Austin or others as the new leader of their Texas Army was peculiar at best. He stood six feet two inches, a powerful man with a colorful past that included a fondness for the bottle. As a youth in Tennessee, he had run away from home in 1809 to live for three years among the Cherokee Indians of Chief Oolooteka (John Jolly), who adopted him and gave him the Indian name Colonneh, or "the Raven." Houston viewed Oolooteka as his "Indian Father" and the Cherokees as his surrogate family, thus instilling in him a great sense of sympathy toward Indians in general during his future political career.

At age eighteen, Houston left the Cherokees to set up a school. In 1813, he joined General Andrew Jackson to fight the British. Within the year, Houston had been promoted to third lieutenant for his noted bravery and devotion to duty. Under the command of Jackson, Houston participated in the pursuit of one thousand Creek Indians in early 1814 with some three thousand U.S. infantrymen, militiamen, and allied Indians. The Creeks fortified themselves in a loop of the Tallapoosa River known as Tohopeka, or Horseshoe Bend. General Jackson's forces made a determined charge against their breastworks that escalated into hand-to-hand combat. Lieutenant Houston was shot through the lower right groin with an arrow in the charge. He nearly passed out from the flow of blood when he ordered another officer to pull the barbed arrow back through his leg.[8]

Although Jackson ordered him out of the fight, Sam Houston soon joined another charge against the fortified Creek position. He was again badly wounded in the process by two musket balls that tore into his right arm and shoulder. Surgeons saved the lieutenant that night while Jackson's men proceeded to kill some eight hundred of the Creeks in the battle and by torching their fortification. Houston emerged as one of the heroes of Horseshoe Bend. He was left scarred and in pain for decades as chips of bone from his shoulder slowly worked their way out, causing drainage that persisted for years.[9]

Houston became a lawyer in Tennessee with a swift and successful political career aided by his battlefield reputation. He served in the U.S. House of Representatives and was elected governor of Tennessee in 1827. His personal life was a mess, though. He became distraught over a failed marriage in 1829 and resigned from office to flee back to the comforts of his adoptive Cherokee family under Chief John Jolly, whose tribe had taken up residence in what is now Oklahoma.

The fallen leader married Diana Roger Gentry (also known as Talihina), a half-blood Cherokee woman who was a sister of another Cherokee leader, John Rogers. Rogers was a likely successor to Chief John Jolly, who had become the principal chief of the Western Cherokees. Within the Western Cherokee Nation, the Raven sustained himself as a lawyer and as a merchant. Houston imported barrels of whiskey, cognac, gin, rum, and wine to sell from his trading post. Political opponents sneered that he was importing the liquors for his own use. By late 1830, his consumption of alcohol was disgusting enough to his own Cherokees that he was sometimes referred to as "Big Drunk." He spoke the Cherokee language, wore traditional Indian dress, and participated in their activities, but Sam Houston's desire for the political spotlight could not be contained. In December 1832, he departed his Cherokees to seek his fortunes in Texas, abandoning his wife, Diana.[10]

Houston shared a Christmas dinner with celebrated knife fighter Jim Bowie, and he was thereafter escorted to Béxar by Bowie. Those who distrusted the former Tennessee governor's motives believed he was scouting the Texas territory for his friend Andrew Jackson—who had been elected president of the United States in 1828. Houston was viewed as a rambunctious drinker with salty language but he also spoke in a language that pleased many revolutionary types—talking of liberty and the dawning of Texas's "morning of glory." He was elected the Nacogdoches delegate to the Consultation, and his past military experience helped him seize the opportunity to command the Texas Army.[11]

Few thought Sam Houston looked the part of commander in chief of the Texas military. Delegate Anson Jones, a doctor from Brazoria, found the new general wearing greasy buckskins and a garish Mexican blanket, looking like "a broken down sot." Jones was kept awake all night by "a drunken carouse" involving Houston and Dr. Branch Archer drinking and denouncing Stephen F. Austin. Ironically, Austin was near Béxar trying to command an unruly mob. Houston, an elected delegate, duly remained at San Felipe during the hiatus of the Consultation versus going to take his command.[12]

The army was to number 1,120 enlisted men. It would include regular soldiers who enlisted for two years and "permanent volunteers" who served only for the duration of the war with Mexico. Major General Houston would also hold authority over the mounted ranger system and its superintendents. He could also choose his own staff of an adjutant general, an inspector general, a quartermaster general, a surgeon general, and four aides. For the moment, however, Houston was granted no authority over the volunteers already serving under Austin's command.[13]

STEPHEN AUSTIN'S ARMY WAS engaged in a siege, a military blockade of San Antonio de Béxar to compel its Mexican troops to surrender.

General Cos was worried little about the blockade and had

no intentions of rolling over. Austin sent a surrender demand to Cos on November 1. The Mexican commander sent the document back unopened, saying that honor and duty forbade him from accepting correspondence from rebels. Cos sent out Padre Garza with a white flag to say to Austin that he would defend this place until he died, even if he only had ten men with him.[14]

Austin held a council of war with his senior officers. His men decided to maintain the siege until they could be aided by reinforcements with a powerful eighteen-pound cannon. Colonel Ed Burleson and a force of men took possession of a nearby mill for the use of its corn and also as a headquarters.

Jim Bowie became tired of this game. He sent a letter of resignation to Austin the following day and rode to San Felipe, where he proceeded to spend much of his time drinking to excess. During the next week, there were minor skirmishes and shots exchanged between the Texas Army and the holed-up Mexican troops. Discipline was virtually nonexistent among the Texas volunteers. Drunk men wandered about camp, firing their guns and wasting ammunition, while others frittered away time gambling and cockfighting. Austin fired off a letter to the General Council. "In the name of Almighty God, send no more ardent spirits to this camp," he wrote. "If any is on the road, turn it around or have the head [of the barrel] knocked out."[15]

The first norther of fall blew in on November 6. Volunteer Samuel Maverick noted in his diary that the thermometer had plunged from 75 degrees the previous day to a mere 49 that morning. Captain William Travis, patrolling with a dozen of Andrew Briscoe's mounted riflemen, achieved a significant feat on November 9 by making a surprise charge on a camp of Mexican soldiers. They seized three hundred horses and captured the *soldados* without having to fire a shot. The captured mounts were found to be so wild, though, that they were taken to the ranch of Juan Seguín.[16]

Some of the new recruits passing through Gonzales to join Austin's army near Béxar were not fit for service. Scout Launcelot Smither informed Austin that one company passed through town and nearly beat him to death when he tried to prevent them from abusing the women of the settlement. "The conduct of wild savages would be preferable to the insults of such cannibals," Smither wrote. Stephen Austin was wearing down both mentally and physically. His two years of incarceration in Mexico had weakened his body to the extent that his servant had to help him to mount his horse. He was unafraid to point out his own lack of military experience to others, even if it did little to inspire his men. But when he was notified from San Felipe on November 18 that he had been appointed as a commissioner to the United States and had been relieved as commander of the Army of the People of Texas, he refused for the time being to abandon his post.[17]

Austin had been encouraged by the arrival of Captain Thomas H. Breece's company of properly uniformed New Orleans Greys, who reached camp pulling two cannon. The Texian volunteers were now firing upon General Cos's troops in San Antonio. The volunteer artillerymen placed the cannon they had captured at Concepción in a battery constructed west of the Alamo. Some placed bets on whether their cannon shot would hit a particular building, the old barracks, between the third and fourth windows. When the man fired the cannon and missed, he spent the next day paying for his bet by casting one hundred lead musket balls. Another man bet his pistols, the best in camp, against the worst pistols for anyone who could make a better shot.[18]

The wager was accepted by forty-eight-year-old Erastus

"Deaf" Smith. Born in New York to a devout Baptist family, the tough old frontiersman had largely lost his hearing to a childhood ailment. He had settled in Texas in 1821, married a tall, beautiful, blue-eyed widow named Guadalupe Ruiz Durán, and proceeded to raise a family of four children. The open environment of Texas seemed to improve his fragile health, caused by consumption (now known as tuberculosis). Smith held divided loyalties between the new Anglo settlers and the Mexican government. By marrying his beloved "Lupe," a Mexican woman, Smith became a Mexican citizen. His intentions to stay neutral were dashed when one of General Cos's Mexican sentries refused to allow him back into San Antonio during October to visit his family. The officer struck Smith in the head with his saber, and he was forced to race from town on his horse, while he fired back at cavalrymen pursuing him. Deaf then joined the Texas rebels and swore that he would one day kill General Cos.[19]

Deaf—called "Deef" by some—had honed his tracking and hunting skills to provide for his family. He lined up the cannon, made adjustments for altitude and distance, and won the fine pistols of his fellow volunteer with his next shot. Smith then offered to fire the cannon again. If he missed, he would return the wagering man's good pistols. He did not miss, and a cannonball smashed right where he had called his shot. His comrades cheered old Deaf wildly and he kept the pistols.

On November 21, General Austin ordered his army to prepare to storm Béxar the next day. That afternoon, however, he received reports from Colonel Burleson and Lieutenant Colonel Philip Sublett that the army was not in support of the attack, and no more than one hundred men planned to follow Austin. The volunteer general reluctantly countermanded his order. He wrote to his brother-in-law James F. Perry the next day that he was "really so worn out" that he required rest. Austin felt that he could have done his new country more justice had he been serving in the convention at San Felipe. "I can be of service to Texas by going to the U.S. and I wish to go there." [20]

Austin paraded his men on the morning of November 24 to find out how many were willing to maintain their siege on Béxar. Some 405 pledged to remain under a leader of their choosing, and voted for forty-two-year-old Colonel Burleson to take command of them. They also elected Francis W. "Frank" Johnson as adjutant and inspector general, with William T. Austin retaining his post as aide-de-camp.

Stephen Austin rode out of camp on November 25 toward San Felipe and, ultimately, the United States. Some believed that his plans had been shared with Sam Houston, who had plotted to subvert them. Key officers such as Jim Bowie, Fannin, and Sublett had taken sides with Houston, and Sublett for one had shared his views on the foolishness of Austin's planned attack on Béxar with the volunteers. Fannin had written to Houston, accepting his offer of a commission in the regular army. Bowie, who had quit the army and spent time getting drunk in San Felipe, may well have shared drinks with Houston. Some believed he was acting as Houston's secret agent when he returned to Béxar shortly before Austin resigned.

Such was the state of affairs within the volunteer army of Texas that continued to hold the six hundred–plus Mexican soldiers of General Cos under siege at Béxar in late November.

AS THE STANDOFF IN San Antonio continued, the General Council reconvened on November 21. After a full week's break, the delegates moved swiftly on strengthening the military of Texas.

On November 24, the council decreed that the regular

Texas Army was to consist of 1,120 men, divided into both infantry and artillery regiments. Each regiment would be further divided into two battalions composed of five companies of fifty-six men. Officers and men would be paid in the same fashion as those of the U.S. Army. The council additionally agreed to pay each soldier with 640 acres of land for service. In order to entice more men to join the regular army for two years, this land bounty was increased with an additional 160 acres plus twenty-four dollars in cash. The delegates also approved the purchase of weapons for the regular troops: three hundred jaeger carbines, six hundred muskets, two hundred braces of cavalry pistols, one hundred butcher knives, and a thousand tomahawks. Orders were placed for proper military manuals, including a hundred copies of Major General Winfield Scott's *Infantry Drill* tactics book and twenty-six of Crop's *Discipline and Regulations*.[21]

John A. Wharton of the Committee on Military Affairs presented a new proposal to protect the citizens of Texas with an organized ranging corps. The resolution, passed by vote on November 24, called for a three-company "Corps of Rangers" of 168 men, to be headed by a commanding major. Each private would be paid $1.25 per day to cover his own clothing, rations, pay, and horse service. Each ranger was to be constantly armed with one hundred rounds of musket balls and sufficient powder. Should a private be unable to provide his own horse, bridle, and blanket, the captain of his company was to purchase them and deduct it from his quarterly pay.[22]

Officers of this new ranging corps would be paid the same daily rate, plus be entitled to pay equal to that of officers with equal rank in the cavalry of the U.S. Army. This act was signed into effect on November 26. The new major of rangers in this battalion had supreme command—as opposed to four regional superintendents previously installed—and would report directly to the commander in chief of the Texas Army. The three new ranger companies would boast fifty-six men each, with one captain, one lieutenant, and one second lieutenant per company.

The council met again at 7 P.M. on November 28 to handle special elections for municipal judges and for the officers of both the infantry regiment of the army and the new corps of rangers. Ten men were named captains of the regiment of infantry, including early revolutionary leaders Robert Coleman, George Collinsworth, and Andrew Briscoe. For the Corps of Texas Rangers, the council named Isaac Watts Burton, William Arrington, and John Tumlinson Jr. as captains. In the voting for major commanding the ranger corps, it was close between James Kerr and "Three-Legged Willie" Williamson. The latter, present as a representative of the Mina Municipality and who had previously commanded rangers during Colonel Moore's 1835 Tawakoni campaign, won the election by a one-vote margin.[23]

Major Williamson's new ranger battalion would struggle to fully organize itself due to the state of war within Texas. In the meantime, the previously authorized regional ranging system remained in place—although it too had not yet fully mustered in. The most active companies in late 1835 were those under superintendents Silas Parker and Daniel Friar. By the end of November, Friar had twenty rangers under his command and they had fought one engagement with Indians who raided their camp on the San Gabriel River. There were no casualties, but two horses were killed by the Indians, including that of First Lieutenant Ennes Hardin.[24]

The General Council of the provisional government of Texas was generous in offering both regular army and ranger units to serve during and after the current revolution. The challenges would prove to be filling the ranks, enduring the hardships of winter, and keeping a rowdy bunch of volunteers in unity against the Mexican Army. General Sam Houston knew there was no substitute for properly disciplined soldiers and for the moment he held no authority over the volunteers maintaining the siege of Béxar.

SOME OF THE SOLDIERS lounging about the camp of the volunteer army were startled by the sudden commotion.

Ahead of a cloud of dust, whipping a lathered horse was an eager scout racing in on November 26. Colonel Burleson immediately made out Deaf Smith, the valiant frontiersman who had so recently won the pair of pistols with his marksmanship prowess. Smith reported that he had sighted a column of Mexican soldiers advancing northward on the old Presidio Road.

The news filtered through camp that the column was likely that of Colonel Domingo Ugartechea, who was known to have departed twelve days earlier with a hundred dragoons to seek reinforcements. Deaf Smith, who had been watchful for their return along with other scouts, now reported that he had seen at least a hundred soldiers and as many pack animals. Rumors spread that Ugartechea's column was also hauling a fortune in silver on its mules to pay the Béxar garrison. Wary of a possible ambush, Burleson managed to restrain his eager volunteers from racing into action. He instead sent Jim Bowie, Deaf Smith, Henry Karnes, and a cavalry force out to reconnoiter the Mexican force but not to attack unless success seemed favorable. Many other volunteers, greedy to seize the fabled silver hoard, grabbed their rifles and dashed from camp without orders to do so.[25]

The cavalrymen intercepted the Mexican force about a mile south of Béxar along Alazan Creek. Bowie immediately called a charge. His men fired their belt pistols and slashed at soldiers with their Bowie knives, unable to use their long rifles effectively on horseback. General Cos observed the skirmish from town and quickly ordered about fifty infantrymen out to assist his dragoons. Bowie's men were soon outnumbered and took cover in a dry arroyo. The Mexicans charged the dry creek bed but were forced back three times by accurate rifle fire.

At this opportune moment, William H. Jack arrived on the field with about a hundred infantrymen. They advanced and forced the Mexican soldiers into a hollow. The firing was at close range as the Mexicans took cover in dense mesquite brush. One of the volunteers was twenty-two-year-old Robert Hancock Hunter, who had come to Texas in 1822 with his family to settle in New Washington, on San Jacinto Bay. He had left home the previous month for San Antonio to join the rebellion against General Cos.

Hunter was armed with a .54-caliber Harpers Ferry Yaeger (Jaeger) musket rifle, its lock tied on with a buckskin string. "We took advantage of the pack mules, and got on the Mexicans before they seen us," Hunter wrote. "The Mexicans backed down in the hollow, which was about 10 or 12 feet deep. We were not more than 15 feet apart." The Texians shot down on their opponents and inflicted heavy casualties. Only one volunteer, Mr. Murphy, was slightly wounded by a spent musket ball that glanced off his forehead. He staggered over to Daniel Perry, who asked, "Are you hurt?" [26]

"No," said Murphy, as he wiped his hand across his brow. Noticing the heavy blood flow from his forehead, he angrily snapped, "By God!" and commenced loading his gun again.

Jack's infantrymen exchanged several rounds with the Mexicans concealed in the thick mesquite brush. The Texians moved forward swiftly, sweeping around both enemy flanks, and soon drove their opponents from the hollow. Bowie and Jack's men chased the dragoons and infantrymen to within three hundred yards of Béxar before they were forced to seek cover in a dry gulch when the Mexican artillery opened fire. "We had a bad show for our lives, eight or ten men to one against us," said Hunter, "but we pulled through."

General Cos and his men soon broke off the fight, opting not to test their short-range muskets against the long rifles of the entrenched Texas volunteers. The mule train was captured but the Texians did not find silver. Inside all of the packs was fresh-cut prairie grass. The treasure train was not Ugartechea's men but merely soldiers sent out that morning to cut fodder for the starving horses of the Béxar garrison. This minor battle was later named the Grass Fight by the disappointed Texians.

Burleson reported only four men wounded in the Grass Fight, while the Mexican losses ranged widely from three to fifty soldiers killed. More important, the foragers proved to the Texians that their siege was working in slowly creating desperation among the Mexican troops as their animals starved. Truth be told, the Texas Army was struggling almost as much to provide for its own mounts.[27]

Major Robert Morris of the New Orleans Greys estimated that the Texian force had dwindled to 225 men by November 29. During the next few days, Burleson debated on moving his troops back to Goliad due to limited supplies and winter conditions. By the morning of December 4, Samuel Maverick found that the Texas Army was beginning to break up. "The volunteers cursed the officers and 250 or 300 set off for home," he wrote in his diary. The dejected Texians were finally given a shot of inspiration close to sunset: some of the Mexican soldiers were beginning to desert.[28]

Scout Ben Milam rode back into camp and found his fellow troops disorganized and preparing to fall back to Gonzales. He sought out Colonel Frank Johnson and argued for the continuation of the effort. The two then proceeded to the tent of Burleson and had a heated exchange. The enemy was weakening, reasoned Milam, and an attack should be made. Burleson finally agreed that Milam could call a meeting of the volunteers. Those in favor could storm the town while he held the remainder of the men to cover a retreat in case the assault failed.[29]

Outside the colonel's tent near the old mill, Milam confronted the soldiers. "By the animating manner and untiring zeal of Colonel Milam," Sam Maverick found that the larger portion of the remaining Texians were still motivated to fight. Milam finally stood and asked, "Who will go with old Ben Milam to Bexár?" He called for those in favor to step to his side of the road. Three hundred of the five hundred present responded to the call, and Milam began organizing the attacking force into two divisions.[30]

Colonel Milam took charge of the first division, assisted by Lieutenant Colonel Louis B. Franks of the artillery and Major Morris of the New Orleans Greys. They would be guided into Béxar by red-haired local carpenter John W. Smith and Hendrick Arnold, a freed black man and son-in-law of Deaf Smith. The first division company commanders were Captains John York, Thomas Alley, William H. Patton, Almeron Dickinson, John English, and Thomas W. Ward.

The second division was placed under Colonel Frank Johnson, assisted by Colonel James Grant and aide-de-camp William T. Austin. Locals Deaf Smith and Sam Maverick would help guide this division into the city, which was unfamiliar to many of the volunteers. The companies of the second division were under captains William Gordon Cooke, Plácido Benavides, Thomas H. Breece, John W. Peacock, James G. Swisher, and Haden Harrison Edwards.[31]

The morning of December 5 opened with Colonel James Clinton Neill leading a division of artillerymen in a feint against the Alamo, opening fire on it to divert the enemy's attention. The other two divisions hugged the adobe walls, breaking down thick wooden doors on two stone and adobe houses on the north side of San Antonio's plaza. The firing became tremendous as the Mexican Army was engaged in what would become a five-day conflict that was occasionally marked by hand-to-hand struggles. During the first day, the Texans suffered one killed, plus twelve privates and three officers wounded. Their enemy kept up a constant firing during the night, while the Texan divisions reinforced their positions.

After daylight on December 6, the Mexicans were discovered to be occupying the rooftops in key positions around the plaza. From there they maintained a steady small arms fire upon the Texans. A detachment under Lieutenant William McDonald from Captain John Crane's company took a key house after a hard fight and managed to extend the Texan line. Five more Texans were wounded throughout the course of the day, including Captain John Peacock, who later died.

The fighting was intense again on December 7. Mexican defenders held a key house in the path of Johnson's division, and they poured heavy small arms and artillery fire down on the Texans. A six-pound cannon was wheeled into town and finally pounded the Mexican troops from the house. As it was farther advanced, however, two of its gunners were shot down and three others were wounded. Second Lieutenant William Carey and two other men continued the fight, even when Carey's skull was creased by a musket ball. Ben Milam led a final push toward Main Plaza, and made his way through the rubble to confer with Johnson at the grand Veramendi house. Dressed in a white blanket coat, Milam stepped into the courtyard with a spyglass to get a better look at the Mexican command post.[32]

A puff of smoke appeared in a cypress tree a hundred yards away on the bank of the San Antonio River. Ben Milam died instantly as a bullet pierced his right temple. The Mexican sniper, Felix de la Garza, was quickly killed by several Texian riflemen. The stunned volunteers buried Colonel Milam in a trench that evening and selected Frank Johnson to carry out the assault plans that their fallen leader had put in motion.

Mexican artillerymen pinned down a group of Texians near several old houses and an adobe wall in the afternoon of the fourth day. Grapeshot quickly reduced the wall and sent Tennessean Henry Karnes leaping into action. Carrying a rifle in one hand and a crowbar in the other, he dashed across a street under heavy fire toward a crucial position on the north side of the plaza loaded with Mexican sharpshooters. Karnes used his crowbar to smash in the door while Captain York's company laid down cover fire. Men from the companies of Captains Lewellen, English, Crane, and York charged on foot to take possession of the house, chasing out the enemy soldiers who did not immediately surrender.

On December 8, Colonel Ugartechea returned to San Antonio with more than six hundred replacements, although the majority were untrained conscripts. One of the few career officers, Lieutenant Colonel José Juan Sánchez-Navarro, was shocked by the sight of Cos's army when his men entered the Alamo. He found the starving cavalry horses were "eating the capes of the troops and even the trails of the artillery." The Texans pierced the thick partitioning walls between houses and steadily advanced on the key Mexican positions about the central part of town. After dark on December 8, Burleson sent reinforcements to help hold the command of the enemy's northwest portion of defenses.[33]

Fighting continued until the remaining Mexicans retreated into the Alamo before daylight on December 9. Four companies of Cos's cavalry decided not to fight and rode away. Lieutenant Colonel Sánchez-Navarro found that morale was gone. Mexican soldiers were mumbling, "We are lost." Cos summoned his officer during the predawn hours and determined that a truce was the only way to save his remaining men. He authorized Sánchez-Navarro to approach the rebel commander under a white flag of truce. The more defiant men under Colonel Nicolas Condelle condemned such an action but reluctantly agreed to the orders of General Cos.

Sánchez-Navarro advanced into the streets of San Antonio with his white flag and met with Colonel Burleson. The two sides agreed upon a cease-fire, but the terms of the truce were discussed until 2 A.M. on December 10. For the Mexicans, the terms were quite generous. They would be allowed six days to recover in Béxar. Then they were to retire with their personal arms, ten rounds of ammunition, and one four-pound cannon to protect themselves against Indian attack while retiring toward the Rio Grande.[34]

The assault on Béxar had cost the Texans the lives of Ben Milam, Captain Peacock, and two others. Another fourteen had been wounded, some seriously. As many as 150 Mexican soldiers had been killed in the conflict. A renewed sense of confidence swept through the volunteer army. James Grant and others pushed the idea of carrying forth with an offensive expedition all the way to Matamoros.

German-born Herman Ehrenberg hoped that the news of the defeat in Béxar would sweep through the Mexican nation, compelling its occupants to "rise in revolt in order to overthrow Santa Anna and his administration." Many of the volunteers took shelter in the Alamo to protect themselves from the cold. Others, like Colonel Ed Burleson, headed for their homes to take care of their loved ones. Juan Seguín disbanded his mounted *tejano* company and rejoined his wife and children as numerous Béxareños cautiously made their way back into the battered town to inspect their homes.[35]

News of the great Texas victory spread through the U.S. papers with reference to the rebels of 1776. By the end of December, theaters in New York and New Orleans were preparing to open plays that celebrated the frontiersmen of the Texas Revolution. It was good that the Texians could finally rejoice for a time, but some were left to wonder if President Santa Anna would sit idly by and accept such a defeat.

6

REVOLUTIONARY RANGERS

JOE PARKER WAS PLEASED to be spending Christmas with his brother. In the past week, he had driven a wagon and horse team some 170 miles from Fort Sterling down the Old San Antonio Road to San Felipe. He was making a supply run for the rangers presided over by his brother Silas back at the Parker family's fortress.[1]

Daniel Parker Sr. was pleased to see his brother arrive safely. He was still engaged in the ongoing business of the General Council. On December 19, the council had sent orders to Major Willie Williamson to proceed to Mina to establish his headquarters for his new Corps of Rangers. Orders also went out to the three new ranger captains to begin recruiting their companies for Williamson's command. Captain Isaac Burton was to proceed to the Sabine River to establish his recruiting station, while Captains John Tumlinson and William Arrington were to similarly organize their rangers in their respective communities of Mina in Robertson's Colony and Gonzales in DeWitt's Colony. Major Williamson's new ranger battalion would require at least some weeks to recruit men fresh from the Béxar campaign. This left the detail of frontier protection largely to the four-district regional ranger system as the new year of 1836 commenced.[2]

Joe Parker was a full three weeks in making his round-trip covered wagon provision run to San Felipe. His team hauled back one hundred pounds of lead for musket balls, one and a half kegs of black powder, corn meal, bacon, beef, pork, bushels of corn, horse feed, and countless other necessities required of mounted frontiersmen serving in the winter elements.[3]

By the time Parker unhitched his wagon within the stockade fence of Fort Sterling on January 9, 1836, things had changed. Captain Eli Hillhouse, commander of Silas Parker's original company, had passed away. In his place the company had been taken over by Captain Eli Seale, who had been with the unit since its creation in October. The General Council had approved a secondary company of rangers in Silas Parker's region and on January 1 Captain James Wilson Parker (brother to Silas) had mustered in his ten-man unit. They would remain in service through April 27, 1836. Captain Seale's company completed three months of service in late January 1836, at which time Captain James A. Head took command for another three-month period. The rangers under superintendent Silas Parker thus covered the East Texas frontiers for a full six months of the Texas Revolution from the Parker family's fortification.[4]

Another ranger unit was brought into operation on January 1 about sixty miles to the northeast in the adjacent regional ranger district presided over by superintendent Garrison Greenwood. He had been tasked by the General Council to raise ten men to range the frontiers between the Neches and Trinity rivers. Greenwood and five other families had been the first Anglo settlers in this region when they departed Nacogdoches in July 1835 to start a new community fifty miles beyond the extremes of existing frontier settlements. They selected a site eight miles east of the Trinity River with fertile soils and ample water supply from several creeks. They named their town Houston in honor of Sam Houston, the prominent Nacogdoches settler and former Tennessee governor the families had become acquainted with.[5]

The approach of winter kept the pioneers busy. They constructed proper log homes and also a pine blockhouse, for protection against Indians, which was named Fort Houston. Greenwood selected William Turner Sadler, one of the bachelor pioneers with experience in the Seminole and Creek Indian wars, to command his new ranger unit. Born in Lincoln County, North Carolina, thirty-eight-year-old Sadler had first surveyed this area of East Texas in 1822 before selling his Georgia farm to settle permanently in the new frontier. He traveled over land and water en route with another Texas-bound immigrant named Mirabeau Buonaparte Lamar, a fellow Georgian who was destined for great fame in the Mexican-owned territory. Lamar, who learned that he was distantly related to William Sadler by marriage, considered his companion to be "an unassuming and intelligent gentleman."[6]

Captain Sadler formally enrolled his ten-man ranger company on January 1, 1836, at the Fort Houston settlement. Among his volunteers were Dickerson Parker and Daniel Parker Jr., sons of the San Felipe representative who had introduced the act to form the regional rangers months earlier. Sadler's rangers had little trouble with Indians during early 1836 and worked on fortifying their blockhouse in between scouting patrols.

In the district to the west of those presided over by Greenwood and Silas Parker was that of Captain Daniel Friar. His ranger company operated from the settlement at the Falls of the Brazos River during early 1836, using Fort Viesca as their staging post. The town's only fortified blockhouse was renamed Fort Milam in December 1835 in honor of Ben Milam's sacrifice during the recent Béxar siege. Friar's rangers were armed with both traditional flintlock and percussion cap rifles and they drew provisions as needed from San Felipe. The General Council considered Friar's company and his superintendence to be a temporary condition, existing only until Major Williamson could properly raise his new ranging corps. Daniel Friar's men served through February 1, covering three months of duty during the Texas Revolution.[7]

One other ad hoc ranging company was formed in January in Robertson's Colony to handle a temporary Indian crisis. James and Thomas Riley, a pair of brothers in the business of surveying, were attacked by about forty Caddos and Comanches near the San Gabriel River. Thomas was killed but James Riley escaped with four severe wounds. Empresario Sterling Robertson took to the field with sixty-five volunteer rangers for several weeks but did not manage to engage any of the hostile forces.[8]

It would be one of Willie Williamson's new companies that carried out the first successful Indian battle of 1836 for the Texas Rangers.

THE TATTERED, BLOND-HAIRED WOMAN was bloodied and looked to be in a state of shock.

Noah Smithwick was preparing his supper over a campfire when young Sarah Creath Hibbins stumbled from the brush. Her arms and legs were caked with dried blood, her flesh and clothing lacerated by thorns. The woman dragged herself into the little ranger camp and collapsed. "It was some time before she could give a coherent explanation of her situation," Smithwick recalled.[9]

Once she could control her emotions, Sarah Hibbins said that she had been traveling in an oxcart from Columbia-on-the-Brazos with her husband, John, her son John McSherry Jr. (from a previous marriage), her new infant, and her brother, George Creath. They were still about fifteen miles from their home when they stopped to make camp for the night on Rocky Creek. They were attacked by a party of about thirteen Comanches, who swiftly killed the two older men. Sarah, her infant, and three-year-old John McSherry were taken captive while the Comanches plundered the settlers' belongings.[10]

Smithwick listened in horror as Sarah described how the Comanches became irritated with the wailing of the Hibbins baby. "The Indians snatched it from her and dashed its brains out against a tree," he recalled. A bitter norther set in and the Indians made camp near where the city of Austin now stands. Once they were sound asleep in their buffalo robes, Sarah escaped from camp at night—leaving her young son behind. She fled on foot, covering her tracks by moving along the cold Colorado River toward the nearest settlements. She moved nearly ten miles in twenty-four hours, working through heavy brush and unforgiving briars until she came upon a herd of grazing cattle late the next afternoon.[11]

The first white men she encountered before dusk on January 19 were Smithwick and his party of eighteen rangers, who were camped on the headwaters of Brushy Creek some thirty miles northwest of the future capital city of Austin. The company was commanded by Captain John Tumlinson, one of Major Williamson's three units of the new Corps of Rangers. He had recruited rangers for a one-year service period and mustered in his original men on January 17 at the settlement of Hornsby's Station. Noah Smithwick, a veteran of the Battle of Concepción, had returned to Mina in December to recover from a nasty fever, thus missing the battle for Béxar. The rangers of Captain Tumlinson had set out from Hornsby's Station to build a frontier blockhouse near the head of Brushy Creek, where Sarah Hibbins happened upon them.

Tumlinson ordered his rangers to finish their supper and to mount up as Sarah pleaded with them to save her boy from the Comanches. They rode hard through the night under the direction of guide Reuben Hornsby, pausing only a short while before daybreak to rest their horses. Scouts found the trail of the Indians after daybreak on January 20. Tumlinson came upon the camp of the thirteen Indians around 9 A.M. on Walnut Creek. "The Indians discovered us just as we discovered them, but had not time to get their horses," said Captain Tumlinson.[12]

He ordered Second Lieutenant Joseph W. Rogers to take eight rangers around the camp to cut off their possible retreat. The Comanches left their horses and raced for the hillside thickets. Tumlinson and Rogers's two contingents immediately charged. Just as Tumlinson leapt from his horse, it was killed by a rifle ball through the neck. The captain turned his own weapon on the Comanche who had just fired and dropped him dead. Smithwick shot down another fleeing Indian and stopped to load his rifle. "A limb knocked my hat off and one of my comrades, catching a glimpse of me flying bareheaded through the brake on foot, mistook me for a Comanche and raised his gun," he recalled. "But another ranger dashed the gun aside in time to save me."[13]

The Comanche shot by Smithwick proceeded to reload his gun while lying wounded on the ground. Ranger Conrad

Rohrer, a burly Dutchman from Pennsylvania, quickly grabbed the Indian's own gun and smashed in his skull. In the brief fire-fight, Private Elijah Ingram had his arm shattered by a musket ball and Methodist minister Hugh Childress was shot through the leg. Captain Tumlinson's company killed four of the Co-manches before the balance, some wounded, escaped into a thicket too dense for safe pursuit. Lieutenant Rogers and sev-eral rangers managed to capture all of the Indians' camp goods and horses. Young John McSherry, wrapped in buffalo robes and tied to a mule, was nearly killed when the beast ran from camp following the battle. Fortunately, the ranger who tried to gun down the fleeing "Indian" missed his mark and only suc-ceeded in bringing down the runaway mule.[14]

Joe Rogers and his men selected the best horse from their captured lot to replace the one lost by their captain. The rang-ers decided that Smithwick's shot on the wounded Comanche afforded him the honor of scalping his first dead Indian. He modestly waived his claim, saying that Conrad Rohrer had fin-ished off the Comanche with his rifle butt. Rohrer scalped the Indian with his knife but said that the pelt belonged to Smith-wick, to whose saddle he tied "the loathsome trophy." Smith-wick later wrote, "I permitted it to remain, thinking it might afford the poor woman, whose family its owner had helped to murder, some satisfaction to see that gory evidence that one of the wretches had paid the penalty of his crime."

Tumlinson's rangers made their way back to Hornsby's Sta-tion to seek medical attention for their wounded. Lieutenant Rogers presented the recovered boy, John McSherry, to his grieving mother, Sarah Hibbins. "Not an eye was dry," recalled Tumlinson. "She called us brothers, and every other endearing name, and would have fallen on her knees to worship us."[15]

Captain Tumlinson's rangers would remain in the area

during the next two months as they completed construction of their fortification beside a huge live oak tree where the present town of Leander stands. They had no further Indian encounters during the Texas Revolution but maintained vigilant patrols during that time from west of the Colorado River to east of the Brazos River.

John Tumlinson's January 20, 1836, fight near Walnut Creek was the first between Comanches and Texas Rangers. There would be plenty more engagements between these rival frontiersmen in the decades that followed.

7

"YOU MAY ALL GO TO HELL AND I WILL GO TO TEXAS"

PRESIDENT SANTA ANNA WAS plotting his return to Texas even before he learned of the embarrassing loss General Cos had suffered at San Antonio de Béxar.

He already had a reputation for saving his people. He moved swiftly after hearing of the seizure of the Goliad presidio and the conflict at Gonzales. Santa Anna now saw the chance to put down the unrest in Texas just as he had crushed opposition in Zacatecas before. He traveled to Mexico City in early November to begin organizing his Army of Operations, which would surpass six thousand men in short order. His country's war chest was depleted, forcing Santa Anna to finance his new expedition with high-interest loans from the church and private lenders.[1]

El Presidente ordered units from around his country to supply men to fill out his Army of Operations' infantry, cavalry, and artillery forces. His expedition would include an almost equal number of regular army forces or *permanentes* and the active militia or *activos*. His senior leaders were veterans he trusted. General Vicente Filisola, a forty-six-year-old born in Italy, was Santa Anna's second in command. General Manuel Fernández Castrillón, his aide-de-camp, was a seasoned military man who had fought alongside Santa Anna for more than a decade. Castrillón, born in Cuba before changing his allegiance from Spain during the Mexican Revolution, was one of the few who dared stand up to their commander in chief when necessary.[2]

News of General Cos's besiegement at Béxar reached the capital and Santa Anna quickly sent reinforcements to his aid. General Joaquín Ramírez y Sesma, a forty-year-old cavalry leader renowned for his bravery, was sent toward Béxar with a Vanguard Brigade of one cavalry regiment, three battalions of infantry, and a battery of light artillery. His troops departed Zacatecas on November 11 for Laredo, the Rio Grande settlement that would serve as the primary base of operations for the march into Texas. Santa Anna temporarily left his political duties behind in Mexico City and moved to the city of San Luis Potosí in early December to organize his army. Once assembled, the army was moved about 120 miles north to the mountain city of Saltillo for final preparations.

On December 20, Santa Anna learned of the defeat of Cos at Béxar. He made plans to eventually cross his troops over the Rio Grande at Guerrero, eighty miles upriver from Laredo, to catch the enemy rebels off guard. Days later, Cos's weary survivors straggled into Laredo, where they were met by General Ramírez y Sesma's Vanguard Force. Santa Anna's main contingent of his army remained in Saltillo well into January as the commander in chief worked to bring his soldiers up to military par.

Many of his men were raw recruits with little or no army experience. The infantrymen were drilled on marching and basic formations but little lead or powder was wasted on practice firing of their muskets. The foot soldiers carried India-pattern Brown Bess smoothbore musket rifles with seventeen-inch bayonets that had been used by British troops for nearly a century. These muzzle-loading flintlocks fired massive .75-caliber lead balls but were not reliable beyond about seventy yards. Inferior Mexican gunpowder often compelled the infantrymen to use double loads of powder that produced a powerful kick and a large powder flash in the pan near a man's face and eyes.[3]

Each infantry battalion, on paper at least, comprised eight companies of eighty men each—although Santa Anna's army did well to have half that number in most companies. Each battalion included six line companies of regular soldiers and two companies of the elite members, known as the *granaderos* (grenadiers) and the *cazadores* (hunters). The *granaderos* were veteran soldiers usually held in reserve when a conflict commenced. The *cazadores* were elite marksmen, often armed with superior British Baker .61-caliber rifles, which were easier to reload and were accurate up to three hundred yards.

Santa Anna's Army of Operations was fitted out with colorful uniforms, a striking contrast to the frontier rags worn by the Texians they would face. Mexican cavalrymen wore short red coats and blue cloth trousers, black leather crested helmets with brass plating, waist-belt sabers, long wooden lances with steel tips, holster pistols, and short-barreled British Paget carbines.

Infantrymen wore white or blue trousers, blue pigeon-tailed jackets with red trim and white crossbelts, and stiff black shako hats adorned with brass plates and small red plumes.

Mexican officers wore more formal attire: black riding boots, blue jackets with scarlet frontpieces, cuffs, and high collars, embroidered with golden leaves of olive, palm, and laurel. The staff wore white or gray trousers, golden epaulets, and wide waist sashes of green or blue color. Certainly, the "Great Napoleon of the West"—as Santa Anna fancied himself—had an impressive-looking military.

The drilling of his troops at Saltillo consumed the better part of January 1836. When his forces prepared to move out, Santa Anna was faced with great difficulties. Scarcity of water was a constant issue, and common men had to be hired to drive the supply carts. A small army of women and children followed the soldiers, with many of the women serving as cooks, nurses, and foragers. When the five-thousand man army pushed north, its artillery corps had but twenty-one pieces of ordnance, the largest being two twelve-pound cannons.[4]

Santa Anna's occupation force finally moved from Saltillo on January 31. The first leg of their journey was through mountain peaks on the old mule trail known as El Camino Real—Spanish for "the Royal Road" or the more Anglican translation of "The King's Highway." The Camino Real roadway was the most direct artery from Mexico City, stretching all the way across the Texas territory into Louisiana. The Mexican Army marched some 150 miles north from Mexico City to Monclova. Béxar lay another 300 miles farther, through vast areas with little grass for their animals, little water for their men, and a brutal winter that taxed the foot soldiers as they trudged endlessly through bitter winds and driving rains.

En route to Monclova, Santa Anna organized his forces into

five units. By January 16, General Ramírez y Sesma's 1,541-man Vanguard Brigade had reached Guerrero on the Rio Grande. General Eugenio Tolsa's 1,839-man Second Infantry Brigade was on the march from Saltillo by January 31. General Antonio Gaona's 1,600-man First Infantry Brigade departed on February 1, along with General Santa Anna, his staff, fifty escorting lancers, and, finally, General Juan Andrade's 437-man Cavalry Brigade.

Lieutenant José Enrique de la Peña, a twenty-nine-year-old aide for Colonel Francisco Duque's Toluca Battalion, wrote that Santa Anna "was more renowned for the success with which he stirred up rebellions that tended to destroy his homeland than for his military feats." The general was a man "whose irascible temperament did not lend itself to discussion." [5]

There would be no mercy for the rebel Texians when the Mexican Army next confronted them. Santa Anna instructed his soldiers on the various bugle calls, including the Spanish *degüello* ("slit throat") call for "no quarter." The commander in chief made his intentions perfectly clear in his issued instructions. The Texas foreigners waging war on Mexico had violated all laws. "No quarter will be given them," Santa Anna declared. "They have audaciously declared a war of extermination to the Mexicans and should be treated in the same manner." [6]

The Anglo colonists and anyone who assisted them were to be treated just as treasonous barbarians or pirates. They were to be executed.

THE VOLUNTEER ARMY OF Texas was showing its weaknesses.

Men not bound to a constant service period had families and private lives to tend to and the provisional government was still in its formative period. By the end of December, a mere hundred men remained on duty in Béxar. The senior officer present was Lieutenant Colonel James Neill, who had most recently commanded artillerymen during the siege. He kept quarters in town while about half his men, led by thirty-year-old Captain William Carey, moved into the vacated Alamo compound.

The men who had not headed for their homes had taken most of the ammunition, supplies, and horses from the old Spanish mission to follow Dr. James Grant on his planned Matamoros expedition. Colonel Johnson was seeking approval from Governor Henry Smith and the General Council in San Felipe. Neill was left frustrated, and he wrote angry letters to Smith and to Sam Houston about the ill state of affairs at the Alamo. Should the Mexican Army return for a counterattack, he and Carey were managing an unruly bunch of volunteers who continued to dwindle. Their lack of proper winter clothing, sufficient meals, and payment of any kind compelled others in San Antonio to drift away. Those who remained turned to gambling, women, and alcohol to alleviate their boredom.

One of the more valuable men who remained proved to be Green Benjamin "Ben" Jameson, the appointed garrison engineer. He was convinced he could improve the fortifications of what he called the Fortress Alamo. The former attorney took inventory of the necessary materials and drew up plans to repair the crumbling compound. He used the available officers and men to haul the captured Mexican cannon through the main gate and place them on platforms built along the mission's perimeter. The largest artillery piece was an eighteen-pounder that Captain Philip Dimitt had brought in from the coast shortly after the departure of General Cos. It was hoisted onto a wooden platform erected above a partially collapsed one-story house at the northwest corner of the Alamo compound.[7]

Rumors reached San Antonio in early January that a thousand Mexican troops were marching from Laredo on the Rio Grande. Lieutenant Colonel Neill was also visited by a Comanche spokesman on January 8, who informed him that their nation was in a hostile attitude toward the rebels who had stirred up the Mexican forces. Neill continued his correspondence with Governor Smith, seeking relief for his men against two potentially deadly groups.

The governor and the General Council had in the meantime given in to the pressures of Dr. Grant, Frank Johnson, and other volunteers who desired to move in force against Matamoros. Smith gave the nod to commander in chief Sam Houston to make a "demonstration" against the Mexican town. Houston began making plans in late December to use Jim Bowie's forces in Goliad and other companies under Colonel James Fannin to carry out the Matamoros expedition. The council proceeded to confuse the entire issue by authorizing both Johnson and Fannin to lead the march, and each man claimed the role of commander. Governor Smith then ordered General Houston to move from Washington-on-the-Brazos to Goliad to personally assume command of the offensive.[8]

The confusion spilled over into a division between Henry Smith and his General Council at San Felipe. Harsh words ensued between the leaders, and Smith finally proclaimed the council dissolved. They responded by impeaching Governor Smith and continued to operate with Lieutenant Governor James W. Robinson serving as the acting governor. Confused leaders such as James Neill in the Alamo were left writing to both sides of the quarreling government for support. When Sam Houston reached Goliad on January 14, he found Bowie still in town. The veteran knife fighter had not received the orders to take command of the Matamoros offensive from Dr. Grant. Houston then sent Bowie and a company of volunteers on to

Béxar on January 17, with discretionary orders to "blow up the Alamo and abandon the place" if necessary.[9]

General Houston then joined Grant's army on its march to Refugio. His efforts to win over the men were dashed when word reached Refugio that the council had deposed Governor Smith, ousted Houston as the supreme commander of the military, and authorized James Fannin to lead the expedition. Houston departed Refugio on January 28 and reported to Henry Smith two days later. The man who still claimed the title of governor instructed Houston to visit with his old friend Chief Bowles in East Texas. Bowles, known also as Duwali in his native tongue, had led his band of Cherokee people into eastern Texas in 1819. Houston's goal was to persuade the Cherokees to remain neutral to the Texians with a treaty that persuaded them to ignore any lures of allegiance to the Mexican Army.

Bowie's company, although small in number, was a refreshing site to Alamo commander James Neill when they arrived at Béxar in January. Bowie was impressed with the character of Colonel Neill, and he wrote to Governor Smith that "no other man in the army could have kept men at this post under the neglect they have experienced." He also found Ben Jameson fully engaged in shoring up the Alamo with his cannon on the walls. Jameson proudly boasted that if the Mexicans should try to storm the fortress, his defenders could whip them ten-to-one with their artillery. Bowie abandoned any orders that he might have received to blow up the Alamo. By February 2, he was so convinced of the fort's defenses that he wrote to Smith, saying he and Neill would "die in these ditches" before surrendering the Alamo.[10]

Smith was in agreement for bolstering the Béxar garrison, as he had already issued orders to Lieutenant Colonel William Travis to raise a company and march to San Antonio. Travis sent a written protest on January 29, even threatening to resign his commission, about having to take such few men without proper provisions. In the end, Travis gave in to the orders and arrived at the Alamo on February 3. Other volunteers began trickling in to Béxar, and Travis soon became more motivated to defend the place.[11]

The biggest morale boost for Travis, Bowie, and Neill came on February 8, with the arrival at the Alamo of a group of volunteers led by Davy Crockett, a Tennessee frontier legend.

David Crockett had won early fame as a militiaman in the Creek Indian War serving under Andrew Jackson. He was elected into the Tennessee legislature in both 1821 and 1823. During the next decade, he would be elected three times to the U.S. Congress, where his reputation as a storyteller, sharpshooter, and bear hunter captured national attention. He was the model for the hero of a play that opened in New York City in 1831, and two years later a book on Colonel Crockett's life and adventures was published. He would even be immortalized in a series of comic almanacs beginning in 1835. Most of the adventures therein were merely tall tales, but the literature forever branded him with the public nickname of "Davy" versus David.[12]

Crockett published an autobiography in 1834 to help correct some of the stories previously written of his life's adventures. He was marketed as an anti-Jackson candidate in his 1835 congressional campaign but Tennessee voters abandoned him over peg-legged Jackson favorite Adam Huntsman in what Crockett felt was a rigged election. Crockett's pride was wounded and his finances were tapped, so he decided he would move his family to Texas if the prospects there proved pleasing to him. He headed west on November 1, 1835, with three companions in tow. Reaching Memphis the first evening, the foursome enjoyed a farewell drinking party with other friends. Before the night was over, Davy Crockett uttered a soon-to-be famous declaration: "Since you have chosen to elect a man with a timber toe to succeed me, you may all go to hell and I will go to Texas."

Crockett played up his public image before departing Memphis the next day. He kept his dress clothes tucked into his saddlebag and instead donned his hunting shirt and a fur cap, to the pleasure of the crowd. He and his companions journeyed down the Mississippi River, made their way to Fulton, Arkansas, and then moved across the Red River into Texas. Two of his friends headed for home once they had reached San Augustine, but Crockett, William Patton, and others pushed on toward Nacogdoches in late December. The ladies of the town threw a banquet in his honor, where Crockett was not afraid to use his story that concluded with "you may all go to hell and I will go to Texas." He was pleased with the opportunities he saw in Texas, calling it "the garden spot of the world." In the same letter, penned to his oldest daughter on January 9, Crockett added, "I am rejoiced at my fate."[13]

The legendary Davy Crockett felt that Texas offered him the chance to start a new chapter in his political career. He opted for military service despite being nearly fifty years of age and took the oath of allegiance on January 12 before Nacogdoches judge John Forbes. He then signed the printed document, promising his allegiance to the provisional government of Texas or any future "republican" government that may be thereafter declared—Crockett carefully adding the word *republican* to his paper.

The former Tennessee congressman soon headed west along the Old San Antonio Road to report to General Houston. He rode with about sixteen other new volunteers, many of whom had been lawyers and professionals in Tennessee and Kentucky.

They began to refer to themselves as the Tennessee Mounted Volunteers. When they arrived at Washington-on-the-Brazos some 125 miles later, they found that Sam Houston was absent during his efforts to control the Matamoros expedition. Crockett and his men were directed to report to San Antonio. The men of the Alamo threw an impromptu fandango when the Tennessee Mounted Volunteers arrived on February 8 and they requested a speech from the much-celebrated Davy Crockett. The coy politician quickly won over the Béxar Texians by saying that he had come to aid their noble cause. He said he had no desire to be a senior officer. He wished to fight alongside them as a mere private soldier for "the liberties of our common country." [14]

TEXAS REMAINED WITHOUT CLEAR leadership during February.

James Robinson continued to serve as the acting governor since the General Council had impeached Henry Smith—who continued to send orders of his own to those loyal to him. There was, however, hope for an end to the bitter feuding, as elections were held throughout Texas on February 1 for delegates to represent all municipalities one month later at a formal convention at Washington-on-the-Brazos. The interim General Council at San Felipe would thus cease to exist as the new convention went to work drafting a formal declaration of independence and organizing a proper government body for Texas.

During the delegate election in the town of Tenoxtitlan, the citizens also cast ballots for a new company of rangers to patrol their district to replace the outgoing company of Captain Daniel Friar. They elected Captain Louis Franks, a surveyor and former lieutenant colonel of artillery during the December Béxar assault. The Franks rangers operated during February and March from the Falls of the Brazos area in Robertson's Colony.

A second volunteer ranging company was formed on February 1 under thirty-six-year-old Captain Stephen Townsend in the Colorado River settlements to deal with recent Indian violence.[15]

The General Council did address pressing issues, some of them aimed at bolstering the Texas Ranger system. With the Texas Army grappling over who was in command and whether it was more important to defend Béxar or assault Matamoros, frontier protection was still crucial to the settlers. The council found during early February that the two previously authorized ranger systems had not been fully developed due to the state of affairs in Texas. One of the four regional ranger superintendents had yet to raise a company in his district, while only two-thirds of Major Willie Williamson ranger battalion had been raised.

The companies of Captains John Tumlinson and Isaac Burton were still not fully manned as of February. Williamson's third captain, William Arrington, had not raised his company at all. The General Council's special advisory committee informed Governor Robinson that two main reasons seemed to curb ranger recruiting efforts: the volunteers were not pleased with the rate of pay offered and they were unwilling to serve in Williamson's battalion since the government had already appointed the ranger officers for them.[16]

The council thus proposed to add two new ranger companies to help overcome the recruiting deficit. Mathew Caldwell, Byrd Lockhart, and William A. Mathews were named ranger-raising commissioners for the Municipality of Gonzales. In the Municipality of Milam, Daniel Friar, David Faulkenberry, and Joseph Parker were charged with drumming up new frontiersmen. The council directed the field recruiters to let the men elect their own officers, to help appease them. Once twenty-eight men were raised, the rangers could elect a lieutenant to muster them into service. The commissioners were to then recruit another twenty-eight rangers, at which time the collective fifty-six men were to elect their captain and two lieutenants. Privates would be paid the same $1.25 per day rate as the previous rangers were being paid, but there was now an extra five dollars per month thrown in to offset personal expenses for provisions.[17]

The new ranger commissioners soon became aware of the two ad hoc ranging companies under Captains Franks and Townsend but did nothing to oppose them. They decided that Townsend's company was necessary and should be stationed at the head of Mill Creek, a recommendation seconded by Major Williamson. Since Townsend had not raised a full fifty-six rangers, however, the commissioners believed that he should be considered a first lieutenant for the time being.

The council further prodded Willie Williamson to get involved in the recruiting of his own companies and to build blockhouses at points on the frontier deemed best suited for defense. The peg-legged leader would maintain his ranger headquarters at Mina and was to make regular reports to the governor and the council of the actions of his men. The rangers would prove vital to both the frontier settlers and to the Texas Army in the weeks ahead. A new challenge was entering the rebel nation that would challenge all the defenses it could muster.

JOSÉ ENRIQUE DE LA Peña was not prepared for such a blizzard.

As the Mexican Army pushed northward from Monclova during the second week of February, it was greeted by the most severe winter on record. Vicente Filisola recorded that the blizzard encountered on the evening of February 13 dumped more than fifteen inches of snow on the ground. The green trees the men could find to burn for fires smoked heavily and were soon extinguished by heavy snowfall. "At dawn it was knee-deep," said Peña. "One could not remain standing or sitting, much less lying down. Those not taking care to shake their clothes frequently soon were numb with cold." [18]

The Tampico Regiment left its mules and horses fully loaded. Many of the animals were badly injured or killed as they slipped and fell on the icy grounds. "The snow was covered with the blood of these beasts, contrasting with its whiteness," Peña recorded. In spite of such great hardships, the Mexican Army valiantly pushed forward during the ensuing days. Santa Anna crossed the Rio Grande at Paso de Francia with his staff on February 16. His plan was to surprise the Texians by driving up the Camino Real to approach Béxar from the west. One day later, General José Urrea moved across the river at Matamoros with 550 men. His orders were to sweep the coastal prairies and then retake Goliad.[19]

Santa Anna's force caught up with Ramirez y Sesma's Vanguard Brigade as the weather began warming. The commanding general turned forty-two on February 21, a day that his combined forces reached the Medina River, the official boundary between the Mexican states of Texas and Coahuila. Santa Anna made camp twenty-two miles east of Béxar to rest his exhausted troops and pack animals. They had covered some five hundred miles through torturous conditions, but their goal was now close at hand. Mexican sympathizers rode into his camp on February 22 and provided El Presidente with the latest intelligence on the Texians holed up in Béxar.[20]

Santa Anna ordered the 160 lancers of the Dolores Cavalry Regiment to mount up on the best horses they could obtain. He believed that they might just catch the rebel defenders off guard before they could take shelter in the old Spanish Alamo garrison.

8

"I SHALL NEVER SURRENDER OR RETREAT"

LIEUTENANT COLONEL TRAVIS WAS beginning to doubt himself.

He and many of his men had not expected the Mexican Army to reach San Antonio before mid-March. When some of the local Béxareños began packing their belongings and evacuating town on February 20, he began to feel there might be some truth to the intelligence reports of the enemy's advance from the Rio Grande.

William Barret Travis had reached the Alamo on February 3 with his small group of volunteers and his twenty-one-year-old slave, Joe. He found that engineer Ben Jameson had done solid work in placing cannon about the fortress walls, shoring up the battered north wall, and piling felled trees to create a barrier along the most exposed area of the three-acre compound. Small parties of volunteers under Philip Dimitt, David Crockett, and others had arrived at Béxar in the days that followed.

The command situation suddenly shifted when Colonel James Neill departed on a twenty-day leave from the Alamo to tend to family matters. He transferred command of the fort to twenty-six-year-old Travis, who held a proper commission in the army. Jim Bowie had a colonel's title given to him by volunteers and Crockett had expressed his desire to remain a private soldier. Formal commissions mattered little to the volunteers of the Alamo, many of whom resented having regular officer Travis forced upon them. They insisted on an election, to which Travis had little choice but to agree. The volunteers voted for Bowie while the regulars generally preferred Travis.

Bowie became the people's choice, and he proceeded to celebrate his victory with an embarrassing two-day drinking binge. In his stupor, he ordered the release of all prisoners being held in town and had his men detain any families from leaving Béxar. He also had some of his drunken soldiers parade around Main Plaza under arms to defy the authority of Juan Seguín in trying to return one convict to jail. Travis was outraged with the behavior, particularly when word arrived from Seguín's spies that a thousand Mexican troops were on the move near the Rio Grande. He wrote to Henry Smith, begging to be relieved of his command. "I am unwilling to be responsible for the drunken irregularities of any man," Travis relayed. He suggested he would remain only until Smith could send a regular artillery officer to return order to the Alamo.[1]

Bowie soon sobered up on February 13 and expressed remorse for his wild behavior. He and Travis then reached a compromise: Bowie would command the volunteers and Travis the regulars, with both men signing all official papers until Neill could return. Bowie would not be in shape to command for long, however. His health declined over the next few days due to a respiratory ailment deemed to be typhoid fever by some or even tuberculosis or pneumonia by others. In any event, he was soon spending most of his time confined to bed in the Ve-ramendi house while Travis slowly took over the duties of running their garrison.

The Alamo defenders continued fortifying their position until February 22, the birthday of American hero George Washington. The men held a fandango that night, eating, drinking, and dancing with the local Béxar women into the early morning hours. As they awoke the next morning feeling the effects of their corn liquor, tequila, and mescal, the Texians found the townspeople scurrying about in a frenzy. Some of the Béxareños explained that they were merely going out to work in their fields, but Travis ordered a halt to any further exodus. One of the friendly Mexicans finally informed Travis near noon on February 23 that the Mexican cavalry had arrived within a few hours of the town while the soldiers were partying into the night.[2]

Travis had the main horse herd driven back into town and posted a sentry in the bell tower of the San Fernando church, the highest position in town. The garrison commander surveyed the area from this point and then climbed back down, leaving the sentry with orders to ring the bell if enemy soldiers were spotted. A half hour later, the lookout rang the church bell and cried, "The enemy is in view!"

Others climbed up to see for themselves but could not make out anything. The sentry insisted that the soldiers he had seen had taken cover in the mesquite bushes, but many dismissed it as a false alarm. John Sutherland and garrison storekeeper John W. Smith then offered to ride out west about a mile and a half from town to survey the area. Sutherland advised Travis that if they were seen returning at any pace other than a walk, it was a sign they had encountered the enemy.

Heavy rain had delayed the movements of the Mexican Army the previous evening, but they were on the move during the early hours of February 23. Just after noon, Santa Anna's vanguard forces caught up to Ramirez y Sesma's advance lancers at Alazan Creek, a mile and a half from the Alamo. El Presidente dispatched Colonel José Vicente Miñon with sixty *cazadores* from the Matamoros Battalion to ride ahead and seize the church. Santa Anna pulled on his finest uniform and ceremonial sword as his soldiers checked their weapons in preparation for battle.

Sutherland and Smith arrived on horseback and peered down on Alazan Creek from a low hill. Below them were more than a thousand Mexican troops in uniform. The scouts raced for town along the muddy slope. Sutherland's horse slipped, throwing him to the ground and injuring his right knee, left arm, and neck in the process. Smith helped him back into his saddle and they galloped into Béxar with their alarming signal. The sentry began clanging the church bell, sending townspeople and volunteer soldiers scurrying for cover in their homes and in the Alamo. It was 3 P.M.

Lieutenant Colonel Travis was already scribbling a hasty note to Gonzales alcalde Andrew Ponton. He said that a large force of Mexican troops was now in sight, and he needed more men and provisions. "We have 150 men and are determined to defend the Alamo to the last," Travis wrote. "Give us assistance." He handed this note to thirty-five-year-old scout Launcelot Smither, who rode from Béxar around 4 P.M. for Gonzales.[3]

John Sutherland, injured and unfit now to serve in able fashion, agreed to take another note from Travis on to Gonzales. He departed with his companion John Smith. Travis then selected cavalryman John B. Johnson to carry another note to Goliad with a similar request. He knew that James Fannin commanded hundreds of men at the La Bahía presidio in Goliad but had thus far been reluctant to move any of his forces to San Antonio. "In this extremity, we hope you will send us all the men you can spare promptly," wrote Travis. "We have one hundred and forty-six men, who are determined never to retreat." Johnson took the note, rode through the plaza, and turned northeast toward Goliad.

Davy Crockett approached Travis and asked that his Tennessee boys be assigned a proper position in the Alamo to defend. The able marksmen under Crockett were given the most vulnerable part of the garrison's perimeter—a 115-foot wooden palisade between the church and the low barracks. Mexican troops were already entering the west side of Béxar as they took station. Many of the Béxar citizens fled town. By late afternoon on February 23, Travis's couriers were on their way and the majority of the Texian volunteers were inside the Alamo mission.[4]

Mexican soldiers raised a red banner atop the bell tower of the Church of San Fernando. Its message was clear: *degüello,* or no quarter for anyone who defied the Mexican Army. The rebels were offered the chance to surrender unconditionally, to which Lieutenant Colonel Travis informed a Mexican courier that his answer would be given soon. His reply was one of blatant defiance. The Alamo's eighteen-pounder erupted with a single shot as the garrison's gunners cheered from their posts.[5]

Mexican cannoneers responded with several rounds of howitzers fired at the mission's adobe walls. The Texians who had carried out the siege against General Cos's troops in Béxar months before were now the besieged. Several brief attempts at a parley ended when the Mexican Army refused to agree to any terms demanded by the rebellious foreigners inside the garrison. Travis thus made it clear to his men when he gathered them for a speech that evening: he would resist his enemy to the end.

The Mexican Army began taking up positions within town that evening, but the Alamo defenders held out hope. Sam Houston, the new commander in chief of the Texas Army, was probably organizing new companies to come to their aid. James Fannin had four hundred men only ninety-five miles away who could make a big difference with the current situation. General Cos had endured the Texian siege in late 1835 for more than a month. Surely they could manage a few days until the Texian reinforcements arrived.

GENERAL SAM HOUSTON'S THOUGHTS were far removed from aiding the Alamo on February 23.

He and John Forbes were deeply engaged in carrying out orders of deposed governor Henry Smith with the East Texas Cherokee village of Chief Bowles. In return for their loyalty to the new revolutionary Texas government, the Indians were finally promised their own land in East Texas, a territory fifty miles wide by about thirty miles long. Bowles and his head chief, Big Mush, signed the treaty on February 23, an agreement that covered a dozen Texas tribes: the Cherokees, Shawnees, Delawares, Quapaws, Kickapoos, Biloxis, Ionies, Alabamas, Coushattas, Caddos of the Neches, Tahocullakes, and the Untanguous.[6]

Houston made a ceremonial presentation of goodwill items to Chief Bowles, including a silk vest, a handsome sash, and a brass-hilted military sword. The Cherokee leader would treasure these items until his death, even if the new Texas government never did carry through with any of its land promises for his Indians.

Houston and Forbes immediately rode for Washington-on-the-Brazos, where the general had been voted in as the delegate for Refugio for the March 1 convention. They arrived, ragged and tired, on Monday, February 29. A true army had yet to be raised in Texas, so the commanding general decided it best to let the various factions of volunteers handle things until his present duties with the convention were concluded. The Texas delegates had a declaration of independence to write.

The Matamoros expedition under Colonel Frank Johnson and Dr. James Grant was no closer to offering aid to the Alamo defenders than Sam Houston. They were near the coastal settlement of San Patricio, trying to round up sufficient horses for their offensive on the Rio Grande town. Other Texas companies were widely scattered in southern Texas as of late February: James Fannin's command was at Goliad; Captain Burr H. Duval's company of Kentucky Mustangs was at Refugio for a time; and other soldiers held duty at Copano, one of the principal Texas ports on Aransas Bay.

The Alamo defenders now under siege by some fifteen hundred Mexican troops had no properly organized Texas Army ready and willing to come to their immediate relief.

Efforts to drive the Texas rebels from their Spanish fortress resumed on February 24. The skilled frontiersmen atop the Alamo walls were quite deadly with their long rifles, picking off Mexican soldiers at two hundred yards without any great fear from the enemy's inferior Brown Bess muskets. Inside the compound, Jim Bowie's health continued to decline to the point that he could not function effectively. Bedridden, he ordered his volunteer forces to obey the commands of William Travis.

Engineer Ben Jameson and parties of men worked continually to mend damages inflicted by Mexican cannons that maintained a steady bombardment against the compound's walls. At least two pieces of Alamo artillery were damaged during the second day of the siege but they were soon brought back into operation. By day three, February 24, Lieutenant Colonel Travis was again using his best weapon—his inspirational messages to inspire reinforcements to come to their aid.

His latest paper was addressed "to the people of Texas and all Americans in the world." He called on them "in the name of Liberty, or patriotism & everything dear to the American character, to come to our aid, with all dispatch." Travis estimated Santa Anna's army to number more than a thousand men. "The enemy is receiving reinforcements daily & will, no doubt, increase to three or four thousand in four or five days." He related that his fortress had been continually bombarded for twenty-four hours, but he had yet to lose one of his 150 defenders. "I shall never surrender or retreat," Travis proclaimed. "I am determined to sustain myself as long as possible & die like a soldier who never forgets what is due to his own honor & that of his country—Victory or Death." [7]

To emphasize his determination, Travis underlined the "never surrender or retreat" line, and he underlined "Victory or Death" three times before signing his name to the appeal. He selected Captain Albert Martin, a storekeeper from Gonzales originally from Rhode Island, to ride from the Alamo with his message that night. Martin burst through the main gate and charged through the Mexican lines toward his hometown.

Santa Anna ordered his artillery to resume its bombardment of the Alamo during the morning of February 25. The Texans returned fire and the sharpshooters continued firing from the walls. Around 9:30 A.M., General Castrillón and Colonel Miñon led the Matamoros Battalion and several companies of *cazadores* to within a hundred yards of the fortress. Texas artillery Captains Almeron Dickinson, Samuel Blair, and William Carey directed their men to pound the Mexicans with canister and grapeshot as their enemy took possession of several small adobe huts near the fort's south wall. The Mexican batteries roared back with canister, grape, and cannonballs of their own in a two-hour exchange. In the end, Santa Anna's men suffered two killed and six wounded, and they retreated back out of range.[8]

El Presidente responded by sending a courier down El Camino Real to order up three of General Gaona's best battalions from his First Infantry Brigade. The great Napoleon of the West was not fully consumed with the business of war, though. Castrillón reported to him that he had encountered a widow of a Mexican soldier in one of the houses with her attractive daughter. Santa Anna expressed desire to see the girl, seventeen-year-old Mechora Iniega Barrera, but the mother refused him any contact with her daughter unless sanctified by marriage. The general found a wily soul among his *soldados* who was willing to don the apparel of a priest and he took young Barrera as his wife in his quarters on the Main Plaza. Santa Anna, already married, then retired in the company of his new wife. She would later be sent on to San Luis Potosí in the general's private carriage while Santa Anna conducted his campaign.[9]

The Texian leaders in the Alamo maintained outward optimism. Davy Crockett was animated in pointing men to various duties. He even took up his fiddle at times to boost morale. Bowie, ravaged with illness, had his cot hauled out into the open so he could speak words of encouragement to his volunteers. Artillery exchanges and minor skirmishes carried on until nearly midnight. Lieutenant Colonel Travis wrote a letter to Sam Houston that night in which he singled out Crockett and two other defenders, Charles Despallier and Robert Brown, for their inspiration and bravery thus far. Travis again made strong pleas for reinforcement, adding, "it will be impossible for us to keep them out much longer." [10]

Once again, his letter concluded with "Victory or Death!"

The Alamo leaders held a council of war and voted for a man to be sent to James Fannin at Goliad. They elected Juan Seguín over the objections of Travis, who preferred the key Béxar citizen to remain as his aide and interpreter. Travis was overruled. His comrades offered encouragement to the brave *tejano*. "Ride like the wind," advised Jim Bowie. David Crockett, who had bet he could outshoot Seguín against wild turkeys, chided him: "Don't you forget, we still have a shooting match to attend to. So don't go and get yourself killed." Seguín crawled out of the compound in the darkness, eased his way along a waterway past the Mexican sentries, and met one of his companions, Antonio Cruz y Arocha. Cruz and Seguín spurred their horses and rode into a cold northern wind toward Goliad, hoping they could convince someone to care enough to come to the aid of the Alamo defenders.[11]

The only forces that made positive response to the calls from William Travis were neither regulars nor volunteer army soldiers. They were mustered in as Texas Rangers.

Courier Launcelot Smither had reached Gonzales on the morning of February 24. The message from the Alamo was clear regarding Santa Anna's intentions. "They intend to show no quarter," Travis had written. "If every man cannot turn out to a man, every man in the Alamo will be murdered."

Smither found the Gonzales townspeople armed and ready. Ranger recruiter Byrd Lockhart, appointed as such by the General Council in early February, had already recruited twenty-two men who were not attached to the regular army. He had mustered them into service on February 23 as the "Gonzales Mounted Ranger Company." In keeping with the council's regulations, the rangers needed a full fifty-six-man company to elect a captain. Their original elected leader would be a second lieutenant until full muster could be obtained. They elected Lieutenant George C. Kimbell, a thirty-three-year-old former New Yorker who had settled in Texas in 1825. Kimbell lived with his wife and two young sons in Gonzales, where he was co-owner of a hat factory. His business partner, Almeron Dickinson, was busy commanding an artillery company in the Alamo.

The Gonzales Rangers were a mixed bag, including farmers like Andrew Kent and Dolphin Floyd; Marcus Sewell, an English shoemaker; and Jesse McCoy, who had taken the vicious beating in September that helped start the revolution. They were still in town when a second courier, Captain Albert Martin, arrived from the Alamo during the early morning hours of February 25. He passed his latest appeal to Smither, now rested up from his ride into town the previous morning. He then rode on toward the convention in San Felipe, passing Travis's note once again to another rider en route. On the back of the letter, Smither scribbled his own additional plea: "I hope that everyone will rendezvous at Gonzales as soon as possible, as these brave soldiers are suffering. Don't neglect them." [12]

Major Willie Williamson, commander of a battalion of

Texas Rangers, was also in Gonzales when Captain Martin arrived with the Travis letter. He quickly sent his own orders to Captain John Tumlinson, whose ranger company was still engaged in building its blockhouse on the headwaters of Brushy Creek. They had seen no further action since their January 20 battle with Comanches in which they had recovered the captive young boy. Williamson related the determined "victory or death" pledge of the Alamo defenders and asked Tumlinson to move his company to Bastrop (Mina), keeping spies out to watch for Mexican troops, until he could join them. Major Williamson sent copies of his orders to the governor in San Felipe and then departed Gonzales on February 26 to join his rangers in Mina.[13]

Captain Martin and the new Gonzales ranger leader, Lieutenant George Kimbell, spent another two days scouring the local areas for more volunteers to join them for the trip to San Antonio. Some of the men who had originally mustered into the Gonzales Mounted Ranger Company opted to stay behind and protect their families, replaced by new volunteers. The rangers departed the Gonzales town square on Saturday, February 27, at 2 P.M. They were guided by returning Béxar scout John W. Smith and accompanied by Captain Martin, who was returning to his Alamo command. The twenty-five men who set out included Thomas R. Miller, the richest man in town, and three teenagers—seventeen-year-old Johnnie Gaston, his nineteen-year-old brother-in-law, Johnnie Kellogg, and sixteen-year-old Galba Fuqua.[14]

Lieutenant Kimbell's ragged ranger group might not have been impressive in size or training, but it was a hell of a sight better than anything being dispatched by the Texas Army. Express rider John Johnson had reached Goliad on February 25, two days after riding from Béxar. He delivered the note from

Travis to Lieutenant Colonel James Fannin, who pledged that he would march in the morning with 320 men. He would leave about one hundred men behind in the Goliad presidio, which his men had renamed "Fort Defiance."

Fannin and his men set out on the morning of February 26, but they did not go far. Three of their supply wagons broke down just two hundred yards from Fort Defiance. It was nearly sunset by the time his men wrestled their four small cannon across the San Antonio River. Due to cold weather, they went back into the Goliad fort to sleep for the night. The men returned the next morning to find some of their oxen had wandered away. Without provision carts, the men would have to carry their own supplies, food, and ammunition. They decided they were ill-prepared for any large force of Santa Anna's troops that might be encountered on the road. "It was deemed expedient to return to this post and complete the fortifications," he wrote as justification to acting governor Robinson in a letter that day. Fannin knew that abandoning Goliad would leave the path wide open for General Urrea's advancing soldiers.[15]

THE FOUL WINTER WEATHER did little to slow the determined march of General José Urrea's forces. The night of February 26 was "very raw and excessively cold," Urrea noted in his diary. The near-freezing rain that fell had his dragoons "so numbed by the cold that they could hardly speak." [16]

His men were nevertheless brave and faithful as they swept across the coastal plains of Texas, cutting down other potential Alamo defenders while Fannin's reinforcements were stalling out. Colonel Frank Johnson had divided his rebel command into five separate parties. Three groups were camped in and around San Patricio while two seven-man parties protected the horse herds. General Urrea struck with speed. Johnson was badly surprised and had no time to collect his command. By dawn of February 27, he had taken the Lipantitlán fort and the town. Nine or ten Texans were killed and eighteen men were taken prisoner. Only six, including Colonel Johnson, escaped.[17]

Dr. James Grant and his horse-hunting party were returning to San Patricio, unaware that Urrea had taken the town. Urrea learned that Grant was approaching and he set an ambush along Agua Dulce Creek, about twenty-six miles south of town. Grant and twenty-six men were driving several hundred head of horses toward town on March 2, when more than sixty dragoons came out of the woods.

Plácido Benavides raced toward La Bahía, while Grant and Ruben R. Brown charged to aid their cut-off comrades. Many of the Texans were quickly killed. Grant and Brown tried to escape and raced about seven miles before they were surrounded. They dismounted and prepared to fight to the end. A Mexican cavalryman ran his lance into Brown's arm but Grant quickly shot the soldier from his saddle. Several other Mexicans ran their lances through Grant. Others lassoed Brown and dragged him to the ground.

Ruben Brown was lashed to a horse and taken to Matamoros for interrogation. Before he was escorted from the Agua Dulce Creek battlefield, he witnessed more Mexican officers running their swords through Dr. Grant's corpse. He also saw another wounded Texan begging for mercy. Several dragoons approached him and smashed his skull with the butt of a carbine.[18]

Benavides made his way to La Bahía on March 1 and informed Fannin of the deadly attack. Fannin had chosen not to

TEXAS RISING

march to the aid of the Alamo defenders, and now many of the
men in his area had been killed. His inability to take decisive
action was beginning to foreshadow his own future.

JAMES FANNIN COULD HAVE tripled the manpower of the Texans holed up in the Alamo, but it was not to be. The only relief
party to reach San Antonio was the mounted ranger company
under Lieutenant Kimbell. Captain Martin and guide John
Smith led them cautiously through the brush as they eased
around Mexican campfires near the mission on the night of
February 29. As Kimbell's Gonzales men approached the fort
around 3 A.M on March 1, they were suddenly fired upon by a
nervous sentry.

The thirty-two reinforcements raced into the Alamo as the
gates were swung open. Travis had hoped to see hundreds of
men arriving from Colonel Fannin's command, but any new
faces were welcomed at the moment. It was the beginning of
the eighth day of the siege but Travis allowed his artillerymen
to fire two shots toward Santa Anna in honor of his new arrivals. One cannonball ripped the roof off a house that had been
serving as Santa Anna's headquarters, while the other slammed
into the town's military plaza. David Crockett entertained his
men with his fiddle while Scotsman John McGregor joined in
with his bagpipes.

Santa Anna's troops had continued with their persistent artillery attacks on the Alamo compound's walls each day. Travis
urged his men to conserve their own cannon shot and ammunition. He estimated that at least two hundred shells had fallen
within his compound without causing a single injury. He had
been encouraged by the arrival of the Gonzales rangers, but
was perplexed at why nine days had passed since he and Bowie

had summoned Fannin for help. How could it possibly take so long for reinforcements to march ninety-five miles to Béxar?[19]

The answer arrived just hours later at 11 A.M. on March 3. Courier James Butler Bonham rode into the fortress from Goliad with the disturbing news that Fannin would not be coming. He had elected to maintain his defense of the La Bahía mission. Ten days of fighting the Mexican troops and watching them continue to grow in number was enough to make William Travis realize the inevitable: he would likely be fighting this battle on his own.

Travis took up the pen that evening and wrote a lengthy appeal to the Texas Independence Convention meeting at Washington-on-the-Brazos. "I feel confident that the determined valor and desperate courage heretofore exhibited by my men will not fail them in the last struggle," he wrote. "Although they may be sacrificed to the vengeance of a Gothic enemy, the victory will cost the enemy so dear, that it will be worse to him than a defeat."

Lieutenant Colonel Travis then detailed his remaining resources. He had provisions to last another twenty days for the number of men he had on hand. He needed more lead, more gunpowder, and "two hundred rounds of six, nine, twelve, and eighteen pound balls" for his cannon. Travis defiantly signed this latest plea with "God and Texas—Victory or Death."

AS SANTA ANNA'S TROOPS swarmed into San Antonio, delegates gathered 180 miles to the east at Washington-on-the-Brazos. They met in an unfinished building—with no doors and no glass in its windows—a quarter mile up from the Brazos River landing. The forty-one convention members shivered from the cold air that blew through the little hall.

A committee of five was authorized to write a formal declaration of independence for Texas. It was headed by George C. Childress, an attorney and former newspaper editor, who modeled their document closely on the United States' 1776 declaration. When the draft was read aloud on March 2, 1836, it was approved. Texas was officially declared free from Mexico. Enough mistakes were found in the Texas Declaration of Independence to delay its final signing until the next day, March 3—delegate Sam Houston's forty-third birthday. Two *tejanos,* José Antonio Navarro and Francisco Ruiz, were among the fifty-nine signers of the Texas independence document.

Houston had returned from his Cherokee peace negotiations just in time for the historic convention, and he remained after the independence document was signed. He was determined not to leave until he had been granted absolute control over all military forces, including regulars, volunteers, and rangers. He had seen firsthand the empty powers of a commander in chief over only regular soldiers during the ill-fated Matamoros expedition. The convention's military committee granted Sam Houston the powers he desired, but he stayed on hand at Washington for two more days to partake in the celebrations that ensued for the new nation.[20]

The convention members approved yet another act to provide for frontier rangers on March 3. The resolution for a "Regiment of rangers" was presented by empresario Sterling Robertson, and two of his old acquaintances, Jesse Benton and Griffin Bayne, were appointed as the senior commanders. Colonel Benton and Lieutenant Colonel Bayne were directed to immediately begin recruiting ranger companies to serve during the war, subject to the order of General Sam Houston. Their first was that of Captain William C. Wilson, who had already started mustering in rangers at Milam that week. One other small ranging company was organized in Robertson's Colony near Washington-on-the-Brazos under Captain Thomas Hudson Barron in early March.[21]

Jesse Benton would have little involvement in the recruiting of rangers for his battalion. He soon departed Washington-on-the-Brazos with some recruits to complete a proper military road to the United States, leaving Lieutenant Colonel Bayne to assemble men in the Texas settlements. The Texas convention had done its part to properly provide for the frontiers and to structure the main military. Any reinforcements for Travis and his gallant defenders in Béxar would now be directed by Sam Houston—who seemed content for the moment to continue enjoying the celebrations in Washington.

BY MARCH 4, DAY eleven of the Alamo siege, the Mexican artillery had weakened the walls. His men had rolled a battery of cannon in close enough so that each round caused a portion of the north wall to collapse. Chief engineer Jameson worked his men tirelessly through the night to make hasty repairs with old pieces of timber.[22]

Some of the Texian defenders were beginning to feel despair. Susannah Dickinson heard David Crockett say during the siege that he would prefer to march out and die in the open. "I don't like to be hemmed up," he said. Susannah spent her time working with the other women inside the Alamo cooking for the men, grinding corn, cooking it into cakes and tortillas, and roasting beef. She also assisted in the hospital, where dozens of men lay sick and wounded. Her fifteen-month-old daughter Angelina charmed everyone with her personality. Susannah paid visits to her husband, Captain Dickinson, atop the platform over the church's eastern end when the Mexican bombardments had ceased. She visited with enough men of the fort to understand how much their minds and bodies were suffering from the confinement and realization of their likely fates. Susannah noted that Colonel Crockett was quite the performer with his violin "and often during the siege took it up and played his favorite tunes." [23]

Santa Anna called a meeting of his officers on March 5. Some of his men believed they should just wait. Travis would run out of provisions soon enough and lives could be spared. Lieutenant Colonel Peña did not see the need for such sacrifice over just a handful of men. Santa Anna, however, insisted on attacking and he was supported by at least some of his top officers, including General Ramirez y Sesma and Colonel Juan Nepomuceno Almonte—who had been educated in the United States and was once an envoy to London.

Inside the Alamo, Travis called his men together. He said if anyone wished to escape, they should do so now. Travis drew his sword and used its point to draw a line in the dirt. "I want every man who is determined to stay here and die with me to come across this line," he said. "Who will be first? March!"

Tapley Holland, a twenty-six-year-old artilleryman from Ohio who had participated in the Béxar siege, was the first to cross the line. One by one and in groups the Texians stepped across. Even Jim Bowie asked that his cot be carried across. As Susannah Dickinson watched, the only man to refuse was fifty-year-old Frenchman Louis Rose from Nacogdoches—whose skin was dark enough to pass for a Mexican man. Rose scaled the low wall of the cattle pen in darkness and followed the San Antonio River out of town toward the colonies. [24]

Only one other Texian left the Alamo that night. Travis called for a courier to make one last desperate attempt to solicit aid from Colonel Fannin. Twenty-one-year-old James Lemuel

Allen mounted his mare bareback and headed out the main gate before the moon could rise. He raced past the Mexican sentinels and galloped toward Goliad with his verbal instructions.

The remaining defenders prepared to accept their fates. Travis made the rounds, stopping to visit with Susannah Dickinson and her daughter. He removed a gold ring embedded with a black cat's-eye stone, put it on a string, and placed it around the neck of little Angelina. David Crockett donned a pair of clothes recently washed by the women of the fort, saying in jest that he wished to die in clean clothing in order that he might be given a decent burial. Other defenders gave watches, jewelry, and other valuables to the women for safekeeping.[25]

Travis did consider the option of surrendering his men, on the terms that their lives would be spared if they gave up their guns. One Mexican woman left the fort that night and passed the word to Santa Anna. Both Peña and General Filisola recorded that El Presidente would offer no such terms. He demanded that the Texas rebels surrender with no guarantee of life itself, since they were viewed as nothing more than traitors. "With this reply it is clear that all were determined to lose their existence, selling it as dearly as possible," Filisola recorded.[26]

Santa Anna then began preparing his men for action during the late hours of March 5. He split his force into five units. Four columns would attack the Alamo from each direction, while he would personally command the reserves. His lancers would form around the fort to prevent anyone from escaping. His artillerymen were ordered to cease their firing at 5 A.M. His men were ordered to get some rest. They would storm the rebel fortress at 5 A.M., when Santa Anna hoped he could catch Travis and his men napping.[27]

After twelve days of artillery action and rifle fire, a welcome but strange silence fell upon the darkened Alamo compound. Travis turned the watch over to adjutant John Baugh so that he could get some rest. Every man, on both sides of the walls of the old Spanish mission, was aware of what they would face the following day.

Victory or death.

9

THE FALL OF THE ALAMO

ALL WAS IN READINESS by 5 A.M.

The Mexican troops sat shivering for another half hour in the predawn chill before Santa Anna finally passed the word to move out. General Cos took his lead column toward the northwest corner. Colonel Francisco Duque led the second column toward the patched breach in the north wall. Colonel Juan Morales advanced his men toward the chapel, while Colonel José María Romero brought his column in behind the fort from the east. They caught snoozing Texas sentinels outside the walls of the compound and silently disposed of them with blades and bayonets to their throats.[1]

Santa Anna's hopes of reaching the Alamo with complete surprise were dashed when an excited soldier shouted, "Viva Santa Anna!"

Another hollered back with, "Viva la Republica!"

Hundreds of voices soon broke the silence just after

5:30 A.M. Several Texans suddenly spotted the masses of troops closing in on their compound. John Baugh saw the columns advancing and raced across the Alamo plaza. "Colonel Travis!" he yelled. "The Mexicans are coming!" Joe, the personal servant of Travis, also awoke and both men grabbed their rifles. They ran for the north battery wall as Travis shouted, "Come on, boys, the Mexicans are upon us and we'll give them hell!"

Artillerymen were quick to light off their first rounds of lethal shot. Each tube had been packed with all the scrap iron that could be scavenged, and the ferrous projectiles ripped through the leading infantrymen below like a murderous hailstorm. The gunners followed by firing solid iron balls into the advancing ranks, mowing down even more enemy soldiers.

Because of the close range of the Mexican Army, the once-deadly Texian sharpshooters were now terribly exposed as they stood to take shots. The Baker rifles of the Mexicans were good from long range but the distance had been closed sufficiently to make even the aged Brown Bess muskets deadly. William Travis was among the early victims of the Alamo assault. He had just emptied both barrels of his shotgun into an advancing column. A Mexican bullet then caught him square in the forehead, causing the Texas commander to tumble down the earthen ramp on which he was perched. His slave Joe then took shelter in one of the rooms along the west wall.

The Mexican assault force took heavy casualties but they were forced onward by their officers. First Sergeant Francisco Becerra, a veteran of seven years' service in the Mexican army, recalled: "The firing of the besieged was fearfully precise. When a Texas rifle was leveled on a Mexican, he was considered as good as dead." Santa Anna released his reserves to join the fighting but he stayed out of rifle range. Many of the Mexican soldiers were cut down by grapeshot and became disorganized for a time. José Enrique de la Peña saw Colonel Duque tumble to the ground as metal ripped through his left thigh. Captain Herrera then fell dead to the effect of another cannon blast as the *cazadores* charged forward. Morales, leading the assault on the palisade, found himself in heavy fire from a cannon and from David Crockett's riflemen.[2]

The surviving Mexicans began climbing over the makeshift barricade at the base of the wall. General Juan Amador and some of his men made it over the twelve-foot north wall and raced across the plaza to open the north wall postern and swing it open. The Texians abandoned the north wall as waves of Mexicans began rushing through. Alamo gunners blasted the incoming uniformed soldiers and cut others down with rifle fire. The long-range rifles were slow to load, though, and members of the Morales battalion soon seized an opportunity to advance over the south wall. The outflanked Texians fell back to the final defensive line inside the long barracks as enemy troops swarmed over the front and rear walls.[3]

Andrea Castañon Villaneuva, wife of a San Antonio innkeeper and better known as Madam Candelaria, recalled hearing the ominous sounds of the Mexican bands playing the *degüello* tune outside the Alamo. The Texans first heard a chilling, dancelike melody but its eerie nature was quickly replaced by *degüello*'s march—a more sustained sound with the pounding movement of percussive energy like that of marching soldiers. Mexican cavalry manuals of the 1840s would carry the *El Degüello* bugle call, which was to be blown at the climax of a cavalry charge to signify "no quarter" to the enemy. As mentioned earlier, in Spanish, the word *degüello* meant cutting the throat—utter destruction to an enemy.[4]

Crockett and his men fell back into the chapel. The barracks was well fortified to make a good position from which to fire upon the Mexican soldiers. Unfortunately, the retreating artillery crew on the northwest battery failed to spike their guns before retreating. Now the Mexicans seized the rebels' cannon, swung them toward the barracks, and began blasting away at the heavy door.

Some of the Texans inside the barracks tried to surrender by waving white cloths. The Mexicans offered a brief lull and advanced. When they entered the barracks, however, they were gunned down by other Texians who did not wish to surrender.

Much angered, Mexican soldiers swarmed into the barracks and fought in close quarters, taking no prisoners. Even the wounded, including Jim Bowie lying in his bed, were killed. Captain Dickinson ran down the ramp and back through the church to find his wife, Susanna, and daughter, Angelina, huddled with the other terrified women and children. "Great, God, Sue, the Mexicans are inside our walls!" he said. "All is lost. If they spare you, save my child." [5]

Dickinson hugged and kissed them both, drew his sword, and raced back into the fight. Sixteen-year-old Galba Fuqua, one of the Gonzales Mounted Rangers who had so recently joined the Alamo, stumbled into the room moments later. He tried to speak to Mrs. Dickinson by holding his shattered jaw with his hands but she could not understand him. The wounded teenager shook his head in frustration and departed. [6]

One group of Texans fled from the Alamo through an opening and raced for cover. General Ramírez y Sesma ordered a company of lancers in pursuit, spearing and shooting every man who tried to escape. The last defenders to fall were in the chapel. The Mexicans took possession of the eighteen-pounder, swung it around, and blew down the wooden door and sandbags guarding the main entrance. Bonham and Dickinson died beside their cannon on the battery at the rear of the church.

Crockett and six of his men fought on until they were overwhelmed in the small lunette midway around the west wall.[7]

At least one servant woman within the fort was killed, but the other women and children were spared. Susannah Dickinson and her daughter witnessed the final minutes of several men near them in the church sacristy who were shot and stabbed to death. Dickinson and the other women were removed from the fort as Mexican soldiers pilfered all of the watches, jewelry, and valuables that some of the soldiers had left in their possession. As she passed through the courtyard, she could see countless Mexican soldiers moving about—finishing off the wounded with musket shots or bayonet thrusts while others stripped the Texian corpses of their shoes, clothing, and valuables. It was little more than an hour since the first bugle call had sounded as the Mexican Army stormed the Alamo.[8]

Santa Anna finally ventured into the fort once he heard that it had fallen. General Castrillón brought forth five prisoners who had been found hiding. Although Castrillón tried to intercede on behalf of the defenseless prisoners, Santa Anna gave a gesture to execute them. Peña and others were outraged by the senseless murders. Staff officers and others who had not participated in the real fighting now drew their swords and slashed the five men to pieces.[9]

THE MEXICAN ARMY PAID dearly for their victory at the Alamo. As many as six hundred men were killed or wounded, a full one-third of the assault force. José Juan Sánchez-Navarro remarked: "With another such victory, we will all go to the devil." [10]

Santa Anna's personal secretary, Ramón Caro, recorded that more than a hundred wounded Mexican soldiers died after the Alamo battle from a lack of proper medical attention. Santa Anna showed no remorse for the Texians as he surveyed the carnage. As the corpses were being dragged outside away from the fort, a small man named Henry Warnell was found hiding among the bodies. Warnell begged for mercy when he was brought before Santa Anna, but the general ordered the Texan executed on the spot.[11]

Santa Anna said that his men had killed six hundred Texans, a number that was an outright lie. The Mexicans took possession of the New Orleans Greys flag as a special trophy of war. The bodies of the slain Texans were heaped in piles, layered with firewood, and set ablaze that night. Barely a dozen people had survived the massacre, mainly women and children and one Mexican defender who pleaded that he had been a prisoner of the Texans. Juana Navarro de Alsbury, recently married to a Texas soldier, had taken refuge in the compound with her sister and her sister's infant son when the siege began. The only American-born survivors were Susannah Dickinson, daughter Angelina, and Joe, the loyal servant of Colonel Travis.[12]

Santa Anna was not swift to carry on his war against the Texians. He spent a considerable amount of time dallying about in San Antonio, interviewing the female survivors of the fort, and enjoying the company of his seventeen-year-old "bride." On March 11, he decided to send a special message to the rebels in the nearby town of Gonzales. He had Dickinson and her daughter placed on a pony. They were sent eastward in company with Colonel Almonte's cook, a freed black named Ben Harris who carried papers from the colonel. As they rode from San Antonio, Susannah saw two long pyres of ashes, wood, bones, and charred flesh—the last remains of her husband and at least 180 other Alamo defenders. As the trio passed the Salado River outside of town, they were suddenly joined by Travis's ex-servant Joe, who had been released by the Mexicans after a lengthy interrogation.[13]

Santa Anna knew the grieving widow and her daughter would make fitting symbols. The Texians who found them would learn what they could expect if they too dared to stand up to his Mexican Army.

GENERAL SAM HOUSTON remained in Washington-on-the-Brazos two more days after the signing of the Texas Declaration of Independence before riding to take command of his army.

He claimed to be settling various affairs with the convention. Some of his critics had other ideas. Former ranger captain Robert Coleman wrote: "The whiskey of the town of Washington had more charms for him than the honorable service of his country in the battlefield." On the morning of March 6—as the Alamo was being overrun—the final appeal from Travis reached the convention. Nacogdoches delegate Robert Potter moved that the convention rush to the aid of Travis. Houston called this idea "madness" and said that he would ride to the front to organize the troops while the government remained in session.[14]

General Houston left Washington that afternoon in company with young volunteer Richardson A. Scurry, Captain James Tarlton, and three members of his new staff: Colonel George Hockley (adjutant and inspector general of the army), Major Alexander Horton (aide-de-camp), and Major William Cooke (assistant inspector general). Hockley, a former war department clerk who had gotten to know Houston during his time with the U.S. Congress, was a close friend of the Texas general and had followed old Sam to Texas in 1835.

Seventy miles east of San Antonio, a growing number of
Texas volunteers were assembling. The fate of the Alamo would
be unknown to them for days as eager bodies rode in from
the outlying settlements. Among them was thirty-five-year-
old José Antonio Menchaca, who had been born in Béxar and
considered it to be his home. Menchaca had served in Captain
Juan Seguín's *tejano* company but Seguín and Jim Bowie had
deemed it advisable for the *tejano* to move his family to safety
during February.[15]

Menchaca, a tall man of more than six feet in height, could
speak and write English as fluently as Spanish. He was well
aware of the ways of General Santa Anna, a leader he had met
before. After spending a week securing his family on the ranch
of Juan Seguín, Tony Menchaca made his way to Gonzales.
When he arrived on March 5, he found one fully organized
company had preceded him, the Mina Volunteers under Captain Jesse Billingsley.

Billingsley, a noted twenty-six-year-old frontiersman, had
already participated in Colonel John Moore's 1835 ranger campaign. He mustered in his new company near Mina at the home
of Edward Burleson. His first lieutenant, Micah Andrews,
hoped to avenge the loss of his brother Richard, who had perished in the October battle at Concepción. The next Texian
volunteer company to reach Gonzales on March 5 was that of
twenty-nine-year-old Captain William Hill, who had also held
command on the 1835 ranger expedition. His Colorado River
settlers had first organized under Captain Joseph P. Lynch and
then rendezvoused with another small unit commanded by
Captain Philip Haddox Coe. Once the combined group reached
Gonzales, Coe and Lynch departed to organize more men, and
Hill stepped into command of the unit.

By March 6, more than seventy Texians from these two groups had gathered in Gonzales. They were joined that day by a company of U.S. volunteers who had traveled nearly one thousand miles in more than two months to join the freedom fight in Texas. Tall, brown-bearded Captain Sidney Sherman had sold his own cotton-bagging factory in Newport, Kentucky, to cover the costs of uniforming, arming, and equipping a fifty-man company. Sherman's men called themselves the Kentucky Riflemen, and they were given a gala ball send-off at a mansion across the river by citizens of Cincinnati, Ohio. The ladies of Newport presented Captain Sherman with a special white silk battle flag. In its center was a half-nude maiden clutching a sword over which a streamer draped bearing the phrase "Liberty or Death." Cincinnati-area leaders continued with a fund-raising drive for Texas that would fund a pair of cannon for the revolution.

The properly uniformed Kentucky company was in sharp contrast to the frontier garb worn by the other Texians who had reached Gonzales. Juan Seguín arrived with twenty-five *tejanos* whose families lived in and around Béxar. All had been born in Texas, with the exception of Mexican native Antonio Cruz, who had accompanied Captain Seguín from the Alamo on February 25. In Gonzales, Seguín added another fourteen loyal *tejanos* and his men elected Salvador Flores as their first lieutenant and Tony Menchaca as their second lieutenant.[16]

Three other Texian volunteer companies had reached Gonzales by March 6: Captain Moseley Baker's San Felipe group; another San Felipe company under Captain Robert McNutt; and the men under Captain Thomas Rabb, who had recruited settlers along the Colorado River and mustered them into service in the little community of Egypt. Baker, a lawyer and former newspaper editor, was chosen by the company commanders to take charge of the collective volunteers in Gonzales until a superior army officer could arrive. Baker estimated there to be about 270 total, "as brave men as ever shot the rifle, the most of whom had been in the Mexican and Indians fights of the country." The Alamo was in peril, and Baker found his fellow Texians "anxious for a fight." [17]

The first army officer to reach the town did so that afternoon. He was Lieutenant Colonel James Neill, returning from a twenty-day leave of absence from the Alamo. He found the eight newly arrived volunteer companies and proceeded to purchase supplies for the Alamo from local merchants. Neill and forty-eight men departed the next morning for Béxar. His force included volunteer scouts from various companies and Captain Seguín's *tejanos*.[18]

Neill and twenty-seven of his men returned in three days, forced back by Mexican patrols around San Antonio. Lieutenant William H. Smith and the remaining scouts remained on duty to keep tabs on the movements of Santa Anna's army. A large contingent of infantry troops under General Antonio Gaona and newly arrived General Eugenio Tolsa would remain in Béxar, while the balance moved out after the Texas rebels on March 11.

Colonel Morales was sent with the Jiménez and San Luis battalions to report to General Urrea in Goliad. The remaining seven hundred soldiers, under General Ramírez y Sesma and Colonel Eulogio González, started for San Felipe. General Vicente Filisola, one of the senior officers accompanying Ramírez y Sesma, noted that their men had one hundred horses, two six-pound artillery pieces, and plenty of supplies.[19]

The San Felipe–bound army would pass directly through Gonzales, where the Texians were gathering.

THE COMMANDER IN CHIEF of the Texas Army was quite a sight.

Sam Houston and his staff rode into Gonzales about 4 P.M. on March 11. He wore a Cherokee coat, a buckskin vest, a broad cap topped with a feather, and high-heeled boots adorned with silver spurs and three-inch rowels in a daisy pattern. On his waist were a belt pistol and a ceremonial sword presented to him by his Cherokee friends. General Houston found before him some three hundred volunteers, low on rations and possessing only two operational cannon.[20]

Houston proceeded to read the new Declaration of Independence and his orders appointing him as major general of the Texas Army, militia, rangers, regular, volunteers, and all others. Like a true politician, he continued to play to the audience gathered before him at DeWitt's tavern in Gonzales. "He delivered a short speech setting forth in stirring words the complications or troubles that threatened our Republic," recalled John Jenkins, a thirteen-year-old member of Captain Billingsley's Mina Volunteers. "I now began to take in all of the responsibility, danger, and grandeur of a soldier's life."[21]

Houston scarcely had time to give his speech before disturbing news began reaching Gonzales. The first word came in from two of Juan Seguín's scouts: the Alamo had been overrun, and all within had been killed, including seven men who were bedridden. Sam Houston immediately denounced the two men, Anselmo Bergara and Andrew Barcena, as "spies" for Santa Anna and had them detained to prevent any further alarming of the local townspeople. It did not take long before William Smith, Captain Seguín, and other trusted scouts rode in with intelligence that supported the grim situation in San Antonio. Houston then wrote orders to Colonel James Fannin at Goliad, instructing him to fall back to Victoria, abandon La Bahía, and "blow up that fortress." He wrote a separate letter, describing the stories brought in by the two *tejanos* he had held as "spies." Houston privately admitted, "I have but little doubt that the Alamo has fallen." [22]

General Houston took steps to organize his volunteer troops into a true military regiment the following day. He named Ed Burleson his colonel commanding the First Regiment of Infantry, and promoted Sidney Sherman of the Kentucky Riflemen as the lieutenant colonel. Several other small companies of volunteers had continued to arrive in Gonzales, forcing the general to set up camp several hundred yards from the Guadalupe River in the edge of a prairie. The following morning, March 13, he had his army paraded for inspection and Lieutenant Colonel Neill made a formal report. The total number of officers and men present was 374.

Sam Houston, hoping to verify the accuracy of the Alamo rumors, selected three of the ablest Texian scouts to find out the truth. Deaf Smith, Henry Karnes, and twenty-nine-year-old Robert Eden Handy raced for Béxar—Smith pledging to enter the city if necessary and to be back within three days. Deaf had joined the Texas Army the previous week to offer his services once again. Following the December assault on Béxar, he had retired to Columbia-on-the-Brazos to spend time with his wife, Lupe, and their four children—Susan, Gertrudes, Travis, and Simona, who ranged in ages from twelve down to six. Smith had moved them to Columbia for their protection from the Mexican Army during the Béxar siege. He was idolized by his kids and by Lupe, who fussed over the musket ball wound he had endured in San Antonio.

Deaf had ridden to Gonzales to help answer the call of Tra-

vis's besieged defenders in early March. He, Karnes, and Handy
had only ridden twenty miles from Gonzales to check rumors
of the Alamo's fall when they found their answer: a party of
four survivors. They were Susannah Dickinson—holding her
baby, Angelina, while riding horseback—Colonel Almonte's
servant Ben, also on horseback, and Travis's former servant Joe
on foot.

Dickinson related the demise of the Alamo and handed the
scouts the dispatches from Almonte. Deaf Smith—dirty and
grizzled from days in the saddle—took pity on young Angelina
and swung her up on his horse to let her ride with him for a
while. Karnes raced for Gonzales to spread the news, while
the remaining party arrived several hours later at 11 A.M. The
wives of Lieutenant George Kimbell's Gonzales Mounted Rangers listened in horror as the young woman described the thor-
oughness of the executions at Béxar. "Not a sound was heard
save the wild shrieks of women and heart-rendering screams of
their fatherless children," wrote scout Handy. Teenage volunteer John Jenkins would never forget the "despair with which
the soldiers' wives received the news of the death of their hus-
bands." The effect of the news created a panic. Private John
Milton Swisher of Captain Hill's company recalled, "The terri-
ble massacre struck terror to every heart." [23]

General Houston dispatched couriers toward other towns
to spread the word of the Alamo's fall. He also decided to have
his volunteers abandon Gonzales and retreat east to a more
defensible position while calling for more support. The townspeople furiously packed what they could carry away. Houston
allowed three of his four supply wagons to be donated to the
desperate citizens for hauling their belongings toward the Sabine River. The Texas Army's only artillery, two brass cannon,

were dumped into the Guadalupe River to prevent the Mexicans from taking possession of them. The fourth wagon was maintained for hauling ammunition.

Henry Karnes and a party of scouts were left behind to burn down the town in order to deny shelter and aid to Santa Anna's advancing troops. Like many others, merchant Horace Eggleston sadly watched his home and business being reduced to ashes as he fell out with the army around midnight. Everything was torched—hotels, an unfinished schoolhouse, Andrew Sowell's blacksmith shop, and even the hat factory of the late Alamo defenders George Kimbell and Almeron Dickinson. The ensuing rush of settlers fleeing eastward ahead of the Mexican Army was a mass chaos that became known in Texas as the "Runaway Scrape."[24]

THE VOLUNTEER TEXAN ARMY moved ten miles overnight, halting for breakfast at Peach Creek early on March 14. They were greeted there by another company of ninety volunteers raised at San Felipe by Captain John Bird, a forty-one-year-old former Tennessean who had fought with Andrew Jackson in the War of 1812.

The eastward march was soon resumed. Captain Jesse Billingsley was disturbed during the day by the sight of "families flying in terror from a foe well known as paying no regard to age or sex. Men were flying barefooted in every direction, spreading terror and dismay all over the country." During the forced march, Sam Houston showed compassion for teenager John Jenkins when he noted the boy struggling to keep up. The general ordered his servant Willis down off his horse to let Jenkins ride for a while. His kindness flipped to rage when Jenkins was unable to prevent his spirited horse from dashing ahead.[25]

"God damn your soul!" Houston roared. "Didn't I order you to ride right here?"

Jenkins dismounted and handed the horse back to Willis. He understood the general's need to rebuke him but lost all respect for the man with the manner in which he was called out. "I'd rather die than ride this horse another step," he said.

Houston doggedly pushed his troops until sunset, when he allowed them to make camp at the homestead of Williamson Daniels on the Lavaca River. The men ate boiled or roasted strips of beef from slaughtered cattle and used a portable corn grinder to work the ears of corn they carried.[26]

General Houston ate little and slept less. He seemed to chew tobacco constantly, napping occasionally on the ground with a saddle blanket and his saddle for a pillow. He carried a vial of ammoniacal spirits, made by his Cherokee friends by distilling liquid from the shavings of deer antlers. Some who saw the general slip the hartshorn vial from his breast pocket and apply the spirits to his nostrils believed their leader was partaking of opium.

Young John Swisher was feeling less enchanted with the life of a soldier. He had been hauling his rifle and heavy knapsack to the point where he could barely move one foot before the other. "Forty-eight hours without sleep, and all the time on duty, was about as much as a sixteen-year-old boy could stand," Swisher related. "When I reached camp I did not even stop to cook my supper, but dropped down upon my blanket and fell into a sleep at once."[27]

10

FANNIN'S BATTLE AT COLETO CREEK

LIEUTENANT COLONEL JAMES FANNIN was not leaving Goliad.

Couriers David Boyd Kent and Ben Highsmith had arrived on March 13 with orders from General Sam Houston. Fannin was told to forward one-third of his men to join the army's main body and then fall back to the town of Victoria with the rest of his command. "Previous to abandoning Goliad, you will take the necessary measures to blow up that fortress," Houston had written.[1]

Kent and Highsmith waited impatiently around Goliad for Fannin to reply. Highsmith finally asked, "Are you going to answer the general?"

"No," snapped Fannin. "Tell him I will not give up Fort Defiance."

The Texan scouts thus rode back for Gonzales, delivering the news on March 15 that Fannin had no intentions of blowing up the La Bahía fortress or retreating to Victoria. Fannin's scouts told him that General José Urrea was advancing on the town of Refugio with Mexican soldiers, so Fannin dispatched Captain Amon B. King with a small party of men. They were to use their wagons to help the Refugio citizens evacuate in the midst of the great Runaway Scrape. His men wasted time, punishing *rancheros* who were loyal to the Mexican Army, and they were soon confronted with Urrea's advance cavalry force on March 12. King sent a messenger to Goliad for help while his men took shelter in Refugio's Mission Nuestra Señora del Rosario.[2]

Fannin dispatched Colonel William Ward's 120-man Georgia Battalion to reinforce Captain King, and they arrived in Refugio around 3 P.M. on March 13. The forces became divided on what actions to take and thus did not depart straight for Goliad. King took his men out that night with some of Ward's force to a nearby ranch to attack *tejanos* believed to be spies. They killed eight of the *rancheros* and scattered the rest. As they returned to the Refugio mission on March 14, they found Colonel Ward's men under attack.

The long rifles of the Texians turned back three Mexican assaults. Amon King's company fell back to a grove of trees on the Mission River and inflicted heavy losses on any of Urrea's soldiers who came within range. The Battle of Refugio soon taxed the powder and lead ball supply of Texians both inside and out of the fort. Both parties hoped to escape after dark rather than surrender. King's men crossed the Mission River but were overtaken on March 15 by Tories, the loyalist *rancheros* they had so recently punished. His men had nothing but wet gunpowder and were forced to surrender. Colonel Ward's group was more fortunate. Instead of retreating toward Fannin in Goliad, they dodged through swamps and woods and headed southeast along the Copano Road. King's men were marched back to the Refugio mission, where they were shot to death on March 16—in accordance with Santa Anna's December 30, 1835, decree that commanded death to all armed rebels. Colonel Juan José Holsinger spared only eight of the rebels from execution.

Lewis T. Ayers, one of those spared, learned firsthand what Anglos who supported the rising against Mexico could expect: "The rest of our party were barbarously shot, stripped naked, and left on the prairie about one mile from the mission." [3]

JAMES FANNIN HELD HIS position at Fort Defiance, reluctant to move his supplies and ammunition without the carts and teams being used by Captain King. His Goliad soldiers were joined on March 14 by another forty-man volunteer company under Captain Albert C. Horton. Fannin sent couriers out for two days to ascertain the fate of the men under Ward and King, but most of his scouts were captured.

One courier finally returned to Goliad at 4 P.M. on March 17 with news of the defeat of his men in Refugio. Some of his officers felt Fannin had been mistaken in splitting his command days earlier and he now showed no intentions of departing Fort Defiance. His garrison's force totaled about 330 Texians. Captain Horton's cavalrymen went out on the morning of March 18 to engage approaching units of Urrea's cavalry. Fannin and his officers had finally decided to retreat but his men were forced to hold their position throughout the day as Horton's force toyed with the Mexican cavalrymen. Urrea's men would chase the Texians to within gun range of their artillerymen and then turn back. Horton's mounted volunteers took up the pursuit until they were forced to retreat. The fruitless game of chase and be chased consumed precious hours and exhausted all horses.[4]

Colonel Fannin resolved to move from Fort Defiance on the morning of March 19, but his long delay in so doing would prove costly. He insisted on hauling extra baggage, nine brass cannon, and five hundred spare muskets on oxcarts. Fannin could have used the early morning heavy fog to slip away, but he procrastinated even longer in having his men burn the nearby houses of the La Bahía settlement and destroy anything that might aid the Mexican Army. The rising pillars of smoke only gave clear indication to Urrea that the rebels were pulling out.[5]

The comedy of errors did not cease. The carts were overloaded and the unruly oxen stubbornly stopped to graze after traveling less than four miles. One of the carts broke down. The large artillery piece rolled off into the San Antonio River and an hour's delay was spent in retrieving it. By midmorning, Fannin's troops realized that no one had thought to pack any food—all of which had been burned in the confusion of destroying the town. The final, and most costly, error occurred just six miles from Goliad. Fannin ordered his column halted to rest his men and allow the hungry oxen to graze in an open prairie just five miles from tree-lined Coleto Creek. Captain Jack Shackelford of the Alabama Red Rovers was among those who demonstrated loudly that they should push on toward sufficient cover before resting.

Fannin assured Shackelford that the Mexicans would not dare to attack a force of more than three hundred men. Some of the men sneered at Shackelford, who they felt was only worried about protecting himself. Shackelford believed that Fannin naively placed "too much confidence in the ability of his own little force," and that the man of such little military experience "could not be made to believe that the Mexicans would dare follow us." [6]

Fannin resumed his march about 12:45 P.M. on March 19. They had advanced a mere four miles when a large force of Mexican cavalry was spotted emerging from the timber two miles behind. Charles Shain, a Kentuckian serving in Captain Burr Duvall's company, realized the mistake of Fannin's previous time wasted on the open prairie. "Had we proceeded, we could have reached the woods in safety," he recalled. Urrea's mounted men swiftly split into two groups to block the Texians from reaching either the protective cover of the woods or the route to Coleto Creek. Fannin had his men unlimber their cannon and fire several rounds, but it was without effect. [7]

The Texians formed a hollow square with artillery pieces posted on each corner. Instead of racing for the timber, Fannin's men would have to fight it out on an open prairie without food or water. The Mexican dragoons dismounted and advanced on foot. Their first volley from a quarter mile away had no effect. The dragoons continued to advance and fire two more volleys while Fannin shouted at his men to hold their fire until the enemy was at point-blank range. The third round from the Mexicans created some casualties. Only when his enemy had advanced within one hundred yards did Fannin order his troops to commence firing with artillery, muskets, and rifles.

The Texas artillerymen created heavy losses but the Mexican dragoons slowly picked off many of the rebel sharpshooters. Captain Horton and about thirty of his mounted men who had gone ahead to the Coleto crossing saw that Fannin's men were hopelessly outnumbered. Instead of sacrificing his men, Horton opted to ride for Victoria to seek reinforcements.

The Mexican soldiers took advantage of high prairie grass to cover themselves, rising only long enough to fire into the tightly packed Texians. Anyone who had criticized James Fannin's courage previously now found the young leader to be stalwart in action. Although painfully wounded by a shot in his thigh, he coolly refused to leave the front ranks of the action. The fighting carried on into the late afternoon as parched Texans drank the last water from their canteens. Both sides were relieved when dusk brought an end to the fighting.

Fannin's rebels had suffered nine killed and fifty-one wounded. They had inflicted severe losses on Urrea's troops in the form of fifty killed and 140 wounded. Shain heard some of the officers proposing to make a retreat in the dark toward the distant woods. Enough of the men objected to leaving the wounded behind that the idea was rejected. Shain and his comrades instead worked to construct a breastworks overnight, using carts, dead oxen, and horse carcasses to form their protection. Others used spades to dig a three-foot-deep trench. Mexican bugles and sporadic sniper fire made it evident that they were completely surrounded on the prairie. "They kept sounding their bugles every five minutes during the night, and we expected a charge every minute," said Shain.[8]

Dawn on March 20 brought more bad news. Urrea had been reinforced by another hundred infantrymen, two four-pound cannon, and a howitzer. The Mexican commander opened the day by peppering the Texan bastion with several rounds of canister and grape. He was making a show of force that was clear: he could simply pound the rebels from long range with artillery until they were annihilated. Fannin's men agreed that they should surrender if Urrea could offer them honorable terms. Colonel Fannin thus limped forward under a flag of truce.

General Urrea denied him any conditions of surrender, however. The Texians were to lay down their arms and end the matter or Urrea would simply renew his bombardment. Fannin had no choice. He returned to his men and lied. He told them Urrea had accepted their offer and would spare their lives. Fannin's men then lay down their arms and surrendered. They were marched back to Goliad under guard, arriving late in the evening. "They gave us nothing to eat that night and nothing till late next day," said Shain. "Then they gave us about as much for twenty-four hours as we could eat at one meal."

General Urrea's men took swift possession of Victoria as well on the morning of March 21. Captain Horton's men, arriving ahead of the Mexicans, found little assistance from the locals and chose to flee town. The other separated contingent under Colonel Ward was largely killed or captured upon trying to enter Victoria that day. By the following day, only ten of Ward's men had managed to escape death or capture. The surviving members of Ward's battalion were then marched back to Goliad to be held with Fannin's captured command.

Fort Defiance was now a prison for more than 370 Texians.

SAM HOUSTON'S LITTLE ARMY was continuing to fall back to the east.

His men broke camp on the morning of March 15 and marched toward the Colorado River. Houston ordered Major William Austin, one of his aides-de-camp, to ride to the coastal town of Velasco to requisition more horses, supplies, cannon, and ammunition. The general spent his morning cursing those who showed insubordination and threatening to court-martial a young sentinel who had fallen asleep at his post during the night.[9]

One of the few bright spots of the day for General Houston came during the noon hour, when his army was joined by about two dozen Brazoria-area volunteers under twenty-nine-year-old

Captain Peyton R. Splane. The Texas Army halted its march around 1 P.M. on the Navidad River and made camp on the land of settler William Thompson. The ragged force, unskilled in military maneuvers, had been on the march for about twenty-six of the past thirty-eight hours.

Mexican troops were not far behind. General Ramírez y Sesma and his seven hundred infantrymen reached Gonzales on March 14 and found some of the buildings still smoldering. Santa Anna, having elected to remain in Béxar awaiting solid intelligence, finally received the news. On March 17 he dispatched General Eugenio Tolsa with six hundred of his Second Infantry Brigade to meet Sesma—already in pursuit of Houston's army—on the Colorado River. He sent the balance of Tolsa's brigade to reinforce General Urrea at Goliad.[10]

General Houston was wary of the movements of the Mexican Army. He took a diversion on the morning of March 16. Instead of continuing east toward Columbia-on-the-Brazos, he headed north from the Navidad River. The Texas Army, now numbering about five hundred souls, halted at 4:30 P.M. at Jesse Burnam's crossing of the Colorado River. Houston promoted William Smith to captain of cavalry this day, trusting the Béxar veteran's ability to command such squad leaders as Deaf Smith and Henry Karnes. A cool, drizzly rain fell on the five hundred Texians bivouacked on the west bank of the Colorado during the next morning. Houston sent orders to Colonel Fannin to take position on Lavaca Bay to protect the army's munitions stored at Cox's Point and Dimitt's Landing. He said that his own force would "remain for a time" before marching down the river.

The convention at Washington-on-the-Brazos, having received word late on March 15 of the Alamo's fall, was at work while the army rested. The delegates resolved to create an ad interim government for the free and sovereign Republic of Texas. The new leaders were sworn into office at 4 P.M. on March 17, and Governor Henry Smith's provisional government ceased to exist. Forty-seven-year-old David Gouverneur Burnet was named as the new president. A stocky man with bushy brown whiskers, Burnet was a native of New Jersey who carried a Bible in one pocket and a pistol in the other.

Vice President Lorenzo de Zavala, whose plantation sat along the San Jacinto River, had been born in the Yucatán state of Mexico in 1788. He had been a strong supporter of President Santa Anna until the dictator had denounced the Constitution of 1824 the previous year. The balance of Burnet's cabinet included Secretary of Treasury Bailey Hardeman, Attorney General David Thomas, Secretary of State Samuel P. Carson, Secretary of War Thomas Jefferson Rusk, and Secretary of Navy Robert Potter. Secretary Potter, who had been a junior officer in the U.S. Navy, had once been jailed in North Carolina for castrating two relatives whom he suspected of having sexual relations with his wife. He was later elected to the state's legislature but was run out of office for cheating at cards. Potter was loyal to President Burnet, and his great distaste for the characters of both General Houston and Secretary of War Rusk would soon surface.[11]

Burnet immediately called upon the people of East Texas to join his republic's army against their Mexican aggressors. With the new government in place, the convention adjourned on March 18. Many delegates headed for the army or to their families. Burnet and most of his cabinet moved to a temporary station at Groce's Retreat, a plantation located downriver from Washington-on-the-Brazos. Secretary of War Rusk was committed to protecting the citizens who remained in Washington, so he commissioned Captain Andrew Briscoe and John Henry

Moore to recruit and organize a spy company for the town's defense.

The Runaway Scrape was in full motion. Settlers continued to flee from the advancing Mexican Army. General Houston and the new government thus saw little need to maintain frontier protection via the Texas Rangers, so orders went out for the various units to join the main army. Captain Stephen Townsend's rangers, camped on the east bank of the Colorado River in Robertson's Colony, received the word on March 16. Captain Louis Franks's thirty-man Robertson Colony unit was largely broken up by late March and some of its members soon became part of the army. The ten-man regional ranger company of Captain William Sadler was finishing work on Fort Houston in East Texas when they got news of the fall of the Alamo. Sadler disbanded his unit but most of his men opted to cross the Trinity River on March 19 and ride with him down the Old San Antonio Road to join the Texas Army.

Major "Three-Legged Willie" Williamson's ranger regiment was also notified of the crisis. Captain Isaac Burton, recruiting on the Sabine, headed out with some of his men. Williamson, headquartered in Mina with the company of Captain John Tumlinson, received orders from Sam Houston on March 18 to monitor the movements of General Gaona's upper division of the Mexican Army as it advanced. News of the tragedy in San Antonio spread panic among the remaining Mina townspeople. Williamson's rangers sank all the ferryboats on the nearby Colorado River to prevent the Mexican Army from crossing. Tumlinson and some of his rangers were allowed leaves of absence to help escort their families to safety during the Runaway Scrape. Acting command of the remaining twenty-two Mina rangers fell upon Second Lieutenant George M. Petty.

Mexican troops soon appeared across the Colorado

River, prompting Williamson and Petty to move their rangers toward the Brazos River. The unit's advance was slowed by muddy roads and two rangers without horses. Major Williamson, eager to join the Texas Army, rode on ahead toward Washington-on-the-Brazos with two of his junior rangers. He arrived on March 20 and found John Henry Moore assembling a spy company that was known as the "Washington Guards." Captain Joseph Bell Chance, a thirty-five-year-old from Tennessee, was elected into command by his peers—the preferred nomination style in which ranger captains gained the respect of their subordinates.

Three-Legged Willie, utilizing his power as ranger commander, took supervisory authority of Chance's company. One-quarter of the three dozen members of the Washington Guards had already been in service with the Texas Rangers during 1836. Williamson used them to guard the ferry crossing of the Colorado River, per orders from General Houston. Any man heading eastward toward the United States was to surrender all rifles, powder, lead, and horses possible for the use of the Texas Army. Major Williamson's rangers were to maintain such duty until Houston sent new orders or they encountered the Mexican Army.[12]

The various Texas Ranger companies in operation during March 1836 would eventually contribute more than eighty men to Sam Houston's army as the campaign progressed. These seasoned frontier fighters would prove to be invaluable as scouts for the cavalry and fierce soldiers in combat.

The Texas Army spent March 18 helping frantic citizens cross over the Colorado River. The five-hundred-man army had completed its own ferrying across by late afternoon and then moved several miles farther down the river.

Houston's scouts scoured the countryside to provide intelligence on the movements of the Mexican Army. In addition to Captain Smith, Henry Karnes was promoted into command of a second cavalry unit on the Colorado. Karnes gathered up Deaf Smith, Robert Handy, and six other horsemen and rode west of the main army to seek news on the enemy. They ate supper on the Navidad River and slept under a large oak tree in the prairie, maintaining a cold camp—no fires burning. "We took this precaution on account of the Indians, or any straggling band of Mexicans, who might have been out, like ourselves, spying," recalled scout John Sharp. Cavalrymen Karnes, Deaf Smith, and the like would prove to be invaluable scouts—one of Sam Houston's strongest assets in the field.[13]

Captain Karnes's scouts set out on the morning of March 20 for the Beason's Ford crossing of the Colorado. They soon found fresh horse tracks and, upon examination, Deaf Smith said that at least ten or twelve horses had passed through no more than an hour before. Smith's men pushed forward at a brisk gait and soon came upon six Mexican soldiers on horseback who were leading other horses behind them. The Texas scouts pursued, and fired their pistols as they closed the distance. Washington "Wash" Secrest shot down one of the Mexican soldiers but the balance took shelter in the river bottomlands, abandoning their horses in the process.

Karnes and his scouts plunged into the thicket on foot, too. He, Smith, and David Murphree captured one of the enemy cavalrymen. They tied his hands behind his back and extracted intelligence from him that General Ramírez y Sesma was advancing close behind with at least six hundred infantrymen, two pieces of artillery, and at least sixty cavalrymen. The scouts hauled their prisoner back to the main Texas Army camp that evening, where his sight created quite a stir. Even more disturbing to Colonel George Hockley was the fact that one of the

Mexican horses captured by Karnes contained clothing belonging to a person who had been killed in the Alamo.[14]

Sam Houston's army proceeded to the Beason's Ford crossing of the Colorado and made camp. More volunteer companies, totaling about 150 men, arrived from the lower Texas settlements. Among these new company commanders was feisty Captain Wyly Martin, a sixty-year-old Georgian who had fought with William Henry Harrison in 1812 and Andrew Jackson at the Battle of Horseshoe Bend. Martin was promoted to captain in the U.S. Army for his bravery, but he was forced to resign his commission in 1823 and head for Texas after challenging a man to a duel and killing him. Captain Martin's fighting spirit would do much to energize other Texians in the weeks to come but the same boldness would prove troublesome to General Houston.[15]

The Texas Army positioned itself to cover Beason's Ford. Houston also sent a fifty-man detachment under Sidney Sherman to move several miles downstream to cover the next major crossing, Dewees's Ford. General Ramírez y Sesma's division began arriving that day, March 20, and his men made camp at a bend in the Colorado River about midway between Dewees and Beason fords. According to General Filisola, Sesma had 725 men and two cannon when he reached the west bank of the Colorado. His men were exhausted from their march from Gonzales, and heavy rains had soaked their firearms. The general had his men dry and clean their weapons before he would entertain any thoughts of challenging the river crossings that were well guarded by the Texian rebels.[16]

Sherman's detachment, having taken up station at the shallow water ford at Dewees, grew in number on March 20. He was met throughout the day by five more companies marching in to report. Captain William Ware's eighteen-man volunteer unit, raised on the San Bernard River, had already reached the crossing by the time Sherman arrived. A short time later, they were joined by the volunteer infantry unit of Captain Joseph Bennett and the twelve-man ranger company of Captain Stephen Townsend, who had been previously mustered to control Indian attacks along the Colorado.

Sherman's men fortified themselves by digging an entrenchment in the sandy beach along the river's edge. "This was designed as a defense in case of an attack by the enemy from DeWee's Bluff on the opposite side," noted sixteen-year-old William Physick Zuber, whose father had granted him permission to join the company of Captain William Patton. Sherman's men were still digging their trenches when a forty-man regular army company under Captain Henry Teal arrived.[17]

The fifth group to reach Sherman's force at Dewees was that of former ranger captain William Sadler, whose men had departed Fort Houston in East Texas after receiving pleas to aid the Alamo defenders. He had only seven of his former rangers with him, but Sadler's small numbers were welcomed on March 21. Captain Teal's regulars soon moved to join General Houston's main body. Their arrival meant that his two musicians, Frederick Lemsky and Martin Flores, were able to bring more military process to camp. Tattoo and reveille were then played on a regular basis at dawn and in the evening to organize the troops.[18]

Sam Houston had his men fortify their position near Beason's Ford by chopping down trees to build a proper breastworks. From the prisoner captured by Karnes and Smith, he learned that more than a thousand Mexican soldiers were on the march to intercept his Texas Army. He decided on March 21 to send about 150 mounted men and foot soldiers across the Colorado River to probe the enemy's position. The detachment was under Major Benjamin Fort Smith, a thirty-seven-year-old from Kentucky who had fought under General Andrew Jackson in the 1815 Battle of New Orleans.[19]

Major Smith led one hundred of his men toward the camp of General Ramírez y Sesma during the morning of March 22. They were spotted by Mexican guards and came under fire. Karnes and his cavalrymen retreated as Sesma's artillerymen opened fire with the camp's cannon. Smith had his men retreat back across the river and take up defensive positions. General Ramírez y Sesma was not eager to yet make a full-scale engagement, but a number of his riflemen did advance to the riverbanks to engage in long-range shooting against the Texas rebels. Major Smith ordered the boardinghouse and other dwellings of Benjamin Beason torched to prevent them from providing any shelter to the Mexican troops. There were no reported casualties from the little skirmish, but the surprise attack did inspire many of the Texas troops who were most eager to get on about the business of fighting a war.[20]

11

"DAMNED ANXIOUS
TO FIGHT"

SIDNEY SHERMAN WAS PROVING to be quite capable with his small command at Dewees's Ford.

On the morning of March 23, his spies overpowered three Mexican soldiers who were out foraging for food. They were marched under armed guard that afternoon into General Houston's camp, where they were interrogated by Moses Austin Bryan of Captain Baker's company. A nephew of empresario Stephen F. Austin, Bryan was fluent in Spanish. He learned that General Ramírez y Sesma's troops, camped on the opposite bank of the Colorado about three miles away, were struggling with meager clothing in the cold weather but had plans to build a boat for crossing the river.[1]

Sam Houston sent written updates to his new superior, Secretary of War Thomas Rusk. The general was worn down from lack of sleep and nearly two days' time he had gone without eating. Houston had been "in constant apprehension of a rout" and was greatly disturbed by the panic created by some of his men who had deserted in recent days. An additional curse on his command was the humanitarian efforts his men had to afford the homeless families of the Runaway Scrape, who sought his protection at every turn.[2]

Houston informed Rusk that he had just received news via courier that Colonel Fannin's men had been attacked a few miles from La Bahía. The results of the encounter were still not known to him, but the general blasted the man who had refused to follow his orders to abandon Goliad. "If what I have heard from Fannin be true, I deplore it, and can only attribute the ill luck to his attempting to retreat in daylight in the face of a superior force," he wrote. "He is an ill-fated man." Houston also criticized President Burnet's government for retreating from Washington and leaving a full company of good men under Major Williamson to guard the river crossing there. His army had just received forty-eight extra muskets and ammunition, and he knew that Sesma's nearby force was no larger than seven hundred men. Given more volunteers, Houston vowed, "We can beat them."

The general's own troops were growing restless with guarding three river crossings. Sherman, motivated by his recent reinforcements, requested that he be allowed to make an attack on the Mexicans. He was ordered not to provoke an attack, as *tejano* Tony Menchaca recalled: "Houston told them that not a single man should move out, that the Mexicans were only trying to draw him out and ascertain his strength, which he did not intend to let them know."[3]

Several important Washington-area citizens joined the

Texas Army at the Colorado crossing. Of them, Houston was pleased to add proper medical attention to his troops in the form of thirty-eight-year-old Dr. Anson Jones, a graduate of the Jefferson Medical School in Philadelphia. Also arriving was Colonel John Austin Wharton, a Texas Army agent recently returned from securing supplies in New Orleans. He joined Houston's staff as adjutant general, a position that Major Ben Smith had been filling in the interim. Houston also took the advice of President Burnet in adding to his staff Dr. James Hazard Perry, a former New Yorker who had studied at West Point.

General Ramírez y Sesma's nearby troops were reinforced while Houston loitered near the Colorado. General Eugenio Tolsa arrived on March 24 with his two battalions, fifty horses, and an additional artillery piece—bringing their combined force to 1,300 troops and 150 cavalrymen. The Texian troops were further disheartened on the night of March 25 when a volunteer named Peter Kerr arrived from Goliad. He brought word that Colonel Fannin's command had been overtaken and captured by the enemy. Soldier William Zuber felt the news so intimidated the troops that General Houston acted to preserve their courage by denouncing Kerr as a spy.[4]

Houston put his troops on the move again the next day. His opponents were growing in number, including cavalry, infantrymen, and even artillery. He did not expect a favorable outcome with battle at this point: many of his men were untrained and he had no artillery pieces yet. He consulted none of his staff in making the decision on March 26 to fall back to the Brazos River. He merely stated to some of his men that they needed to find new grass for the army's horses and mules to graze on.[5]

At the time, his volunteer force had swelled to perhaps thirteen hundred men—many of whom were not eager to be retreating from General Sesma's troops. General Houston moved about in animated style, barking at his men to get moving. Heavyset wagonmaster James Wilson swore profusely, saying that he had worn out his shoes on the march to the Colorado and now his legs and feet were torn up from walking through sawbrier plants. Houston in turn cursed the man and ordered him to get his teams moving. Pointing at his bloodied feet, Wilson snapped, "Do you think I am going to drive a wagon for a damned little one-horse army and my feet in that fix?"[6]

Scout Daniel Shipman noted that Houston then offered up his own boots to Wilson in order to get the belligerent man moving. Many of the volunteers murmured their discontent about falling back. James Tarlton considered it a "shameful retreat." Private John Swisher felt that "nine-tenths of the army was anxious to fight." In hindsight, he admitted, "There are times when it requires more courage to retreat than to stand and fight, and this was the case at the Colorado." As many as two hundred men left the army at this point, opting to go take care of their families since the army showed no signs of fighting soon.[7]

Sidney Sherman, still stationed at Dewees's Ford with three hundred troops, was also disturbed to be falling back. His command had just been joined by another volunteer company from Nacogdoches, to whom he assigned Captain Sadler's eight rangers. Sherman's men reluctantly loaded up beef from freshly slaughtered cattle and followed their orders to rejoin General Houston's main body. They marched about seven miles and made camp around midnight in the river bottomlands.[8]

Sherman's force was on the move again early on March 27. Prior to reaching the Texas Army, they were greeted by three new companies under Major John Forbes, with upwards of 150 men. The first to arrive on March 26 was the company of Captain Amasa Turner, who had visited the saloons in New Orleans to round up American volunteers for the revolution. His group sailed from Louisiana but faced great difficulty in making it to Texas soil when their vessel was wrecked on a sandbar off Velasco. Once ashore, the Americans were organized into companies during late January and early February. Two other infantry companies were mustered in under the command of Captains William S. Fisher and Richard Roman.[9]

Major John Forbes, an aide-de-camp of General Houston, had moved from Washington-on-the-Brazos on March 5 to forward troops to the army. He arrived in Velasco and found the New Orleans–raised infantrymen to be fully armed and ready for action. Captain Fisher's company had been in Texas longer than the Americans under Captains Roman and Turner, but the whole lot was a true melting pot of cultures. The occupations of the new Forbes battalion ranged widely: farmers, carpenters, printers, clerks, a musician, and even a Baptist minister from Georgia. While most had been born in the United States, Forbes found his volunteers also included immigrants from England, Italy, Scotland, Germany, Poland, France, and Portugal.[10]

Forbes procured sufficient wagons and ox teams from local citizens and began a forced march up the Brazos River past the town of Columbia. Captain Turner's company reached Sidney Sherman's division by 11 A.M. on March 26. The companies detailed to march with the ox teams and wagons, those of Roman and Fisher, were another fifteen hours in making their rendezvous.

Captain Robert Calder was as eager as any to figure out old Sam Houston's plans. He rode alongside the general during some of the retreat from Beason's Ford toward San Felipe. Calder commented that the Texians could have whipped Sesma's troops at the Colorado, but that he guessed Houston was hoping to draw the enemy deeper into the heart of the Anglo settlements before fighting. Houston agreed, offering that more supplies and more men would be available, and that any casualties would have been impossible to transport away from the Colorado River area.[11]

"You may tell those fellows who are so damned anxious to fight," Houston remarked to Calder, "that before long they shall have it to their heart's content."

Sherman's men were still roasting a freshly slaughtered cow when the main contingent of General Houston's army finally reunited with them shortly before noon on March 27 at the San Bernardo River. The Texas Army continued its retreat throughout the day, covering some twenty miles before halting at 9 P.M. near the home of Samuel May Williams—located on Spring Creek, just two miles from San Felipe.

Several new volunteers had joined Houston during the day's march, the most notable being a trio previously attached to the command of Colonel Fannin. Thomas Jefferson Adams, Garrett E. Boom, and Dr. John Walker Baylor each joined one of the volunteer companies, with hopes they would soon be able to effect some revenge on Santa Anna's army. They had been among the mounted horsemen of Captain Albert Horton's command who escaped the Coleto Creek battle on March 19. Their last sight of Fannin's troops showed them to be hopelessly surrounded on an open prairie in the midst of a terrific battle.

JAMES WALKER FANNIN AND his 375 Goliad defenders had spent a week as prisoners of war in a 113-year-old Spanish mission.

The old La Bahía presidio that Fannin had renamed Fort Defiance was filthy, cramped, and the scene of great suffering. Captain Jack Shackelford found that throughout it all "Colonel Fannin was quite cheerful, and we talked pleasantly of the prospect of our reaching the United States." The wounded men suffered with poor medical attention, and all of the Texians struggled to take in enough rations to survive. Some used whatever money they had to buy a meager corn tortilla, hardly enough food to feed a child.

Abel Morgan, tasked by Mexican soldiers with tending to the wounded, reported that they were only allowed to feed them the soup of a stillborn calf boiled in a large copper kettle. "I cut the feet off and threw them down close to the kettle," Morgan related. "Some of our men came and picked up those feet and roasted them and ate them, hide and all." [12]

General Urrea was given direction by Santa Anna to execute the "perfidious foreigners" being held at Goliad. Perceiving some reluctance from Urrea, Santa Anna sent orders on March 23 directly to the twenty-seven-year-old officer in command of the La Bahía fortress, Lieutenant Colonel José Nicolás de la Portilla. The Texans were not to be treated as prisoners but rather as pirates who should be immediately executed. Portilla received the command on March 26 and, though it weighed heavily on his moral convictions, he passed the word that the Texians were to be shot at dawn.

Soon after sunrise on Palm Sunday, March 27, Colonel Portilla carried out El Presidente's orders. Twenty men were spared their lives because of their value as physicians, interpreters, orderlies, or mechanics. The kind and brave intervention of Colonel Francisco Garay and a Mexican woman named Francita Alavez also helped spare some. The other 370 Texans were divided into three separate groups. Young Charles Shain believed the Mexicans intended to comply with their truce and would simply march them to Matamoros for the duration of the revolution. "The first division was led out on the Victoria road," he wrote. "The second, the division I belonged to, was taken out on the San Antonio Road." Shain's group was moved toward the San Antonio River. As they reached a brush fence, he suddenly heard a firing of guns commence either in or near Fort Defiance.[13]

The guards immediately ordered Shain's division to halt. The rear of the group was still coming to a stop when one of the Mexican officers barked, "Prepare!" Shain stared in horror as the infantrymen only yards away from the Texans raised their guns level and began firing. Dozens of men dropped instantly as lead bullets ripped through their chests and foreheads. The scene was played out at the same time through the other Texas divisions as they were summarily executed at point-blank range.

Some were merely wounded by the first volleys fired at them. Others survived the first shots when bullets tore into an adjacent man or when a few of the old Brown Bess muskets had a flash in the pan and failed to fire on the first strike. Those who could do so fought back or immediately fled for the nearby San Antonio River. Artillery captain Benjamin Holland desperately smashed a Mexican soldier in the face with his fist, ripped away the soldier's rifle, and sprinted for the river. John C. Duval was not hit but he collapsed under the weight of a fellow Texan who was shot in front of him. Duval wisely played dead until the Mexicans took off in pursuit of fleeing Texans before he headed for the water.[14]

Sergeant Isaac D. Hamilton had his left thigh shredded by a ball from the first volley. He ran for his life and was bayoneted in the right thigh in the process. Somehow, in the midst of the killing frenzy, he escaped through waist-high prairie grass into the nearby timber. Former cavalryman William Haddin made it across the river but the three Texans he fled with were not as fortunate. Many of those who reached the river were shot along its banks or were picked off as they swam. Hundreds of the Texans were killed by either the first rifle volleys or were cut down with sabers and guns as they fled. Miraculously, at least twenty-eight of them escaped, many badly wounded.[15]

One who survived against all odds was William L. Hunter. He had been shot, stabbed with a bayonet, clubbed with the butt of a gun, stripped, and finally had his throat partially slashed. After nightfall, Hunter managed to crawl away and hide in a thicket. He was later found by a kindly Mexican woman who brought him food and water until he was able to set out for help. The first volley missed Charles Shain and he raced for the river. "While I was swimming they shot five times at me, at a distance of not more than fifty yards," he wrote. He met fellow survivor Daniel Murphy—wounded in the left knee—on the other shore and took cover during the next few hours while Mexican soldiers chased down and slaughtered every Texan they could catch. They moved about two miles to some heavy timber and found another survivor, John Williams, hiding in a treetop. The trio remained hidden until nightfall before moving toward Coleto Creek overnight.

Inside the La Bahía mission, the men who were too wounded to walk were put to death under the direction of Captain Carolino Huerta of the Tres Villas battalion. Colonel Fannin, suffering from the bullet wound to his thigh, had to be helped to the courtyard of Fort Defiance. Joseph H. Spohn, one of the Texians being spared for his skills as an interpreter, was ordered to convey to Fannin that he was being chastised by the Mexican government "for having come with an armed band to commit depredations and revolutionize Texas."[16]

Fannin was denied his request to speak to Colonel Portilla. He then offered Captain Huerta his gold watch, a small purse of doubloons, and a double handful of cash from his overcoat.

Fannin asked in return for these gifts that he be given a proper burial and that they spare scorching his face by shooting him in the chest. He then sat down on a chair and was blindfolded. Huerta pocketed the cash and gold watch, and had Fannin shot through the face. Instead of a Christian burial, his body was later thrown upon a funeral pyre with the other victims.[17]

Approximately 341 Texians were slain in what became known as the Goliad Massacre. Lieutenant Colonel Portilla reported to General Urrea that he felt "much distressed" over carrying out Santa Anna's orders. "It is my duty to do what is commanded me, even though repugnant to my feelings." Santa Anna could have hauled his prisoners to Mexico or shipped them off to the United States. By choosing to execute and butcher entire companies of both U.S. and Texian volunteers, he had succeeded only in creating an image of himself as the most barbaric of murderers.[18]

Those who had been spared and the twenty-eight who escaped would in due time relate the horrors they had witnessed. Charles Shain, Daniel Murphy, and John Williams fell in with two more survivors of the Goliad Massacre the next day. They continued their flight for five days without any proper food. "On the sixth in the morning, we found a small turtle," Shain related. "We immediately kindled a fire and cooked and ate it." Feeling rejuvenated from such a meager meal, the survivors pushed on toward the Guadalupe River, hoping to make contact with anyone from the Texas Army.

SAM HOUSTON'S REBELS WERE on the move again on March 28, ignorant of the cold-blooded massacre that had taken place the previous day in Goliad.

The Texas Army moved from the Samuel Williams homestead into San Felipe de Austin, where the companies were furnished with all the clothing and supplies the town could offer. The merchants were issued promissory notes. It was little surprise to many when the word was passed on March 29 that the Texas general had no intention of making a stand at San Felipe. Instead, Houston had decided to move upriver to Groce's Landing, the settlement of fifty-four-year-old Jared Ellison Groce, the richest man of Austin's Colony. He hoped to find food supplies there. He had also learned the steamboat *Yellow Stone* was at Groce's Landing, taking on cotton for transport down the Brazos.

A direct-line march would be fifteen miles, but following the snaking Brazos would stretch the journey to twenty. Captains Moseley Baker and Wyly Martin at this point refused to retreat any farther. At age sixty, Martin had been a captain under Andrew Jackson at Horseshoe Bend, where Houston had been a lieutenant. Martin now found it difficult to continue retreating under a leader seventeen years younger and once his subordinate. General Houston wisely opted not to call out his recalcitrant juniors and risk dividing his volunteer army.[19]

He rode back and issued orders for Captain Baker to post his company on the east bank of the Brazos, opposite San Felipe, to prevent the Mexican Army from crossing. Baker had already sent seven of his men to do this hours earlier. Captain Martin was similarly directed to station his men at the key crossing of Fort Bend, or Old Fort, located twenty-five miles downstream from San Felipe.[20]

Other men refused to move north as well. Captain John Bird and a portion of his men decided to stay in town to ensure that a certain barrel of whiskey did not go wasted. Lieutenant John McAllister took the balance of Bird's company and joined Captain Baker at the river crossing. The army, having reached its largest size at about fourteen hundred men, now faced two hundred men splitting off as the retreat continued.[21]

Deaf Smith and scout John York arrived with news they had spotted an advance Mexican guard within a few miles of San Felipe. Although the "cavalrymen" were later determined to be a distant herd of cattle, the report was apparently enough to cause Houston to order Baker's men to burn down Stephen Austin's original town. Baker's third sergeant, Moses Bryan, refused to do so when he was asked to supervise the destruction. "I did not want to be the one who destroyed the first town my uncle Stephen F. Austin had laid out in the beginning of his colonization enterprise," he reflected.[22]

General Houston would flatly deny issuing such orders, but the fact of the matter is that Santa Anna's troops would have soon looted and burned the town anyway. Houston turned to Isaac Moreland of Captain William Logan's company and asked if he had heard any direct orders to burn the settlement.[23]

"General, I have no recollection of it," Moreland said.

"Yet they blame me for it," Houston muttered.

The entire town was a raging inferno as he led his men on a two-day march north to the Groce plantation. En route, Houston wrote a sharp letter to Secretary of War Rusk in which he criticized the Texas government for retreating from Washington to Groce's and now down to Harrisburg. "Your removal to Harrisburg has done more to increase the panic in the country than anything else that has occurred in Texas, except the fall of the Alamo." Houston added that he conferred with no man outside of Colonel Hockley in reaching his decision to move out. "Had I consulted the wishes of all," he wrote, "I should have been like the ass between two stacks of hay."[24]

Houston found few true friends within his army aside from Hockley and his trusted top scout, Deaf Smith. He was able to confer with the short, sturdy frontiersmen in solitary engagements. Smith was not entirely deaf but he was unable to follow an ordinary conversation, especially in a crowd. When Sam needed to get a point across to old 'Rastus, he could do so well enough as long as he was addressing Smith face-to-face.[25]

The march to Groce's was challenged by steady rains that turned the road into bogs. Troops labored at clearing the timber and brush in areas that were not wide enough for the baggage wagons. Private Felix G. Wright, who had become gravely ill, died the next morning and was buried in camp. Colonel George Hockley recorded his passing as the first Texian death of the campaign.[26]

Two other companies from the upper Red River settlements, those of Captains William Kimbro and Benjamin Bryant, joined with the army during its move toward Groce's. Kimbro's company was ordered to assist Captain Baker's men in guarding the San Felipe river crossing. Houston's army made camp on the afternoon of March 31 on the west bank of the Brazos while work parties continued to widen the road ahead for the remainder of the march. Houston and Hockley estimated that approximately eight hundred men remained with their main contingent.[27]

General Houston's men proceeded to camp for the next two weeks in their new location west of the Brazos River, opposite Groce's Landing. George Hockley wrote that the new camp was "in a secure and effective position, with excellent water from a lake immediately ahead" near the road leading to Groce's ferry. In sharp contrast, Dr. Nicholas Labadie felt that the army now pitched its tents in a deep ravine that was nothing more than a "miserable hole." Houston did find relief in the fact that the 144-ton steamboat *Yellow Stone* of Captain John E. Ross was at the landing, taking on cotton from the Bernardo Plantation of Leonard Groce. He placed a guard detail aboard the riverboat and pressed its seventeen-man crew into service of the army in case its services were needed to move the troops across the river.[28]

The cold, rainy weather helped spread a few cases of measles, so Houston had the sick men transported across the river to a field hospital established on the opposite bank on April 1. The army had at least eight skilled doctors to help tend to the wounded, including surgeon general Alexander Wray Ewing, a twenty-seven-year-old Irishman who had studied his trade in Edinburgh. Few of the doctors enjoyed their task of treating the sick, many of whom increasingly suffered diarrhea from drinking foul water. Dr. Anson Jones, for one, demanded that he be permitted to maintain his rank as a private soldier and resign his medical duties once action was imminent.[29]

Houston received welcome news in the fact that a pair of much-needed cannon were en route to his army from the coastal port of Velasco. The pair of artillery pieces had been cast by leading citizens of Cincinnati, Ohio, to aid the Texans in their war for independence. They had been transported down the Ohio and Mississippi rivers to New Orleans, where they were moved on a sailing ship to the Texas Gulf Coast. Aboard the packet sailing for Texas was the family of Dr. Christopher Columbus Rice. Those on board the vessel suggested a formal presentation of the cannon be made and that Rice's twin daughters should act as sponsors. The pair of American artillery pieces were thereafter dubbed the "Twin Sisters."[30]

The news that the artillery would soon reach his army compelled Houston to promote Leander Smith from captain of the Nacogdoches Volunteers to major of artillery on April 1. While he waited, General Houston used the time to drill his green troops on proper military discipline. Two of his soldiers were brought up on formal court-martial charges for insubordination and desertion. A review board of a dozen Texas Army officers on April 2 found both men guilty and sentenced them to be shot to death the next day. General Houston approved the proceedings and declared that Captain Richard Roman's company of regulars was to carry out the executions at noon.[31]

If Houston hoped to use the rebellious soldiers as an example, his point was made with the rest of his troops. Captain Amasa Turner and two others from his company petitioned the general the next day to pardon one of the condemned men—Private Abraham Scales, who had deserted from their company and been captured. Houston gave in to their wishes and Scales was released. Days later, he would successfully desert the Texas Army again.[32]

Sam Houston pushed the execution of the second prisoner, Private John T. Garner, back one day. This time he allowed the execution process to be carried out until the last possible second. Teenagers like John Swisher and Bob Hunter were shocked as their companies were made to parade in formation for the execution. "The grave was dug and a coffin was there," Hunter related. "The man was blindfolded, and made to kneel on the ground by the coffin, and there was 12 men to shoot him." Captain Robert Calder found the affair to be a "solemn and impressive" ceremony.[33]

Captain Roman gave the order, "Present arms. Take aim."

At that moment, Colonel Hockley raced up and hollered for Roman to halt the execution. He and Houston played the drama to the last possible second before granting clemency to Private Garner. Houston wrote in his reprieve that he hoped the mercy he had shown would be repaid with good conduct and strict obedience to all army regulations. He then took the opportunity to advise his entire army as they stood at attention that any further prisoners found guilty of mutiny and desertion "will suffer the penalty of the law." The near-death experience served its intended purpose with John Garner: he would remain loyal to the Texian cause for the remainder of the campaign.[34]

GENERAL SANTA ANNA HAD fewer discipline concerns with his men.

He had crushed the enemy's resistance in San Antonio, and his subordinates had literally wiped out the Texas rebels in the Goliad area. By late March, his troops were dispersed to put down aggression in several sectors. General Antonio Gaona was on the march toward Nacogdoches with artillery and seven hundred men. Colonel Augustin Amat moved on March 27 toward San Felipe with the Sapper Battalion and most of the Guadalajara Battalion. The "Great Napoleon of the West" hoped to surround Sam Houston's troops, with Gaona moving in from the northeast and General Urrea's thirteen-hundred-man division coming up from the south through Victoria. Houston's men would be followed by General Ramírez y Sesma's men until the other divisions could close in.[35]

Lieutenant Colonel Peña led his First Infantry Brigade from San Antonio de Béxar at 4 P.M. on March 29. Heavy rains caused General Santa Anna to linger in Béxar until March 31, when he, his staff, and thirty dragoons finally departed. El Presidente's group caught up with Colonel Amat's division near the Guadalupe River on April 2. He hoped to punish the rebellious colonists swiftly, but heavy rains had swollen the Guadalupe. Santa Anna was delayed several days in crossing the river. He soon became annoyed with the lack of progress, leaving General Vicente Filisola behind to help his army shepherd their wagon trains and artillery over the angry river.

Santa Anna pushed on toward the Colorado River to rendezvous with Sesma's forces. He soon learned that the Texas Army was nowhere to be found in early April. Sam Houston and his rebels—the last faction of Texians in need of eradication— appeared to Santa Anna at the moment to have "completely disappeared." [36]

12

THE FORK IN THE ROAD

PRESIDENT DAVID BURNET WAS also wondering just what General Houston was doing.

His cabinet, now keeping time in Harrisburg near the Gulf Coast, was discontented with Sam Houston's apparent unwillingness to engage the Mexican Army. The fact that Houston had sent letters condemning the "flight of the wise men" of the Texas government did little to soothe the nerves of the republic's top executives. In a meeting with his cabinet, Burnet decided that Secretary of War Thomas Rusk should be sent to find the general "to stop a further retreat of our army, and to bring the enemy to battle." Colonel Robert Potter read the orders aloud to Rusk, informing him of his authorization to take command of the Texas Army, if necessary.[1]

On April 3 Colonel Rusk reached San Felipe, where he sent words of encouragement to Captain Wyly Martin for his efforts in continuing to hold the key Brazos River crossing at Fort

Bend. The first news of the massacre of Colonel Fannin's men in Goliad was just making the rounds this day. William Haddin, the first of the twenty-eight survivors to reach friendly forces, was originally thought to be the only man to escape death.[2]

George Erath, the Austrian-born surveyor who had made his first campaign in Texas with rangers in August 1835, learned more of military procedure as a Texas Army volunteer. Sam Houston finally had time to begin training his recruits during the rainy days in camp near Groce's Landing. "The delay had a good effect in disciplining us, and giving us information about military tactics," Erath recalled. The general forced his men to stand round-the-clock guard details, often spent "knee-deep in water." Erath, a member of Captain Jesse Billingsley's company, benefited from the drills but found little variety in the food available near the Brazos River: "Supplies were beef principally, scant of salt, an ear of corn for a man a day, which had to be ground on a steel mill."[3]

Sam Houston was prone to curse out those whose who defied him or impeded his army's progress. But he was also seen to display a fatherly side to some in times of need or when he needed to instill some motivation. One young volunteer approached Houston in Groce's camp to seek advice on his soaked firearm.[4]

"General, I've got my gun wet and it won't fire," he said. "What shall I do with it?"

Houston calmly explained that the soldier should warm his pocket handkerchief by the fire, open the gun's powder pan, wrap the handkerchief around the lock, and let it remain for several seconds.

"Repeat the operation two or three times, then pick a little dry powder into the touchhole," said the general. "I think you'll have no difficulty in blowing the bullet out."

A small crowd had gathered to watch their commander in chief school the young recruit. After the general retired to his tent, Private John Swisher noted that some of the men could not resist having some fun with Houston. Another young man new to the army announced that his old flintlock was broken. He was told to go see the camp blacksmith, and was pointed toward the tent of Sam Houston.

He appeared in the general's tent, saying, "I can't make my gun stand cocked. What shall I do with it?"

"Go to hell!" Houston snapped as he realized the prank. "Damn it, I'm no gunsmith!"

The young soldier retreated, leaving his weapon behind. In solitude, Houston removed the gun lock, cleaned the old flintlock piece, and reassembled it. The boy was soon informed by the camp fun-lovers that he had not visited the blacksmith but instead the army's top man. He was urged to go beg forgiveness, and he did so with his hat off, trembling as he explained his mistake to Houston.[5]

He was surprised by the generosity now displayed by General Houston, who was well aware that he was the cause of the snickering outside his tent. "My friend, they told you right," he said. "I am a very good blacksmith."

Houston snapped the gun several times and handed it back to the soldier. "She is in good order now," said Houston. "I hope you are going to do some good fighting."

THOMAS RUSK REACHED THE Texas Army camp on the evening of April 4. He was met by a number of the more rebellious officers who were displeased with their general's continual retreating from the Mexican Army. Many hoped that Colonel Rusk would use his authorization to seize command of the troops.

Colonel Rusk, however, was able to see past the venting to coolly analyze the situation. He soon realized the former Tennessee governor, a veteran of the U.S. Army, was doing all he could to hold together such a motley bunch of men: American mercenaries, volunteer colonists, and a few companies of uniformed regulars. Rusk gave his support to Houston and proceeded to appoint Stephen Austin's nephew, Moses Austin Bryan, as his own staff secretary and interpreter soon after his arrival in camp. Houston was itching to acquire fieldpieces for his troops and had sent his new artillery captain, Leander Smith, to Harrisburg to fetch the two artillery pieces. The Twin Sisters from Cincinnati were loaded on board the steamboat *Ohio* and moved from Galveston to Harrisburg, where they would arrive on April 8.

During this waiting period, Houston and President Burnet continued to duel with each other in ink. In response to Burnet's latest critical letter, Houston fired back on April 6: "I hope a just and wise God, in whom I have always believed, will yet save Texas." Secretary of War Rusk displayed his support for Houston in his own update to Burnet. "I find the Army in fine spirits, ready and willing to measure arms with the enemy," Rusk wrote. He estimated the total Texian strength to be fifteen hundred men, although a portion of this number was detached guarding the major river crossings.[6]

The main body of the army was suffering in its rank position. The most ill were moved across the Brazos River to the field hospital established on Jared Groce's Bernardo Plantation. More men fell ill by drinking stagnant water, adding dysentery to the measles outbreak that had already swept through the lines.

General Santa Anna did not have to ponder Sam Houston's whereabouts for very long after his staff caught up to Ramírez y

Sesma's troops on the Colorado. They marched into the torched town of San Felipe on April 7 and surprised three of Captain Baker's guards who were sleeping near the river. Two escaped across the Brazos but Private Bill Simpson was seized by Mexican cavalrymen. Under interrogation, he told Santa Anna that Houston's rebels were camped in the woods near Groce's Landing and numbered about eight hundred. El Presidente had snipers take shots at Baker's company, entrenched across the river. The Texans fired back, killing two soldiers and a mule during the day.[7]

The skirmishing intensified the next morning. Private Isaac Hill was awakened in his trench by the booming of a Mexican artillery piece from across the river. "Many rounds of roundshot, grape, and canister were discharged at us, throwing the sand upon us and knocking the bark from the cottonwood trees that extended their branches upon us," he said. Private John Bricker of Baker's company was killed by grapeshot striking his head as he moved about to retrieve spent cannonballs—thus becoming the first casualty of enemy action on General Houston's campaign. The Texans returned fire throughout the day, trying to suppress the Mexican soldiers' steady work of building wooden rafts for use in crossing the river.[8]

Near Groce's Landing, Sam Houston and Colonel Rusk took the time on April 8 to better organize their army. They created a Second Regiment of Infantry, placing Colonel Sidney Sherman and Lieutenant Colonel Joseph Bennett in command. The original First Regiment of Infantry remained under Colonel Ed Burleson, with Lieutenant Colonel Alexander Somervell now his second in command. The regular companies of Captains Amasa Turner and Henry Teal were placed under the direction of Lieutenant Colonel Henry Millard.[9]

Although the booming of the Mexican cannon at San Felipe could be heard from the Texian camp, Houston held most of his men in check. He sent Lieutenant Colonel Bennett with forty-five men to reinforce Captain Baker while he struggled with the rising number of sick men in his filthy river bottom camp. General Santa Anna took some 550 grenadiers and infantrymen on April 9 and moved down the west bank of the Brazos, away from Groce's. He left General Ramírez y Sesma and about 850 men to continue firing on Baker's troops and to finish building the river rafts. Santa Anna's force reached the tavern of widow Elizabeth Powell on the San Bernard River on the evening of April 10. They pushed on the next day toward the next major crossing point of the Brazos River, Thompson's Ferry, near Fort Bend.[10]

Moseley Baker's San Felipe detachment fell back from the Brazos to Iron's Creek on April 9. He sent word to General Houston the following day that the majority of the Mexican soldiers were on the move. Word also reached President Burnet in Harrisburg that Santa Anna's army was preparing to cross the Brazos. He wrote angrily to Sam Houston that his intelligence told him the Mexicans had "jeeringly threatened to smoke him out" of his Brazos bottomlands campground. "The enemy are laughing you to scorn," Burnet said. "You must retreat no further. The country expects you to fight. The salvation of the country depends on your doing so." [11]

General Houston received word on April 11 from his detachments that the Mexican Army was crossing the Brazos at Thompson's Ferry. He was coming under increasing criticism by some of his own men for lying idle. Major James Perry, a volunteer aide-to-camp and friend of President Burnet, wrote a mutinous letter to Colonel Robert Potter, the Texas secretary of navy. In it he said the Texas soldiers "are completely without discipline" and were little more than "an ordinary mob." Potter reported that General Houston had discontinued his use of alcohol, but some said he was partaking of opium, keeping him "in a condition between sleeping and waking, which amounts to a constant state of insanity." The opium reference was the Cherokee hartshorn powder used by the general to ward off colds.[12]

Potter's letter was apprehended by Houston, who sent it on to President Burnet, but had spies thereafter keep track of Potter's action. The general defended his perceived angry character and attributed his behavior to lack of sleep. "I am worn down in body by fatigue, and really take my rest most in the morning, for I watch nearly all night," Houston wrote. "Instead of being in a state of insanity, I fear I am too irritable for my duties." He struck back at the Texas president, saying that if he had been elected into office, there would be "more men to defend it."

A more shocking event that took place in the Texas Army camp this day was the arrival of some of the Goliad Massacre survivors. Texas scouts came upon a half dozen of them the previous day at Mill Creek, north of San Felipe. The long-suffering group included Charles Shain, Daniel Murphy, Thomas Kemp, David Jones, William Brenan, and Nat Hazen. When they rode into camp with the scouts on April 11, Dr. Nicholas Labadie found them to be "wounded, barefooted, and ragged."[13]

Colonel Ben Smith took young Shain under his wing, offering him proper clothing and the assistance of his servant, Mack Smith, until his body was healed. These Goliad survivors would join two of the Texas Army companies. Shain took the time to write a long letter to his father back home in Kentucky, explaining the great hardships he had endured. He also made a pledge to his family: "I will try to avenge the death of some of my brave friends. All of my company were killed."

The Texas cabinet in Harrisburg received word on April 12 that the Mexican Army had crossed the Brazos and was on the move. Acting Secretary of War David Thomas sent a blunt message to General Houston that day: "The country expects something from you." President Burnet sent his own orders to Colonel Rusk that day, indicating that he was still incensed with Houston's jabs about the flight of the government. He made it clear to Rusk that the country expected the Texas Army to engage in battle. "A further retreat without a fight would be infinitely disastrous," Burnet said. "Houston's force is numerically greater than the antagonists."[14]

A small party of the men stationed at the Fort Bend crossing exchanged shots with Mexican troops during the afternoon. Sam Houston sent orders to Captain Wyly Martin to gather up his men and leave the river crossings. They were to proceed to the home of Charles Donoho on the road from Groce's to San Felipe and there make camp until further orders were issued. Sam Houston hoped to gather all of his forces in the vicinity of Donoho's and then march toward Harrisburg—where he fully expected Santa Anna's forces to be headed.[15]

The first groups of weary, muddy Texan soldiers began boarding the riverboat *Yellow Stone* at 10 A.M. on April 12. The vessel's steam engines were barely enough to maneuver through the swollen Brazos River's angry currents. In moving many hundreds of men, baggage, supply wagons, ox teams, and about two hundred horses, Captain John Ross's *Yellow Stone* would require numerous trips. It took until late the following afternoon to get the entire army across.

The most welcome site at Leonard Groce's Bernardo Plantation on the east side of the river was the arrival of Major Leander Smith and his companions. They had finally succeeded in hauling the six-pound iron cannon, known as the Twin Sisters, from Harrisburg all the way to Groce's. Many of the volunteers toiled through the night to prepare proper canister shot for their new artillery. General Houston shared dinner on the night of April 12 at the Groce home with Dr. Anson Jones. In their conversation, Jones was not afraid to state that "if the retreating policy were continued much longer, he would be pretty much alone." Jones advised Houston that his next move should be toward his enemy.[16]

The sentiment that it was now time to fight was spreading, even among the newest arrivals. One of them was a blue-eyed, thirty-seven-year-old of medium height named Mirabeau Buonaparte Lamar. The former editor and poet had walked fifty miles from Harrisburg in company with several other volunteers. Lamar had recently arrived in Texas for the second time, planning now to settle permanently. He left his savings of six thousand dollars in the trust of Vice President Lorenzo de Zavala and headed for the army. Lamar reported in to General Houston at Bernardo, and the influence of the Texas cabinet on him quickly became apparent. Lamar was critical of Houston's laxness and proceeded to talk of plans to attack the enemy. He advocated taking a large party of men on board the *Yellow Stone* to conduct guerrilla raids on Mexican forces near the riverfront. Upon learning of this scheme, Houston posted notices in camp that anyone who attempted to raise an unauthorized force would be executed for mutiny.[17]

Rusk and Houston spent much of April 13 sending appeals to other settlements for men to join the cause of the army. By late afternoon, Colonel Sidney Sherman and the last of the army had crossed the Brazos on the *Yellow Stone*. The only loss throughout the mass transfers had been two oxen that had fallen overboard and drowned.

GENERAL SANTA ANNA'S MEN used trickery to cross the Brazos. He led a column downriver toward Thompson's ferry above Fort Bend, leaving General Ramírez y Sesma with eight hundred men to deal with Captain Baker's detachment. Santa Anna's force reached the crossing on the morning of April 12 and spied a black servant on the far shore. Colonel Juan Almonte, the squarely built, good-natured officer once educated in the United States, called over in perfect English for the man to bring the flatboat across to get them, as the Mexican troops hid in the bushes. Once the servant reached the other shore, he was taken prisoner and the Mexican Army began crossing the Brazos. A courier was sent back to fetch Sesma, whose soldiers hurried downriver and effected their crossing on April 13.[18]

Santa Anna's men struggled to cross the Brazos bottomland, particularly one swollen creek. Secretary Ramón Caro noted that His Excellency had a profound fear of water. He dismounted at this creek, cautiously inched across a log, and had one of his soldiers swim his horse across. Santa Anna then watched the show as his infantrymen struggled and slipped on the steep, opposite bank. Mules overloaded with pack saddles slipped and fell, jamming up officers, men, and horses. "This, together with shouts and curses, completed a scene of wild confusion, which His Excellency witnessed with hearty laughter," Colonel Delgado wrote in his diary.[19]

Santa Anna gave orders for General Filisola to send General Martín Cos with five hundred infantrymen to seize Fort Velasco on the coast with the use of two eight-pound cannon and a howitzer. Filisola was also detailed to take cavalrymen out to San Felipe to make contact with General Gaona and to guard the ford near Thompson's Ferry. Santa Anna believed it would be useful if his men could capture the steamboat *Yellow Stone* once it moved downriver.[20]

General Filisola's men did encounter the riverboat as it chugged down the Brazos on the morning of April 15. Lieutenant Colonel Peña found that the Guadalajara Battalion soldiers posted on the river were "dumbfounded by the sight of a machine so totally unfamiliar and unexpected." Colonel Juan Almonte ordered the troops to open fire on the vessel. Captain Ross had his steamboat well covered with cotton bales to help absorb the lead balls fired at the *Yellow Stone* as he maintained steam and plowed past Thompson's Ferry with his ship's bell clanging.[21]

Santa Anna failed to pull his army together to make one cohesive strike against the retreating Texas rebels. Instead, he ordered General Jose Urrea to investigate Matagorda and then set up a general headquarters at Brazoria. Filisola's division was left near Fort Bend while El Presidente and more than seven hundred troops pushed forward with a new goal. Lorenzo de Zavala and other members of the Texas government were nearby in Harrisburg. "Their capture was certain if a few troops marched on them quickly," wrote Santa Anna. With President Burnet as his captive, he could then take care of Sam Houston's little army.[22]

SAM HOUSTON WAS STILL like the ass between two stacks of hay. On the one hand, he had President Burnet ridiculing him into fighting. On the other, he had Texas secretary of state Samuel Carson urging him to continue falling back. Carson had arrived at Fort Jesup in Natchitoches, Louisiana, on April 13 to meet with General Edmund Pendleton Gaines. He hoped to draw the U.S. troops into the Texas Revolution by showing that the

Mexicans had incited hostile Indians to commit depredations on either side of the national line. Carson also called upon the governors of Louisiana, Tennessee, Mississippi, and Alabama to send brigades of volunteers to help halt the Mexican dictator who was sweeping through Texas.[23]

Carson wrote to General Houston on April 14: "You must fall back, and hold out, and let nothing goad or provoke you to a battle, unless you can, without a doubt, whip them, or unless you are compelled to fight." Carson pledged that U.S. troops would be gathered at the Sabine River to assist, and would move swiftly into Texas if the Mexicans were found to be stirring the Indians into committing bloodshed.

Houston could not count on the promised American volunteers arriving from distant states in time to help him. He also ran the very real risk of his entire army disintegrating if he continued to do nothing. He therefore sent the steamboat *Yellow Stone* downstream on April 14 and began marching his army down the road from Groce's to Donoho's home, where he had ordered his detached forces to remain. Lieutenant Colonel James Neill, once the commander of the Alamo, was back in command of artillery. He organized companies of men to help haul the smoothbore Twin Sisters artillery pieces down the boggy road.

The Texas Army camped on the night of April 14 at the plantation of Charles Donoho, where they were rejoined by the companies of Captains Moseley Baker and Wyly Martin. Finding the trees too green to burn, soldiers tore down all of the wood railing around the Donoho home to use for firewood. Captain Baker openly criticized General Houston for failing to join him in fighting the Mexicans along the riverfront. Houston ignored all those who badgered him, and held no councils of war to seek the various opinions of other officers that would have been offered. He studied the intelligence that was received daily and made his decisions with little input, save perhaps his close ally Colonel Hockley.[24]

One such piece of advice was forwarded to the general on April 14 from cabinet member David Thomas in Harrisburg. Thomas said that Santa Anna's army was moving through the Brazos bottomlands and that the Texas Army should hasten toward Galveston, where they would be close to provisions and ammunition. General Houston faced mutiny on the morning of April 15 as he tried to get his troops marching east again toward Nacogdoches. Captains Baker and Martin gave various reasons for refusing to march. Tired of shepherding pitiful citizen refugees and facing such insubordination, Houston ordered Wyly Martin to feed his company and then guide the Runaway Scrape families toward safety by leading them down the road to the Robbins's Ferry crossing of the Trinity River.[25]

"Thus was the insubordination gotten over," Houston later detailed. "Captain Baker fell into line." He offered furloughs to some men to help care for their families, and an estimated three hundred or more soldiers left the army at this point with Captain Martin's rebellious company. Those who remained with Sam Houston marched across open prairie land along the well-traveled road from Washington-on-the-Brazos. Each passing mile brought them closer to a crucial fork in the road near the home of Abraham Roberts. The left-hand fork of the road led toward the Trinity River, Nacogdoches, and the eastern settlements. The right-hand fork led toward Harrisburg.[26]

Colonel Robert Coleman, the former ranger commander who was now an aide-de-camp for Sam Houston, made his thoughts known that day. He felt any attempt to take the left-hand road near Roberts's home would "throw everything into confusion." Coleman believed that men would either leave the army or demand a new commander in chief if Houston was perceived to be continuing his flight. Houston had no intention of sharing his thoughts with a subordinate who was becoming less of an ally with each passing day. He simply let the issue pass by telling Coleman he would consider the advice that had been offered to him.[27]

SANTA ANNA WAS HELL-BENT on catching David Burnet's government.

He marched his men steadily on April 15, pausing only long enough at the plantation of William Stafford to loot it and burn down the structures. Santa Anna, his staff, and their escorts eagerly rode ahead toward Harrisburg, leaving General Castrillón to supervise the march of the infantrymen. Once in town, Santa Anna and his advance party captured three printers who were busy setting type for the next issue of the *Telegraph and Texas Register* newspaper.

The printers informed El Presidente that one of the two editors, Gail Borden, had left town just an hour before. They also said that President Burnet, Vice President Zavala, and their cabinet had departed at noon that day on the steamboat *Cayuga* for Galveston Island. They believed the Texas government was moving toward the settlement of New Washington, located on a peninsula where Galveston Bay meets San Jacinto Bay. Santa Anna was so furious at having just missed capturing the Texas government that he ordered the printing presses destroyed and thrown into the river. These presses had produced the first issues of the *Telegraph and Texas Register* newspaper, and, most recent, copies of the brand-new Texas Declaration of

Independence. Colonel Juan Almonte was ordered to take fifty dragoons and scout out as far as New Washington and the pass at Lynchburg.[28]

Houston's army halted after dark to make camp at the homestead of Samuel McCarley. The troops were within three miles of the crucial forks in the road. Once again, they used the McCarley home's fencing for firewood and cut sharp sticks to use in roasting their raw beef over the campfires. The march along the muddy road was resumed early the next morning, April 16. Captain Conrad Rohrer's artillery and provision wagons led the procession this day due to the poor road conditions.

About three miles from McCarley's place and some fifteen miles east of Donoho's home, the Texas Army finally reached the split in the road near the Roberts homestead. The time had come for "Old Sam" to show his true colors. Would he choose fight or flight? Captain Jesse Billingsley and other company leaders had already made their decision. "Many of us signed an agreement to support each other and take the road leading in the direction of the foe, whatever the order might be," Billingsley wrote.[29]

Colonel Sidney Sherman was certain that Houston would lead the men toward East Texas. He felt that Colonel Rusk used his influence to coerce the general to turn toward Harrisburg to fight. Houston did have fresh intelligence from Secretary Carson that U.S. regulars might be to his benefit if he did choose to head for the border. But "Old Sam" never commented to his subordinates on what his true plans were or if anyone influenced him. Captain Robert Calder, leading some of the advance guard, only commented later that he received an order to take the right-hand road. Houston may very well have let the will of his troops play in his favor by letting the masses move down the path of their choice. He commented later that only Rusk and George Hockley were familiar with his true plans. Captain William Heard and his orderly sergeant, Eli Mercer, said that word had been spread through the army that if Houston chose the left-hand road toward Nacogdoches "the volunteers would call out for a leader to go at their head to Harrisburg to meet the enemy." [30]

Regardless of who ultimately made the choice for the right-hand road, the fork in the road marked a pivotal point in the campaign for Texas. The leading companies moved right and they were followed by the baggage wagons, the artillery, and hundreds of foot soldiers. It was finally time to fight!

The little band of Texian musicians marched right amid shouts of joy throughout the ranks. Captain Amasa Turner of the regulars felt the turn toward Harrisburg to meet their enemy "revived our drooping spirits."

General Houston sent Major Williamson, commander of a ranger battalion, to ride ahead and find Captain William Kimbro's company, which had been on detached duty for two weeks. They were to rejoin the main army as it headed for Harrisburg. The troops could only move as fast as the heavy Twin Sisters cannon could be hauled through the sloppy road bed. Houston soon found a new problem. His men were using two wagons and ox teams borrowed from one of the fleeing civilians, Pamelia Mann. She now confronted the general and told him her teams could only be used if the army was to continue on toward Nacogdoches. Houston had given her his word that morning that they were continuing in that direction. [31]

The army had then turned right at the fork and proceeded on toward Harrisburg. Mrs. Mann was furious when she finally overtook the teams hauling the cannon with her oxen miles later.

"General, you told me a damn lie!" she snapped. "You said that you was going on the Nacogdoches Road. Sir, I want my oxen!"

"Well, Mrs. Mann, we can't spare them," Houston politely replied. "We can't get our cannon along without them."

"I don't give a damn for your cannon!" she barked. "I want my oxen!"

Private Bob Hunter watched as the determined widow drew a large knife from her saddle and sawed off the rawhide tug holding the chain to her oxen. "Nobody said a word," recalled Hunter. Mrs. Mann then mounted her horse and rode off with her oxen as the Twin Sisters bogged into the mud. Houston told his men they would have to get by as best they could dragging the cannon. Conrad Rohrer had other ideas. He grabbed one of his teamsters and said that he would convince Mrs. Mann to return the oxen to his use.

"Captain Rohrer, that woman will fight," Houston hollered.

"Damn her fighting!" shouted Rohrer.

Sam Houston then waded into the mud, grabbed a wheel mounted to one of the cannon frames, and asked his men to help him get the artillery moving to drier ground. The army was able to move another six miles before making camp for the night in some heavy timber near Cypress Creek (present Telge Park).

When Captain Rohrer rode back into camp that night, he said that Mrs. Mann had refused to give up her ox teams. Several soldiers noticed that his shirt had been torn in several places. Rohrer explained that she had asked for some of it for baby rags. Private James Winters, however, heard several men laughing that the tough old widow had torn it off him.[32]

13

"DARING CHIVALRY": THE FIRST DUEL

COLONEL JUAN ALMONTE'S DRAGOONS came within a musket's shot of capturing the Texas government.

President David Burnet, his wife, Hannah Este Burnet, and several cabinet members departed the steamboat *Cayuga* at the Lynchburg landing. They took their horses, crossed San Jacinto Bay aboard the ferry, and rode the final ten miles to the settlement of New Washington. At the plantation of Colonel James Morgan, they found a flatboat hauling supplies from the Morgan warehouse out to the schooner *Flash* in Galveston Bay. Morgan's Point, a parcel of land extending into San Jacinto Bay, was the sprawling plantation of cattle and orange trees owned by Morgan.[1]

Colonel Almonte and his fifty soldiers received word that

the Texas president was at Morgan's plantation and rode there in great haste. Burnet's party had just enough warning to climb into a large skiff and a large flatboat. The cabinet members and several plantation servants pulled hard on the oars to clear the beach as Almonte's dragoons arrived at the bay shore. The Mexican cavalrymen dismounted and took aim on the fleeing Texian executives. David Burnet and his party were spared only by the chivalry of Juan Almonte, who refused to let his men shoot into the boats on account of a woman and child being present.[2]

The Texas government leaders thus narrowly escaped capture on April 16 as they rowed across to Galveston Island. Almonte's men seized James Morgan's warehouses—stocked with food and other provisions—and sent word for General Santa Anna to join them at New Washington. His Excellency's troops had lingered in Harrisburg through the day, continuing to loot the town. Lieutenant Colonel José María Castillo y Iberri recalled that Santa Anna was so enraged at missing the capture of President Burnet that he even lent a hand to the troops he ordered to burn the town.[3]

Santa Anna moved from Harrisburg around 3 P.M. on April 17, crossing Buffalo Bayou en route to New Washington. He had 750 soldiers and fifty horses at his disposal. He sent Lieutenant Colonel Castillo y Iberri as a courier toward the port of Velasco to order General Cos to march to his assistance with five hundred foot soldiers. Santa Anna's own force crossed a tributary to Buffalo Bayou known as Vince's Bayou on a sturdy cedar bridge built by the William Vince family. When the mules hauling the Mexican cannon known as the Golden Standard refused to cross the bridge, Santa Anna ordered General Castrillón on what proved to be a nine-mile circumvention through boggy prairies.[4]

Colonel Juan Bringas, an aide to Santa Anna, relieved the Vince ranch of a large, black Thoroughbred stallion called "Old Whip," which he made his own. The general's force suffered through a violent storm that evening and reached New Washington by noon on April 18. Colonel Pedro Delgado noted that his troops found many items of luxury in the warehouses on James Morgan's plantation, including soap, tobacco, and flour. A much worn-down bunch under General Castrillón finally arrived with the Golden Standard cannon around 5 P.M.[5]

Santa Anna found another item of interest that particularly caught his eager eye. Among the indentured servants working on Colonel Morgan's plantation was a beautiful mulatto girl named Emily who was assisting with the loading of supplies on a flatboat. Less than thirty years in age, Emily D. West hailed from New Haven, Connecticut, where she had been born among blacks not held as slaves. On October 25, 1835, the light-skinned Miss Emily signed a contract with agent James Morgan in New York City to return to his New Washington hotel at Morgan's point. She agreed to work for one year as a housekeeper for the annual contract of one hundred dollars. Emily arrived in Texas in December aboard a schooner carrying thirteen other laborers and the wife and children of Texas vice president Lorenzo de Zavala.[6]

Santa Anna ordered the town of New Washington burned to the ground after his soldiers finished looting all of the Morgan supplies they could haul with them. El Presidente's troops marched from Morgan's Point and made rendezvous with Colonel Almonte's group of dragoons. They were taken under fire near the banks of the bay by a little armed schooner of the new Texas Navy. Santa Anna decided to keep moving, hoping to surprise Sam Houston's rebel army near the Lynchburg ferry.[7]

As his troops moved to set an ambush site, Santa Anna took

into the custody of his entourage the most prized seizure of his campaign—the beautiful Miss Emily.

SAM HOUSTON'S RAGGED ARMY was moving steadily closer to a forced rendezvous with His Excellency's army.

On April 17, the Texas Army marched fifteen miles closer to Harrisburg, which Santa Anna was reported to have reached with his forces. The Texians had trudged more than two hundred miles since departing Gonzales on March 13 by the time they arrived in the charred town of Harrisburg around noon on April 18. The men made camp within sight of town, about eight hundred yards away on the left bank of Buffalo Bayou. Many collapsed in exhaustion after the steady marching through muddy roads. Captains Henry Karnes and William Smith crossed the bayou and went out with their scouts to search for the nearby Mexican Army.

Deaf Smith, Karnes, and several of their men soon proved their value in the field once again. Twelve miles down the road toward the Brazos, they came upon three Mexican horsemen and overpowered them with little fight. One of them was Captain Miguel Bachiller, a special courier from Mexico City. His deerskin saddlebags were inscribed with the name "W. B. Travis," the late commander of the Alamo. More important was the discovery of important letters intended for Santa Anna. The prisoners were bound and ridden back to the Texian camp at Harrisburg that evening.

Sergeant Moses Bryan and others erupted into laughter at the site of Deaf Smith. The wily, weathered-skin old scout had traded his ragged coats and pants with those of Captain Bachiller. Soldiers howled at the site of the Mexican prisoner whose toes now stuck out of the holes in Smith's tattered shoes.

"Smith had on the Mexican courier's fine suit of leather, a broad brim sombrero, a heavy bead band and trinkets attached, fine shoes and socks," recorded Bryan. "But the suit was too small and too tight and pants not reaching nearer than six inches of the top of the shoes." [8]

Bryan, called to act as interpreter for Sam Houston, questioned the Mexican captain. Bachiller indicated that Santa Anna was moving with at least six hundred troops and one brass twelve-pound cannon. Sergeant Tony Menchaca of Captain Juan Seguín's company read another dispatch from General Filisola to Santa Anna that indicated to Houston that the Mexican Army's divisions were currently separated. Major Lorenzo de Zavala Jr. and others who could read Spanish pored over the other letters. Sergeant William Swearingen heard that the most important intelligence gleaned came from a dispatch from General Cos to the Mexican general. In it, Santa Anna stated that he would move the next morning to join Cos at Lynch's Ferry on Buffalo Bayou. [9]

Sam Houston's spirits were greatly revived. He now had the upper hand, having learned of the position of his enemy's troops and the planned rendezvous site of the divisions under Cos and Santa Anna. His first challenge would be in crossing Buffalo Bayou. Colonel Sidney Sherman and 150 men were sent across on the evening of April 18, but crossing the swollen waterway proved difficult and dangerous. Only the cavalry company of Henry Karnes swam its horses across before orders were sent to halt the move while a more favorable crossing method was determined.

General Houston decided on April 19 that he must leave behind everything that encumbered his march to engage Santa Anna. He detached a number of men at Harrisburg to guard the army's baggage wagons and to care for the dozens of men ill with measles, fever, diarrhea, and flu-like symptoms. Major Robert McNutt, third senior officer of the First Regiment of Infantry, was placed in command of the camp at Harrisburg.

The frontiersmen who had most recently been serving as Texas Rangers were targeted as candidates to help guard the baggage teams and the sick. Major Willie Williamson, who had returned to the army in company with Captain Joseph Chance's Washington Guards ranger company, assigned Chance's company to McNutt. Captain Stephen Townsend's small Robertson Colony ranging company was also assigned to McNutt. The order to remain behind as camp guards did not go over well with many of the rangers, however. Captain Townsend and his brother Spencer temporarily joined the cavalry. Williamson also joined the cavalry, along with two of his other ranger officers who temporarily abandoned their commissions, Captain Isaac Burton and Lieutenant Thomas Robbins. Captain John Tumlinson and two of his rangers attached themselves as private soldiers in Texas infantry companies. William T. Sadler and seven of his former Fort Houston rangers also blended into infantry and cavalry companies. More than eighty men who had served as Texas Rangers were present to either help guard the army baggage or march toward Lynchburg.[10]

Texas officers gave every man the chance to stay behind at camp if he was not willing to go into battle. There were no takers, aside from those too sick to walk. Two other infantry companies were assigned to Major McNutt, plus small numbers of guards picked from various other companies. Teenager William Zuber was ordered by Captain James Gillaspie to remain behind. Frustrated, he broke down in tears. Captain Juan Seguín's *tejano* unit was also assigned to guard camp, as Houston considered their skills at herding to be of good value.

Sergeant Tony Menchaca questioned this decision and asked that his superior, Colonel Sherman, visit the commander in chief with him.[11]

Menchaca told Sam Houston he had joined the Texas Army to fight and he did not agree with his commission being deprived. "I did not enlist to guard horses and I will do no such duty," he informed the general.

Menchaca stated that he would instead head for Nacogdoches to take care of his family in their flight to safety. Houston could hardly turn away such strong patriotism. "Spoken like a man," he conceded. He pledged to Menchaca that he would allow Seguín's *tejanos* to fight. To avoid being mistaken for the enemy, Houston had Seguín's men insert colored playing cards into their headbands. Some added white scraps of cardboard with printed lines of "Recuerden en Alamo" and "Recuerden Goliad." [12]

Some three hundred men remained behind at Harrisburg when the Texas Army began moving on April 19. Buffalo Bayou was swollen to more than three hundred yards wide in places, causing the troops to hike two miles below Harrisburg until a more suitable fording site was found below the mouth of Sims Bayou. There the troops used wood from a nearby home to shore up a leaking old ferryboat that would take them across the bayou.

Prior to crossing Buffalo Bayou, Sam Houston delivered his first formal speech of the campaign. Perched atop his large gray mare, Saracen, he reminded his men that if anyone did not feel like fighting, they could stay behind with Major McNutt's detachment. "Some of us may be killed and must be killed," he said. George Erath recalled that Houston "promised us that we should have full satisfaction for all we had gone through."

Houston concluded his speech by urging his men to "remember the Alamo, the Alamo! the Alamo!" His soldiers roared back with "Remember the Alamo!" [13]

A battle cry had been born.

"After such a speech, but damned few will be taken prisoners," remarked Lieutenant Colonel Alexander Somervell. Private Patrick Usher was equally inspired: "Had General Houston called upon me to jump into the whirlpool of the Niagara as the only means of saving Texas, I would have made the leap." [14]

Colonel Rusk, the secretary of war and a signer of the Texas Declaration of Independence, spoke next. His words were equally inspiring. "May I not survive if we don't win this battle!" Rusk declared. Moses Bryan found the colonel's talk soul-stirring and it was met with great applause. Tony Menchaca felt that Rusk addressed the men with enough effect that some were moved to tears. He advised his men to not only remember the Alamo but to remember Goliad and the brave men who had been slaughtered there. [15]

The pep talks achieved their desired effects. Rusk ended his speech abruptly with "I have done." The Texians broke into animated shouts of "Remember La Bahía! Remember Goliad!" and "Remember the Alamo!" Lieutenant M. H. Denham felt that he and his fellow soldiers were now "determined to conquer or die." [16]

The Texas Army began crossing Buffalo Bayou after the speeches were complete. The patched-up ferryboat proved effective enough in poling the Twin Sisters across, along with load after load of officers and men. By 5 P.M. on April 19, all were across and the men took cover in the bushes along the road to watch for the arrival of expected Mexican reinforcements. Once it was completely dark, General Houston put his troops on the move toward Lynchburg. He believed he would catch General Santa Anna at the ferry, awaiting the arrival of General Cos.

He finally halted his troops at 2 A.M. on April 20, about two and a half miles from Lynch's Ferry. Those not on guard duty quickly fell out and tried to get some sleep, clutching their rifles close to their growling bellies. The fact that the bay-area ground was wet did not help when a cold norther settled in over the weary Texians.

Most had little on their minds save the hope for real action that might well come with morning.

NEW WASHINGTON WAS IN flames as Santa Anna's troops marched toward Lynchburg on the morning of April 20.

En route, Colonel Delgado suddenly noted Captain Marcos Barragán racing up the road at full speed on horseback. He had been sent with about fifty of his men to Lynchburg Pass to observe the movements of the Texas Army. There he ran afoul of Texian scouts under Sidney Sherman and lost four cavalrymen in a brief encounter. Barragán wheeled his horse about and raced for Santa Anna to spread the news. He reached the general around 8 A.M. and said the Texans were hot on his heels.[17]

General Santa Anna was so alarmed that he jumped on his horse and galloped off at full speed for the road. He barreled right through men and mules, plowing over two soldiers in his haste. Colonel Delgado worked to quickly restore order to his momentarily panicked troops. He moved his men and artillery across the tall grass of the prairies to establish a good defensive position during the late morning hours. The Mexican Army made preparations for battle near the San Jacinto River and Buffalo Bayou on the sprawling cattle ranch of widow Margaret "Peggy" McCormick. The forty-eight-year-old cattle-woman originally from Ireland had continued to run the cattle ranch with her two sons following the accidental drowning of her husband, Arthur, in 1824. The McCormicks had fled their league of land as the Mexican Army approached.

Santa Anna was pleased with the position of his troops on the vast McCormick ranch. He found that Sam Houston's Texas rebels had taken possession of a small wooded area that was surrounded by the bayou. "His situation made it necessary for him to fight or go into the water," thought Santa Anna.

THE MORNING BRUSH WITH Captain Barragán's scouts put the Texian camp in a brief panic as well.

Dawn at General Houston's camp was quite cold for late April, as an unusually late norther had blown through overnight. Soggy with dew and quite chilled, the Texas soldiers had been put back on the march again at 6 A.M., just four hours after they had paused for the night to rest. They marched to Lynchburg Ferry and paused while Sam Houston picked out a suitable stretch of ground on which to make his camp. Only then did he allow his men to stake their horses and mules and begin collecting kindling wood for breakfast fires.[18]

Three of Peggy McCormick's cattle were slaughtered to feed the troops. Dr. Shields Booker scavenged a dozen eggs to add to the surgeons' pot of brackish water and half-pounded coffee. The campfires had not been burning long when some of Colonel Sherman's and Captain Karnes's scouts galloped back into camp with news of their skirmish with Captain Barragán's cavalrymen. Houston barked at his troops to grab their arms, break camp, and kill their fires. George Erath saw Colonel Rusk ride into camp, shouting to all that Santa Anna had burned New Washington and was advancing on the Texas force.[19]

The surgeons each quickly downed their share of boiling coffee and pulled the eggs from the coffee water. Dr. Labadie noted that the eggs contained small chickens inside. "I surrendered my share to others who, finding them well cooked, swallowed them quickly." Several of the soldiers found great delight in the momentary fear that consumed Colonel John Forbes when he heard the Mexican Army might be rushing down on them. The commissary general jumped on his saddled mule and tried to get it to run. All the beast could do was jump about, as its legs had been tied to keep it from wandering off from camp. Private Thomas Corry recalled that Forbes "sat surrounded by laughing men, until one of them walked some fifty feet and cut the hobbles off." [20]

Sam Houston found no humor in the fact that hundreds of men began priming their weapons for action with fresh powder. In order to load fresh, each man discharged his weapon. Dr. Labadie said there was "a perfect roar of musketry, till over 400 were fired across the bayou." Houston flew into a rage. "Stop that firing!" he roared. "God damn you, I say, stop the firing!"

Several other soldiers proceeded to clear their muskets until the general drew his sword and threatened to run through the next man who fired his gun. Many of the soldiers griped aloud that they could not go into battle with wet weapons that had not been freshly loaded in many cases for at least two weeks. Another musket roared in defiance of Houston, at which point he gave up his threat. His ragged volunteer army was primed for the fight, and he realized there was little he could do to control them. [21]

Around 10 A.M., Houston had his men move into a small grove of live oak trees near the elevated banks of Buffalo Bayou, along with their Twin Sisters artillery. The position offered perfect cover to await the advancement of Santa Anna's troops across the grassy half-mile-wide prairie that lay ahead. Buffalo Bayou skirted along the northern boundary of this field and fell away to the southeast as it ran into the San Jacinto River just above Lynch's Ferry. The eastern boundary of the field was San Jacinto Bay, which flowed down toward Galveston Bay. Several significant bodies of water lay along the eastern edges of the field, including Peggy's Lake—large enough to look like a bay itself. Thick groves of trees and coastal marshes pocketed the fringes of this massive point of land that Houston's men now surveyed.[22]

Houston had his men turn the horses and oxen loose to graze while his scouts went out for more intelligence. Nine new volunteers presented themselves at General Houston's newly erected command tent during the late morning. They had rowed an eight-oar cutter across Galveston Bay and reported in to the army at its place of concealment in the timber a half mile below Lynch's Ferry. One of these volunteers, Captain Benjamin Cromwell Franklin, later documented the vivid scene of the army of irregulars he was now joining. "Around some twenty or thirty campfires stood as many groups of men, English, Irish, Scotch, French, Germans, Italians, Poles, Yankees, Mexicans, all unwashed, unshaven for months, their long hair, beard and mustaches, ragged and matted, their clothes in tatters, and plastered with mud. In a word, a more savage band could scarcely have been assembled; and yet many—most indeed, were gentlemen, owners of large estates, distinguished some for oratory, some for science, and some for medical talent."[23]

Houston kept a scouting patrol of six soldiers under Colonel Robert Coleman posted to watch Lynch's Ferry. During the late morning, his party fired upon and captured a small ferry flatboat that was moving up Buffalo Bayou. Several of Coleman's men swam over and commandeered the supply boat after the Mexican soldiers dived overboard. They found it loaded with flour, coffee, meal, salt, and other goods stolen from Colonel Morgan's New Washington warehouse with the intent of sailing the goods along the bayou to Santa Anna's troops. Coleman's scouts sailed the little flatboat to a convenient landing place near Houston's new camp. The Texians were elated to have barrels of flour to make dough for bread. "We feasted that day," said Private Alfonso Steele.[24]

SANTA ANNA WONDERED JUST how many troops old Sam had brought to the McCormick ranch to fight him. He decided to probe the Texian forces hiding in the woods near Buffalo Bayou to determine their number.

He ordered the Toluca company to move forward as skirmishers to draw out the rebels. Santa Anna had his musicians play the dark *degüello* music that had been used by his army in March when the Alamo was overrun. The message was clear to those who understood: no quarter would be offered for traitors to the Mexican government. They would be laid to waste just as El Presidente's troops had done with the Alamo and La Bahía defenders.[25]

It was 11:30 A.M. on April 20, 1836.

Sam Houston was cautious not to tip his hand as Santa Anna tried to call him out. He ordered his men to lie down in the tall grass to conceal their numbers, and he ordered the Twin Sisters to remain tucked into the tree line. The only sound was the ever-increasing blare of the Mexican trumpets as they moved forward. Houston glanced over to where Lieutenant Colonel James Neill stood by with his two artillery teams, commanded by Captains Isaac Moreland and George Poe.

Houston called over to his friend, "Moreland, are you ready?"

Moreland informed the general that the range was still too far. Each six-pound cannon was managed by a team of three gunners plus their team of assistants who would sponge, ram, point, and haul the cannon into firing position.

Houston had waited long enough. He did not even give his comrade's team time enough to properly lower their cannon's elevation.

"Clear the guns and fire!" Houston barked.

The Twin Sisters roared to life with ear-ringing blasts that spit fire from each barrel and shook the ground beneath the gunners' feet. Neither American-made artillery piece had even been test-fired due to a scarcity of cannonballs. Their aim mattered little. The sudden roar of an unseen cannon from the edge of the woods scared the hell out of the advancing Mexican cavalrymen—even if the first shot by the Texans was too high.[26]

The Mexican cavalrymen retreated back across the open prairie. General Santa Anna accepted the challenge from Houston and soon had his artillerymen roll their own cannon out into the open field. A thick little island of oak trees stood roughly 150 yards from the thicket where the Texas rebels were hiding. Captain Fernando Urriza's artillerymen towed their much larger, nine-pound brass Golden Standard piece to this spot. Once positioned, the Mexican cannon erupted with a roar. Deadly grapeshot whistled through the tree limbs above the Texians' heads, raining leaves and limbs down on them. The heavy iron balls splashed harmlessly in Buffalo Bayou and on the opposite bank.

General Houston then ordered his cannon advanced. Lieutenant Colonel Neill's artillerymen rolled the two little Texas pieces forward ten paces onto the prairie and commenced firing. One of their early shots killed two pack mules harnessed to the Golden Standard, splintered the Mexicans' ammunition box, severely wounded Captain Urriza, and killed his horse. Both sides continued trading rounds of canister and grape for a good half hour. The Mexican artillerymen achieved their own destructive round by knocking out former Alamo commander James Neill, his hip shattered by grapeshot.[27]

Sam Houston held his cavalry and infantrymen in check while the two sides slugged it out with their fieldpieces. He finally gave the nod to Sidney Sherman to lead half of his mounted men toward the island of timber in the center of the prairie to take command of that vantage point. Upon charging into the little thicket, however, they were badly surprised to find a huge number of Mexican infantrymen waiting for them. Sherman immediately yelled at his men to retreat, but several of their horses were killed in the process. Houston allowed about fifty of his best sharpshooters to move forward and fire one round with their long rifles to support the retreat of the cavalrymen. Captains Poe and Moreland turned the Twin Sisters toward this thicket of woods and fired. The splintering of trees above the heads of the Mexican infantrymen was enough to force them into their own hasty retreat.[28]

The Golden Standard team rolled their cannon from its advanced position back into the little thicket at this point. The action began to dwindle as Sherman's cavalry reached safety. Santa Anna's men fell back around 3 P.M., three and a half hours after the action had commenced on the McCormick ranch. Sam Houston chalked up round one to the Texans, estimating that his men had inflicted eighteen to twenty casualties.

In return, only two Texans had been injured: Neill and Private Thomas C. Utley, the latter hit in the left arm by a round of grapeshot.[29]

The Texas Army paused to take lunch, baking bread from the captured flour. George Erath and others made the flour into dough and wound it around a stick with a chunk of beef on top before roasting their concoction over campfires. As hunger pains were subdued, the inevitable griping resumed that General Houston still did not intend to fight the Mexican Army. "By his long retreat, Houston had made himself extremely unpopular, especially with the western men who in consequence of it had had their property destroyed, houses burned, and land devastated," said Erath.[30]

Santa Anna used the downtime to fortify the area he had selected for his army's campground. He chose a small thicket near the San Jacinto River, backed by marshlands and the vast body of water known as Peggy's Lake. Colonel Pedro Delgado's men were ordered to move his twenty mules' worth of unloaded ordnance supplies one mile up to the new camp from where it had been offloaded earlier. Delgado complained that his men were subject to being pounced upon by the Texas rebels in the process. Lieutenant Colonel Juan Bringas replied to him that it was not worth the effort to complain to His Excellency while he was in such a "raving state of mind."[31]

COLONEL SIDNEY SHERMAN WAS not content to waste the rest of the day.

Around 4 P.M. he rode to General Houston's side with a pitch that he be allowed to seize the Mexican cannon. Houston was opposed but Sherman's persistent badgering finally won over Colonel George Hockley. The general finally consented to let the battle-hungry Kentuckian "reconnoiter" the enemy's forces.[32]

As this mission was deemed voluntary, he would take only those cavalrymen from the companies of Henry Karnes and William Smith who willingly chose to accompany him. A number of other eager Texans quickly borrowed horses from those who were less excited about charging into the enemy's lair. Among those offering his service was the Georgia poet who had walked to join the Texas Army at Groce's plantation, Mirabeau Lamar.

Sherman drummed up sixty-eight mounted men willing to ride into action with him. General Houston pledged only two regular army companies under Captains Amasa Turner and Andrew Briscoe as infantry support, if needed. Sherman slyly conversed with other infantry and artillery company commanders to solicit their support—with or without the general's approval.[33]

While Sherman organized his offensive, the Mexican troops were preparing as well. Colonel Delgado's men had succeeded in moving their ordnance stores into Santa Anna's new camp. Lieutenant Ignacio Arenal stepped in to replace the wounded Captain Urriza in command of the Golden Standard. He was ordered to load his cannon with grapeshot but not to fire until the enemy was within close range. Santa Anna, seeing the Texian rebels forming again across the field, ordered his cavalry commander, Captain Miguel Aguirre, to advance his mounted men in preparation.[34]

Sidney Sherman's horsemen advanced across the field in three squads. Major Lysander Wells of the Second Regiment had the left wing, Captain William Smith commanded the center, and Captain Henry Karnes with Deaf Smith took the cavalrymen on the right side. Secretary of War Thomas Rusk could

not resist joining the procession. Private Walter Lane, riding
with Karnes's right wing, could hear Mexican officers taunting
them with "Venga aquí (come here)." 35

Sherman took the offer.

"Charge!" he hollered as he spurred his horse forward.

The Golden Standard opened fire as the Texans raced ahead.
Major Wells heard the whiz from a shower of grapeshot that
showered harmlessly overhead. Sherman's men fired their long
rifles but were forced to dismount to reload the awkward weapons. Mexican infantrymen immediately dashed forward to fire
upon them, but Sherman ordered his men to charge forward
again. Two Mexican soldiers fell wounded, compelling their
comrades to fall back toward safety again. Santa Anna, watching the drama from a safe vantage point, ordered his bugler to
play the "no quarter" *degüello* piece again. He also ordered
two companies of his riflemen to join the fight. 36

As Sherman's men came under increasingly heavy fire from
Mexican cavalry, infantry, and the artillery piece, Sam Houston
finally allowed one of the Twin Sisters to be advanced. Captain
Moreland and seven men rolled their six-pounder into the skirmish. One of the volunteer artillerymen, Dr. Nicholas Labadie,
dashed from his position to help one of Sherman's wounded
men. Thirty-year-old Devereaux Jerome Woodlief, shot in the
hip during the cavalry charge, was led back to the safety of a
large oak tree. 37

A second Texan, artilleryman Olwyn Trask, was soon felled
by a round of grapeshot that shattered his thigh bone. He was
helped across the field to waiting surgeons, while Captain Aguirre ordered his men to charge for a second time upon Sidney
Sherman's men while they were reloading again. Three Texians
had their horses shot out from them. They ran for their lives as
Mexican cavalrymen charged toward them.

Colonel Rusk had charged so far forward that he found his horse surrounded by Mexican lancers as they closed in. He was spared as Mirabeau Lamar suddenly barreled in on a large stallion, slamming headlong into a Mexican on a smaller horse. Lamar knocked down the lancer and his horse, allowing Rusk to ride to safety. He then spotted another comrade in peril. Nineteen-year-old Walter Lane found his powerful horse had "more zeal than discretion" as it charged headlong into the midst of the Mexican lancers.

Lane threw up his double-barreled shotgun to ward off the blow of a Mexican officer's saber. His rifle empty, the teenager aimed his horse pistol at his adversary's head and fired. He missed, and in the same instant, Lane was knocked from his horse by a Mexican lancer. He hit the ground hard and was momentarily senseless. Captain Karnes ordered his wing to turn and support their fallen man. Lamar made his second save by shooting the enemy lancer before he could finish off the horseless Texan. Karnes raced in on his old sorrel, ordered Lane to jump on, and rode the boy out of harm's way while Lamar held off their attackers. "I would know her hide if it was dried on a fence even now," Lane later said of the bony horse that bore him to safety. "She had the sharpest backbone it has ever been my fortune to straddle."[38]

Sidney Sherman wisely pulled the remainder of his troops back away from the action at the urging of Colonel Coleman. General Houston had angrily refused to allow his riflemen to join the fight. Seeing that Sherman had stirred up not only the enemy's artillery, but cavalry and some two hundred infantrymen, he turned to his aide-de-camp, Colonel Hockley. "What are they about?" Houston demanded. "I ordered a reconnoiter only! Call off the infantry!"[39]

Major Wells was irritated by the lack of support from his

own army's infantry. "We were lucky to escape the hornets' nest with only two men badly wounded," he said. The sixty-eight volunteer horsemen failed to seize the Mexican cannon, but they earned the respect of their peers. Captain Robert Calder characterized their actions as "fearlessness and true patriotism." Captain Jesse Billingsley was moved enough to try to lead his Bastrop company onto the field despite being ordered by Houston to restrain his men.[40]

The action was largely over by this point and both sides withdrew their artillery pieces. Round two of the April 20 duel went to the Mexican army. Colonel Delgado felt the Texians "retired sluggishly and in disorder." General Houston noted in his official report only that his cavalry had a "sharp encounter" with the Mexican cavalry, "in which ours acted extremely well, and performed some feats of daring chivalry."[41]

Colonel Sherman had earned the respect of nearly every Texan present, and Mirabeau Lamar was hailed as a hero for helping to save the lives of two cavalrymen. Captain William Heard believed that the commander in chief had sent the Kentucky colonel out to fight on April 20 against long odds in the hope Sherman "would get killed off out of his way." Sherman had nearly succeeded in what might have been his ulterior motive—forcing Sam Houston and Santa Anna into an all-out engagement. Four Texans had been wounded but only the leg wound of Olwyn Trask would eventually prove to be a fatal one. The wounded were helped across the bayou to the home of Vice President Lorenzo de Zavala, which became the army's makeshift hospital.[42]

Santa Anna kept his troops busy through the night, building a defensive breastworks out of saddles and supplies. His *soldados* could see the flickering campfires of the Texas rebels, only about a mile away across an open prairie.

The Texas Army had plenty of heroes to talk about that evening around the campfires as they roasted beef, made bread, and sipped captured coffee. There was speculation among the key officers as to whether General Houston would ever allow his army to fully engage that of Santa Anna. Captain Billingsley wrote that many company commanders "entered into a solemn engagement to fight the enemy on the next day, General or no General!" [43]

George Erath felt the Texans had been conservative throughout the day's action. In his view, the afternoon skirmish proved the Mexican strength was "considerably inferior to ours, and their position [w]as very badly chosen for their defense." The cries around the campfires had grown stronger. Erath felt there was a "determination to retreat no further; and it was only by the advice and example of a sprinkle of old men among us— some of whom had been in the Revolutionary War and that of 1812—that we kept order and discipline to await the developments of next day." [44]

14

SLAUGHTER AT SAN JACINTO

ONE MILE AWAY FROM the Mexican Army on the cattle ranch of Peggy McCormick, the Texian camp was stirring first. At 4 A.M. on April 21, 1836, a former slave from New Orleans named Dick tapped reveille on his drum in the brisk morning air while Sam Houston slept soundly. Some wondered aloud if their commander in chief would sleep all day.[1]

Colonel Robert Coleman could hear the reveille of Santa Anna's army an hour later. General Houston, who had never slept more than three straight hours since the start of the campaign, snored soundly for another two hours while his troops stood under arms. Santa Anna, on the other hand, had been awake since long before sunrise studying the Texan camp with his spyglass. His Golden Standard cannon was held in readiness on the left side of camp, protected by his cavalry and a column of companies under command of acting Lieutenant Colonel Santiago Luelmo. On the right of His Excellency's camp were

three companies of men to guard the woods while the permanent Matamoros Battalion held battle formation in the center.[2]

Santa Anna was awaiting the arrival of his brother-in-law,
General Martín Perfecto de Cos, with five hundred reinforcement troops. In the meantime, Colonel Pedro Delgado discussed
with General Manuel Castrillón his displeasure of their leader's
chosen campground location. The young *soldados* were busily
constructing a defensive breastworks with boxes, grain bags,
and pack saddles, but Delgado feared it would not be nearly
enough. The Texians would be able to advance through some
wooded cover and had ample space for retreat to their rear
and to their right side. Santa Anna's troops, in contrast, were
backed by marshes and bay shores that offered no opportunity
for easy flight if they were overpowered. "The camping ground
of His Excellency's selection was, in all respects, against military rules," Delgado felt. "Any youngster would have done
better." [3]

The late spring sun soon warmed the pasturelands as the
opposing armies sat idle. General Houston soon sent his trusty
spy Deaf Smith and Captain Henry Karnes to ascertain the enemy's strength. While Smith was rumored to have a passion for
alcohol, he was also a master of espionage. Texas folklore has it
that the dark-skinned spy wandered aimlessly into the Mexican
camp barefoot, wearing a large sombrero and ragged pants and
shirt. When confronted by armed soldiers, Smith pretended to
be a simple-minded Mexican worker. He played stupid or only
mumbled brief Spanish answers to his interrogators. The Mexican soldiers reportedly tired of quizzing the fool and Smith
later stumbled away from their encampment. Karnes met him
out of sight, offered Deaf his horse, and away they rode to en-
lighten old Sam as to their enemy's strength.[4]

Santa Anna enjoyed a bright moment around 9 A.M. when

General Cos finally arrived with his reinforcements. His joy was short-lived, however, as he found that 20 percent of Cos's five hundred troops had been delayed in their march due to heavy pack loads. While Santa Anna had ordered select infantrymen, his brother-in-law arrived with what he considered to be "raw recruits." Even worse, the soldiers had been subjected to a forced march that had not allowed them to eat or sleep for more than twenty-four hours.[5]

Sam Houston dressed for the day in his Cherokee coat, buckskin vest, and silver-spurred riding boots. He wore a broad cap and from his pistol belt dangled his ceremonial Cherokee sword. As the morning hours whittled away with inactivity, the Texians who were already disgusted with Houston's perceived lack of desire to fight became more vocal. By noon he was informed that some of his officers were anxious to hold a council of war.[6]

General Houston pulled together his senior officers: Colonel Burleson and Lieutenant Colonel Alexander Somervell of the First Regiment; Lieutenant Colonel Henry Millard of the regulars; and Colonel Sidney Sherman, Lieutenant Colonel Joe Bennett, and Major Lysander Wells of the Second Regiment. There was some discussion about building a floating bridge across Buffalo Bayou, to be used for retreat if necessary. As word of this idea filtered back to the battle-eager troops, some were appalled. Captain Amasa Turner said that his men despised such a plan, saying, "We will go out and whip the Mexicans while Old Sam builds his bridge."[7]

The bridge idea was dismissed and a vote was finally put before the very officers who had long criticized Houston's every move. "Should we attack the enemy in their position, or shall we await his attack?" That was the question. Surprisingly, two-thirds of the officers voted in favor of waiting on Santa Anna to make the first move. Should the Mexican Army fail to advance on the Texian camp by late afternoon, however, the officers were in favor of initiating the action. With that, Houston announced, "Gentlemen, you are adjourned." [8]

The Texian officers moved back to their respective commands to spread the word: the mind-numbing waiting game was to continue.

SANTA ANNA DID NOT press an offensive. The Texians were not completely idle during those next hours, however.

Deaf Smith conferred with Sam Houston on a plan to use a pair of axes to chop down or set afire Vince's Bridge. Any reinforcements for Santa Anna traveling down the main wagon road between Harrisburg and Lynchburg would thus be greatly slowed in reaching the battlefield while circumnavigating the rain-flooded Vince's Bayou. Smith and six other cavalrymen raced the eight-mile distance on horseback while Karnes, Captain William Smith, and their comrades created a brief diversion. Deaf Smith's party found the wood of the bridge would not burn sufficiently so they chopped and broke it apart. [9]

"Deef" Smith could not resist having fun with his young recruits during the return trip. About three-quarters of a mile from the Texas camp, he halted them in a deep, dry hollow. He said that he would ride ahead to check for Mexican troops. Moments later, Smith came racing back, shouting that the prairie ahead was filled with newly arrived Mexican cavalrymen.

"My orders are to return to camp," announced Smith. "I will do it or die!"

He told his men to prepare their guns and follow him Indian file through the dry hollow to where it joined Buffalo Bayou. Smith took off, with his men close in tow. Once he broke into the open prairie, he whipped his horse on and raced ahead, howling with laughter. Perry Alsbury and the other anxious cavalrymen realized their nerves had been put to the test by old Deef: not a single Mexican horseman was in sight on the prairie.[10]

Santa Anna returned from his reconnaissance of Sam Houston's forces around 2 P.M. Corporal Juan Reyes of the permanent Matamoros Battalion noted that His Excellency allowed the cavalry's horses to be unsaddled and watered while the infantrymen proceeded to eat their meals. Toribio Reyes, a private of the Grenadier Company of the Matamoros Battalion, stated that Santa Anna "ordered a pound of flour per garrison to make tortillas and take mess." Santa Anna then retired to his fancy campaign tent.[11]

By 3 P.M., Colonel Ed Burleson galloped up to where George Erath was surveying the distant Mexican camp. "George," called Burleson. "Run down and tell your captain and the captains on the right to come up here instantly and meet me." Erath gathered the captains and some of the lieutenants of Burleson's First Regiment for a conference with their leader. Burleson told them the Mexican Army appeared to be reinforcing itself with no intention of commencing battle. Another vote was taken: should the Texians attack immediately or wait until just before daybreak?[12]

Captains Moseley Baker and Bob Calder preferred a 4 A.M. assault, but most desired to commence the action right away. Lieutenant Colonel Bennett similarly called together Sidney Sherman's Second Regiment. Their company commanders also voted in favor of an immediate attack. Bennett soon reported that the men were ready to fight, so Houston passed the word at 3:30 P.M., "Parade your companies."[13]

"The announcement of the decision to fight acted like

electricity," wrote Erath. George Brown and Dick, the former slave, called the men together with a gentle tapping of their drums to signal general parade. Sam Houston's four divisions of men fanned out in front of the mossy hardwood grove where they had camped overnight. The Texian general, mounted on his fine grayish mare, Saracen, made a final inspection of his troops. By best count, he had some 930 men present on the battlefield.[14]

Only two of General Houston's officers, Colonels John Wharton and Sidney Sherman, wore proper military uniforms. Captain William Wood's Kentucky Riflemen, financed by Sherman, was the only Texian company sporting uniforms. Every other foot soldier, artilleryman, or cavalryman wore their citizen's clothing. In the case of most humble frontiersmen, this consisted of buckskin pants, moccasins, fur caps, and homespun shirts. Deaf Smith and a few others sported Mexican sombreros. Captain Alfred Wyly's fourteen-man company from Harrisburg was the smallest unit while Captain Moseley Baker's San Felipe company was the largest present with fifty-nine men. The median age of Houston's troops was twenty-eight. Sixty percent were single men and the majority of them were Caucasian.

The Texas Army did have at least five blacks and twenty-nine *tejanos* either present on the battlefield or guarding the baggage at Harrisburg. The majority of the *tejanos* were members of Captain Juan Seguín's twenty-four-man company. One of the black men who fought for Texas was Hendrick Arnold, an efficient member of Deaf Smith's spy company who had previously helped guide the Texas Army into San Antonio during its December 1835 assault to oust General Cos.

The Texians sprawled before their meager campground in parade formation as Houston rode slowly down their lines.

To the extreme right were the cavalry companies of Captains Henry Karnes and William Smith. They would be led into battle this day by a valiant new leader, Mirabeau Lamar—newly promoted to colonel. By saving two lives in the previous day's skirmish, the poet from Georgia had earned the respect of his peers. General Houston had offered him command of the artillery but Lamar declined. Colonel Rusk then offered to have him join his staff as an aide-de-camp but Lamar instead accepted a third offer. The men under Karnes and Smith insisted that Colonel Lamar command their forces since he had saved two of their comrades.[15]

Standing ready beside Lamar's cavalry were the ninety-two regulars of Captains Andrew Briscoe and Amasa Turner. The six-piece Texas band—two drummers and four fifers—would march near them. The two six-pounder Twin Sisters cannon stood slightly ahead of the regulars and the thirty-two artillerymen were headed by Colonel Hockley. To the left of the artillery stood the eight companies and 386 men of Colonel Burleson's First Regiment. Colonel Sherman's 330-man Second Regiment, composed of ten companies, formed the left wing of the Texas Army.

Baker, Calder, and other company leaders seized the moment to give quick motivational speeches to their young patriots. Goliad survivor Charles Shain needed little encouragement as he heard Sam Houston state that those who could not brave the enemy's bayonets should remain behind. Shain and the other massacre survivors hoped to avenge the loss of their brave comrades who had been slaughtered at the La Bahía and Alamo compounds.[16]

It was around 4 p.m. when General Houston trotted Saracen before his paraded companies and gave the long-awaited marching order, "Trail arms! Forward!"

SANTA ANNA'S FORCES, NUMBERING about thirteen hundred souls, could not have been caught less prepared for battle.

His cavalrymen had been allowed to unsaddle their horses to graze. General Cos's reinforcement troops, exhausted from their long march, took the opportunity to sleep while other troops who had been constructing the defensive breastworks enjoyed a late afternoon meal. Santa Anna asked General Castrillón to advise him of any enemy movements while he retired to his command tent to take a siesta. One of the more controversial stories later circulated was that El Presidente was actually keeping company in his tent with Emily West, the indentured servant captured two days earlier on Colonel Morgan's plantation at New Washington. The mulatto girl was reportedly the inspiration for the song "The Yellow Rose of Texas." Exactly what the commander in chief of the Mexican Army was doing with young West during these climactic moments will long be debated, even if many historians dismiss the whole event as grandiose Texas folklore.[17]

The Texians at that moment were advancing stealthily across Peggy McCormick's cattle ranch. Sidney Sherman's Second Regiment moved quickly through the mossy live oaks and tall grasses of the little thicket running along the edge of the marsh. The cavalry and other infantrymen of the regulars and of Colonel Burleson's infantry eased forward over the open prairie. Tree cover, waist-high coastal grass, and a slight rise in the ground toward Santa Anna's camp perfectly disguised their movements. Eager artillerymen pulled the heavy Twin Sisters cannon with leather straps toward the slight rise in the center of the field.[18]

Moseley Baker's company advanced with a hoisted red

handkerchief, a sign that his men planned on offering no quarter to their enemy. Captain Wood's Kentucky Riflemen carried the only true flag for the Texans, one that had been presented to them by the ladies of Newport, Kentucky, before they departed the United States. The flag featured a half-nude maiden who clutched a banner reading "Liberty or Death"—the very opportunities facing the 930 advancing Texians.

Sherman's men encountered a division of Mexican soldiers in the woods near camp and were the first to commence firing. Stephen Sparks of Captain Hayden Arnold's Nacogdoches volunteers recalled, "We were ordered not to fire until we could see the whites of the enemies' eyes. When we got within 300 yards of the ditch, we were ordered to charge, and we charged in double file." Only one other man fired his weapon before Sparks touched his own trigger.[19]

Most of Sherman's men were within sixty yards of the napping Mexican Army as they opened up with their muskets. Each man quickly reloaded with lead balls and continued charging forward, firing point-blank into the mass of troops who sprang for their own weapons. Sherman's regiment quickly became engaged in hand-to-hand combat as the action forbade the time to properly load and prime another round. Cries of "Remember the Alamo!" and "Remember Goliad!" rang out through the rising musket smoke and screams of death.

The stunned Mexican Army began firing back in earnest at the mass of frontiersmen sweeping down on their campgrounds from all sides. Their own cannon, the Golden Standard, opened fire with a mighty roar on the Texas cavalry. Colonel Rusk raced across the battlefield on horseback to report to General Houston that Sherman's men had taken the napping enemy completely by surprise. En route, his young aide, Dr. Junius

William Mottley, was blasted from his horse by a rifle ball to the stomach.

As Rusk approached Houston, the general's horse was cut down by a volley of shots. Saracen's gray coat was splattered crimson red as five shots pierced the animal's chest. Houston landed on his feet as his mount collapsed under him. Private Achelle Mare caught a small, riderless horse for the general, whose long legs now dangled below the stirrups as he pushed forward.[20]

The conflict was now in full rage. Deaf Smith raced across the plains with a filthy, foaming horse to alert Houston that Vince's Bridge had been successfully destroyed. No one else would be joining the battle. Conversely, neither army's combatants could easily escape. Flashes of smoke and fire erupted along the Mexican breastworks as Ed Burleson's regiment moved toward camp. The stunned Mexican soldiers initially fired too high. Private Ed Miles felt that his enemy's first shots "passed over us like hail." The *soldados* adjusted their aim as the Texans descended the slight slope leading toward camp, and some of their musket balls began hitting home. Thomas Mays crumpled from a musket ball that smashed into his left thigh.

George Erath was marching in double file behind buckskin-attired, scraggly-bearded Captain Jesse Billingsley. They descended into a low spot in the field and then marched through the high coastal grass up over a slight rise. As they crested the little hill, bullets filled the air and Private Ed Blakely crumpled with a mortal wound. Erath had fired his gun from 150 yards but choked his barrel while hurriedly ramming in his next musket ball. Disgusted, he threw down his gun and grabbed Blakely's weapon and shot pouch. Erath saw that the whole

Mexican line ahead of him was falling into chaos as he charged forward.[21]

The Texans had advanced in perfect silence but now that the hellacious thundering had erupted, the little Texian band began to play with their drums and fife. They opened with Thomas Moore's number "Will You Come to the Bower?" once the shooting commenced. Private John Hassell recalled that Colonel Burleson ordered "Yankee Doodle" to be played as well.[22]

The Twin Sisters were first fired from about two hundred yards from the Mexican breastworks. The ground-shaking roar was inspiring to many, who sprang forward with renewed energy. The artillerymen quickly loaded new rounds of canister and towed the iron weapons steadily closer to Santa Anna's campground to continue pounding the defenses.

El Presidente sprang from his tent as chaos befell his napping army. He would claim that Colonel Castrillón was negligent in visiting the guard lines a single time while he and Cos were resting. General Vicente Filisola wrote that most leaders were merely following the example of their senior officers and that those who were still awake "were completely relaxed." Corporal Juan Reyes said "the enemy fell upon us with such violence that when the bugle of the right [flank] signaled the enemy on that side, it was lost in the din of battle." Private Toribio Reyes found that none of the senior Mexican officers was able to maintain any order in the immediate confusion and uproar of the explosions. Some of the companies engaged in return fire but Reyes saw that General Cos's newly arrived Aldama and Guerrero battalions were the first to begin fleeing from the battlefield.[23]

Other Mexican units engaged the Texans in valiant fashion. Colonel Manuel Céspedes led an attack column—consisting of the Guerrero permanent battalion and detachments from

LEADERS OF TEXAS

James DeShields, *Border Wars of Texas.*

Stephen Fuller Austin *(left)*, the "Father of Texas," and commanding general of the volunteer army in 1835.

(Below, left) David Gouvernor Burnet served as the interim president of the Republic of Texas in 1836.

(Below, right) Samuel Houston, known in Cherokee language as "the Raven," was the troubled commanding general of the Texas Army after the fall of the Alamo.

San Felipe de Austin, located on the banks of the Brazos River, was the political center of the colony empresario Stephen Austin started in 1824. "San Felipe Townscape" *by Charles Shaw, San Jacinto Museum of History, Houston.*

EARLY TEXAS RANGERS

Noah Smithwick, an 1836 Ranger who later commanded his own men against Comanches.

Ranger battalion commander Colonel Robert "Three Legged Willie" Williamson.

Captain William Turner Sadler was one of the early Ranger leaders in the 1836 revolution.

Austrian-born early Ranger George Bernard Erath.

Colonel John Henry Moore, revered Indian fighter.

Garrison Greenwood, an early Ranger superintendent.

Fort Parker, also known as Fort Sterling during the Texas Revolution, was the rendezvous site for Colonel Moore's Ranger companies in 1835. It was also the site of a bloody Indian attack in 1836.

Portrait of Lieutenant Colonel William Barret Travis, the Alamo commander. Reportedly drawn in 1835 by his friend Wiley Martin, this only likeness of Travis is questioned by many historians.

David "Davy" Crockett, Tennessee politician and folk hero who went to Texas to fight in the revolution.

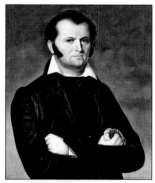

James Bowie, fabled knife fighter and co-commander of the Alamo, fell gravely ill before the Mexican assault on the fortress.

Alamo survivor Susanna Dickinson, wife of Captain Almeron Dickinson.

Juan N. Seguín, in uniform in 1837 for a portrait while serving as lieutenant colonel of Texas Cavalry. Seguín was one of the last couriers from the Alamo and later commanded a *tejano* company at San Jacinto.

Colonel James Walker Fannin, commander of the men at Goliad, failed to come to the aid of the Alamo defenders.

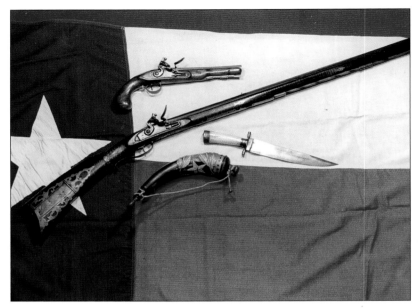

Selection of the early weapons used by Texan settlers in the 1830s. At top is an 1820s-era .48-caliber Pennsylvania/Kentucky flintlock rifle, a type carried by many early frontiersmen. Above it is a .60-caliber flintlock pistol. Below the rifle are a Bowie knife and a nineteenth-century powder horn. *Photo by Tom Knowles, courtesy of the Texas Ranger Hall of Fame and Museum.*

In an early action of the Texas Revolution, Andrew Briscoe was arrested in October 1835 by Mexican authorities in Anahuac. William Barret Travis led a Texan mob that stormed the jail and secured his release. *Oil on canvas painting by Charles Shaw, San Jacinto Museum of History, Houston.*

The Texas Revolution opened with the battle of Gonzales on October 2, 1835. Mexican troops advancing on the town were met at the Guadalupe River on September 29 by eighteen militiamen. They had one small cannon and a defiant flag printed with the phrase "Come and Take It." *"Battle of Gonzales" by Charles Shaw, San Jacinto Museum of History, Houston.*

Robert Jenkins Onderdonk painted *The Fall of the Alamo* in 1903. This depiction portrays Davy Crockett with an upraised rifle fighting off Mexican soldiers who have breached the walls of the mission on March 6, 1836.

A modern view of the Alamo church in San Antonio.

Courtesy of Donald Yena and Frank Horlock.

(Above) Texas prisoners are marched from the Mission La Bahía in Goliad on March 27, 1836, by order of General Santa Anna. *Painting by Donald Yena.*

(Below) More than 300 Texans are executed in the so-called Goliad Massacre. "Remember Goliad" *illustration by Norman Price, Texas State Library and Archives Commission.*

News of the fall of the Alamo and the subsequent Goliad Massacre created chaos amongst Texas settlers. The mass exodus of citizens toward the east became known as the Runaway Scrape. *"Runaway Scrape" by Charles Shaw, San Jacinto Museum of History, Houston.*

On April 16, 1836, Sam Houston's army reached the pivotal fork in the road. One road led toward Nacogdoches and the United States, the other toward Harrisburg and San Jacinto. *Oil on canvas painting by Charles Shaw, San Jacinto Museum of History, Houston.*

Sam Houston delivered a motivational speech to his soldiers from horseback prior to their crossing Buffalo Bayou on April 19. "General Sam Houston" *equestrian portrait by Stephen Seymour Thomas, 1903, San Jacinto Museum of History, Houston.*

THE TEXAS ARMY AT SAN JACINTO

Colonel Edward Burleson, commander, First Regiment of Texas Volunteers.

Colonel Sidney Sherman, Second Regiment of Texas Volunteers commander.

Captain Jesse Billingsley, Bastrop frontiersman and future Ranger commander.

Captain Robert James Calder, Company K, First Regiment, at San Jacinto.

Erastus "Deaf" Smith, favored scout of Sam Houston.

Captain Henry Wax Karnes, cavalry leader at San Jacinto and later frontier leader.

Colonel Thomas J. Rusk, Texas Secretary of War at San Jacinto.

Colonel Alexander Horton, aide-de-camp to General Houston.

Mirabeau B. Lamar was promoted to be commander of the Texas Cavalry.

THE MEXICAN ARMY IN TEXAS

General Martín Perfecto de Cós, the brother-in-law of Santa Anna, brought reinforcements to the San Jacinto battleground.

President Antonio López de Santa Anna Pérez de Lebrón, leader of the Mexican forces that entered Texas.

General Vicente Filisola, the Italian-born second-in-command of the Mexican Army of Operations.

(Above) Colonel Juan Almonte, the English-speaking advisor to Santa Anna.

(Right) General José Urrea, commander of one of the divisions of the Mexican Army.

Deaf Smith and his volunteers, unable to burn the bridge over Vince's Bayou, destroy the remnants on the morning of April 21 to prevent Mexican reinforcements from reaching the San Jacinto battleground. "Destroying Vince's Bridge," *by Charles Shaw, courtesy of the San Jacinto Museum of History, Houston.*

Walter Paye Lane *(right)* survived San Jacinto and later served with the Texas Rangers in the 1840s. Lane rose to the rank of brigadier general during the Civil War.

Private Walter Lane is rescued on April 20 by Captain Henry Karnes while Mirabeau Lamar, future Texas president, holds off Mexican soldiers. "Sherman's First Skirmish," *oil painting by Charles Shaw, courtesy of the San Jacinto Museum of History, Houston.*

Henry Arthur McArdle's 1895 painting *Battle of San Jacinto*. The original artwork hangs in the senate chambers of the Texas State Capitol.

(*Above*) Colonel Sidney Sherman's Kentucky Volunteers carried this "Liberty or Death" battle flag at San Jacinto.

(*Left and above*) These photos—taken during the annual San Jacinto reenactment ceremonies— depict Texans charging the Mexican breastworks, the Mexican Guerrero Battalion firing back, and Texan artillery crews preparing to fire the Twin Sisters cannon. *Courtesy of the San Jacinto Museum of History, Houston, and author's collection.*

After being routed in a mere eighteen minutes, Mexican soldiers fled into the boggy grounds and the bay called Peggy's Lake. Vengeful Texans cut them down until order could be restored to the troops. "Massacre at Peggy's Lake" *by Charles Shaw, courtesy of the San Jacinto Museum of History, Houston.*

Taken in the late 1800s, this photo shows the large post oak tree in the Texan camp where Sam Houston was lying when Santa Anna surrendered. Buffalo Bayou lies in the background. This early Kodak was sent to San Jacinto artist Henry McArdle.

HOUSTON, SANTA ANNA, AND COS.

Sam Houston—and his long rifle—accept Santa Anna's surrender.
Library of Congress

(Above) This Donald M. Yena painting of the Neches River battle shows Cherokee Chief Bowles being shot down on July 16, 1839. The Cherokee War of Texas drove most of the surviving people of Bowles from the republic.

(Right) Chief Bowles, known in his native tongue as Duwali, was the leader of the Cherokees who came to settle in Texas in 1819.

(Below) "Battle of Plum Creek." More than five hundred Comanches, sporting war paint and stolen clothing, are met in battle by Texan forces on August 12, 1840.
USTA's Institute of Texan Cultures, No. 088-0055. Artist: Lee Herring. Courtesy of Mrs. William Adams.

John Coffee Hays, the most respected Texas Ranger of the 1840s. He was known to his foes as "Captain Jack" or "Devil Jack."

Ben McCulloch was first lieutenant of Captain Hays's Rangers in 1844. He helped man the Twin Sisters cannon at San Jacinto.

CAPTAIN JACK HAYS AND HIS RANGERS

Cicero Rufus "Rufe" Perry (right) joined the Texas Rangers in 1836 and fought Comanches with Jack Hays in the 1840s. Perry was severely wounded in an 1844 Comanche ambush on his Ranger camp.

Pasqual Leo Buquor (below, left), later the mayor of San Antonio, rode with Captain Hays in 1841 and 1844.

Samuel Hamilton Walker (below, right), survived the Mier Expedition and rode with Hays in 1844.

Jack Hays sat for this oil painting in later years in California. It depicts his famous solo stand against Comanches in late 1841 atop Enchanted Rock in present Llano County. *Gift of Mrs. Roblay McMullins, Texas Ranger Hall of Fame and Museum.*

William Alexander Anderson "Bigfoot" Wallace, famous Texas Ranger and survivor of the Mier executions.

Early firearms of the Texas frontier used during the 1840s. Shown left to right are: an 1838 model .52-caliber revolving carbine (often used by cavalrymen); a .36-caliber Patent No. 5 "Texas" model Colt revolving pistol; and an 1837 model ring-lever action .52-caliber revolving rifle. *Photo by Tom Knowles, courtesy of the Texas Ranger Hall of Fame and Museum.*

Toluca and Guadalajara—forward to contain the main fire of their enemy. The Golden Standard gunners managed to get off at least three rounds of return fire before a shot from the Twin Sisters hit the Mexican cannon's water bucket, wounding or scaring off most of the gunners. By this time, countless Texans were jumping over the Mexican breastworks.

Colonel Céspedes was seriously wounded and he retreated. Others began following suit. General Castrillón and twenty-five-year-old Lieutenant Ignacio Arenal, however, fought until the bitter end to keep the Golden Standard manned. Castrillón stood atop ammunition boxes and shouted at soldiers to hold their ground. He became a martyr, defiantly glaring at the advancing Texians with his arms folded across his chest. Volleys of rifle balls ripped through the proud artillery general's body and he expired near the cannon.[24]

Colonel Sherman's Second Regiment swept into the Mexican camp. Unable to reload their guns quickly enough, they used their rifles and muskets as war clubs to bash Mexican soldiers in hand-to-hand combat. Others pulled their Bowie knives. Former Ranger captain William Sadler fought off a Mexican soldier wielding a dagger, wrestled him down, and kept the dead man's dirk as a prized trophy of the conflict. Deaf Smith was thrown from his horse near the breastworks. He grabbed one of his belt pistols and aimed it at the head of a Mexican soldier, but the percussion cap exploded without the pistol going off. Smith threw the gun at his opponent and then wrestled the *soldado*'s rifle away from him. Cavalryman James Nash saw the plight of old Deaf and used his horse to run down a nearby Mexican officer, whom Smith finished off with the officer's own saber.[25]

Sam Houston later credited Juan Seguín's *tejano* company with fighting valiantly for the Texian cause. Seguín's men fired their first volley and they crouched low to reload near the Mexican camp. First Sergeant Manual Flores, seeing the chaos unfold ahead of them, shouted at his fellow *tejanos*: "Get up! Santa Anna's men are running!" As they swept into the Mexican camp, one enemy officer cried out to Tony Menchaca for mercy, calling him a "fellow Mexican." Menchaca howled back angrily, "No, damn you, I'm no Mexican! I'm an American. Shoot him!"[26]

The Texans were able to fire their weapons numerous times before the close-action combat ensued in Santa Anna's camp. "I shot old Betsy six times and a holster pistol one time," said Private John Hassell of Burleson's regiment. "In the seven shots, I know that I killed four." George Washington Lonis of Captain David Murphree's company fired his rifle thirteen times and claimed a dozen kills before he fell seriously wounded by a musket ball that ripped through his right lung.[27]

Colonel Burleson's First Regiment and Colonel Millard's two regular companies soon cleared the Mexican breastworks and seized the Mexican cannon. "Our rifles created dreadful havoc among them, and they gave way in every direction," said Captain Robert Stevenson. All Mexican resistance had been broken in "about eighteen minutes" per General Houston's postbattle report. Goliad Massacre survivor Charles Shain agreed that the Texan army was across the breastworks in less than twenty minutes and "the Mexicans were then running in all directions."[28]

GENERAL SANTA ANNA HAD lost all control of his army.

He tried in vain to rally his men but they were fleeing now in all directions. Santa Anna found that it was "every man for himself. My desperation was as great as my danger." Colonel

Delgado felt that his soldiers had been reduced to "a bewildered and panic stricken herd." Santa Anna reportedly announced, "The battle is lost." He accepted a stallion from one of his aides and raced from camp toward Thompson's Pass. His aide Ramón Caro mounted another horse and galloped after the fleeing general.[29]

General Houston, by contrast, was highly visible to his men during the first eighteen minutes of conflict. He placed himself at the head of his First Regiment in front of the Mexican breastworks, shouting at his men to continue firing. The general was riding before his companies of regulars when his second horse was killed by a volley of five shots. Another musket ball shattered Houston's left ankle but he was quickly helped onto his third horse of the day. Few soldiers were even aware at the time that old Sam had been winged.[30]

By this point the Mexican Army had been completely broken. The Texian companies were widely scattered. Captain Robert Calder later noted, "I very much doubt if any captain could, at short notice, have formed any five of his men together." Although Santa Anna's troops had been routed in eighteen minutes, heavy fighting would continue for another two hours. It was nothing short of a slaughter.[31]

Vengeful Texans showed no mercy. Mexican soldiers cried out for it, though, as they were overtaken beyond their campground. Most were dispatched with a lethal blow to the head amid screams of "Remember the Alamo!" The fleeing *soldados* were doomed by the soggy grounds along the bayou behind their encampment. Horses that tried to cross Peggy's Lake bogged down and began sinking. Some Texans literally crossed the huge mud bog by jumping across horses and other debris like stepping-stones. Peggy's Lake was actually a small bay separated from the main San Jacinto Bay by a small strip of land.

Texas riflemen cut down the fleeing soldiers who tried to escape through the marshes. Some Texans who ran out of ammunition or did not want to waste time to reload splashed into the water to use their Bowie knives and hatchets. A few bloodthirsty souls even removed scalps.

Private Walter Lane refused to fire on the helpless Mexican soldiers who "took to the water like ducks to swim across, our men firing at their heads." Corporal Bernardino Santa Cruz, one of the elite grenadiers, noted with disgust that entire battalions of his army had fled, leaving his unit no other choice. Santa Cruz and his companions plunged waist-deep through the body of water and effectively lost their chance to fight any further as their ammunition pouches and powder became soaked. Lieutenant Denham found Peggy's Lake to be "a scene of slaughter which defied description." Private James Winters found that the dead horses and soldiers "made a bridge across the bayou." Colonel Wharton tried without success to save one young Mexican soldier by pulling him up onto the horse behind him. Wharton declared him to be a prisoner, but old Jim Curtis, who had recently served in Tumlinson's ranger company, defiantly shot the Mexican from the colonel's horse.[32]

"It was nothing but a slaughter," recalled Sergeant William Swearingen, who watched his comrades shoot the swimmers as fast as they could reload their guns. Wharton tried ordering the men to cease firing.

"Colonel Wharton, if Jesus Christ were to come down from Heaven and order me to quit shooting Santanistas, I wouldn't do it, sir!" yelled Private Joe Dixon of the regulars.[33]

Wharton angrily reached for his sword. Dixon stepped back and cocked his rifle, forcing the colonel to discreetly ride on to check the bloodlust elsewhere. Dr. Nicholas Labadie tried to secure Colonel José Batres—on his knees and pleading for mercy—as his prisoner. Several Texans leveled their rifles at Batres, splattering his blood and brains across Dr. Labadie. The Texan leaders were far from immune from barbaric actions. Near Peggy's Lake, a pair of Texas regulars secured a Mexican man and a female camp servant as prisoners. They were soon implored by a Texan officer on horseback: "Kill them, God damn them. Remember the Alamo!" [34]

The two regulars attacked the man with bayonets even as Private Thomas Corry attempted to prevent the senseless execution. At the same time, Colonel John Forbes, the commissary general of the Texas Army, ran his sword through the Mexican woman's chest and left her expiring body to quiver on the ground.

"Damn you!" shouted Corry. "You have killed a woman!"

Other Texans witnessed the event and Forbes was later put before a board of inquiry on charges of murder. His fellow Texan would acquit Forbes of any unsoldierlike or improper conduct. [35]

Peggy's Lake was not the only slaughtering ground during the late afternoon hours of April 21. One large group of Mexican officers and cavalrymen fled down the road leading toward Vince's Bridge. They were badly surprised to find that Deaf Smith's men had already disposed of their only easy exit from the McCormick ranch. Cavalry captains Karnes and Smith led about eighteen mounted men, one of them a Goliad Massacre survivor, in pursuit. Another slaughter ensued when the Mexican horsemen reached the swollen bayou.

Some fell to their knees after their horses became bogged down. "Me no Alamo!" said some. "Me no La Bahía!" Most were executed by carbines at close distance. William Taylor, one of the pursuing cavalryman, explained, "We felt compelled to kill them. We saw it was impossible for us to take prisoners, and we had little disposition to do so." One of the stronger Mexican soldiers turned on Jack Robbins and tackled him. The pair wrestled in the mire until Robbins could pull his knife and end the duel. A Mexican officer riding Old Whip, the fine black stallion recently stolen from William Vince's ranch, tried to pass himself off as Santa Anna once he was detained. Henry Karnes swung his sword, scoring a glancing blow off the Mexican officer's head. He then leapt into the bayou to escape. His exodus was prevented by a volley of lead fired by Taylor and other cavalrymen.[36]

There were no other prisoners taken near Vince's Bridge, although a few had escaped the scene. Foremost among them was General Santa Anna, who had lost his horse and taken refuge for the moment in a thicket of small pines. Secretary Ramón Caro also ditched his mount and hid in the woods. Karnes's men poked about the thicket, some calling out in Spanish for Santa Anna to surrender himself and be spared. There was no reply. Deaf Smith then mounted Old Whip and rode back toward the battlefield to secure more men to keep the woods surrounded through the night. The capture or execution of El Presidente would certainly seal the Texan victory.[37]

On the main battlefield, Sidney Sherman and his men began taking prisoners of those Mexicans who chose to surrender. Some of the regular army soldiers moved about near the breastworks, running bayonets through wounded *soldados*. Hundreds of other Mexicans threw down their weapons and surrendered en masse. Among them was Colonel Juan Almonte, one of Santa Anna's English-speaking aides.

General Houston became disgusted with the actions of many of his men as evening approached. They had fired most of their ammunition and had splintered many of their rifles while bashing skulls. He feared that even a small force of fresh

Mexican troops arriving on the scene might overpower his rejoicing troops. He had to call off Colonel Wharton, who was eager to continue attacking Cos's reinforcement troops, from further action. Houston, weak from blood loss and riding his third horse, tried in vain three times to order his men to form into line and fall back to camp. No one paid him the least bit of attention.[38]

Wheeling his horse back toward the Mexican camp, Houston snapped, "Men, I can gain victories with you, but damn your manners!"

The sun was setting behind the big trees around the Mexican camp. Houston congratulated Sidney Sherman en route to the camp area. He then noticed Colonel Rusk approaching through the fading light and leading several hundred Mexican prisoners. Perhaps light-headed from blood loss and unable to make out the throng clearly, Houston reportedly exclaimed, "My God, all is lost!"[39]

Captain Turner of the regulars quickly handed the general his spyglass to see that Rusk was marching with prisoners. Bill Millen, Turner's first lieutenant, could not help from chiding Houston: "General, Colonel Rusk has a very respectable army, eh, sir?"

General Houston was helped from his borrowed horse and the Texian surgeon general, Dr. Alexander Ewing, began working on his shattered left leg. His wound was later diagnosed as a compound fracture of the left tibia and fibula, just above the ankle. Hundreds of Mexican prisoners, many of them wounded, were marched back into Santa Anna's old camp as darkness approached. A crude stockade of battlefield debris was constructed to contain them. Artillerymen turned both the Twin Sisters and the Golden Standard on the prisoner pin, ready to rain down grapeshot if any escape was attempted.

More than six hundred Mexican officers and soldiers had been slain in the battle at San Jacinto. More than seven hundred soldiers were eventually captured and more than two hundred of them were wounded. Colonel Thomas Rusk would write of his nine-hundred-odd fellow Texan troops, "This brave band achieved a victory as glorious as any on the records of history, and the happy consequences will be felt in Texas by succeeding generations." [40]

During the battle, only seven Texans had been killed outright. Four others were so badly wounded that they would not survive, but only thirty others had been wounded. Sergeant William C. Swearingen penned a letter back home to his family in Kentucky, summarizing the good fortunes the frontiersmen had enjoyed at San Jacinto. "To see the number, the position, and the termination and the time in which it was done (time 18 minutes), it at once shows that the hand of Providence was with us." [41]

James Tarlton, a well-educated Kentucky politician, poetically summed up San Jacinto in writing on April 22, "Such slaughter on the one side and such almost miraculous preservation on the other have never been heard of since the invention of gunpowder." [42]

15

TEXAS RISING

PRIVATE GEORGE ERATH WAS in awe of the pile of Mexican booty seized by the Texas Army. Colonel Burleson had detailed him and William Simmons, another volunteer from Jesse Billingsley's Bastrop company, to guard the mass of goods seized in Santa Anna's camp throughout the night of April 21.

Erath saw ornate furniture, fine silverware, considerable food supplies, and other treasures "such as a European prince might take with him into the field." The most tempting prize to the haggard victors of the day's battle, however, was a six-foot-tall pyramid containing several dozen baskets of champagne that was discovered. Burleson had instructed the two soldiers to guard the valuables well, but said they could share some of the food with hungry Texans.[1]

Simmons decided that the champagne fell under the "food" category and began liberally distributing bottles to stragglers as they returned to the camp. Word of the champagne spread and

Erath found "we had plenty of company of officers for the rest of the night. I don't think much of the wine was left. I took my carouse in eating sugar while others drank."

Dr. Lorenzo de Zavala's home, located across Buffalo Bayou from the battlefield, served as a makeshift hospital through the evening. Henry Karnes and the Texas spies were busily searching long before daybreak for other Mexican soldiers who had escaped the main field. Generals Cos and Santa Anna eluded their pursuers for the time being, but the horsemen did round up other prisoners. The main battlefield was a grisly scene, with clusters of dead and dying *soldados* lying in every direction. Samuel Hardaway, gazing upon the scene, found that only the recollections of the dreadful massacre his fellow Texans had endured at the Alamo and at Goliad relieved his feelings from the horrors of the present landscape.[2]

One of those captured was Ramón Caro, the personal secretary of His Excellency. Vengeful Texans were eager to kill him, but he was brought before Sam Houston for questioning. The Texan general knew that the victory at San Jacinto would be a hollow one should the Mexican commander in chief manage to elude his scouts. Santa Anna had spent the night hiding in tall grass near the bayou. After dawn, he crossed the waist-deep creek before finding a deserted servants' quarters on the Vince ranch. He pulled some old slave clothes—including a blue cotton round jacket and cotton pantaloons—over his fine diamond-studded linen shirt. Santa Anna then donned an old hide cap, wrapped a horse blanket around himself as a serape, and then set off again down the bayou, still wearing his morocco slippers.

His good fortunes expired in the late afternoon of April 22 when he was approached by a six-man scout patrol under Sergeant James Sylvester. They had actually spotted a herd of four or five deer on the west side of a branch that fed into Buffalo

Bayou. Sylvester had dismounted from his horse, crept closer to the deer, and was raising his rifle to fire on them. The deer were suddenly spooked, raised their white tails, and bounded away with their flags flying. The sergeant shifted his gaze and spotted the culprit: a Mexican soldier racing for a nearby bridge had startled them.[3]

Sylvester's party surrounded the Mexican, who was dressed in a dingy-looking common soldier's uniform. Joel Robison, who could speak Spanish, interrogated their prisoner. He stated that he was not an officer, but a cavalryman who had been displaced from his horse in the previous evening's battle. The scouts hauled their captured man back to the former Mexican Army camp to deposit him in the prisoner bullpen. There arose some commotion among the other prisoners, who recognized Santa Anna instantly. Wise officers yelled at the others to shut their mouths, but it was too late.

Privates James Winters and Stephen Sparks noticed many excited Mexican soldiers jumping to their feet, clapping their hands, and saying, "Santa Anna." Private Sion Bostick, one of the captors, recalled, "We knew then that we had made a big haul." Former ranger captain William Sadler stepped up to the prisoner and ripped open his ragged blue cotton round-jacket—clearly revealing the fine linen shirt beneath with its sparkling diamond studs.[4]

Sam Houston was lying on a blanket dozing beneath a large oak tree in camp when President Santa Anna was led before him. The general had his wounded left leg propped up. Colonel Forbes shook him awake as Santa Anna addressed Houston, telling him that he was surrendering as a prisoner of war. Not understanding the language, Houston had Forbes fetch a proper translator. In the meantime, the crowd grew restless.

"Shoot him!" some shouted.

"Hang him!"

Soldiers pressed in closer to curse and shout at the Mexican leader who had ordered the murders of the Alamo and Goliad survivors. Colonel Hockley had to place a guard group around the general's area to control the unruly crowd, many of whom shouted for Houston to execute Santa Anna.

Moses Austin Bryan helped translate for Sam Houston until guards could fetch Ramón Caro. Bryan recalled that Santa Anna's confessions before the Texas leader translated as: "I am Antonio López de Santa Anna, President of Mexico, Commander-in-Chief of the Army of Operations, and I put myself at the disposition of the brave General Houston. I wish to be treated as a general should when a prisoner of war." [5]

Angry Texans shouted that Santa Anna deserved only death. General Houston demanded that Colonel Almonte be summoned to verify the identity of Santa Anna. The great Mexican conqueror, perceiving that Houston enjoyed the attention of praise, continued to pepper him with compliments. He called Houston "the Wellington of the times" and compared the Texans' victory with that of the British and Prussian victory over the French in 1815 at Waterloo. Colonel Forbes soon returned with Almonte, the senior Mexican officer who spoke fluent English. The early interrogations only inflamed the Texian crowd more. When asked to explain the massacre of Travis and his men at the Alamo, Santa Anna stated that it was customary to "put all to the sword" when such a small force refused to surrender and forced such casualties on a superior attacking force. [6]

Santa Anna's initial attempts at diplomatic negotiations soon crumbled. He became frazzled under the grilling he endured from Houston and Rusk. Secretary Caro, sent to fetch the general's official correspondence papers, also returned with El Presidente's medicine box. Santa Anna reportedly restored his own calm with a quick dose of opium from the box. After some discussions, he agreed to issue orders to have his remaining troops in country fall back toward Mexico. Caro wrote out three sets of orders for Generals Filisola, Gaona, and Urrea to withdraw their forces. Filisola was further ordered to release any prisoners and send them to San Felipe de Austin. Santa Anna signed the official papers with the dateline from "camp of San Jacinto, April 22, 1836." [7]

DEAF SMITH RODE INTO the night of April 22 with two companions. He carried with him copies of Santa Anna's truce agreement and the dispatches written to his subordinate officers. En route, he unknowingly apprehended a Mexican man traveling on foot who was none other than Santa Anna's own brother-in-law, General Martín Cos. The identity of Cos was not determined until he was hauled back into the Texian camp.

On April 23, Vice President Zavala and Colonel James Morgan reached the San Jacinto battlegrounds from Galveston via the steamboat *Cayuga*. The victorious Texans remained camped at San Jacinto for several days as General Houston continued his talks with Santa Anna. The four-thousand-plus Mexican troops still stationed in Texas slowly received the news and the official dispatches that ordered them to retreat toward their home country. They were followed by Texian forces and their retreat was a long, trying struggle through lowlands bogged with mud.

Ranch owner Peggy McCormick returned to her property to find it strewn with some two hundred rifles smashed to pieces and hundreds of dead bodies. She furiously approached General Houston where he lay wounded in his camp, demanding that he "take them dead Mexicans off my league." She said they would "haunt" her the rest of her life. [8]

"Madam, your land will be famed in history as the classic spot upon which the glorious victory of San Jacinto was gained!" Houston replied. "Here was born, in the throes of revolution, the infant of Texas independence! Here that latest scourge of mankind, the arrogantly self-styled 'Napoleon of the West,' met his fate!"

McCormick was unimpressed. "To the devil with your glorious history! Take off your stinking Mexicans!"

Houston's army finally moved six miles from the battlefield on April 26 to get away from the stench of rotting bodies. There the victors held a booty auction. Some twelve thousand dollars from Santa Anna's personal war chest was split among the soldiers who had fought at San Jacinto. Each man was allowed to bid on the various spoils of war captured from their opposing army. Colonel Sidney Sherman walked away from the auction with a fine officer's sword, adorned with heavy gold on its hilt and scabbard. Santa Anna's decorative saddle sold for eight hundred dollars. Texans draped their newly purchased mules and horses with red and green cords and glittering Mexican Army epaulets. Colonel Pedro Delgado felt the victorious frontiersmen looked like "bull-fight clowns." [9]

SURGEON ALEXANDER EWING FEARED that Sam Houston might die if he did not receive proper medical attention for his badly infected leg wound. As he prepared to depart for New Orleans on May 3, Houston resigned his commission and Thomas Rusk took over as major general of the Texas Army. Rusk's resigned position as secretary of war was filled by the election of Colonel Mirabeau Lamar. The Georgia poet who had been a lowly volunteer private three weeks before had thus reached the highest military position in Texas in less than a month. Such were the opportunities in a renegade fledgling nation where battlefield valor could determine one's entire future.

The Mexican prisoners of San Jacinto were herded onto the steamboat *Yellow Stone* and moved to Galveston. They were detained there until mid-August under deplorable conditions until they were released to make their way back to their home country. President Burnet and his cabinet worked out a treaty with Santa Anna at the port of Velasco and signed it on May 14. The Velasco Treaty spelled out that all hostilities would cease between Texas and Mexico and that all Mexican troops would evacuate Texas. Santa Anna signed a second document in which he swore to use his influence once he was returned to Mexico to have his country acknowledge Texas independence.[10]

Santa Anna was held prisoner until the fall of 1836, when he was escorted to Washington, D.C., to be questioned by the U.S. government. Colonel George Hockley and a small party departed Brazoria County in late November to deliver El Presidente and his top English-speaking officer, Colonel Almonte. They traveled by horses and by boat, reaching the capital on January 18, 1837. President Jackson greeted Santa Anna warmly and honored him with a dinner attended by many dignitaries. The defeated Mexican dictator reportedly proposed to cede Texas to the United States for a fair price, but "Old Hickory" was aware that Santa Anna was in no position to carry out such a bargain.[11]

Santa Anna would eventually return to power within Mexico after defeating French troops in 1838. For the moment, however, he was a broken man. Andrew Jackson arranged for a sailing vessel to transport him back to his home near Veracruz, where Santa Anna remained in seclusion for some time— disillusioned and resentful. He later wrote, "It seemed that my country had abandoned me to my enemies."

16

NEW CHALLENGES FOR A NEW NATION

THE TEXAS RANGERS GAINED a new level of importance during the early months of independence in the new Republic of Texas.

None of the three legally created ranging systems had ever reached full capacity during the Texas Revolution, but each had served an important role in maintaining frontier peace during the absence of regular army companies. These rangers were instrumental in building or manning at least four frontier outposts. Two companies had skirmishes with Indians during the revolution and one entire ranger company had paid the ultimate price for Texas independence in being sacrificed at the Alamo. At least eighty-three men involved in the ranging service during the Texas Revolution were either present on the San

Jacinto battlefield or were stationed at Harrisburg guarding the baggage on April 21.

The great Runaway Scrape was contained as word of the Texan victory spread. The Texas Army and its cavalry monitored the slow retreat of Mexican troops from their country as peace negotiations were conducted with Santa Anna on the Texas coast. The Texas Rangers were revamped to help maintain order throughout the republic. Major Willie Williamson had ceased to be involved with his battalion and the regional ranging system headed by area superintendents had largely lapsed. Three of the council-approved superintendents— Garrison Greenwood, Daniel Friar, and George Davis—were no longer functioning in such a role. As of May 1836, only Silas Parker remained, in charge of Captain James Parker's small ranging unit at Fort Sterling.

The third ranger organization that had been approved by the Constitutional Convention did remain in service after San Jacinto. Colonel Jesse Benton was absent in the vicinity of the U.S. border on the Red River but his subordinate, Lieutenant Colonel Griffin Bayne, became the active organizer and commander of the various ranging units still in the vicinity of the San Jacinto battleground.

Bayne promoted several officers on May 8 to regroup three companies to carry on his ranger regiment. The first company was headed by Captain E. L. Ripley Wheelock, a New England native who had attended the West Point military college and had served in both the War of 1812 and the Black Hawk War. Griffin Bayne directed the activities of three other ranger companies under Captains William Wilson, John Tumlinson, and Isaac Burton. The latter two units had largely scattered during the Runaway Scrape and the San Jacinto battle but both men had since resumed command of their rangers.[1]

TROUBLES WITH THE INDIANS returned to the pioneer settlements almost as soon as the Texas Revolution was concluded.

Near Bastrop on May 14, a party of about a dozen Comanches appeared in one of the fields near the home of Reuben
Hornsby. They carried a white flag of peace as they approached
a group of Anglo settlers working the crops. John Williams
and Howell Haggard, two former Tumlinson rangers, were the
closest as the Comanches moved forward. Without warning,
they were suddenly speared with lances and shot down in cold
blood. The other men ran for cover and swam the river to escape while the marauding Indians rounded up all the cattle in
the settlement and moved on.[2]

Only days later, one of the most famous Indian raids of
early Texas history took place at a revolutionary ranger outpost. Around 9 A.M. on May 19, hundreds of Comanches and
Kichai (known as Caddos to the settlers) appeared in the open
prairie near Parker's Fort, which had been known in earlier
months as Fort Sterling.

Thirty-eight settlers resided at the dual-blockhouse fortress
but most of the adult men were in the field tending to crops at
that moment. Sarah Parker Nixon quickly ran for her thirty-
eight-year-old father, Captain James Parker, on his nearby farm
to spread the warning. Captain Parker was still on the payroll
of the regional ranging system that was presided over by superintendent Silas Parker. Most of the other women of Fort Parker
departed with their children to seek hiding places in the woods.

Four men were left in the fort to defend the women and
children who remained. They were Silas Parker, his younger
brother Ben Parker, Samuel Frost, and his son Robert B. Frost—
all of whom had been involved in the ranging service during

the previous months. The vast Indian party halted about two hundred yards from Parker's Fort and two Comanches were sent forward displaying a white flag of truce. Ben Parker volunteered to meet with them. He returned, saying that the Indians intended to fight and that everyone should prepare themselves.[3]

Ben then said he would try to make a compromise with the Indians while the others prepared, although his brother begged him not to go. As he approached, the Comanches and Kichais erupted into dreadful war whoops and drove long spears through the body of the ranger. "Their united voice seemed to reach the very skies whilst they were dealing death," recalled Rachel Parker Plummer, the seventeen-year-old auburn-haired daughter of Captain James Parker. Rachel snatched up her sixteen-month-old son, James Pratt Plummer, and raced out of the fort's back gate.[4]

A large Indian knocked her unconscious with a wooden hoe and snatched her infant from her arms. When she awoke, she was being dragged by her hair back into the fort past the mutilated body of her uncle Ben. Silas Parker and the two Frost men died trying to defend the other women and children from the Comanches and Kichais swarming into the fort. Young Comanches proved themselves as being brave in combat by physically striking an opponent versus shooting them from long distance. An even greater feat involved using a sharp knife to remove an opponent's scalp and ears while he was still alive. Among the bloody scalps young captive Rachel would see that morning was at least one she could identify by its gray hair as being that of her grandfather, Elder John Parker.

The Indians overtook another party of settlers who tried to flee the fort. John Parker and his wife, Sallie White "Granny" Parker, were stripped and then the reverend was run through with an arrow and scalped. Granny and another woman were physically assaulted, speared, stabbed, and left for dead on the prairie. Only the youngest female of the party, Elizabeth Kellogg, was taken hostage and dragged back into Fort Parker. There the scene was utter chaos as the whooping Indians looted and ransacked the pioneer fort. Other Indians overtook Lucy Parker, wife of murdered ranger superintendent Silas Parker, as she fled with her four children. Several of the men from the fields arrived in time to help defend her but two of Lucy's children—Cynthia Ann and John Parker—were overtaken by the Indians before they moved on.

The Parker's Fort survivors fled into the wilderness and sent for help from Fort Houston. James Parker returned to his family's settlement one month after the massacre and buried the bones of those who had fallen. The Anglo captives were hauled away by the raiding party. Elizabeth Kellogg was eventually ransomed and delivered to Nacogdoches six months later. Rachel Plummer's father, James, would make three perilous trips into Indian territory before he was able to finally help secure her ransom via Mexican traders in Santa Fe on June 19, 1837—exactly twenty-two months after her capture. During that period, Rachel had given birth to a child but it was brutally murdered in her presence. She died at age twenty, one year after being returned to her father, not living long enough to see the ransom of her son James Pratt Plummer, who was taken to Fort Gibson in 1842.[5]

The most famous of the Parker family hostages were siblings Cynthia Ann and John Parker. John became a famous Indian warrior who later quit his tribe to fight for the Confederacy during the Civil War. Cynthia Ann, nine at the time of her abduction, lived with the Comanches for twenty-five years and gave birth to two sons—one of whom became the famous chief Quanah Parker. She did return to Anglo civilization, where her uncle Isaac Parker helped her to remember her childhood name before she passed away in Anderson County in 1864.

Ben and Silas Parker were later approved for payment for their services as rangers until the date of their murders. Their brother James Parker was officially paid as a Texas Ranger for the period of November 17, 1835, through May 19, 1836. The Parker's Fort Massacre effectively terminated the existence of any regional ranging system in East Texas for the time being.

THE PARKER FAMILY'S TRAGEDY became the strongest incentive to maintain a proper ranging service to protect against such frontier violence. Daniel Parker Sr. demanded of Sam Houston that summer that his area be afforded proper armed units. Houston thus sent orders for Parker to oversee the construction of a blockhouse and ferry on the Trinity River above Comanche Crossing and near Fort Houston.[6]

General Rusk, the new commander in chief of the Texas Army, was in agreement that a proper ranging system should remain in place. He commissioned former ranger captain Sterling Robertson to travel through the major settlements to drum up volunteers for the service, even though he was as yet unaware of the Parker's Fort Massacre.[7]

Rusk kept the ranging companies under Lieutenant Colonel Bayne in operation with or near his army as it pushed the remnants of Santa Anna's soldiers back toward their home country. On May 29, he sent Captain Isaac Burton's unit to patrol the flat coastal plains from the Guadalupe River to Mission Bay near Refugio to watch for Mexican incursions. Burton's men received word of a suspicious vessel in the Bay of Copano on June 2, and he decided to set an ambush.[8]

That night, they spied on the schooner *Watchman* from a

bluff overlooking the bay. At 8 A.M. on June 3, two of Burton's rangers sent a distress signal to the Mexican vessel. The schooner's skipper ran up the U.S. stars and stripes on the mainmast but received no response from the men ashore. His crew then hoisted the red, green, and white Mexican flag. The two men on the beach excitedly beckoned for the Mexican crew to come ashore. The *Watchman*'s skipper and four other sailors rowed ashore in a small boat and were thoroughly surprised to be arrested by Captain Burton's rangers.

Burton left four rangers to guard the five Mexican sailors and took a sixteen-man party in the boat back out to the *Watchman*. They seized the remaining crew and the cargo of the ship, which was found to be loaded with supplies intended for the Mexican Army. General Rusk received word of Burton's seizure and was alarmed that the action might trigger negative repercussions that could violate the recent Velasco peace treaty. Captain Burton either failed to receive Rusk's orders in a timely fashion or chose to ignore them. He remained with his captured schooner for another two weeks.[9]

The rangers of the Texas Gulf Coast were far from finished with their naval adventures. Two other Mexican sailing vessels, the *Comanche* and *Fanny Butler,* approached Copano Bay on June 17 and both were loaded with supplies for the Mexican Army. Burton ordered the *Watchman*'s skipper to invite the other two captains via signals to join him on his ship for a glass of grog. The unsuspecting skippers came aboard with thoughts of partaking in fine spirits and ended up under the guns of Texas Rangers.[10]

Burton split several of his rangers between the three schooners and forced the Mexican crews to sail on June 19 from Copano Bay to the northeast for Velasco. The *Watchman, Fanny Butler,* and *Comanche* were then ordered to Galveston, where their cargoes were forfeited to the Republic of Texas. Auditors assessed the freight—food, muskets, gunpowder, ammunition, and bayonets—to be worth twenty-five thousand dollars. It would go a long way to support the Texas Army. If General Rusk was less than pleased with Isaac Burton's actions, Lieutenant Colonel Bayne was ecstatic. He promoted Burton to major commanding his ranger battalion on June 24. President David Burnet allowed Burton to be paid $2,848.90 from the captured spoils and divvied up healthy payments to those of his men who had helped board and sail the Mexican vessels.

The peaceful seizure of three enemy vessels by mounted frontiersmen—in which not a single shot was fired—was drama better than any novelist might pen. Major Burton's crafty rangers were soon dubbed "Horse Marines" as word of their adventure spread through the republic and into the United States.[11]

STERLING ROBERTSON WAS DISGUSTED.

The land *empresario* of his namesake colony returned from his ranger recruiting trip in mid-June. He had recruited only fifty-odd men, and during his time stumping through Nacogdoches and San Augustine, Caddo Indians had carried out more atrocities against his colonists. The "rangers" Robertson had been able to enlist were a sorry lot at best.

Most were newcomers to Texas who had neither horses nor guns. They had the notion to press the same from private citizens, sometimes relieving pioneer families of the only weapons they had to use for hunting or for defense against Indians. Robertson informed Rusk that his people were more angered and afraid of the new frontier guardians than they were cheered by their sight. Some families hid in the woods as soldiers marched past. The citizens of his colony were greatly alarmed by news of the Parker's Fort Massacre and of fresh assaults that other Indians had carried out against settlers on the Little River. A new frontier ranging system was sorely needed.[12]

There was less concern about the strength of the Texas Army, which continued to swell during the summer of 1836 as more opportunists poured into the republic. By early August, the army sported fifty-three companies and more than 2,500 men—almost three times the strength Sam Houston had at his disposal on April 21 at San Jacinto. Only fourteen of these companies were composed of men who had fought in the Texas Revolution or had previously lived in the republic.[13]

Indian violence continued to escalate during the summer of 1836. Tom Rusk commissioned Colonel Ed Burleson to raise and command another six ranger companies to serve between the upper Colorado and Brazos rivers to keep the Indians in check. Unlike the ill-mannered volunteers Robertson had rounded up on his recruiting mission, the men recruited for the Burleson battalion were largely Texas settlers with good reason to help protect their fellow citizens. Many of them, in fact, had previously served in revolutionary ranger companies and had also taken part in the summer 1835 ranger expedition through East Texas.

Colonel Burleson's First Division of Rangers took on provisions from local residents, who were issued vouchers for their goods. These were often unpaid for years during the early republic era. Horses, corn, potatoes, beef, pork, clothing, tobacco, and other goods were obtained to sustain these rangers as they patrolled the frontiers between the Colorado and Brazos rivers. Captain William Hill's company had a brush with Indians during August while scouting on the San Gabriel River near the mouth of Brushy Creek. His rangers overtook a group of twenty or more Caddos in thick post oaks in the Yegua River bottomlands close to sundown.

"Dismounting, we prepared to attack them in camp, but a straggling warrior hastened the issue by coming out and meeting us accidentally and unexpectedly," thirteen-year-old ranger Cicero Rufus Perry recalled. The Indian was killed but not before he had raised a war whoop to alert his comrades. Captain Hill's company rushed into the campground and engaged in a brief firefight. Three Caddos were killed and several others were wounded. Andy Houston was the only Texan injured when he was hit in the wrist by an unspiked arrow. The rangers seized the camp equipment abandoned by the fleeing Indians. Perry, who turned fourteen while on this expedition, was shocked to see "a large number of human scalps, taken from white people of both sexes and all ages." [14]

By mid-September, the corps of Texas Rangers was at an all-time high in terms of companies and men enrolled in the service. There were thirteen companies, comprising approximately 450 men in four battalions—a number the ranger service would not surpass until 1839. Colonel Burleson's rangers saw little other action during their three-month tenure. Major Isaac Burton's three-company battalion helped provide for itself by rounding up loose cattle and horses on the plains of the Nueces and about San Antonio during the summer of 1836. Many of the herds had been owned by Mexican citizens who had lived between the Nueces and the Rio Grande rivers. The Texas Army even erected its first cattle pens at Goliad, and the first sweep by these "cowboys" netted 327 head of cattle for use in sustaining the troops.[15]

Still, Major Burton struggled to keep his rangers properly provisioned with horses, equipment, and food due to the destitution of the revolution-ravaged republic. Several of his companies continued to operate into the fall of 1836, by which time their services were negated by the creation of a more properly equipped ranger battalion formed under the command of Colonel Robert Coleman—one of Sam Houston's former staff members during the San Jacinto campaign. Coleman's promptings to Texas leaders in 1835 had helped formally create the Texas Rangers, so it was little surprise that he was given the nod in mid-August 1836 to take another ranger command.

On August 12, Coleman was authorized to recruit three companies of rangers to protect the frontier inhabitants of the upper Brazos, Colorado, Little, and Guadalupe rivers. He had raised his third company by September 21, and he moved his men to the Colorado River area on Walnut Creek, about six miles below present Austin. There his rangers built a blockhouse and a cluster of log cabins surrounded by a stockade fence. The new ranger headquarters became alternately known over the next two years as Fort Colorado, Coleman's Fort, and Fort Houston.[16]

George Erath, a veteran of ranger service in 1835 and the Battle of San Jacinto, had just completed three months of service in one of Colonel Burleson's ranger units. He now jumped at the chance to join Coleman's new ranger battalion. "We were promised twenty-five dollars a month and 1,280 acres of land for every twelve months' service," he said. "The government furnished ammunition and rations, but we furnished our own horses and arms. We lived for the most part on game out of the woods." Erath witnessed several men enlist who exchanged their claims to money and land for horses, saddles, and bridles with which to serve. Coleman's ranger battalion was productive in establishing new frontier outposts during its early months of service.[17]

President Houston authorized the enrollment of three ranger companies in East Texas during September but he would find some of them to be far less productive than those under Coleman. Major James Smith of Nacogdoches supervised the first two East Texas ranger companies, commanded by Captain Michael Costley and Elisha Clapp—whose men vigilantly patrolled to pursue small Indian bands when they were not working on new blockhouses on the Trinity River.[18]

Major Smith's third company proved to be nothing but trouble. It was led by businessman George Washington Jewell, who had raised his men in Tennessee in August and marched to Texas. Captain Jewell's men were ordered to complete the construction work on Fort Houston, a project that had been abandoned when Captain William Sadler's rangers had answered the call to join the San Jacinto campaign. By late fall, James Smith left his position to attend to other business. The Fort Houston rangers under Captains Jewell and Costley then promoted Major Jewell into command. Sam Houston ordered these men to construct two additional blockhouses and a ferryboat at the upper crossing of the Trinity River. Captain Squire Haggard, the new commander of Jewell's company, sent a defiant reply to President Houston: "By God, we came to fight, and we'll be damned if we are going to work for anybody, or obey any such orders to build blockhouses." [19]

Costley's company completed its three-month service period on December 11 and was mustered out of service. Major Jewell maintained his position, although Houston flatly refused to acknowledge his promotion. Jewell and Captain Haggard were left in command of forty-odd rangers for another three months as they worked on Fort Houston and patrolled the immediate vicinity. The recalcitrant rangers were troubled by Indian depredations in early 1837 and three of Haggard's men were killed on the Trinity in late January. President Houston blamed their deaths on the rangers' own failure to build the fort and ferryboat he had directed them to do, and he ordered Texas auditors not to pay anyone who had served under Jewell, Haggard, and Costley. Major Jewell's last rangers were mustered out of service on March 19. The defiant Captain Costley was shot through the heart months later during an altercation with another man. One of Houston's allies wrote to the president that because of his character, Costley "well deserved his fate." [20]

THE NEWLY CONVENED FIRST Congress of the Republic of Texas took care of the need for such rowdy East Texas rangers.

Sterling Robertson, a member of the Standing Committee on Indian Affairs, introduced a bill on October 21 calling for further protection of the Indian frontier. President Houston signed the bill into law on December 5. It provided for a battalion of "mounted riflemen," consisting of five companies of fifty-six men each. These men would furnish their own horse, a good rifle, and a brace of pistols. The president was authorized to use these men to build blockhouses, forts, and trading posts, and to prevent Indian depredations. [21]

Congress further refined the role of the frontier battalion on December 10. These Mounted Riflemen, "now and hereafter in the ranging service on the frontier," were to be paid twenty-five dollars per month, plus the same bounty of land as other volunteers in the field. In terms of officers' pay, the captain was to receive seventy-five dollars per month, a first lieutenant sixty dollars per month, a second lieutenant fifty dollars per month, and the orderly sergeant forty dollars per month. The Texas Congress acknowledged all officers and men who had been engaged "in the ranging service since July 1835" as eligible for pay. Less formalized ranger companies had operated within Texas since 1823, but the First Congress recognized Robert Coleman and his 1835 unit as the driving force behind the service's true organization.[22]

The Texas legislators appointed Major William H. Smith, a former cavalry company commander at San Jacinto, as commander of the new Mounted Rifleman Battalion. He was to organize five ranger companies in Texas that would cover the new counties of Gonzales, Shelby, and Mina (Bastrop). The new rifleman battalion would soon replace the three-company battalion under Colonel Coleman's command and would obviate the need to continue Major Smith's East Texas battalion.

In late December, the First Congress also approved legislation to provide for a new Texas Army with one regiment of cavalry, one regiment of artillery, and four regiments of infantry. The Senate named Brigadier General Albert Sidney Johnston as the new commander in chief, with Colonel Henry Karnes to lead the First Regiment of Cavalry. Karnes's horsemen would serve primarily on the western frontiers of Texas beyond the reaches of the mounted riflemen and rangers. During late December 1836 and early 1837, Colonel Karnes deployed his cavalrymen. Captain Lysander Wells's men would operate at San Patricio on the lower Nueces River; Captain James W. Tinsley stationed his men along the coastal areas near Copano Bay; Captains Deaf Smith and Juan Seguín would tackle the San Antonio area; and Lieutenant David L. Kokernot's small detachment of cavalry was assigned to command Post Sabine on the Texas–Louisiana border.[23]

By November, Robert Coleman's ranger battalion had already built Fort Colorado, and a second blockhouse at Milam; another detachment under George Erath was making good progress on a new fort on the Little River. "By the first of December I will show the government, as well as all others, what a Kentuckian can do," Coleman wrote to Congressman Robertson. Misfortunes soon sidetracked the colonel's good intentions, however. Coleman left First Lieutenant Alexander Robless in charge of Fort Colorado while he was in the field during December laying out a new frontier road. One of the rangers, Private Fee C. Booker, was known for his love of the bottle. After one particular binge, Booker was disciplined by Lieutenant Robless, a former U.S. Army soldier. Ranger Noah Smithwick recalled that Robless "ordered him tied up to a post all night to sober off. The man was so completely under the influence as to be unable to maintain an upright position; his limbs gave way, and he sank so that the cord around his neck literally hung him." [24]

Lieutenant Robless tried to dismiss the event as a suicide, but his rangers were in an uproar. Robless deserted his post and left Colonel Coleman holding the bag for his actions. President Houston relieved Coleman of command in early January 1837 and ordered him to report to the War Department in Columbia. He was held under military arrest in Velasco pending the outcome of an investigation into the wrongful death. Before he could be brought to trial, Robert Coleman—the man who had been most instrumental in the formal creation of the Texas Rangers—drowned in a fishing accident in early July 1837. [25]

THE MOST SIGNIFICANT INDIAN encounter for the Coleman battalion occurred on January 7, 1837. Sergeant George Erath took ten rangers and three volunteers out from his Little River Fort to follow a fresh Indian trail.

His men tracked them to Elm Creek in present Milam

County and attacked early the next morning. Erath's men killed several Indians with their first shots but then realized a serious problem. Instead of being about a dozen in strength, Erath found the Indians were actually "about a hundred strong." The rangers were surrounded in the Elm Creek forest and were forced to retreat in small groups while under heavy fire. Two men perished before Erath's surviving force reached their Little River Fort that night. A snow storm prevented reinforcements led by Major William Smith from reaching the scene of Erath's fight until January 15. Sergeant Erath later believed that if all his men had been equipped with pistols or the six-shooters that evolved several years later, he could have dominated the Elm Creek battle.[26]

During early 1837, Major Smith was directed by Sam Houston to absorb Coleman's companies into his own new Mounted Rifleman Battalion. Smith's rangers suffered from improper clothing during the winter months. The Texas government did purchase surplus U.S. Army uniforms to help replace their buckskin suits, but the supplies were limited. Noah Smithwick noted that Private Isaac Castner, a large man of about two hundred pounds, was given a uniform that "would have been snug for a man of 140" pounds. Commissary Samuel Wolfenberger's pants reached only halfway down his legs, his jacket missed the top of his pants by six inches, and his arms extended a foot beyond the sleeves. Smithwick and other rangers howled with laughter as Wolfenberger "stalked up and down like an animated scarecrow, trying to negotiate a trade."[27]

William Smith's Colorado River area battalion was all that remained by late March in terms of rangers to protect the Texas settlements. He directed his men to continue building frontier forts during the winter to help stave off the occasional murders committed by marauding Comanches. The more distant settlements were protected by frontier posts, each manned by companies of Colonel Henry Karnes's cavalry. The first company to form, that of Captain Deaf Smith, remained on the San Antonio River below town during the early weeks of 1837. The experience that some of his men gained in the cavalry would serve them for years to come as they later turned to the ranger service. The most notable of this category was one John Coffee Hays, who reached his twentieth birthday while camping with Deaf Smith's spies in early January 1837.[28]

Jack Hays had been born on his family's plantation near Little Cedar Lick, Tennessee. His Scotch-Irish father, Lieutenant Harmon Hays, named his son after General John Coffee, under whom he had served in the War of 1812 along with Sam Houston. Young Jack, a fair-complected lad with dark hair and piercing hazel eyes, had the chance to listen to the tales of General Andrew Jackson on many occasions and he was quite impressionable. Jack's parents succumbed to illness when he was just fifteen, leaving him and his siblings to be raised by a Mississippi uncle, Robert Cage.[29]

Young Hays soon struck out on his own, taking a job as a chain boy for a surveying crew. He and another surveyor were locating claims near a Choctaw hunting section one day when they were charged by several Indians. Jack shot and killed his first Indian to secure the possession of the fallen man's horse in his first hostile encounter. He stuck with surveying for two years before entering the Davidson Academy in Nashville, where Jack stood out as the fastest runner in the school. Before his first year of school was complete, illness forced him back to his uncle's Mississippi plantation—where he was working when he heard news of the Alamo's fall.

He decided to fight for the Texian cause. Using some of his surveying money, Jack Hays bought a good knife and a brace of pistols and headed for New Orleans. There he joined a group of southern volunteers and made his way to Nacogdoches. The quiet, slender, five-foot-eight youth became the object of attention of a particular Nacogdoches barroom bully who decided that Hays would make a good victim. The man stared into Jack's face and knocked the drink from his hand. Hays said nothing, but his glaring eyes gave away his inner anger. The bully reached for his gun, but young Jack was faster. In a split second, the larger man was lying on the dirty barroom floor bleeding out. Hays, completely exonerated for defending himself, soon moved on from Nacogdoches and served with the Texas Army during the mopping-up stages of the Texas Revolution.[30]

During his time with the Texas Cavalry, Hays's simple mannerisms and sense of humor quickly endeared him to his fellow soldiers. He and his comrades learned many lessons the hard way in 1837. In mid-February, Captain Smith was forced to move his cavalry to the Medina River just to find grazing grass for their horses. On February 21, his company faced a major setback when their entire herd of horses was stolen. At this inopportune time, Secretary of War Fisher issued orders for Deaf Smith to conduct a mission to Laredo to assert Texas's claim to that area. Smith led Hays and his other men into San Antonio to secure new horses. While there on February 25, they joined Lieutenant Colonel Juan Seguín's company in providing a proper funeral ceremony for the fallen Alamo heroes. Their remains were collected from the ash piles where they had lain for almost a year and were buried in a black coffin with full military honors.[31]

Hays's first fight with Deaf Smith's cavalry came on March 17. Smith's men had reached the old San Ygnacio Ranch on the Arroyo Chacón, five miles east of Laredo, on March 16. They were attacked the next afternoon by forty Mexican cavalrymen from the Laredo garrison. They tied off their horses and took cover in a mesquite thicket as the Mexican horsemen advanced, firing on the Texans. "When they were about fifty yards distant, I returned their fire, giving strict orders that not a piece should be discharged until every man was sure of his aim," said Smith. Jack Hays was stirred by shouts from the Mexicans of "cowardly Texans" and "damned rascals" as they attacked. They were met by such a deadly outpouring of lead shot that Hays felt it "threw them into confusion and completely routed them. The rangers did not surrender."[32]

Captain Smith's company suffered two men wounded, but he believed they killed ten Mexicans and wounded an equal number. He returned to San Antonio on March 26 with twenty captured horses but found no hero's welcome from the townspeople. They showed Smith that "their sympathy was with the enemy." President Houston was later critical of his old pal Deaf Smith for making a campaign without orders—an action the politician no doubt feared could have stirred new controversy with Mexico. Captain Smith, irked by the lack of support and facing failing health, turned command of his mounted men over to Captain Nicholas Mosby Dawson in June. The seasoned hero of San Jacinto then settled with his wife, Lupe Smith, and their family at Richmond in Fort Bend County, to struggle with his health. Smith lost his last battle on November 30, 1837, when he succumbed to his illness. The intrepid scout of the Texas Revolution was honored in 1876 when Deaf Smith County was carved out of the former Béxar Territory.[33]

THE ONCE-POWERFUL TEXAS ARMY began to crumble during 1837.

Albert Sidney Johnston, appointed by the First Congress as

the new senior brigadier general, was challenged to a duel by Brigadier General Felix Huston, the acting army commander. The two Texans faced off with inaccurate horse pistols, firing at each other half a dozen times before Johnston was felled with a severe hip wound. The lack of action took a toll on the regulars during the months that General Huston held acting command. Illegal whiskey became a mainstay in some of his camps and mutinies were soon on the rise. Colonel Henry Teal was murdered in his sleep by another soldier on May 5. By mid-month, President Houston was so angry with his Texas Army that he ordered three of his four regiments furloughed. The remaining six hundred troops continued to dwindle over the ensuing months as more men deserted, were furloughed, or completed their enlistment periods.[34]

By summer 1837, only a few of Colonel Karnes's cavalry companies remained in service on the southwestern frontier. Captain Dawson's spy company was on duty in the San Antonio area, where Sergeant Jack Hays—the assistant quartermaster for the Béxar cavalry—often commanded patrol parties that ranged out to distances of fifty miles from their base camp. Hays led a surprise roundup against Mexican bandits on one occasion in which he attacked them at sundown. His men killed three outlaws and pursued the remaining five on horseback. Hays shot one of the bandits from his horse. The chase only ended after three of the remaining outlaws had been apprehended.[35]

Major William Smith's ranger battalion suffered a number of setbacks in the spring of 1837. Lieutenant Nicholas Wren led fifteen rangers out to attack a small Comanche camp, managing to kill only one Indian in exchange for the life of one of his rangers. Weeks later, another group of Comanches eased up on the rangers' Colorado River outpost, stampeded their horses, and escaped with some of them. On April 28, a similar stampede was carried out against the horses of Captain Daniel Monroe's rangers at Fort Smith on the Little River. This time the rangers were too weak in number to even pursue them. Two weeks after losing his horses, Captain Monroe moved his rangers back to Fort Fisher, near the site of the old Waco village. He sent a party of three rangers and two volunteers to fetch a wagon team. They were attacked by a large band of Comanches on May 15 near Post Oak Springs in present Milam County and all five men were slaughtered.[36]

During the next month, yet another ranger was killed by Indian violence near Fort Milam. The Second Congress of the Republic of Texas responded by authorizing a new battalion of ten mounted riflemen companies to range on the northern frontier. Colonel Joseph Bennett found recruiting difficult at best, and Captain John M. Bowyer's Harrisburg County company was one of the few to fully organize. Bowyer's mounted gunmen arrived at Fort Smith in early October to join an expedition under Captain William Eastland, commanding a small ranger company of Major Smith's battalion still in service. Eastland departed on October 13 with a detachment of Captain Bowyer's company commanded by First Lieutenant A. B. Vanbenthuysen. Disagreements arose between the companies and they parted ways two weeks later in the field.

Lieutenant Vanbenthuysen continued tracking Indians into early November with eighteen of his men. On November 10, they engaged a party of about 150 Indians in present Archer County near a rock formation known as the "Stone Houses." Heavy fighting took place for ninety minutes; the rangers lost six horses and four men in that time. The Indians took a brief hiatus before advancing on the rangers again. This time they lit fire to the prairie grass to drive the Texans from their defensive position. Six more rangers perished as they were forced to charge on foot through the Indian lines into the timber. Among the fallen was Lieutenant Alfred H. Miles, who had been involved in the capture of Santa Anna at San Jacinto. Vanbenthuysen and seven other rangers survived the Stone Houses Fight, three of them being wounded.

Only two ranger companies remained in service by year end 1837 as their enlistment periods ended. President Houston had furloughed most of the Texas Army during the year, and he refused to appropriate any money to support the Texas Militia structure. Henry Karnes's cavalry had dwindled to forty-seven men by late 1837. The lack of military forces prompted the Second Congress of Texas to address the issue, with or without Sam Houston's blessing. In spite of President Houston's veto, a supplemental militia act was passed by the Congress on December 18, 1837. Major General Thomas Rusk was elected into command of the new, single-division Texas Militia, which would be divided into four brigades with regional brigadier generals in command. The four militia brigades for 1838 were: the First Brigade, under General Ed Burleson, including all areas west of the Brazos River; the Second Brigade, under General Moseley Baker, covering the territory between the Brazos and Trinity; the Third Brigade, under General Kelsey H. Douglass, covering the area between the Trinity and Sabine; and the Fourth Brigade, under General John H. Dyer, covering the area north of the Sabine and up to the Red River settlements.[37]

Unlike rangers who served continually, the militiamen would only be called up in times of crisis or to make specific campaigns that did not exceed three months. All able-bodied men within a county between the ages of seventeen and fifty were required to enroll in a militia company. The actions of the Texas Militia were presided over by its adjutant general, the chief militia officer, Colonel Hugh McLeod. Although it was not called into service during the early months of 1838, the new militia structure authorized by the Second Congress would prove to be important as Sam Houston allowed the ranging service to continue dwindling.[38]

By early spring, only Captain William Eastland's ranger company remained in service on the Colorado River at Fort Houston, the post originally built by Colonel Coleman. The last of these rangers were honorably discharged in late April as their service terms expired. Among them was Noah Smithwick, who completed his second one-year service period on April 26, 1838. A ranger was given 1,280 acres of land for each twelve-month service period. "No one cared anything for land those days," Smithwick recalled. "I gave one of my certificates for 1,280 acres for a horse which the Indians relieved me of in less than a week."[39]

The decline of proper military forces in Texas came at a time when Indian violence saw a sharp increase. Many of the encounters in 1838 came as a result of the new General Land Office of the Republic of Texas, which opened for business on January 4, along with other county land offices. A flood of land claimants and surveying parties began invading what was previously Indian-held territory.

This new land rush led to steady work for surveyors such as Jack Hays. His time with the Texas Cavalry had expired in 1837, so he went to work in his familiar profession. He soon became the deputy surveyor of the Béxar District under Robert C. Trimble. Hays and his men had several brushes with Comanches during the year, but he still managed to locate seventy-six certificates during 1838.[40]

Some of the Indian tribes were eager to keep the peace with the expanding white settlers, including the Lipan Apaches. Chief

Cuelgas de Castro signed a treaty for the Lipans on January 18, 1838. The Texans offered them $250 in gifts and for trading houses to be established among them. In return, neither the Lipans nor the Anglos would attack each other. Chief Castro's men became respected scouts who helped the rangers and militiamen with one of their own enemies, the warlike Comanches. The war chief of the Lipans, Chief Flaco, became a close ally to frontiersman and surveyor Jack Hays. Flaco learned from Hays's methods of remaining cool under fire. Hays learned from his new Lipan friend important skills such as trailing a foe, cultural variations of Texas tribes, and the unique methods of fighting employed by various Indians.[41]

President Houston's new secretary of war, Barnard Bee, appointed Albert Sidney Johnston and Lysander Wells to serve as commissioners to treat with the Comanche Indians. Colonel Henry Karnes was added on April 12 as a third Indian commissioner, and they made efforts to meet with the Comanche leaders. Bee and Colonel George Hockley completed a peace treaty with Chief Placido's Tonkawa Indians on April 11 at Houston. Commissioners Johnston, Karnes, and Wells met with a band of about 150 Comanches near San Antonio in May. Chiefs Essowakkenny and Essomanny accepted gifts of friendship and pledged that Essomanny would later appear before the Texas Congress to continue their peace talks. Congress tried to further provide for the frontiers in May by adding mounted gunmen companies within each militia district, but Sam Houston refused. He felt it was his duty alone to decide when to call out the militia, and he did not trust the aggressive nature of some ranger leaders who might stir up the Indians. "Everything will be gained by peace," wrote Houston, "but nothing will be gained by war."[42]

Colonel Karnes succeeded in convincing a party of more than

one hundred Comanches to visit Congress in the city of Houston on May 26. Three days later, Chiefs Muguara, Muestyah, and Muhy pledged that their Comanches would "stand by the white man and be his friend against all of his enemies." The Comanche group left in high spirits, sporting glass beads, blankets, red cloth, gunpowder, and other goods gifted to them by their new Texan friends. Frédéric Leclerc, a French settler, noted that these same Comanches had returned to stealing horses within a week and had murdered three enterprising Texans who were lured to their camp to open new lanes of commerce.[43]

Henry Karnes himself soon found proof of the true intentions of the Comanches. During the summer he led a force of twenty-one men out from San Antonio. His second in command was Benjamin Franklin Cage, a cousin to surveyor Jack Hays—whose mother was Elizabeth Cage Hays. Karnes and Cage were resting their horses on August 10 on the Arroyo Seco, west of the Medina River, when they were suddenly charged by two hundred mounted Comanche Indians. Jack Hays helped divide the attackers by shooting down the leading chief, Essowakkenny—one of the very leaders whom Karnes had made peace talks with in May. The Comanches made two more charges against the Texans to launch their arrows. The Anglos were slightly protected by a ravine and chaparral brush, but Colonel Karnes was struck by an arrow while standing atop the bank to help direct the battle. Many of his men's horses were killed or wounded by the flint-tipped missiles slung at them. The Comanches retreated after losing an estimated twenty killed and as many wounded.[44]

Karnes and Hays won the respect of the citizens of San Antonio for fighting off these aggressors. It was a clear sign to all involved that the Comanche, in spite of their feigns at peace talks, had no real intention of surrendering the prairies to any white settlers.

17

LAMAR'S CHEROKEE WAR OF EXTINCTION

MAJOR GENERAL THOMAS RUSK'S Texas Militia was finally put to the test during the summer of 1838.

General Vicente Filisola, the military commander of northern Mexico, had instigated an effort to unite various Indian tribes of Texas to rise up against settlers encroaching upon their lands. Mexican agent Julian Pedro Miracle moved from Matamoros into Texas during June. His party visited representatives of eight allied East Texas tribes and succeeded in stirring up resentment against the Anglo Texas settlers. One of Miracle's key men was Vicente Córdova, a former Mexican judge and alcalde of Nacogdoches who had become frustrated with the Anglo leaders who failed to protect the property of Nacogdoches-area *tejanos*. Córdova was instrumental in rounding up rebel *tejanos,* at least one former slave, and a few *tejano*-loyal Anglos to their revolt. By August, the *Nacogdoches Chronicle* reported that Córdova's rebel force had grown to about two hundred men. The first outbreak of violence occurred on August 4, 1838, when a Nacogdoches citizen was killed as a group of settlers tried to arrest one of Cordova's *tejanos* who was herding stolen horses. Word of this killing was passed to General Rusk and his regional militia commander, Kelsey Douglass. Three days later, Rusk was informed by Captain John Durst that at least one hundred armed *tejanos* were encamped on the Angelina River with a couple dozen Biloxi and Ioni Indians.[1]

Sam Houston issued orders for the Mexicans and Indians to disperse or be considered enemies of the republic. Córdova and his rebels instead sent a reply on August 10 that they were "ready to shed the last drop of blood" in defense of their principles. His force shot down and killed two brothers around this time, an act that further stirred the local Nacogdoches citizens to react. General Rusk began raising his militia in Nacogdoches and San Augustine against the orders of President Houston. Adjutant General Hugh McLeod helped organize fourteen companies of volunteers, who marched toward the Cherokee village of Chief Bowles, where Córdova's rebels were believed to have taken shelter.[2]

Rusk's force, joined by other volunteer companies, set up camp near the Cherokee village while Rusk held peace talks with Bowles, Chief Big Mush, and other leaders. President Houston wrote to Bowles, strongly urging him to give up any ideas of fighting. By August 18, the so-called Córdova Rebellion was largely quelled when Chief Bowles refused to let his Cherokees take part in the uprising. Córdova's men slipped away, and the Texas Militia forces gradually headed back to their settlements. Houston ordered Rusk to disband his men and maintain peace. Colonel McLeod was irked. He wrote to Vice President Mirabeau Lamar that this "timely demonstration of force" through Indian country had stirred fear in the Indians but that Houston had hindered Thomas Rusk's work "in every way with his orders." The policies of diplomacy versus war with the Indians held by the two top leaders of Texas could not be more conflicting.[3]

No sooner had the militiamen returned to their homes than evidence of the hostile intentions of the rebels was discovered on August 20. Captain Julian Pedro Miracle was killed on the Red River and his captured papers detailed each of the Indian tribes that had been contacted. The smoking gun was more than even President Houston could ignore. Thomas Rusk began forming militia companies again during early September.[4]

Rusk took advantage of the current crisis to implement a constant ranger presence within his militia. President Houston tried to keep the peace with the Texas Cherokees during the fall. He sent instructions for the surveying and marking of boundary lines for the territory he had promised Chief Bowles's people in his February 1836 treaty. On October 1, some of Córdova's rebels captured surveyor Elias Vansickle and held him prisoner for several months. Major Leonard Mabbitt's Fort Houston rangers relayed word of the kidnapping to Major General Rusk. He ordered up additional militia units to move against the forces reported to be camping out near the Kickapoo village north of Fort Houston.[5]

Support for Rusk's desired offensive was gained by a tragic depredation carried out on October 5, 1838, in East Texas, and which became known as the Killough Massacre. Isaac Killough and at least fifteen members of his extended family were murdered or captured that day by Cherokee Indians and their affiliated members.[6]

Three days after the Killough Massacre, a large party of Indians carried out another bloody assault on a group of Texas surveyors surveying land in what is now Navarro County, near present Dallas. William Fenner Henderson's twenty-three-man surveying party was approached by Indians around noon on October 8 as they were running their survey lines across a stretch of prairie. Without warning, the surveyors suddenly came under heavy fire from forty or more Kickapoo, Tawakoni, Ioni, Waco, and Caddo Indians who had been concealed in bushes growing along the banks of a nearby ravine. The Texans took cover in a ravine and engaged in a shooting match that killed a dozen of the surveyors.[7]

San Jacinto veteran Walter Lane and ten other survivors finally fled the ravine after midnight using their last five living horses. Four of the Texans were killed in the moonlit escape, but the other seven made it into the nearby forest. Lane, his leg shattered by a musket ball, made it to Parker's Fort by October 12 with two other men. Another survivor, John Violet, was found by a mounted party days later. His thigh bone broken, Violet had crawled more than twenty-five miles with little food or water. Various accounts of this fight give various numbers of casualties, but it appears that as many as seventeen Texan surveyors perished. The conflict was later known as either the Surveyors' Fight or the Battle Creek Fight.[8]

Major General Rusk was mobilizing his East Texas militiamen on October 11, even as the Surveyors' Fight survivors were struggling toward safety. Rusk departed Nacogdoches with four companies bound for the Kickapoo village in response to the Killough Massacre. He sent word for Major Mabbitt's First

Regiment of Mounted Gunmen—under Captains James Bradshaw, William T. Sadler, Squire Brown, and Jacob Snively—to move out from Fort Houston and rendezvous with him at Fort Duty, located four miles west of the Neches River and ten miles from Fort Houston. Mabbitt's 175 rangers headed out on October 12 but were ambushed along the trail just six miles east of their fort. Four rangers were killed and two other wounded in the hail of musket balls that suddenly rained down on them. One of those who perished, San Jacinto veteran John W. Carpenter, pursued a Caddo chief into the forest, where both men exchanged fatal shots. The ambushing party, a combined bunch of Córdova's Mexican and Indian rebels, vanished into the forest as quickly as they had appeared, leaving five of their own dead.[9]

Mabbitt's rangers rendezvoused with General Rusk's militiamen and the combined forces—numbering about 260 men—marched from Fort Houston on October 15. After covering about thirty miles, they reached the abandoned Kickapoo village by nightfall. Rusk's command staff included Adjutant General Hugh McLeod and Major Isaac Burton, the ranger captain who had captured Mexican schooners shortly after San Jacinto. The Texan force made camp for the night in a horseshoe bend of Kickapoo Creek about a half mile northwest of the Neches River.[10]

Around 10 P.M., Córdova's spies attempted to start a forest fire surrounding the Texan camp. The damp forest grounds refused to spread the fire, so the Texans tied off their horses in the center of camp and posted stronger guard details to keep watch. Just before daybreak on October 16, the forest around the militia camp suddenly erupted in war whoops and exploding muskets as hundreds of Indian and Mexican rebels took Rusk's men under fire. The companies of Captains William

Sadler, James Bradshaw, James Box, and Jacob Snively in the northern edge of camp took the brunt of the initial attack. Many of the rangers who had survived the previous ambush on Mabbitt's force days earlier now had their clothing ripped by rifle balls, although none were killed. Hugh McLeod felt it was the "closest shooting I ever saw to do so little execution." [11]

Thirteen Texans were wounded, including more than a quarter of Captain Bradshaw's men. John Murchison, brother-in-law to Captain Sadler, was knocked down by a musket ball that struck him in the forehead and lodged in the socket of his left eye against his eyebrow. General Rusk, angered by the hidden attackers, advanced from the camp and shouted at them to show themselves like men. After the initial firing died down, Rusk rallied his men and ordered a charge into the forest. They succeeded in scattering the Indians and Mexicans. In a running firefight that stretched for three-quarters of a mile, nearly a dozen rebels were left lying about the battlefield, including one Cherokee. The Texans estimated they may have killed as many as thirty of their opponents based on the blood trails they found after daylight. More than two dozen Texan horses were mortally wounded in the battle and one ranger, James Hall, later died from his wounds. [12]

The Battle of Kickapoo was enough to quell the Córdova Rebellion and send the leader fleeing for Mexico. The Texans regrouped at Fort Houston, where many of Rusk's militiamen headed for Nacogdoches to disband at the conclusion of the so-called Kickapoo War campaign. Captain Sadler's volunteer rangers returned to the Mustang Prairie settlement in Houston County, where Sadler and his brother-in-law had left their families in the care of several older men. They found to their horror that a party of Kickapoo Indians had descended upon the dog-trot cabin of John Edens and carried out what became known as the Edens-Madden Massacre. Ten women and children were shot, tomahawked, scalped, and burned before the cabin was torched. Captain Sadler lost his wife and infant daughter in the bloody massacre near San Pedro Creek.[13]

EAST TEXAS DID NOT possess sole ownership of the frontier violence franchise in 1838.

In Béxar County, a party of Anglo and *tejano* surveyors was attacked on October 18, and at least five of their number were killed. A thirteen-man volunteer party under Captain Benjamin Cage, a cousin to Jack Hays, set out in pursuit toward the Leon Creek massacre site. They were attacked by more than one hundred Comanche Indians. Cage and seven others were killed and four other Texans were wounded. Among those to escape was Judge Joseph L. Hood of San Antonio, who survived an arrow wound and was later elected sheriff of Béxar County.[14]

In Bastrop County, at least two settlers were killed in Indian depredations during November. In present DeWitt County, Comanches preyed upon Guadalupe River settlers, where they captured five young children on December 9. Thirteen-year-old Matilda Lockhart was out gathering pecans with four Putman children when they were seized. Elizabeth and James Putman were eventually ransomed, while their sister Juda would remain captive for fourteen years. Another of the children, Rhoda Putman, became the wife of a Comanche chief and refused to leave them. As for Matilda Lockhart, her captivity would become the focus of a major confrontation between Texan forces and the Comanche more than a year later.[15]

Tom Rusk and Hugh McLeod held peace talks with Shawnee chief Linney in late November before moving toward the

Red River to join with militiamen organized by General John Dyer and Captain Edward H. Tarrant. They pursued a band of rebel Caddos across the border of the Red River into Louisiana and forced them to surrender their firearms. The event ended without bloodshed, but the local *Natchitoches Herald* ran an article in its December 16 issue with the headline INVASION OF THE UNITED STATES BY TEXAS.[16]

Rusk's militia remained vigilant in late 1838 and even employed friendly Indians in the frontier service to serve as spies and scouts. Captain Panther of the Shawnees commanded a thirty-man unit of mounted Shawnees for three months, while another mounted ranger company was mustered in on December 24 under Captain James H. Durst. His unit was composed primarily of Cherokee Indians, with a few Caddo, Shawnee, and Anglo volunteers. Brigadier General John Dyer's Fourth Militia Brigade marched out in late November for another campaign toward the Three Forks of the Trinity near present Dallas. Indian encounters were few but the militiamen and rangers did help build various fortifications in the Red River settlements during the winter months. Rusk and Dyer managed only to destroy some abandoned Caddo villages during December before turning for home as their supplies dwindled. Rusk returned to Nacogdoches "worn down and exhausted," and obviously frustrated that his men had received little support from their government. "I fear if a decisive blow is not struck against the Indians before spring," he wrote, "we shall be much troubled with them." [17]

A major change in Indian policy was in the works during the time Rusk's men were in the field. President Mirabeau Lamar, elected as the new president of the Republic of Texas to replace Sam Houston, was inaugurated on December 10, 1838. He and

Vice President David Burnet made it clear that they would not follow President Houston's policy of pacifying the more hostile Indians of Texas. President Andrew Jackson's Indian Removal Act had forcibly removed Indian tribes from the United States east of the Mississippi River. Army forces were marching some fifteen thousand Cherokees along the so-called Trail of Tears into Indian Territory (present-day Oklahoma) during the winter of 1838–39. The new Texas president intended to be equally aggressive.

Lamar set the tone during his first speech before the Third Congress on December 21. "As long as we continue to exhibit our mercy without showing our strength," he said, "so long will the Indians continue to bloody the tomahawk and move onward in the work of rapacity and slaughter." President Lamar saw Indians as "wild cannibals" who committed killings with the "ferocity of tigers and hyenas." He denounced the 1836 land treaty of Houston with Chief Bowles and pledged to remove the Western Cherokees from Texas. Lamar promised a war of extermination to bring about "their total extinction." The Third Congress of the Republic of Texas went to work right away providing for frontier protection. New mounted ranger companies were approved for counties facing the greatest threat from Indian violence and a new regular army was authorized on December 21, 1838.

The "Frontier Regiment" was to consist of fifteen companies with a total of 840 men, funded by $300,000 in republic promissory notes. Including both infantry and cavalry, the new Texas Army would be stationed along a military road to be laid out from the Red River on the U.S. border to the Nueces River near the border with Mexico. The new leaders of the army would be commissioned during the next month.[18]

Congress additionally authorized President Lamar to use $75,000 to press eight "companies of mounted volunteers" into service for six months' ranging duty for protection against the Comanche and other hostile Indians. The commanders of this new ranging regiment were named on January 9, 1839, as Colonel Henry Karnes, Lieutenant Colonel Jerome Devereaux Woodlief, and Major William Jefferson Jones. Major Jones was ordered on January 21 to proceed with recruiting men through Columbia and Matagorda en route to Washington-on-the-Brazos.[19]

The opening weeks of 1839 were marked by serious encounters between Texas settlers and frontier Indians as these new forces were being organized. The first major confrontation occurred on the evening of January 1 on the upper Brazos River when the home of George Morgan was assaulted by a party of about fifteen Indians. They were led by Anadarko chief José María, who also commanded several Caddos, Ionies, and Kichais. They laid into their Anglo victims with fury, hacking five families to death with tomahawks and scalping knives. Four children escaped to spread the alarm, one of the daughters being severely wounded.[20]

Just two weeks after the Morgan Massacre, another party of forty Indians assaulted the fortified home of John Marlin on the Brazos River. The armed men were better able to fight back this time: they killed as many as seven of their attackers. The next morning, January 15, a fifty-two-man volunteer unit led by Captain Benjamin Franklin Bryant, an officer veteran of San Jacinto, crossed the Brazos in pursuit of the Indians. Near the plundered Morgan home they encountered Chief José María's band of Anadarkos and other allied Indians. The chief fired a rifle ball through the sleeve of volunteer Joseph Boren and then signaled for his men to attack the approaching Texans.[21]

Ranger David Campbell returned fire and his shot struck José María squarely in the breastbone. The chief stayed on his horse until another ranger, Albert Gholson, shot and killed the chief's horse. The Indians took cover in a ravine and retreated toward a densely timbered river bottom as the Texans maneuvered to cut them off. The divided volunteers suffered several men wounded in the process, and Lieutenant Ethan A. Stroud ordered his men to retreat to another point two hundred yards away. Some of the men, however, perceived this to be an order to fully retreat. Panic set in among a few of the Texans. Chief José María capitalized on the moment and ordered his Anadarkos to the charge. Eleven men of Captain Bryant's command were killed, two more were mortally wounded during the retreat, and another five were wounded. The Indians were believed to have suffered similar casualties, but they had routed the Texans in what became known as Bryant's Defeat. Years later, Chief José María visited the Bryant's Station community to smoke the peace pipe with Benjamin Bryant. The proud chief admitted that his Indians had been whipped and were retreating until he observed the confusion among the Texans.[22]

THE TEXAS MILITIA WAS strengthened in East Texas during the following weeks, and President Lamar also appointed officers to his new Frontier Regiment army in late January. Colonel Edward Burleson was elected into command of the First Regiment of Infantry with Lieutenant Colonel William S. Fisher as his second in command. Recruiting for the new army began in earnest at posts staffed in Houston, Galveston, and Matagorda. Some of the original officers of Burleson's new Frontier Regiment were seasoned veterans of service with the Texas Rangers: William T. Sadler, William H. Moore, Isaac Burton, Jacob Snively, and others.

Captain Sadler wrote to his old companion President Lamar on February 22 regarding the current crisis with the Indians. He reported the murder of his own wife, child, and related family members that had occurred in the October 1838 Edens-Madden Massacre, and of the difficulties faced in maintaining control of volunteer forces that were raised to challenge aggressive Indians. Sadler felt that more disciplined regulars were needed to quell the depredations. "We cannot check the Indians unless we follow them to their place of rendezvous or where they have their families and visit them with the same kind of warfare that they give us," wrote Sadler. "We should spare neither age, sect nor condition, for they do not. I know it will be said this is barbarous and too much like the savage. And it certainly is harsh, but it is the only means in my view that will put them down." [23]

The Comanches were already being visited with the very violence that Sadler proposed. Colonel John Henry Moore departed La Grange on January 26 with a 109-man expedition to attack a band of Comanches reported on the San Gabriel River. His force included Captain Noah Smithwick's Bastrop County Rangers, Captain William Eastland's La Grange Rangers, twelve friendly Tonkawa Indians under Chief Castro, and forty-two Lipans led by Chief Flaco. Moore's rangers found and attacked a Comanche village on the San Saba River on the morning of February 15.

His men rushed through the Indian camp, shooting down Comanches sleeping in their wigwams. The Texans were soon forced into a deep ravine by the regrouped Comanches, who made two strong offensive charges against Moore's men. The opposing forces met under a white flag of truce to parley late in the day in hopes of exchanging prisoners. No agreements were made, but the Comanches were whipped. They allowed the Texans to retreat from the battlefield that night on foot since the Indians had managed to steal all of the rangers' horses during the early moments of the battle. The rangers lost one man killed and a handful of wounded in exchange for having killed more than one hundred Comanches. Although Moore had carried out what amounted to a slaughter in the Indian village, the fact that he lost his horses and opted to retreat home on foot left many to consider his Comanche expedition to have been a defeat. Captain Smithwick, for one, deemed the entire affair a "disastrous expedition." [24]

The Comanches mourned their losses for one week, and then rode south to seek the revenge that their culture demanded. On February 24, they attacked the cabin of Elizabeth Coleman—widow of the late ranger commander Robert Coleman—about twelve miles above Bastrop near the Colorado River. They killed the widow and one of her sons and took another son prisoner. The Comanches then proceeded to the home of Dr. Joseph Robertson, where they carried away seven slaves. Word of the Indians on the warpath was spread quickly among the settlements, and two volunteer companies were assembled to counter the Comanches—fifty-two settlers led by Captains James Rogers and Jacob Burleson, the latter a brother of Colonel Ed Burleson. [25]

The Texans made contact with the Comanches about twenty-five miles north of the Colorado River near Brushy Creek on February 25. Captain Burleson ordered his men to dismount to fire with their long rifles but the Comanches quickly charged upon them on horseback. Most of the Texans regained their mounts and escaped, but Burleson was shot in the back of the head as he stopped to help a fourteen-year-old volunteer to escape. Believing they had downed the hated Colonel Burleson, the Comanches scalped Jacob Burleson, cut off his right hand and his right foot, and removed his heart.[26]

The surviving volunteers retreated from the numerically superior Comanche force but they were joined in the afternoon by another large party of volunteers hastily assembled near Bastrop by Colonel Ed Burleson. With eighty-four men, he rode to Brushy Creek, where they found the Indians maintaining a defensive position in the steep-banked creek bed. Captains Rogers and Jesse Billingsley led their men into the creek beds to drive the Comanche out, but they found their foes well entrenched. The Texans and Comanches engaged in a sniping contest throughout the late afternoon in a fight that became known as the Battle of Brushy Creek. Three more Texans were killed and several others were wounded by nightfall. Burleson estimated that his men killed or wounded at least thirty Comanche in the fight.[27]

COLONEL BURLESON'S FRONTIER REGIMENT, authorized for fifteen companies of infantry and cavalry, was unable to muster more than four companies at any point during the first half of 1839. President Lamar thus put out a requisition on six southern Texas counties to help fill out the Mounted Rifleman Battalion for six months under Colonel Henry Karnes. Other support came in the form of the individual county ranger companies that the Texas Congress had also sanctioned.[28]

One of the new menaces was the return of Vicente Córdova, who had led the East Texas rebellion in 1838. He departed the upper Trinity River region in March with plans to move to Matamoros to meet with Mexican agent Manuel Flores and

General Valentin Canalizo, who had succeeded General Filisola as commander at Matamoros. En route with about fifty-three Mexicans, half a dozen Biloxi Indians, and five runaway slaves, Córdova's force was spotted on March 27 at the foot of the Colorado River hills. Colonel Burleson quickly organized two Texas Ranger companies commanded by Captain Jesse Billingsley of Bastrop and Captain Micah Andrews of La Grange.[29]

Burleson set out on March 28 with seventy-nine rangers and volunteers to pursue Córdova's force. They caught up with them before sundown the next day on Mill Creek near the Guadalupe River. Burleson immediately formed a battle line, sending Captain Andrews's company to the right and Billingsley's to the left. Córdova's men fought back in the initial firefight but broke and ran when the Colorado-area Texans made a full charge. Dr. James Fentress managed to wing Córdova himself with a shot through his arm. At least eighteen of Córdova's rebels were killed in the Mill Creek fight, and Burleson's rangers managed to round up nineteen prisoners in the aftermath. Of greater importance to Colonel Burleson were the correspondence papers of Córdova that his men seized.[30]

Córdova's men retreated up the Guadalupe River in search of a crossing point. During the early morning of March 30, his party encountered five of Captain Mathew Caldwell's Gonzales County Rangers returning from a scouting party. The rangers were sound asleep when some of Córdova's men slipped into their camp and stole their horses. Ranger James Milford Day was awakened by the snorting of the horses, and he quickly shot an Indian who was untying his horse. Day was shot in the left hip and left seriously wounded while Dave Reynolds suffered a hit just below his collarbone by another musket ball. Córdova's men fled across the river toward the present Austin area while the rangers struggled back toward the settlements to spread the alarm. Captain Caldwell's rangers, a group of Gonzales volunteers, and cavalrymen under Henry Karnes pursued the Córdova gang to the Nueces River before giving up the chase.[31]

Karnes remained stationed in the San Antonio area while the first of his new mounted gunmen companies moved up from the Houston area. Major William Jones held supervising command of these first two ranger companies under Captains Mark B. Lewis, a veteran of the 1835 Béxar siege, and San Jacinto veteran James P. Ownby. Karnes placed this detachment on the Colorado River to help protect the men who were surveying and building Austin, the new capital city of Texas.

Mexican Indian agent Manuel Flores, ignorant of the running fights Vicente Córdova's men had been engaged in, departed Matamoros in late April to attempt a rendezvous. Traveling with about thirty Mexicans and Indians, Flores committed several depredations. On May 14, they attacked a surveying party's camp near San Antonio. Lieutenant James Rice and another ranger spotted the Flores party the next day and the company of Captain Micah Andrews set out to intercept the rebels. They caught up to Flores near the San Gabriel River. Andrews, a heavyset man, found his horse too worn down to keep up with the constant riding. Rice and sixteen other rangers maintained a fast pursuit of the fleeing Mexicans and Indians, and they engaged in a gunfight late on May 17. Flores and two of his men perished in the brief exchange.[32]

The victorious rangers rounded up extra horses, mules, ammunition, baggage, and other belongings of the Flores party as they fled the scene. On the body of Manuel Flores they found a quantity of important papers detailing the secret agreements between General Canalizo, Vicente Córdova, and chiefs of various Indian tribes. The letters, passed along to Colonel Burleson and Vice President Johnston, showed that Flores and Córdova had been commissioned by Mexican authorities to "harass the Texans persistently, burn their habitations, lay waste their fields, [and] steal their horses." Evidence showed that Flores had contacted chiefs of the Caddos, Kickapoos, Shawnees, Cherokees, and other tribes. In fairness to Cherokee leaders Bowles and Big Mush, there were no reply letters from them, but it was enough to help President Lamar to justify strong actions against the Texas Cherokees.[33]

Lamar ordered Major Baley Walters to take two companies of rangers to occupy the Neches Saline just inside the Cherokees' claim and close to the village of Chief Bowles. Walters and his rangers established Fort Kickapoo at the old Indian village, close to the site of the previous year's Indian battle. Bowles ordered the Texans away from his area, an action that compelled Lamar to call up all available military forces in earnest. Lamar sent a small party to meet with Bowles on May 26, warning the Cherokee leader that his threats were an error that would lead to his ruin if he further challenged the rangers sent into his territory.[34]

John Henninger Reagan, a twenty-one-year-old ranger who was among the messenger party, recalled: "Bowles stated that he could not make a definite answer as to abandoning the country until he could consult his chiefs and head men. So, it was agreed that he might have time for such a consultation . . . about ten days was the limit set." Both sides agreed to meet again in early June. Mirabeau Lamar used that time to mobilize his East Texas militia and to order in Colonel Burleson's Frontier Regiment and Lieutenant Colonel Devereaux Woodlief's Austin-area mounted gunmen. A showdown with the Texas Cherokees looked to be inevitable.[35]

FARTHER WEST, TEXAS RANGERS were engaged in other action.

Captain John Bird's rangers from Austin and Fort Bend counties were stationed at Fort Smith on the Little River. He and several of his men encountered a small party of Indians on the morning of May 26. Bird quickly gathered a portion of his company and a dozen rangers from the command of Lieutenant William G. Evans's "Travis Spies" company to take up the pursuit. The Indians were determined to be an allied force of Caddo, Kickapoo, and Comanche. Bird followed them for about eleven miles and made an attempt to charge them. His men could not get closer than 175 yards due to the speed of the Indian horsemen. He finally ordered his men to turn back, but they found themselves surrounded a half mile later.

The thirty-five Texans took shelter in a welcomed ravine (later named Bird's Creek). The Comanches were led by a war chief named Buffalo Hump, who wore a buffalo hide war bonnet complete with horns. He moved his Indians to a nearby hilltop to hold a council of war and to call for reinforcements. The Comanches were soon estimated to number about 250, many of whom began stripping down to prepare for battle. Buffalo Hump then led his warriors down with terrifying war whoops in a heated advance that lasted a half hour. The Comanches then formed their horses into single file and rode circles around the Texans in the creek bed, taunting them.[36]

Dutch-born ranger William Winkler took cool aim and shot one of the Comanche leaders from his horse. The other rangers shouted hurrahs and blasted away with their rifles until the Indians retreated to the hilltop to regroup. Buffalo Hump made a second charge twenty minutes later. In it the Comanches managed to kill and wound several of the rangers while taking heavy losses of their own. As the Indians fell back a second time, Captain Bird leapt from the creek to encourage his men. In the process, he was shot through the heart by an arrow launched by an Indian from the incredible distance of two hundred yards—making it one of the luckiest, or best, shots of the Texas Indian wars.

By this point, half of the ranger officers had been killed or wounded. Command fell upon Nathan Brookshire, a forty-six-year-old veteran of both the Creek Indian Wars and the War of 1812. He encouraged his men on when the Comanches made a third charge to within the edges of the creek banks. The Texans wisely withheld their fire until the last instant and this time shot down many of their attackers. With evening approaching, the Indians withdrew again to their ridge top, where the rangers could see Chief Buffalo Hump urging his men for a final attempt in dramatic fashion. His Indians had suffered many losses, however, and he found few willing to make another ride into the face of the deadly Texan long rifles. Undeterred, Buffalo Hump gathered about a dozen of his men and started down the hill to assault the rangers once again.

The chief rode to within several paces of the Texan position, fired his gun, and then wheeled his horse around while raising his defensive shield to cover his body. Buffalo Hump left only his head and neck exposed, but it was enough. German ranger James W. Robinett fired a rifle ball through the Comanche leader's neck, dropping him instantly from his horse. The remaining Indians put themselves in grave danger to retrieve the body of their fallen leader, and many of them were shot down in the process. The ornamental buffalo skin and horns were likely a sign of command, as this headdress would be worn in subsequent years by another Comanche chief known as Buffalo Hump.

The Comanche and their allies moved off under cover of darkness to mourn their losses. Brookshire and his men escaped through the forest that night and reached Fort Smith during the early morning hours of May 27, having lost five men killed. In return, they claimed as many as forty Indians killed and many more wounded. The battle, known as Bird's Victory, was the first serious repulse of a numerically superior Indian force. Its effect was much celebrated among the Texas settlers.

San Antonio–area surveyor and frontier scout Jack Hays was involved in his own Indian encounters during June 1839. Although no muster rolls have survived, Captain Hays reportedly took command of a small force of rangers in February in response to President Lamar's appeal for frontier volunteers. One of his men, Charles Wilkins Webber, described Hays as "a slight, raw-boned figure, with a lean Roman face, and an expression of modest simplicity." Unsophisticated and good-natured, the clean-faced Hays stood out among his rougher-looking volunteers. Many wore buckskin suits, with colorful serapes draped about their shoulders and Mexican sombreros on their heads. The rangers were a picturesque lot, smoking Mexican cigarettes atop their horses with braces of pistols and knives tucked into their waist belts.[37]

In late May, several Béxar citizens and surveyors were killed. Colonel Henry Karnes organized two volunteer companies in San Antonio on June 6 in response to orders from President Lamar to go fight the Comanches who were committing depredations in the area. The companies were under Captains Louis Franks and Juan Seguín. Jack Hays attached himself to the company of Captain Franks to serve as a scout. The Indians fled westward ahead of the Texan force as it scouted high above the forks of the Medina River toward the Frio River. On June 19, they found recent encampments where the Comanches were driving large herds of horses. Jack Hays led a little squad out farther to scout around Canyon de Uvalde, where they destroyed several deserted Indian villages and killed a few Indians in brief encounters. Mary Ann Maverick wrote that the Karnes force returned to San Antonio on June 23 "with some Indian ponies, dreadfully ragged, dirty, and hungry." [38]

IN THE EAST, TEXAS military forces were meeting with Cherokee chief Bowles during early June. As the peace talks continued, President Lamar mobilized his army toward East Texas. From Bastrop, Colonel Burleson marched with two regular companies plus Lieutenant Colonel Woodlief and two of his volunteer ranging companies under Captains Mark Lewis and James Ownby. On June 27, Lamar appointed a five-man special commission to deal with the Cherokee crisis: Major General Rusk, Vice President David Burnet, Secretary of War Albert Sidney Johnston, Isaac Burton, and James S. Mayfield. He authorized them to make compensations for the Indians' improvements but to pay them no more than one-fourth of the agreed-upon value in cash. [39]

Rusk and his Nacogdoches militia companies reached Major Walters's Fort Kickapoo camp during the first days of July. They were joined by additional companies of General Douglass's regiment while Colonel Willis Landrum marched toward the area with an additional 262 Third Regiment militiamen raised near the Red River. Colonel Hugh McLeod and several officers opened a round of peace talks with Bowles on July 9, as the size of the Texan camp swelled to roughly 550 men. During the ensuing days, Thomas Rusk advised the Indian leaders that his troops intended no harm unless they were forced to fight. He cautioned Chief Bowles that if his people persisted in being friendly with "the wild Indians and Mexicans, we will be forced to kill your people in defense of our frontier." Rusk made it clear that the Cherokees were "between two fires" and that if Bowles chose to remain, "you will be destroyed."[40]

On July 12, Bowles stated that his tribe intended to leave peacefully but would need time to prepare for such a journey. Spy Buck, representing Shawnee chief Linney, said that his people would need three moons' time, or about two months, to prepare. The commissioners advised him this was far too long but that they would be given ample time to prepare for their move. The parties agreed to meet again in two days, when it was hoped that Chief Big Mush of the Cherokees and the Delaware chief would be present to sign a peace treaty.

General Rusk used this time to organize more companies by sending a rider back to Nacogdoches. A final meeting was held at Council Creek on July 14 between Rusk, Johnston, Burnet, Burton, and Mayfield for Texas and Bowles and twenty Indians. Rusk noted that Bowles, Chief Key, and the other Indian leaders carried war clubs and had painted their faces black with war paint. David Burnet read an agreement, while interpreter Cordray explained the terms to the leaders. The Cherokees, Delawares, and Shawnees were to leave in peace with payment for their improvements and they were to surrender their gun locks to the Texan troops until they had crossed into the United States.[41]

Bowles refused to sign the treaty. He said he would present the demands to the other chiefs and would give Mayfield an answer the following morning. The Indians were likely discouraged from further negotiations by the arrival of Colonel Burleson's regulars on May 14. Added to Colonel Landrum's Red River troops, General Rusk's numbers had surpassed eleven hundred in camp—more Texans than had been available to engage Santa Anna at the Battle of San Jacinto. Rusk, head of the militia, and Burleson, leader of the Texas Army, refused to oppose each other, so they made an agreement to let General Kelsey Douglass—the regional commander of the Third Militia Brigade—take overall command.

Colonel Mayfield rode to the Indian campgrounds on July 15 with four other men to have the Cherokee treaty signed. Bowles informed them that his men were afraid that they would be killed as soon as they surrendered their gun locks. Mayfield warned the Indian leaders that the Texas Army would march against them this day if they refused. Bowles promised to keep the Texans informed as to their movements, and he followed through on this vow around noon on July 15. His son, John Bowles, and a half-breed Cherokee named Fox Fields rode in under a truce flag to inform commissioner Albert Sidney Johnston that the Cherokees were breaking camp to move to the west side of the Neches River.[42]

General Douglass put his Texan troops in motion and sent Colonel Landrum's regiment to the east side of the Neches to move upriver. The Indians were believed to have moved sixteen miles away to the Delaware village of Chief Harris. The first to arrive found the village abandoned, however, and they followed the trail of the retreating large body of Indians. Captain James Carter's spies located the Indians about three and a half miles northwest of the present town of Chandler, west of the Neches River. Carter sent a rider back to alert command while advance groups of Thomas Rusk's began exchanging shots with the Indians.[43]

Ed Burleson quickly arrived with his regular army soldiers and the two mounted gunmen companies under Lieutenant Colonel Woodlief. They made a determined push against the

Indian forces, who were occupying a ravine and thicket near the body of water that became known as Battle Creek. "You would have thought our men were mad," recalled William Hart of Captain Peter Tipps's mounted Nacogdoches volunteer company. Hart felt his own hollering was as loud as any of the war whoops being emitted by the Indians he faced.[44]

The Indians put up heavy fire as the Texans charged the creek bed. Four Texans were mortally wounded and eight others were injured. Two of Captain George T. Howard's regular soldiers crumpled with fatal head shots. John Crane, a member of Henry Karnes's Mounted Rifleman Battalion, paused his horse near the creek as one of his companions, John S. Caddell, hollered that an Indian was taking aim at him. Crane's horse reared up and the Indian's rifle ball struck him under the right arm just under his heart. Crane, who had commanded a company during the 1835 Béxar siege, fell from his horse and died almost instantly. "By that time, I shot the Indian, killing him," said Caddell.[45]

The Cherokees and their allies were driven from their defensive positions, and they fled the battlefield as darkness fell over Battle Creek. The main fighting had lasted little more than a quarter hour. General Douglass reported that eighteen Indian bodies were found on the field and that many other casualties of theirs were seen to be carried away. The Texans seized five kegs of gunpowder, 250 pounds of lead, as well as horses, cattle, and corn the Indians left behind. The Texans set up camp for the night on the battlefield, naming it Camp Carter in honor of Jim Carter's spies.

Chief Bowles and his Cherokees retreated up the Neches River during the predawn hours of July 16. They reached the Delaware village of Chief Harris while the Texans tended to their wounded. The Texan forces saddled up around 10 A.M.

and rode toward the Delaware camp. Captain Carter's spies were again first to spot their adversaries, on a small hilltop overlooking the Neches River. Colonel Burleson's battalion reached the Delaware town around midday. Rifles were already cracking as Carter's scouts exchanged shots with the Cherokees.

Burleson's regulars were taken under heavy fire before they could even dismount. Seven horses and one soldier fell to the Indian guns but General Rusk soon joined the action with the first two companies of his Nacogdoches volunteers. The Texans set fire to the Delaware village. The towering flames quickly added to the misery of the mid-July heat. Bowles and his men were forced into a dry creek bed below the burning village as more of General Douglass's troops reached the scene. Douglass ordered every sixth man to be left behind to guard their horses as he took the majority of his men to sweep around the Indians and their area of entrenchment.

Douglass, Rusk, and Burleson faced approximately six hundred Indians: Cherokees, Delawares, Shawnees, Kickapoos, Quapaws, Choctaws, Biloxis, Ionies, Alabamas, Coushattas, Caddoes, Mataquos, and Tahocullakes. During the next ninety minutes, the Texans attempted three charges upon the Indians' creek bed. Several men were killed and others were wounded in the heavy exchange of gunfire. The heat caused many to suffer from dehydration under the broiling afternoon sun, and the Cherokees nearly succeeded at one point in stampeding the Texan horses. "Under a scorching meridian sun, we again met a rallied enemy," said volunteer ranger Peter Rodden. "The captain of my company was shot down on the first onset. Confusion spread among the ranks, the Indians on three sides of us." [46]

Several doctors moved carefully about the battlefield, tending to their wounded comrades. Kelsey Douglass finally ordered an all-out charge upon the Indians, which was carried out by rangers, regular soldiers, and militiamen alike. This time the Texans did not turn back, and they forced Chief Bowles's men into great panic. Indians fled through the nearby cornfields toward the Neches River bottomlands below. Bowles remained valiantly on horseback, in plain view. He wore a military hat, a silk vest, a sash presented to him years before by Sam Houston, and a fine military sword on his side. "He was a magnificent picture of barbaric manhood and was very conspicuous during the whole battle," wrote militiaman John Reagan.[47]

The fine sorrel horse ridden by Bowles had four white feet and a blaze face. As his forces retreated, the chief became the object of fire for many Texans. His horse collapsed with seven bullet wounds and Bowles suffered a bullet wound through his leg. As the Cherokee leader stumbled away from his fallen mount, ranger Henry C. Conner shot him through the back with a buck and ball load. Captain William Sadler, commanding one of Burleson's regular companies, was given credit by some with having scored one of the musket shots that wounded the eighty-three-year-old chief. Bowles pulled himself up to a sitting position, still clutching his sword, a Bowie knife, and a holster of pistols. Captain Bob Smith approached Bowles.[48]

John Reagan hoped that the chief might be taken as a prisoner as he watched his captain advance. Smith's father-in-law had been murdered by Indians in 1838, however, and he had no sympathy for the gravely wounded Cherokee leader.

"Captain, don't shoot him!" Reagan cried out.

Smith had already pulled his belt pistol. Militia volunteer William Hart recalled, "Bob Smith shot him above the eye with a pistol." Smith then took the prized sword while others removed his red military jacket and even his scalp. Hart collected the bloodstained saddle from Bowles's fallen horse to add to his own bareback mount. The final minutes of the Cherokee battle near the Neches River saw as many as one hundred Indians killed, including Chief Big Mush of the Cherokees. The remainder of the Indians fled the area as darkness soon closed over the battlefield.[49]

Four Texans had perished in the July 16 battle, while another twenty lay wounded, including Adjutant General Hugh McLeod, Vice President Burnet, and Secretary of War Johnston. McLeod suffered an arrow through his thigh, while militia leader Hugh Augustine took another arrow through his leg that would require it to be amputated at the knee. Against the wishes of many of his men, General Douglass ordered pursuit of the fleeing Indians to be halted for the night. The Cherokee War, as this campaign came to be known, was deemed by supporters of President Lamar to be the second most important conflict fought on Texas soil after San Jacinto. Sam Houston and other Indian advocates were openly critical of Tom Rusk and other leaders of the Cherokee campaign.[50]

The body of Chief Bowles, mutilated by some who wished to keep souvenirs, would lie unburied on the Cherokee battleground for years. The combined force of Texas Army, Texas Militia, and Texas Rangers spent the next days following the trail of the slowly retreating Indian survivors, burning villages they found along the way. Bodies of some of those who had perished following the battle were found along the trail for miles like discarded baggage. The Texans countermarched back into the old Cherokee Nation and began disbanding many of their companies in early August.[51]

Leaders of the Shawnees agreed to a peace treaty in the wake of the Cherokee War. They were paid for their improvements and given about two months to prepare for their journey to the United States. With their gun locks removed, they were escorted to the border and removed from Texas without any further bloodshed. The Texas Cherokees remained splintered. The majority of the survivors crossed into the southeastern portion of Indian Territory to settle in what would become Oklahoma. Other small groups, including Chief John Bowles (son of the martyred leader), remained in Texas to face future confrontations with the white people.

The Cherokee War was the greatest assembly of troops to deal with an Indian crisis in Texas history to that point, and the most expensive. The tab for paying the Third Militia Brigade under General Douglass alone amounted to $21,000. Ed Burleson removed most of his Frontier Regiment men back toward the Colorado River settlements to regroup before making his next Indian campaign. The cost of maintaining President Lamar's new Texas Army was going to be hefty. Estimated funds to maintain Burleson's staff, five companies of cavalry, and fifteen companies of infantry were tabulated to be $306,649. The land cost was equally high for Texas. Since the commencement of issuing bounties in 1837 through September 30, 1839, Albert Sidney Johnston reported that more than four million acres of Texas land had been issued in certificates of claim to donation and bounty lands for military service.[52]

Small county ranger companies were maintained through the fall of 1839 in areas that were deemed most needy of protection from frontier marauders. The Texas Militia was still struggling to organize companies. Adjutant General Hugh McLeod found that by October, only sixteen of the Republic of Texas's thirty-one counties had submitted complete muster rolls of their companies. Eight other counties merely submitted proof that companies had been formed.

Texas Army strength had reached 440 men by early December, at which time Secretary of War Johnston decided that the

Frontier Regiment was strong enough to conduct its first major campaign since the Cherokee War. Colonel Ed Burleson moved out from Austin on December 16 with four of his infantry companies, one small company of mounted scouts under Captain Mathew Caldwell, and two large companies of friendly Indian scouts—members of the Lipan tribe under Chief Castro and Tonkawa scouts commanded by Chief Placido. The Frontier Regiment expedition marched up the San Gabriel River, past the Lampasas River, and was about one hundred miles northwest of Austin by Christmas Eve.[53]

Burleson's scouts located an Indian camp on the Colorado River that day and he moved his men into position to attack the next morning. His men had located a small detachment of Cherokees led by Chiefs Egg and John Bowles, whose men were attempting to reach Mexico by passing beyond the outermost white settlements. The Texans approached the Cherokee camp on December 25 and took the Indian prisoner who came out to meet with them. The remaining Cherokees immediately took flight and a general fight ensued. Six Indians were killed, including both Cherokee chiefs. More than two dozen Indian women and children were captured. Burleson's force suffered one wounded Tonkawa and the loss of scout John Lynch of Caldwell's spy company, who received a fatal shot through his chest. The Texas Army had broken up the last major faction of Bowles's Cherokees and spent the last week of 1839 scouring the Texas Hill Country for signs of any more Indians willing to give them a fight. Burleson described his final Cherokee battle on Christmas Day as a "short but decisive affair."[54]

AUSTIN, THE NEW CAPITAL city of Texas, was becoming a boomtown by October 1839. President Lamar and his cabinet transferred the seat of government there during the first of the month and Colonel Burleson's regular army largely took up station in the area that month to construct more blockhouses.

With the Cherokees and Shawnees largely removed, Indian troubles in central and western Texas became more frequent with the Comanches. Captain George Howard fought a skirmish with them on October 24 with portions of his Company D of the First Regiment and a detachment of Captain William H. Moore's Company C. His men killed three Comanches and three of their horses against no losses to the regular soldiers.[55]

The following day, October 25, a Texan regiment of mounted gunmen attacked an Indian village. President Lamar had authorized the regiment in late August for the purpose of conducting a campaign to the upper Brazos River against hostile Indians who had been plaguing the Austin-area settlers. Henry Karnes, the former mounted gunman battalion commander, had resigned his commission by the time Lamar's new battalion was organized in September. Colonel John C. Neill of Harrisburg was chosen by his volunteers to lead the new battalion. His command included six mounted companies, a fifteen-man artillery company, and a twenty-nine-man mounted spy company under Captain John Tumlinson—in all, more than four hundred men.

Colonel Neill's companies proceeded up the Trinity River and moved across the Brazos at the town of old Nashville. They proceeded to the Falls of the Brazos to the old Waco village, and then to the Indian village of Anadarko chief José María, victor of the January Bryant's Fight battle. The Indians largely fled the village, save one Ioni chief who was killed. The Texans looted all worthwhile camp equipage and about forty Indian ponies before continuing their campaign up the Brazos. Tumlinson's spies captured an Indian woman and her two children as the expedition continued to track Indians who were fleeing ahead of them. Near the Clear Fork of the Trinity River, Neill's battalion fought a battle on November 5. Two Comanches were killed. The Texan lost a dozen horses shot by the Indians and Private Laban Menefee was hit in the thigh by an arrow.[56]

Neill's gunmen moved southeast after the battle toward Parker's Fort. Two members of Captain Henry Reed's company were shot and killed by Indians on Richland Creek after they departed the main group of Texans. Colonel Neill marched his companies back toward the settlements and allowed his companies to disband in late November, having fulfilled Lamar's wishes to take an offensive campaign out into the prairies to where the Indians lived.

Another expedition went out from San Antonio during the time that John Neill's men were on the campaign. Henry Karnes, having resigned his commission as colonel of mounted gunmen, returned to San Antonio in late summer 1839 and began organizing men to join him on an expedition against the Comanches. During September, he helped organize a forty-six-man company of *tejanos* and Anglo Texans in San Antonio. Captain José María Gonzales was elected into command of the largely *tejano* ranger company. It did include a few Anglo surveyors and former rangers such as Jack Hays. On September 24, Colonel Karnes met up with Captain William F. Wilson's Galveston Mounted Gunmen, who had orders to join him in San Antonio for an expedition. Karnes and the Wilson company reached San Antonio on October 3 after traveling some 215 miles from Houston.[57]

Captain Wilson's Galveston Mounted Gunmen remained on station in San Antonio for two weeks while Karnes attended to business. The men amused themselves by enjoying fandangos at night. The streets were lighted and men and women enjoyed the festive music, and dancing that ranged from waltzes to the Virginia reel. Wilson's rangers camped within a mile of the San Antonio River, but crafty Comanches were able to slip in during the night and steal three of their horses. Several rangers set out in pursuit, and managed to kill one Indian and recover one horse.

On October 20, Colonel Karnes moved his expedition out from San Antonio with the companies of Captain Gonzales and Captain Wilson. They headed for the Hill Country near the San Saba River. The terrain made for rugged travel through dense juniper brush and rocky passes. Two men were wounded in accidental discharges of guns and both of them eventually died from their wounds. One week into the expedition, two men were already dead and no hostile Indians had even been sighted. Food became a serious concern in this rugged, open country beyond the Pedernales River. The men gathered wild pecans and killed a buffalo and several bear to sustain themselves.

Near the present town of Fredericksburg on November 1, one of the advance spies of Captain Gonzales's company raced into camp to announce that he had spotted Indians. The *tejanos* of the San Antonio company were greatly alarmed and refused to leave camp. Jack Hays gathered three other scouts from his company and headed out to reconnoiter the enemy. Hays located the Indian camp as darkness fell and then had his men quietly crawl forward until they could make out the Indians near their fire. Hays had his men cover him while he crawled to within eighty yards and made a count. The Comanches had quality horses and numbered about thirty men under one of their prominent chiefs, Isomania.[58]

Hays and his men fell back to the main Texas camp to report to Henry Karnes. Half of the Texans were left to guard their own camp and horses, while Karnes sent Hays, his small spy group, and half of Captain Wilson's company back to attack the Comanche camp. They crept up on Chief Isomania's sleeping Indians an hour before daybreak. Surprise was foiled when one of the Comanche horses became alarmed and began making noise. The surprised Indians grabbed their weapons and the shoot-out began. "The Indians were taken by surprise," said Hays, "and thought more of flight than fight." Twelve Comanches were killed and Chief Isomania was shot through with two lead balls. The other Indians fled, leaving the Texans to pilfer their camp goods and some forty mules and horses.

Chief Isomania lay heavily wounded on the ground for two more days. "His countrymen recovered him and he was soon restored to health," Hays related. "He afterwards came to Bexar and there related his fate, stating that he had lain dead three days, and then came to life." The expedition remained in the field, moving toward the Llano River, but the colder weather and lack of proper food supplies soon began taking their toll. Colonel Karnes, still not fully recovered from an arrow wound he had sustained in his Comanche fight on the Arroyo Seco thirteen months prior, fell ill. Jack Hays and his Anglo surveyors decided to head for Austin on their own on November 10. The balance of the group began breaking up during the next week. Karnes, Gonzales, and the remaining men made their way back to San Antonio on November 21 after an exhausting month of marching through trying conditions.[59]

18

WAR WITH THE COMANCHES

WAR ON THE TEXAS frontiers in 1840 became primarily focused on the Comanches.

Colonel Henry Karnes was still recovering in San Antonio from his most recent Indian expedition when three Comanche riders entered town on January 9, 1840. They were members of the Penateka ("Honey Eaters") tribe, one of a dozen regional Comanche bands that had migrated to the North Texas plains almost 150 years prior. As many as forty thousand Comanches had inhabited Texas soil in the 1780s, but epidemics including cholera had reduced their number by the late 1830s to about twelve thousand.[1]

The Comanche representatives expressed the desires of their people to make peace with the Texans and offered up a young boy who had been captured in 1836. Karnes agreed to meet with their leaders but made it clear that any other American captives must be released before any agreements could be

made. After the Penateka Comanches departed w
tomary gifts, Karnes sent word to Albert Sidney J
he recommended San Antonio be reinforced with enough men
to apprehend the Indian leaders if the upcoming negotiations
did not go as planned.[2]

Colonel William Fisher, who had inherited command of
the Texas Army from Ed Burleson just days earlier, moved to
San Antonio to oversee the pending negotiations. Fisher made
his intentions clear: the Comanches were not to come into
town without bringing all of their prisoners. It was not until
March 19, 1840, that the Comanches rode into San Antonio
with about sixty-five men, women, and children of the tribe.
They brought with them only one prisoner—fifteen-year-old
Matilda Lockhart, the niece of early Texas Ranger captain
Byrd Lockhart who had been taken captive in December 1838.

Matilda was not a pretty sight to behold. The young girl's
body was a mass of bruises, sores, and scars where her flesh
had been burned. San Antonio resident Mary Ann Maverick
was shocked to see that the teenager's nose had been "burnt
off to the bone. Both nostrils were wide open and denuded of
flesh." The younger Comanches and the women of the tribe remained in the courthouse yard, while the twelve senior leaders
of the Comanches were led into the San Antonio Courthouse.
This one-story stone building, built in the 1740s, would become
known as the "Council House" for the Comanche negotiations.
The Texan leaders present to lead the talks were Colonel Fisher,
Colonel Hugh McLeod, and Colonel William Cooke, the acting secretary of war at the time. All three officers were staunch
supporters of President Lamar's Indian policies.[3]

The Texas commissioners proceeded to question the twelve
Comanche chiefs within the Council House. They firmly believed that more than a dozen other white captives were in the

possession of the Comanches, who had brought in only Matilda Lockhart. The abused teenager was brought in for questioning, and she told the panel that she had seen several other prisoners within camp just days before. "They brought her in to see if they could get a high price for her, and, if so, they intended to bring in the rest, one at a time," McLeod related. Colonel Fisher turned to Chief Muguara and asked where the other twelve captives were being held. Muguara told the commissioners his tribe had brought in the only prisoner they had. "The others are with the other tribes." [4]

McLeod, Cook, and Fisher sat silent as they soaked in what was an obvious lie.

"How do you like the answer?" Chief Muguara finally said.

Colonel Fisher then ordered one of his regular army companies into the council room to prevent anyone from leaving and had another company take station near the rear of the Council House where the younger Comanches were gathered. He then had his translator tell the twelve chiefs in proper Penateka tongue that they were now prisoners of Texas and would be held as such until all of their prisoners were brought into San Antonio. Seconds later, the Council House erupted into violence.

One of the Comanche chiefs tried to make it out the back door, stabbing a Frontier Regiment soldier in the process. Captain George Howard seized another of the chiefs but was stabbed in his side. One of Howard's men shot and killed the chief before even more hell broke loose. The Comanches drew their knives and bows, ready to fight to the end. Muskets and belt pistols exploded within the tight confines of the old stone courthouse. Lieutenant William Dunnington was shot through with an arrow but discharged his pistol into a Comanche chief's face before he collapsed. Judge John Hemphill defended himself by disemboweling another Comanche leader with his Bowie knife. Once the shouts and gun smoke died down, several Texans lay dead or wounded alongside the bodies of all twelve Comanche leaders.

The war whoops from within the Council House were understood instantly by the younger Indians outside. The Comanches used their bows and arrows, plus a few rifles, in fighting that quickly spread through the streets and into some San Antonio homes. Seven Texans were killed. Another eight lay wounded, including former ranger captain Mathew Caldwell, who was shot in the leg. Hugh McLeod reported that thirty-five Comanches were killed, including three women and two children. Another twenty-nine were rounded up as prisoners and locked in the city jail. Comanches were known to avoid capture, so the Texas commissioners were certainly aware of how violent the matter might become if they tried to arrest these Indian leaders.

The so-called Council House Fight marked the first limited use of a powerful new firearm in Texas, carried by Colonel Lysander Wells and several of his cavalrymen. His men had just taken possession of new Colt "Patent Arms" repeating revolvers, manufactured in Paterson, New Jersey, by Samuel Colt's Patent Arms Manufacturing Company. Many of the one-thousand production run of Colt's Patent No. 5 were shipped to Texas for the use of its army, and they became commonly known as the Texas Patersons. This five-shooter was a light-caliber (from .28 to .36) cap-and-ball firearm with a four-and-one-half-inch octagonal barrel. The Texas Paterson could discharge five rounds as fast as the shooter could work the hammer and trigger. Ill-trained on how to operate the new Colt, Wells and his men a few Comanches with the new repeating revolver in the frenzied initial combat. In time, however, the Colt five-shooter would earn respect on the Texas frontiers.[5]

Chief Muguara was the most influential leader of the twelve Penateka Comanche chiefs killed in the Council House Fight, but few of the senior Comanche chiefs were present in San Antonio. When word spread to these leaders and to their affiliated bands, the massacre in San Antonio caused great anger to sweep through the Comanches. Nine days after the shoot-out, a war party of at least two hundred Comanches rode into San Antonio looking for a fight. They were led by Chief Isomania, who had recovered from his near-fatal wounds inflicted by Jack Hays and his men months earlier.[6]

Isomania, nearly naked with his body streaked in war paint, rode up to the Mission San José and demanded that Captain William Redd's Frontier Regiment soldiers come out and fight. Hoping to still secure the release of other American captives, Redd stated that he must hold to the twelve-day truce that had been promised at the Council House. Isomania and his men called the Texans "liars" and "cowards" before he finally led his men a short distance away to wait out the truce period.

On April 4, heavyset Chief Piava rode into town with an Indian woman to meet with Captain George Howard and Colonel Fisher. The Comanches proposed trading some of their prisoners for some of their own people being confined in San Antonio. They were allowed to leave town under escort with an Indian woman and child captured in the Council House Fight. The Texans returned a half hour later with a twelve-year-old Mexican child and six-year-old Elizabeth Putman, who had been kidnapped from the Guadalupe River in December 1838. The Putman girl could not speak English, was covered in bruises, and her nose was partially burned off. Captain Howard continued to negotiate with Piava and managed to recover seven young Comanche prisoners by day's end, in return for releasing an equal number of Indians.[7]

Chief Piava was particularly eager to secure the release of a wounded Indian woman, who had been the wife of one of the slain chiefs. Howard wisely withheld her, demanding the Comanches bring in more of their prisoners. Booker Webster, one of the recovered captives, said the Comanches "howled and cut themselves with knives" after learning of the Council House massacre. He said that thirteen American captives had then been butchered and roasted. Webster and Elizabeth Putman had been spared only because they had been previously adopted into the tribe. Further negotiations failed to bring in any more prisoners during the next few months, as the Comanches remained quiet. The remaining Indians held in San Antonio were shuffled over time from the city jail to the Mission San José to a camp by the San Antonio River. Several Comanche women and children were taken into San Antonio homes to work, but most eventually managed to flee when lax security permitted their escapes.[8]

Rumors continued to swirl through the republic in early 1840 of a new invasion by Mexican troops.

It was enough to keep Colonel Fisher's Frontier Regiment vigilant. In May, Secretary of War Branch Archer ordered the Texas Militia out into the field to exterminate all Indians from Texas, but his proclamation was only partially carried out. Many men were needed near their homes to harvest their crops. Sporadic Indian attacks kept militiamen and rangers alike active during the summer of 1840. Colonel Henry Karnes was called upon to raise a new western frontier regiment, but he died on August 16 from yellow fever before he could fully raise his men for an expedition.

By late July, the peace maintained by the Penateka Comanches was coming to an end. They had mourned their losses from the Council House Fight for several months, but they moved north during May in search of allies. Their leading chief, Buffalo Hump, held peace meetings on the upper Arkansas River (outside Texas territory) with Kiowa Indians. They offered large numbers of horses to the Kiowas in exchange for guns, blankets, and kettles. The allied Comanches and Kiowas, numbering more than six hundred, descended back into Texas during July to begin what would be the largest of all southern Comanche offensives against the Anglo settlers of Texas.[9]

The first incident occurred on August 5 as the Comanches swept toward the coast and attacked two men east of Gonzales. Dr. Joel Ponton escaped, although wounded by two arrows. Ponton hid in a dense thicket and listened. The Comanches forced his comrade, Tucker Foley, to try to persuade Ponton to emerge from hiding while they slowly tortured, speared, and scalped Tucker to death. Ponton fled to the nearest settlement of Lavaca after dark and spread the warning. Captain Adam Zumwalt raised three dozen volunteers and visited the scene of the attack the next morning. The Comanches were long gone, leaving only the naked, mutilated body of Tucker behind.[10]

More volunteers were organized as word spread through the settlements of the body of Comanches sweeping south. In Gonzales, Captain Ben McCulloch moved out with twenty-four men on August 6 and joined Zumwalt's party the following morning. The group had little trouble in picking up the trail of the massive Indian force and they were joined about noon by sixty-five volunteers from the Cuero and Victoria settlements, commanded by Captain John Tumlinson. As the veteran ranger, Tumlinson was given acting command of the 125 men.

They took up the pursuit but were already too late to prevent the raids.[11]

Chief Buffalo Hump's five-hundred-plus Comanche party reached the outskirts of Victoria by late afternoon on August 6. Four black servants were killed, along with three citizens who tried to confront the attacking Indians. Buffalo Hump's men swept through Victoria, where they seized fifteen hundred horses and mules, killing three more men, and seizing a black servant girl. The following day, the Comanches killed two more men who happened to pass near their camping place on Spring Creek, three miles outside of Victoria. Buffalo Hump took his men south to the little settlement of Nine Mile Point, seizing three generations of women. They were Elizabeth Bryan (a relative of Daniel Boone's wife), her daughter Nancy Darst Crosby—the daughter of Gonzales mounted ranger Jacob Darst, who had perished at the Alamo—and Nancy's young child. Unable to keep Nancy Crosby's baby quiet, the Indians threw it to the ground and speared it to death. By the time the Comanches made camp on Plácido Creek, twelve miles from the coastal town of Linnville, they had already taken sixteen lives since starting their Texas offensive sweep.[12]

Shortly after 8 A.M. on August 8, Chief Buffalo Hump's Comanches rode into the key shipping town of Linnville and began killing again. The citizens took to the bay in boats to save themselves while the Indians looted the vast stores of supplies in the town's warehouses. They hauled off all the goods they could carry, along with vast herds of cattle, and burned down most of the buildings. By the time Buffalo Hump's men moved from Linnville to make camp for the night, the death toll for the Great Comanche Raid stood at twenty, plus another five women and children taken captive.[13]

The men under Captains Tumlinson, Zumwalt, and Mc-Culloch reached Victoria that evening and learned of the atrocities committed. Chief Buffalo Hump had his men on the move early on August 9, and they killed another Texan scout during the morning. The Comanches, burdened by stolen pack animals heavily laden with booty, were easy to track. John Tumlinson brought his men in for a charge against the Indians. Volunteer Washington Miller found the Comanches to be "hideously bedaubed" in war paint, feathers, huge buffalo and elk helmets, while "dashing about with streamers" flying behind them. Tumlinson's men attacked Buffalo Hump's band near Garcitas Creek, where the smaller force of Texans was quickly surrounded. The Comanches skirmished for about twenty minutes, losing four of their own in exchange for one Texan killed. The larger portion of the Comanches used the distraction time to continue heading north with their herd of pack animals.[14]

Ben McCulloch was furious. Captain Tumlinson had refused to allow the Texans to make a full charge, and the Comanches were now riding away. McCulloch took three men from his company and rode hard for Gonzales all night to raise more men who would help him fight the Indians. He sent one of his men racing for the Colorado River to round up frontier leader Ed Burleson, asking him to rendezvous with McCulloch at Peach Creek. Tumlinson's men, joined by forty men from Texana under Captain Clark L. Owen, continued to follow the Comanches through the next day.[15]

McCulloch's scouts reached Bastrop on August 10, and Burleson sent out riders to round up the townspeople who were willing to fight. Thomas Monroe Hardeman was in the midst of a wedding ceremony to Susan Burleson, cousin to the former Texas Army commander. Toast glasses were quickly set aside and wedding guests dashed for their horses. Hardeman, now distantly related to Colonel Burleson, was elected major in command of the Bastrop troops who were hastily assembled. The Anglo volunteers were joined by Chief Plácido and twelve of his Tonkawa scouts soon after Burleson's force headed toward the Gonzales area. By the evening of August 11, more than one hundred new Texan volunteers from many different communities had made rendezvous just east of Plum Creek.[16]

Scout Henry McCulloch sent a rider to the volunteers' camp just before daybreak on August 12 to announce that the Comanches were approaching just several miles away. Captain Mathew Caldwell took the opportunity to offer a motivational speech. The forty-one-year-old signer of the Texas Declaration of Independence was well respected. He had fought in the Texas Revolution, had commanded rangers, and had commanded scouts for the Frontier Regiment. He was given the "Paul Revere of the Texas Revolution" moniker for riding from Gonzales to Bastrop in 1835 to call men to arms to defend Béxar. Most, however, knew him as "Old Paint" because of the white patches in his beard, in his hair, and on his chest.

Despite their small numbers, Paint Caldwell told the assembled Texans: "They must be attacked and whipped before they reach the mountains." Once the Comanches could take cover in the Hill Country thickets, he saw little use in following farther. Old Paint called for a swift assault, and hoped for the best. "If we can't whip 'em, we can try!" he offered.[17]

Chief Buffalo Hump's Comanches were quite the spectacle.

They were herding more than two thousand captured horses and mules, five hostages, and an immense hoard of stolen goods. Jim Nichols of Seguin saw one Comanche sporting a tall beegum hat from which streamed at least ten yards of ribbon in red, green, and blue colors. Robert Hall of Gonzales noted that many of the Indians had new white shields for protection but "presented a ludicrous sight." Many of them wore shirts buttoned on backward in addition to other stolen shoes and clothes from the Linnville warehouses. "They seemed to have a talent for finding and blending the strangest, most unheard-of ornaments," thought John Jenkins of Bastrop. Other Comanches carried umbrellas, some wore buffalo helmets or buck horns, and one leader sported a headdress made from a large white crane with red eyes.[18]

Near Plum Creek, the Comanches were met by about two hundred Texans and friendly Tonkawa scouts. Revered frontier leader Ed Burleson offered command of the mixed bunch to Texas Militia general Felix Huston. The Comanches they faced were spread out over a quarter-mile-wide stretch of open prairie land. Minor skirmishes broke out as the Indians continued herding their stolen livestock northwesterly toward their home camps. Huston had his men dismount and form a defensive square, a command found most distasteful by veteran rangers and Indian fighters who preferred to remain on horseback.

The Texans opened fire with muskets and long rifles. The Indians in turn launched arrows and charged in to riddle some of their foes and their staked horses with musket balls. Jim Nichols was in awe of the fine horsemanship of some of the Comanches: "Lying flat on the side of their horse with nothing to be seen but a foot and a hand, they would shoot their arrows under the horse's neck, run to one end of the space, straighten up, wheel their horses, and reverse themselves, always keeping on the opposite side from us." San Antonio surveyor Jack Hays, among the hastily assembled Texan volunteers, soon spotted an opportunity. He noticed that most of the lead bullets were glancing off the Comanches' rawhide shields. Hays ordered his fellow men to hold their fire until after the Indians had launched their arrows and then shoot as they wheeled their horses away. During the next Indian charge, the Texans did as Hays instructed and were quite deadly. One Comanche chief with ribbons and feathers in his hair turned his horse, raised his shield high, and was then shot by John Smothers of Captain Zumwalt's company.[19]

Nineteen-year-old John Henry Brown of Lavaca noted that the Comanches "set up a peculiar howl" to mourn their chief, who slumped over his saddle horn. Ben and Henry McCulloch urged General Huston to call for a general charge, and the Texans rushed forward. The Comanches quickly broke into smaller parties and fled, firing back at the pursuing Texans all the way. Indians were shot down in small numbers for more than twelve miles from the Plum Creek battlefield as they were chased through boggy branches and thickets. The Comanches shot and stabbed several of their female captives as they fled. In return, the excited Texans killed at least a few Indian women during the running chase that lasted until sundown. General Huston's men suffered one man killed and nine wounded in addition to the female captives killed and wounded. The Comanches were estimated to have suffered more than eighty chiefs and warriors shot down in the clash at Plum Creek.

San Jacinto veteran John Harvey, having survived his third Indian battle in Texas, felt that if Ed Burleson or Paint Caldwell had commanded the volunteers "we would have done more execution." Hamilton P. Bee, arriving in the wake of the battle, agreed that pursuit of the Comanches would have been continued more vigorously had Burleson been allowed to take charge. General Huston, a previous combat virgin, proudly trumpeted his victory—according to Bee—as "a second Waterloo." [20]

The remaining Comanches escaped with a large number of stolen horses and cattle, but they had paid a heavy price for their massive vengeance raid. They lost at least three times as many of their own as they had taken in Texan lives. The Texas Comanches would never again carry out such a major offensive raid so deep into the Texas settlements, but Texas Rangers and militiamen would still clash with these fearless warriors of the plains for many years to come.

THE NEXT MAJOR CLASH between Texans and Comanches occurred on October 24, 1840. General Huston granted veteran Indian fighter John Henry Moore permission to raise an expedition to go into Indian country to follow up on the Plum Creek battle. During early October, Colonel Moore raised ninety ad hoc rangers from Fayette and Bastrop counties, commanded by Captains Thomas J. Rabb and Nicholas Mosby Dawson. Accompanied by a Lipan Apache detachment under Colonel Castro and Lieutenant Flaco, the expedition departed the Austin area on October 5 on a course up the Colorado River. Moore's Lipan scouts found a large Comanche encampment on October 23 on a horseshoe bend of the Colorado River about 250 miles northwest of Austin.[21]

Colonel Moore's men advanced on the sleeping Comanche village—estimated to contain sixty families and 125 men—during the cold early morning hours of October 24. He stationed a detachment of mounted cavalrymen to cut off the Indians' retreat route while he advanced on foot with the remainder of his rangers. A Comanche watchman shrieked an alarm as the Texans moved within two hundred yards of their camp. Moore ordered a charge and his men raced into camp, discharging rifles, shotguns, and pistols at close range. Many Comanches who tried to swim the Colorado River were cut down on the far banks by the waiting cavalrymen. The massacre was devastating. At least 140 Comanches, and likely many more, were killed or drowned in the river after being wounded. Thirty-four others, mainly women and children, were captured in small groups, along with about five hundred horses. Ranger Micah Andrews reported using a new Colt Paterson Model 1839 five-shot repeating carbine in the attack. Horsemen preferred the revolving-cylinder carbines because of their twenty-four-inch or less barrel length, as opposed to thirty-two or more inches of barrel lengths on most rifles of the day. Andrews managed to fire the Colt revolving cylinder carbine ten times while his companions were only able to fire their rifles twice.[22]

Only two Texans were wounded in the bloody rout of the Comanche village. The rangers made their way back into Austin during early November with their large herd of captured horses and Comanche prisoners. Moore's Indian village attack and the Battle of Plum Creek handed the Comanches two back-to-back defeats that they could not easily recover from. Senior leaders of the tribe in future years apparently decided to leave the Texas settlements alone, as Comanche raids were thereafter concentrated primarily against Mexican settlers.[23]

19

CAPTAIN DEVIL JACK

MIRABEAU LAMAR'S PLANS FOR the Frontier Regiment had gone largely unrealized during its first year. Constant Indian campaigns and slow recruiting had hindered his new army of Texas. During the fall of 1840, however, the president gave approval for his regulars to step up their efforts to build frontier forts linked by a military road.

Ed Burleson had resigned from the army, leaving Colonel William Cooke and Lieutenant Colonel Adam Clendenin as the two leading officers. Cooke stationed one company at the San Marcos River to establish a permanent post while he led an expedition to lay out the road toward the Red River. They spent three miserable weeks near the Trinity River in October so starved for supplies that his men were forced to kill and eat their own horses and pack mules. The surveying work continued and several new posts were established at the Red River and in northern Texas. The highest station at Holland Coffee's

Red River outpost, known as Coffee's Fort, was an estimated 270 miles from Austin. Colonel Cooke's men were also instrumental in mapping out the northern areas of Texas and the vast Cross Timbers region, which extended from the Brazos River to the present Texas border with Oklahoma. During the first two years of existence, the Frontier Regiment recruited only 674 soldiers but lost more than one-quarter to desertion.[1]

The Texas–Mexico borderlands were becoming more of a political hotbed by late 1840 as the Mexican Army maintained patrolling forces near the Rio Grande. Secretary of War Branch Archer was authorized to use more volunteer and militia forces to supplement the regular army, which was thinly stretched trying to build frontier posts and the military road. A new resolution was passed on December 26, 1840, authorizing three new ranger companies of fifteen men each, "to act as spies upon the Western and North Western Frontier of this Republic, for the space of four months." The first company raised was under Captain John T. Price, a veteran cowboy with experience in dealing with Mexican forces. His small company of rangers was designated to scout toward Corpus Christi to keep watch on the movements of federalist leader General Antonio Canales, and centralist leaders Rafael Vásquez and Enrique Villareal, who were operating in the area below the Nueces River. The second new ranger company, organized on January 20 in San Antonio, was under Captain Antonio Pérez, who had served on Henry Karnes's fall 1839 Comanche expedition.[2]

The third Texas Ranger company was to be led by a man who had never officially commanded his own ranger unit, Captain John Coffee Hays. The veteran frontiersman had certainly gained valuable experience in leading small squads of scouts in various Indian fights during the previous three years. In between surveying expeditions, Hays had also participated in campaigns under Deaf Smith and Henry Karnes, and had fought the Comanches at Plum Creek in 1840. His service as a surveyor, scout, and spy had given Hays an enviable reputation for bravery, endurance, and skill in commanding men. The boy-faced man who was commissioned by President Lamar to take command as a captain of spies over Texas frontiersmen many years his senior was well respected in his trade. Jack Hays turned twenty-four in San Antonio, now in command of his first small company of Texas Rangers.[3]

He had only a dozen men initially. Among them were James Matthew Jett and his brother Stephen, who had served in Daniel Friar's 1835 ranger company and in many other ranger and cavalry companies thereafter. Each man supplied his own horse, weapons, and equipment with the promise of three dollars per day payment from the government, plus supplied ammunition. The rangers each carried a carbine or rifle, a Bowie knife, and a small provisions wallet generally holding *panola* (parched corn), tobacco, and ammunition. Their horses were fitted with Mexican saddles, hair rope *cabristas* (halters), and rawhide Mexican *riatas* (a form of lariats) for roping horses. The lightly equipped rangers were prepared to move as nimbly over the plains as the Indians did. Hays and at least a few of his men had even acquired the new Colt Patent Arms .36-caliber five-shooter pistols originally purchased for the Texas Navy and the Frontier Regiment's cavalrymen.[4]

Captain Hays scouted from San Antonio in early January, moving along the Nueces River until he met up with the new company under Captain Price. Hays took his men into Laredo to reconnoiter Mexican troops rumored to be assembling there for an invasion. "There were but few soldiers there and the inhabitants were not disposed to offer resistance," he related. His showing of force unchallenged, Hays patrolled his rangers on the western frontier before returning to San Antonio.[5]

During this time, the Texas Army was coming to an end. The House and Senate of the Republic's Fifth Congress squabbled over funding for Colonel Cooke's Frontier Regiment. Acting President Burnet finally passed instructions on March 2, 1841, for the army to disband. Its men, who had largely completed the military road to the Red River and had established a number of fortified outposts, were mustered out of service by early April.[6]

The first real challenge for Captain Hays's San Antonio rangers came during early March. Thirty frontier marauders under Agatón Quinoñes attacked a party of traders and the alarm was spread to the chief justice at Béxar. Hays had added two more former Frontier Regiment soldiers—Mike Chevallie and twenty-one-year-old Pasqual Leo Buquor—to bring his company to fourteen rangers. They set out on March 15 in company with a dozen *tejano* rangers under Captain Antonio Pérez to intercept the robbers before they could reach Laredo. In addition to the Quinoñes gang, the rangers faced another twenty-five-man gang under Ignacio García. Mexican sympathizers in San Antonio sent two couriers toward Laredo with the news that Jack Hays was en route with his armed men.[7]

About ten miles from Laredo on April 7, rangers Buquor and Martias Díaz spotted the first riders of García's force. "They rode up to us, sounding a bugle, firing upon us and ordering us to surrender," wrote Hays. He instead had one of his rangers shoot the Mexican official from his horse, and "a general fight then ensued." The Mexican *escopetas* (shotguns) caused no injury, but the Texan long rifles killed one Mexican and wounded another. García's men quickly took position on a small hill and tried to encircle the Hays and Pérez rangers. Hays ordered his men to dismount and to tie off their horses in a grove of Spanish persimmon trees with five guards, and he moved forward with twenty men to attack. "Being nearly all provided with Kentucky and Tennessee rifles, our shots were unerring," recalled Buquor, who later served as mayor of San Antonio. "On the first fire, we killed two and wounded several, loading as we advanced." [8]

García's other rebels took flight and the rangers scrambled to retrieve their own horses. Mike Chevallie, thrown from his horse during the engagement, was nearly overrun. Captain Hays and Nat Harbert charged forward, killing the nearest Mexican and pulling Chevallie to safety. The marauders made another stand a short distance later. Hays again had his men dismount and charge forward, killing two more Mexicans as *escopeta* blasts and pistol bullets zinged past them. Only Captain García and three of his men escaped. Ranger Buquor said that García "carried a bullet in the left cheek from my rifle." He reported that the rangers killed or wounded nine before they subdued the remainder of García's men for interrogation.

Jack Hays was back in San Antonio for mere weeks before another Mexican force under frontier commander Calixto Bravo was reported in May 1841. Bravo's men attacked a small party of traders bound for the Rio Grande and sent a spy into Béxar to inform the rangers that his party included upwards of two hundred men. Undaunted by the impending ambush, Hays sent word back that he was mobilizing more than one hundred men from Gonzales to challenge the robbers. In reality, he rode out from San Antonio with only his company and a force of *tejano* mounted men under Antonio Pérez that totaled only forty. Outnumbered perhaps four-to-one, Hays and company charged doggedly against the Bravo bandits and chased them nearly to the Rio Grande.⁹

Hays returned to San Antonio on May 10, where he disbanded his "company of spies." The rangers under Pérez disbanded ten days later. The rangers regrouped during the next weeks at a time when the Republic of Texas had authorized the formation of county "minutemen" companies to range against Indian and Mexican attackers. Between May and July 1841, fourteen such minutemen companies were organized in the counties of Béxar, Fannin, Gonzales, Houston, Lamar, Milam, Montgomery, Nacogdoches, Paschal, Red River, Robertson, San Patricio, Travis, and Victoria. Jack Hays would spend much of June pulling together his new "Béxar County Minutemen." ¹⁰

At least half a dozen expeditions were mounted by varioussized groups of rangers and militiamen during the late spring and summer of 1841. Of these, General Edward Tarrant's offensive thrust into the Cross Timbers region produced the most significant Indian battle on May 24. About eighty men under Captains James G. Bourland and John B. Denton swept through a series of Caddo, Cherokee, and Tonakawa villages along the banks of Village Creek near present Arlington and Fort Worth. They killed at least twelve Indians and suffered eight Texans wounded, and Captain Denton was killed in an ambush. Tarrant was forced to retreat when his men were met with increasing numbers of Indians along their route. He would return with a four-hundred-man force in July only to find these Indian villages abandoned.

Life in San Antonio was festive in between frontier engagements. President Lamar's entourage visited town on a recruiting trip in June and enjoyed a grand ball thrown in honor of the president. Lamar opened the evening with a waltz with María

Gertrudis Flores de Abrego Seguín, wife of new San Antonio mayor Juan Seguín. "Mrs. Seguín was so fat that the general had great difficulty in getting a firm hold on her waist, and they cut such a figure that we were forced to smile," wrote local Mary Ann Maverick. Captain Hays, ranger Mike Chevallie, and another man had only one dress coat between them so they took turns wearing the formal jacket and dancing with the ladies.[11]

By late June, Jack Hays had a dozen men enrolled in his new San Antonio Minutemen company. They set out on June 27 in company with a twenty-man *tejano* unit under Captain Salvador Flores to pursue a party of Indians who had driven off cattle from settlements near town. Hays led his group fifty miles west of town to the Canyon de Uvalde at the headwaters of the Frio River, where they discovered a Comanche camp. On June 29, he led his rangers in a charge against ten Comanches traveling through Uvalde Canyon. Ranger John Slein killed one Comanche with a blast from his double-barreled shotgun and the others retreated into a small thicket.[12]

Captain Hays and three of his rangers dismounted and charged into the thicket. "Their fate was inevitable," he wrote of his Comanche opponents. "They saw it and met it like heroes." When the shooting was complete, Hays's men had killed eight Comanches and taken the other two as prisoners. Gathering horses and other Indian property, the Texans withdrew to San Antonio to seek medical treatment for Joseph Miller's wounds. Hays vowed to raise more men and return to the Comanche camp he had discovered.

Jack Hays spent two weeks of July recruiting more men for his return expedition. He succeeded in putting together forty-three men—twenty-five rangers and the rest Lipans and Tonkawas under the leadership of Captain Flaco. Six of Hays's new men were *tejanos* who had previously served in Captain Antonio Pérez's ranging company.

His force departed San Antonio on July 12 and rode to the site of the Comanche camp near the Frio River. They found it abandoned, with only some bodies of murdered prisoners. The rangers doggedly pursued the Comanches for more than a week. "Our horses and men were much starved and worn down by the time we reached the head waters of the Llano," said Hays. There his scouts discovered fresh trails made by large numbers of Indians. On July 24, his men were spotted by a party of Comanche hunters and the Texans pursued them at full speed. About a mile before they reached the camp of their main body, fifty Comanches turned to engage the rangers.[13]

The main body of the tribe retreated while Hays's men fought a two-hour running battle over six miles of rugged country. During the fight, the Comanches would retreat, form a line, and then prepare for battle. Hays decided at one point to make a solo charge toward them, unload his Colt five-shooter, and then retreat. His horse had other ideas, however. The excited animal would not wheel about and instead charged headlong into the Comanches. Chief Flaco, a close friend to the ranger captain, valiantly joined the charge right into his enemy's line. Hays calmly shot down one Comanche who halted his horse to fire at him. Flaco and Hays broke through the Indian lines and emerged on the other side miraculously unscathed. After the fight, Flaco was heard to remark: "I will never be left behind by anyone, but Captain Jack is *bravo too much*."[14]

The battle on the Llano River took a toll on both sides. The Comanches made a strong advance on the rangers. John Slein, a merchant who had joined Hays just a month prior, was killed. Ranger John Trueheart was disabled by a nasty bullet wound in the neck. Another bullet winged Hays in one of his fingers but did not slow him from the fight. He estimated that his force had killed or wounded eight to ten Comanches by the time the fight was terminated. The rangers moved back through the Indian camp, where they saw the eerie remains of a Mexican prisoner who was hanging by his heels, shot and lanced to death. Flaco's Lipans took departure from the expedition when Captain Hays headed back toward San Antonio with the wounded Trueheart being carried on a litter. He considered his Llano fight to have been productive. "This was the last of the Indian difficulties about San Antonio," he wrote. "They never made their reappearance, except one or two small thieving parties who were run off without much difficulty." [15]

JACK HAYS RECOVERED QUICKLY from his hand wound.

His ranger unit increased in size to forty-five men during August in the wake of the Llano River fight, but he trimmed his company back to twenty men during a brief hiatus in action in September. The citizens of San Antonio elected Hays to be the Béxar County surveyor during the summer but his duties as a ranger commander allowed him only to locate five land certificates during the remainder of 1841.[16]

Hays wrote few extant reports during the fall of 1841 but it was during this time that one of his most fabled Indian encounters occurred. He was out on a scout with about twenty of his men near the head of the Pedernales River in present Llano County. Captain Hays was scouting ahead of his men, who had made camp on the banks of nearby Crabapple Creek. Hays rode ahead to the vicinity of Enchanted Rock, a gently sloping pinnacle that is the second-largest granite formation in the United States. He was armed only with a Bowie knife, a rifle, and two Colts.[17]

Hays suddenly encountered three Comanches on horse-back, who began pursuing him. He spurred on his horse in a race for his life. The ranger captain wheeled about to exchange gunfire with the Indians from time to time as the numbers of his pursuers gradually increased. Hays stayed ahead of the Comanches in a chase that stretched more than eight miles. He finally reached Enchanted Rock, where he sprang from his horse to ascend the granite formation. Near the top, he took shelter in an indenture sheltered by loose rocks.

The Indians gathered near the base of Enchanted Rock, firing shots up at their hated frontier opponent some had come to call "Devil Jack." Hays was conservative with his ammunition. He only shot down Comanches as they made their way up the hill toward his hiding spot. In between firing his rifle and reloading it, he relied on his pair of Colt five-shooter pistols to remain constantly armed and dangerous. From his vantage point with superior firepower, Ranger Hays reportedly kept his adversaries at bay for upwards of two hours. He is said to have faced an estimated one hundred Comanches during his solo stand.

The war whoops and cracking of rifles did not go unnoticed on the Texas frontier. Hays's ranger company finally perceived their overdue leader was in trouble and followed the sounds of the action toward Enchanted Rock. They fought their way through the Indian force, pushing them back long enough for Captain Hays to scramble down from his rocky perch.

The story of Jack Hays and his solo Indian battle atop Enchanted Rock became even more legendary around campfires during the years that followed. Texans and their Indian foes alike marveled at the bravado of "Devil Jack." On one occasion when a group of Indians came into San Antonio to make a treaty, several chiefs were overheard talking about and pointing toward Hays.[18]

Pointing to his companion, one chief pronounced, "Blue Wing and I, no afraid to go to hell together."

Pointing toward Jack Hays, the chief then remarked: "*Capitan* Jack, great brave. No afraid go to hell by himself."

THE TEXAS INDIAN WARS had cooled dramatically by late 1841.

The Cherokees and Shawnees were largely gone from the republic. The Comanches had suffered heavy losses and appeared less eager to make raids into the Austin and San Antonio area settlements. Massive expeditions of soldiers and militiamen were no longer needed to quell serious uprisings. One well-equipped Texas Ranger company could successfully range vast areas of the frontier to deal with hostile groups.

The Sixth Congress of the Republic of Texas convened in Austin on November 1, two months after the country's citizens had voted for their next president. Mirabeau Lamar's term ended on December 13, 1841, when Sam Houston was inaugurated for his second term as Texas president. He and Vice President Ed Burleson were quick to shut down the vast military forces built up by Lamar. Their secretary of state, Dr. Anson Jones, recommended maintaining only "a few Rangers on the frontiers" to act in strictly a defensive role. He declared that it would be "cheaper and more humane to purchase" the friendship of the Indian tribes than to fight against them.[19]

County ranging companies ceased to operate. The Sixth Congress refused to appropriate any more funds to Lamar's county minutemen system. Without funding, only three authorized county ranging companies were still operating as of January 1842: Captain William Becknell's Red River County

Rangers, Captain John McDonald's Refugio County company, and Captain Jack Hays's Béxar County Rangers. The work of Hays and his men did not go unnoticed. An article in the December 8, 1841, issue of the *Telegraph and Texas Register* bragged that these rangers had "almost completely broken up the old haunts of the Comanches in the vicinity of Béxar."

The relative peace in the area allowed Hays to return to his appointed duty of county surveyor during early 1842. His party of six came under fire from a group of Indians while running a property line in February. The Indians did not initiate a full assault, so Hays was content to dash about on his horse and fire periodic shots at them. His aggressive nature, and likely his frontier reputation, kept the Indians at a safe enough distance that his surveying team was able to complete its work.[20]

Comanches became a lesser issue for Captain Hays in early 1842. His newest challenge was contending with a force of Mexican Army soldiers who were preparing to march into Texas to restore order in territory once held by Mexico. Rumors had long swirled through the colonies that Mexican troops were preparing to attack but nothing of any consequence had materialized in the six years since San Jacinto. Fears became reality when General Mariano Arista issued a statement from Monterrey on January 9. He announced to Texans that it was hopeless for them to continue their independence struggle. He promised protection to all who would remain neutral to Mexico during his planned invasion.

In San Antonio, the townspeople feared another 1836 Alamo-type episode. They began fortifying their city and pledged money to help pay for Jack Hays's spies and other volunteers. As Mexican troops marched toward the vicinity of Béxar, Captain Hays found no shortage of men to send out on scouting duties. His ranger unit was well seasoned. Matt

Jett, Stephen Jett, John Young, Antonio Coy, Nat Harbert, Archibald Fitzgerald, and Mike Chevallie had served under him during 1841.

One of his newest rangers was William Alexander Anderson Wallace, a twenty-five-year-old from Virginia. The six-foot-two, 240-pound frontiersman had come to Texas to avenge the loss of his brother and cousin, who had perished in the Goliad Massacre. He became known as "Bigfoot" after his moccasin tracks were once confused with the fourteen-inch imprints of a six-foot-eight Waco Indian who was known as Chief Bigfoot. Bigfoot Wallace had previously fought Comanches in the 1840 Plum Creek battle and had participated in General Tarrant's 1841 battle at Village Creek.

Captain Hays sent out his spies to scout for the approaching Mexican forces in late February. Two of his men, Mike Chevallie and James Dunn, were ambushed and captured at the Nueces River by Colonel Calixto Bravo's troops. A third ranger, Antonio Coy, was captured by Mexican forces while scouting for Hays toward the Rio Grande. Hays sent couriers to warn other settlements and to gather volunteers. By the evening of March 4, he had gathered nearly 110 men in San Antonio. They elected him colonel commanding their force of small companies: Captain Daniel Friar's Cuero settlement company; Captain James Callahan's Seguin-area men; and Hays's own ranging unit, which he placed under the acting command of Captain Duncan Campbell Ogden.[21]

The Mexican invasion force, under General Rafael Vásquez, swept into the coastal regions of Texas while Colonel Hays was assembling his forces. The townspeople of Goliad, Victoria, and Refugio surrendered to the Mexican forces who occupied their settlements in early March. By March 5, the 700-man Vásquez force was within six miles of San Antonio. Nine of

Hays's scouts approached the Mexican force and exchanged shots. General Vásquez sent Captain José María Carrasco forward under a white flag of truce to treat with the Texans.

Vásquez informed the Texans they would be attacked if they did not surrender. Ranger James "Keno" Ellison had Captain Carrasco blindfolded and hauled back to the camp of Jack Hays. Their prisoner informed the Texans that Rangers Chevallie and Dunn were being held prisoner in the Mexican camp. Colonel Hays reluctantly agreed to a truce with the Vásquez force, which outnumbered his San Antonio volunteer force by at least seven-to-one. The Texans took a vote and decided to retreat from town back toward the Salado River.[22]

San Antonio was once again in chaos. The locals retreated with the belongings they could quickly haul away, and more than three hundred kegs of gunpowder were thrown into the San Antonio River. Citizens and merchants smoked fine cigars and drank all the liquor they could hold as they destroyed items of value that could benefit the Mexican troops. Flames and explosions lit up the Alamo city as merchants used kegs of gunpowder to blow up their own warehouses. The most inebriated had to be lashed to the artillery oxcarts as they were hauled from town.[23]

General Vásquez took San Antonio without a fight. His men proceeded to loot the town of whatever remained. His intention was not so much to possess the town as to make a statement. By March 7, the invaders had withdrawn from town and had started their march back south toward Mexico. Vásquez released his three ranger prisoners en route. The whole Vásquez Invasion was a relatively bloodless affair, but it succeeded in striking as much terror in the hearts of Texas settlers as the Runaway Scrape of 1836. Jack Hays and his scouts trailed the retreating Mexican forces back across the Rio Grande.

Texas was left in a state of turmoil. Former San Jacinto hero Juan Seguín, the mayor of San Antonio, was accused of aiding the Mexican invasion effort in spite of the fact that he had served under Colonel Hays. His reputation shattered, he resigned his office in April and retreated into Mexico for his own safety.[24]

President Houston executed emergency plans to raise troops to defend Texas against another Mexican invasion. He had full confidence in the ability of Jack Hays, whom he authorized to command a corps of rangers to supply intelligence of enemy movements along the southern frontier. Hays increased the size of his own company during the spring months and supervised the activities of a second ranger company under Captain Ephraim Walton McLean. Citizens so feared a second Mexican invasion that few San Antonio–area families returned to town even after the departure of Vásquez.[25]

CHIEF YELLOW WOLF TOOK advantage of the crisis created by the Mexican Army.

The Comanche war chief assembled eighty of his men shortly after the Vásquez Invasion to raid Béxar County settlements. Yellow Wolf's party succeeded in rounding up horses from the settlers and killing several *tejanos*. They also attacked two sheepherders, killing a black man and taking ranger James Dunn as their prisoner. The Comanches then retired toward the Guadalupe River with their booty.[26]

Jim Nichols, who had recently signed on under Captain Hays to serve as a ranger scout, was still asleep when word reached their camp near the old Mission Concepción. "About sunrise there was sixteen of us in our saddles," he said. Hays led the pursuit party with two of his Lipan scouts hot on the heels of Chief Yellow Wolf's raiders. The rangers overtook the Comanches a short distance from Bandera Pass at the Pinta Trail crossing of the Guadalupe River.[27]

Hays and his men opened fire on the Comanches as they headed up the opposing bank of the Guadalupe. Several Indians were killed and wounded before Yellow Wolf led his men over the hill. There Hays found that the Comanches had formed into a battle line to trap the Texans.

"Steady there, boys!" Hays barked. "Dismount and tie those horses. We can whip them—no doubt about that."

The ranger captain ventured that they were outnumbered ten-to-one. The Comanches, leading a herd of stolen horses and mules, prepared for the fight. Hays took a quick poll and found his men eager to engage.

He then urged them forward with the directive, "When you shoot, shoot to hit."

The rangers scattered Yellow Wolf's party with their first volley. Hays led his men back over the riverbank to reload their rifles. The Comanches charged down upon them but the Texans held their ground as they were showered with arrows and musket fire. "We reloaded as quick as possible and charged them in return," said Jim Nichols. Hays carefully had only half of his men fire at a time so that they could reload while the next half poured lead into their war-whooping adversaries.

Several rangers were wounded, but they cut down many of the Comanches in return. Yellow Wolf—sporting gaudy head-gear and a large, ornamental shield—was shot from his fine black horse. Prisoner James Dunn, who managed to escape after the battle at the Guadalupe, claimed that the Comanches suffered twenty-three killed and three dozen wounded. Yellow Wolf and his survivors retreated, allowing the rangers to round up most of the stolen horses.

THE VIGILANT RANGER COMPANY of Captain Hays maintained frontier patrols from the San Antonio area during the summer of 1842. His men attacked Mexican marauders and raided small camps of Comanches to recover stolen horses.

In between actions, his rangers honed their shooting skills by employing Comanche-like techniques. Jim Nichols recorded that Hays drilled his men earnestly on their riding and shooting techniques. They learned to fire their rifles at full gallop at human-size targets and then discharge their pistols effectively at secondary targets. "We drew a ring about the size of a man's head and soon every man could put both his [pistol] balls in the circle," Nichols said. The rangers became adept at snatching up a hat, coat, or silver dollar from the ground at full gallop. Then they would "stand up in the saddle, throw ourselves on the side of the horse with only a foot and a hand to be seen, and shoot our pistols under the horse's neck, rise up, and reverse." [28]

THE UNREST WITH MEXICO continued in 1842.

During early July, Colonel Antonio Canales marched into Lipantitlán and skirmished with a small group of Texas military personnel. The coastal settlements of South Texas were thereafter ranged by several small companies and Ed Burleson led an expedition out to control the Indians in his region.

San Antonio remained largely unsettled during the summer due to the existing turmoil. Jack Hays, now twenty-five years old, made a trip to the temporary capital of Houston to meet with President Houston for authorization to raise more rangers. The Texas Congress approved more funds for him and Hays was promoted to major, commanding two companies: his own and a small mounted company under Captain Tony Menchaca. Hays and Menchaca both struggled to recruit their allotted number of men. By early September, Hays had only fifty rangers, one-third of his allowed strength.[29]

The Comanche empire, numbering close to twenty thousand people, remained as the principal antagonist for Major Hays in the early 1840s. Four main Comanche divisions operated on the southern plains during this time: the Kotsotekas, the Yamparikas, the Hois, and the Tenewas. Chief Pia Kusa's Hois remained staunchly opposed to treating with the Texans although his tribe primarily conducted plundering raids across the Rio Grande into Mexico. Another prominent Hois leader was Chief Potsanaquahip, whose Comanche name "male buffalo" was translated by the Texans as "Buffalo Hump." Another chief of the same name had been killed in John Bird's 1839 fight, but the Chief Buffalo Hump leader of the 1840s was a blooded veteran. His Hois division of the Comanche had participated in the 1840 Great Comanche Raid and in the subsequent Plum Creek battle. Bands of Hois from Chiefs Pia Kusa and Buffalo Hump would continue to see action with the Hays rangers during the next two years.[30]

President Santa Anna, back in control of Mexico, intended to restore Texas under his country's control as well.

A second invasion of Texas in 1842 was put in motion in late August. General Adrian Woll—a forty-seven-year-old Frenchborn officer of Mexico's Army of the North—crossed the Rio Grande with his troops to retake San Antonio. Bigfoot Wallace soon reported to Major Hays that Mexican spies were present about town. Hays's men arrested several spies and learned that a force of about fifteen hundred Mexican Army soldiers was approaching Béxar.[31]

Hays assumed command of the various volunteer forces that assembled in San Antonio. General Woll's troops slipped through

the rough country north of town and surprised the Béxar inhabitants on the morning of September 11 while Hays was out
scouting with his rangers. Woll took over the city and held many
Texans as prisoners while Hays gathered troops at Seguin, thirty
miles to the east. Colonel Paint Caldwell, elected into command
of the volunteers, rendezvoused with Jack Hays before dawn on
September 13 at their camp eight miles east of Salado Creek.

The Mexican force and the two-hundred-plus assembled Texans clashed on Sunday, September 18. Hays's rangers taunted
the Mexican cavalry into pursuing them from San Antonio. The
frontiersmen were under heavy fire as they raced toward Caldwell's main force on Salado Creek. The opposing forces squared
off, skirmishing for hours with artillery and small arms fire. The
Texans boldly advanced in the afternoon until Woll's force was
finally driven back. Former Hays ranger Stephen Jett was killed
and eight other Texans were wounded. In return, the Mexicans
lost sixty men killed and many more wounded. Among those slain
was Vicente Córdova, leader of the 1838 East Texas rebellion.

During the Salado Creek battle, another company of fifty-
four Texans from La Grange under the command of Captain
Nicholas M. Dawson marched toward the action. His company
was intercepted by a column of several hundred Mexican cavalrymen and a battery of two fieldpieces. Thirty-six of Dawson's
men were killed, three escaped the field, and the remaining fifteen were taken as prisoners. Marched to Perote Prison in Mexico, only nine of the Dawson Massacre survivors would live to
make their way back to Texas.[32]

Colonel Caldwell and Major Hays sent out a small party
on the morning of September 19 to find the mutilated bodies
of Captain Dawson's men on the battleground. General Woll
began a retreat from San Antonio the following morning while
rangers kept a steady reconnaissance of their movements. Hays

and companion Ben McCulloch captured four Mexican prisoners during the day on September 21 while Paint Caldwell reorganized his volunteers.

Caldwell's force moved up the Medina River that evening while Hays continued scouting Woll's movements. He reported at midnight that the Mexicans had broken camp and moved out. The main body of the Texans struggled to cross the river but Hays's rangers rode hard and caught up with the Mexican rear guard around 3 P.M. on September 22. General Woll had put out a five-hundred-dollar bounty for the head of Jack Hays, and his men nearly claimed the prize. As the rangers approached a bend in the creek, they were suddenly fired upon by Mexican soldiers hidden in the creek bottom.[33]

One of the musket shots whizzed past Hays and slammed into the chest of ranger Sam Luckie, who was riding beside his commander. The ball passed out Luckie's shoulder as the force of the impact threw him from his horse. Other rangers helped secure Luckie to a litter and haul him back to the Medina River. Hays and his advance force—a mile and a half ahead of Colonel Caldwell's troops—dismounted and prepared for battle. General Woll opted to keep pushing ahead instead of fighting, however. His men crossed Hondo Creek about fifty miles from San Antonio and set up a defensive position below the mouth of Quihi Creek.[34]

Old Paint Caldwell sent an additional hundred horsemen to race ahead to support Hays with his charge against Woll's force. On a bluff on the east side of the Hondo, Woll had placed a cannon with twenty artillerymen while his troops moved over to the west side. Joined by the additional Texans, Hays and his lieutenant, Henry McCulloch, decided to seize the Mexican cannon on the hill.

"Charge!" Hays shouted.

Rangers and volunteer horsemen alike bounded straight

into the path of the waiting enemy infantrymen and artillery crew. The cannon roared to life but its nervous gunners did not take the sloping ground into account. The first round of grapeshot sailed high over the Texans' heads, as did the second round. By then it was too late: the rangers' Colt pistols began making widows for the Mexican soldiers. Three of Caldwell's men were wounded in the charge and Arch Gibson, one of Hays's rangers, was shot through the right cheekbone.

Hays and his men seized the Mexican cannon but their possession was short-lived. They came under heavy fire from the west side cannon. Hundreds of Woll's infantrymen then charged forward, forcing Hays to retreat until Paint Caldwell could arrive with more volunteers. The shooting died down as dusk fell over the Hondo Creek area. The Texans tended to their wounded during the night while Woll used the evening time to put miles between himself and Caldwell's regrouping forces.[35]

The following day, General Woll's force managed to escape the area due to a complete breakdown of control among the Texans. Caldwell, Hays, and others were chomping at the bit to pursue and punish the Mexican invaders. Many of their volunteers, however, were worn down. Major James Mayfield considered it futile to pursue Woll any farther. The battle-hungry volunteers then held a vote and elected John Henry Moore to take command of them. Those who supported Caldwell were upset with the choice and the men became further divided as they bickered over who should lead them. One of the volunteers, Reverend Zachariah Morrell, wrote, "This was certainly one of the most disgraceful affairs that ever occurred in Texas."[36]

Adrian Woll's invasion force thus escaped to the Rio Grande without another serious fight, carrying a number of Texan prisoners with them. Some of the volunteers who wanted to fight signed on as members of Jack Hays's ranger company.

PRESIDENT HOUSTON WAS APPALLED by the Woll invasion. He authorized one of his militia leaders, Brigadier General Alexander Somervell, to organize men and advance into "the enemy territory" if necessary. He advised Somervell to rely upon "the gallant Hays and his companions" to help coordinate their efforts for revenge and in recapturing their fellow Texians.[37]

Volunteers began assembling in San Antonio during October, but Somervell spent his time leisurely organizing his forces for many weeks. His expedition finally set out on November 13, 1842. General Somervell had about twelve hundred men when he ventured out to the Medina River to make his first camp. His casual nature prevailed. More days were wasted waiting for an artillery piece, but when it showed up, Somervell refused to take it along. He then set out across open country instead of following the Laredo road toward Mexico. His men struggled through mud and cold weather in November while Jack Hays's rangers stayed ahead of the pathetic bunch to scout for trouble. Hays was ready as ever for action. His men rode with a hand-fashioned flag stitched with the motto, "We give but ask no quarter."[38]

By late November, tempers were flaring as Somervell's expedition took a wrong turn that led them farther through mud-bogged prairies. Captain Hays soon set the men on the proper course, but he was challenged by another ranger captain, Samuel Bogart, who desired to have equal status as a leader of the scouts. Hays moved ahead in early December into the border town of Laredo, where his rangers apprehended two Mexican *rancheros*. General Somervell sent six companies of men across the Rio Grande to engage the Mexican forces at the local garrison. The Mexican soldiers retreated across the river, along with many of the townspeople.[39]

Somervell's troops proceeded to pillage Laredo for two days while the rangers under Hays and Bogart retired to a ravine to rest their horses. The town's alcalde was apprehended with a rope around his neck while Texans broke down doors and stole everything of value from the citizens' homes. General Somervell pushed his troops farther into Mexico to the town of Guerrero, located some fifty-four miles below Laredo. By December 19, many of Somervell's troops had become disgusted with the whole campaign, the bitter weather, and the absence of good horses they had hoped to plunder on their expedition. The general then ordered his army to begin a march back toward Gonzales to be disbanded.[40]

Five company commanders, however, announced that they would be continuing their expedition into Mexico without Somervell. They elected Colonel William S. Fisher into command and reorganized their forces. Nine of Jack Hays's rangers split from his company and joined the Fisher expedition. Fisher led his remaining companies down the Rio Grande toward the town of Mier. Captain Hays reconnoitered the town and found it void of Mexican troops. He then advised Fisher that he had completed his obligations in guiding the Texans to Mier and that his services on the southwestern frontier of Texas were his primary concern. Hays warned the colonel that a large Mexican force was reported to be assembling to oppose the Texans, before he departed Mier with most of his rangers on December 24.[41]

The Hays rangers made their way back to San Antonio by the end of December, happy to be free from the strains of the much-troubled Somervell and Mier expeditions. Soon after their departure, Colonel Fisher's men fought a battle with Mexican troops on December 25–26. Heavily outnumbered, Fisher's troops inflicted severe casualties on the Mexicans before they were forced to surrender. The Texas prisoners, including former Hays rangers Bigfoot Wallace and Thomas Jefferson Green, endured a long march toward Mexico City during early 1843. They were jailed briefly at a prison at Hacienda del Salado, but the Texans overpowered their guards and escaped toward the mountains.

Most of them were captured during the next two weeks and were marched to a new prison at Saltillo. President Santa Anna, infuriated by such actions, sent orders that every tenth man of the remaining 176 Texan prisoners should be shot to death. On March 25, the ragged convicts were forced to determine their own fate by drawing a colored bean from an earthen pot. The 159 who pulled a white bean would live. The unlucky seventeen who drew a black bean would face the firing squad. Bigfoot Wallace, carefully watching the process, noticed that the lethal black beans pulled by the unlucky Texans appeared to be larger than the white ones. When his time came, the former ranger carefully sifted beans through his fingers until he found one of smaller size. Bigfoot survived but seventeen Texans— including three former Texas Rangers—pulled black beans and were summarily executed.[42]

The Mier Expedition survivors were marched deeper into Mexico to the little village of Perote, where they were held in an old castle converted into a prison. Eight Texans would manage to escape the Perote castle and return to their republic homes. Twenty others perished during their next eight months of captivity. More than one hundred Mier Expedition prisoners would remain imprisoned in Mexico until they were released in September 1844. The treatment endured by these men would not be forgotten by Texans when the next opportunity arose to fight the country of Santa Anna.

20

TRIUMPH AT
WALKER'S CREEK

THE ENTIRE REPUBLIC OF Texas was patrolled by only one company of Texas Rangers during 1843.

It was no surprise that this distinction fell upon the most revered frontier fighter of his time, Captain Jack Hays. Most of his company had followed him back to San Antonio in late December 1842, leaving the ill-fated Mier Expedition rebels to their fates. President Sam Houston spent the latter part of the year struggling with a nation plagued by fears from the Mexican invasions. The Vásquez raid had compelled the republic to move its capital from Austin to Washington-on-the-Brazos.

The Seventh Congress of the young nation passed a new frontier act on January 16, 1843, to organize six militia brigades throughout Texas. The legislators also approved funding for one spy company to protect the southwestern frontier until the militia act could be passed. President Houston, however, refused to sign the militia act and no other military forces would be legally organized in 1843. Houston thus handed sole military authority in Texas to Hays, whose men were to maintain order throughout the vast Nueces–Rio Grande river countryside.[1]

He began recruiting new men from the Béxar area during February and had fifteen men in active service by the first of March. Among them were Sam Luckie—wounded during the Woll invasion—and brothers Matt and William Jett, whose brother Stephen had been killed on the Salado. Sam Houston and his representatives worked hard to make peace treaties with the Texas Indians in 1843 and found the most resistance to come from the Wichitas and Comanches.

Captain Hays spent much of his time combating Mexican bandits who preyed on the settlements from San Antonio to the Rio Grande. While camped on the Nueces River with a recaptured herd of horses and mules, Hays's rangers were confronted by a band of more than one hundred Mexican soldiers. They were led by bandit Agatón Quinoñes—who had faced Hays in 1842 at Hondo Creek. The next day, Quinoñes skirmished with the rangers in a mounted shoot-out. Hays and his men wounded some of their opponents and escaped without loss. "It was a hot time for a little while," admitted ranger Rufe Perry.[2]

Hays thereafter moved his men back toward the settlements to replenish supplies they had lost during the scrape with the Mexican bandits. En route, they were forced to eat an old mustang to survive. "It was the hardest meal to swallow I ever tried," said Perry. Once they reached the Guadalupe River settlements, the rangers were taken in and fed by Andy Lockhart's family. Perry found Matilda Lockhart, the eighteen-year-old former Comanche hostage, to be a very hospitable hostess.

President Houston proclaimed martial law in the region from the Nueces and Frio rivers to the Rio Grande on April 27. Captain Hays's company ranged against Mexican bandits during the spring with orders to arrest any armed group in the region operating without authority from the Texas government. His unit more than doubled in size during the summer as veteran frontiersmen like Mike Chevallie, Ben McCulloch, and George Howard signed on with him. During early June, the rangers apprehended three armed Mexican bandits scouting for Agatón Quinoñes's gang. Hays, upon interrogating them and finding that they had committed murders and had stolen horses from the settlers, exercised his new authority by having the marauders executed.[3]

LIFE AS A TEXAS Ranger had its moments of humor.

One such episode occurred during an 1843 scouting expedition involving Jack Hays and one of his rangers, Alligator Davis—who earned his nickname by once wrestling an alligator on the Medina River. The pair chased two little bear cubs up a tree. Davis offered to tie one up and take it back to town for Mrs. William B. Jaques, an elegant lady fond of pets who was much admired by the rangers. Captain Hays shook the cub from the tree and then howled with laughter as he watched 'Gator Davis wrestle with the frightened beast. They lashed the bear to the horse of Davis but failed to secure its mouth. When the cub bit into the horse, Davis was thrown to the ground as his mount raced away with the bear tied to its back.[4]

The rangers had more gunfights with Mexican bandits during August and September as they kept the peace in the region. In one of his reports to the government, made November 12, Hays detailed some of his success. "The western settlements for several months past enjoyed, so far as I have been able to ascertain, almost an entire immunity from the incursions of the Indians," he wrote. "The only source from which danger is now apprehended is the robbing parties of Mexicans."[5]

Captain Hays was forced to disband his spy company that month due to insufficient funds to pay them for their daily service. Most of the supplies and services needed to keep his rangers in operation came from San Antonio–area merchants who desired their protection. The Texas government deemed that the rangers under Hays, although small in number, had been "active, vigilant and efficient" in keeping Mexican and Indian forces under control.[6]

Jack Hays spent the 1843 holidays finally relaxing in company with the Judge Jeremiah H. Calvert family of Washington-on-the-Brazos. He had previously met young Susan Calvert in San Antonio, and his thoughts remained with the attractive brown-eyed brunette. Susan, whose family had recently moved to Texas from Alabama, began a courtship that would last for several years with the most famous Texas Ranger.

While Hays passed the holidays in Washington and Seguin, the newly seated Eighth Congress of the Republic of Texas worked out legislation to finally pay the rangers for their previous year's service. Sam Houston met with Hays in early January and listened to his plans on how to maintain order on the southwestern prairies. Houston was an old friend of Hays's father, and he continued to show loyalty to his favored ranger leader. On January 23, 1844, Congress authorized Hays to raise a forty-man ranger company to patrol the frontier from Béxar County to Refugio and westward as needed.[7]

Hays organized his new ranger unit, the only one in operation in Texas, during the spring of 1844. He made Ben

McCulloch his first lieutenant and took in many veteran frontiersmen as privates, including Rufe Perry, Matt Jett, William
Jett, Mike Chevallie, and Christopher Black "Kit" Acklin. One
of his new rangers was Samuel Hamilton Walker, a participant
of the Mier Expedition who had but recently escaped from a
Mexican prison. Walker—who had endured great hardships in
his internment—had little desire to take any prisoners when he
fought.

Captain Hays made a brief visit to see President Houston
in early March 1844. When he signed the guest book at the
local hotel in Houston, Hays was hardly recognizable as a
feared ranger. John W. Lockhart was surprised to see that the
fabled "Captain Jack" of the Texas newspaper stories was a
"small, boyish-looking youngster, with not a particle of beard
on his face." [8]

Those who had encountered Devil Jack on the plains knew
better than to discount the baby-faced ranger. Hays's 1844 company was better equipped than ever. His men were now fully
furnished with the deadly five-shot Colt revolvers. Sam Walker
later praised the Colt factory, saying that their fine weapons
enabled his rangers to be so confident "that they are willing to
engage four times their number." [9]

Walker soon had his chance to prove the value of his trusty
Colts.

JACK HAYS DECIDED HIS men had ridden far enough.

It was June 8, 1844, and his rangers had been in the saddle
for a week. They had moved north from San Antonio to scour
the country between the Pedernales and Llano rivers for Indian
activities. They found plenty of signs but had made no significant contact. Captain Hays thus turned back for San Antonio,

led his fifteen men across the Pedernales River, and made camp for the night on a stream he named Walker's Creek.

Hays, Ben McCulloch, and several others were in the process of unsaddling horses when a warning cry was given.

"Comanches, Cap'n!"

Kit Acklin and Alexander Coleman galloped into camp with the news. Their four-man patrol, stationed well back from camp to cover the company's rear, had been collecting honey from a bee tree. From his high vantage point, Coleman had spotted Comanche horsemen approaching. They wasted no time in alerting their comrades.

"To your saddles, boys!" shouted Hays. "Prepare to fight!" [10]

Captain Hays and his rangers rode out from camp and soon spotted their opponents—later determined to be about sixty Comanche, Kiowa, and Shoshone Indians under the leadership of Chief Yellow Wolf. The Comanches turned away and rode at a slow pace as the rangers approached. They clearly had no great fear of such a small bunch of Texans, only one-quarter of their own number. The Indians drifted toward a wooded area, where Hays presumed they might have other forces waiting to ambush them. [11]

Yellow Wolf made every effort to get the veteran ranger captain to commit to chasing his Indians. "They, however, did not succeed in their design," wrote Hays. The Indians resorted to shouting insults at the Texans in Spanish. Not to be outdone, Hays unleashed his own tirade of cursing at Chief Yellow Wolf. The rangers walked their horses slowly up Walker's Creek until the Comanches finally darted into the forest and disappeared. They soon reappeared to gather on the crest of a nearby slight hill, apparently joined by at least ten other Indians.

The game of taunting resumed. Several Comanches at a time rode down the slope, shouting challenges at the rangers.

as they waved their shields and lances. They obviously hoped to entice the Texans to discharge their rifles at longer range, from which distance their padded shields would likely deflect the lead balls fired at them. Devil Jack was too wise to take the bait, however, and he prepared his men for a little surprise for their adversaries.

The rangers, plainly visible to the Indians, slowly advanced up the gentle slope of the hill. Once they reached the steeper base of the rise, they momentarily fell out of sight of Yellow Wolf's force. Hays then immediately spurred his horse and motioned his company to follow him full speed around the hillside. They then galloped over the top of the hill and surprised the Comanches and their allies from their flank.

Each of the rangers unleashed a round from his rifle. Several Comanches were blasted from their horses. Captain Hays had his men race back down the hill to level ground. Yellow Wolf rallied his Indians and soon led them in a charge down the hill to assault the badly outnumbered rangers. There was insufficient time for the Texans to reload their rifles.

"Drop your rifles, men!" Hays shouted.

The Comanches rushed in, fully intent on slaughtering the sixteen rangers. Their rifles had all been emptied, leaving them with only Bowie knives and pistols. Yellow Wolf's Indians found out too late that they had been drawn into another deadly trap: each ranger sported a pair of Colt five-shooter pistols. Although outnumbered four-to-one, the "helpless" Texans sported 160 ready rounds.

The lower hillside came alive with war whoops, cracking pistols, and the acrid smell of gunpowder as the rangers unleashed round after round of .36-caliber pistol bullets. Hays saw many Indians tumble from their saddles as his "five-shooting pistols did good execution." Yellow Wolf's men wheeled away, giving the Texans enough time to swap cylinders on their Colts.

Hays boldly led his men in pursuit. The opponents exchanged two more rounds of close-action pistol fire. The Comanches made the most of their opportunities each time the rangers stopped to change cylinders. Ad Gillespie was knocked from his horse, his body pierced through with an arrow. Andrew Erskine took an arrow in the thigh and Ranger Peter Fohr was killed outright. James Lee was incapacitated with several severe arrow wounds.

After the third round from the deadly Colts, Yellow Wolf's Comanches had suffered enough casualties that his men fled. Jack Hays charged after them with the balance of his able men. The Indians turned to countercharge several times when the rangers came uncomfortably close. During one of these counterattacks, Rangers Sam Walker and Ad Gillespie were suddenly caught far in advance of their comrades. One of the Comanches raced in to spear Walker, but he was quick on the draw. He coolly shot the Indian from his horse but momentarily lost track of some of his other opponents. Another Comanche barreled in and drove his lance into Walker.[12]

John Carolin came to his aid, shooting the Indian in the head with his Colt just as he ripped his lance back out of Walker's body. Carolin helped Walker into a nearby thicket while Gillespie, lying wounded on the ground, reloaded his rifle to make a longer-range shot. Hays and several others aggressively chased the other Comanches back to allow their more seriously wounded comrades to be helped away.

The running battle stretched out over three miles. At least twenty Comanches remained able to fight, still more than double the rangers who were still mounted and in pursuit. Hays doubted his men could handle another full-scale charge as he watched Chief Yellow Wolf shouting at his Indians to garner their courage for a final attack.

"Who has a charged rifle?" Hays shouted.

"Right here, Captain," the wounded Gillespie announced.

"Shoot that damned chief!" Hays cried.

Gillespie nodded, and rested his Yaeger hunting rifle on a large boulder. His long barrel cracked toward the distant Comanches as Yellow Wolf began to burst into a war cry. Hays proudly noted that Gillespie's aim was dead on, as the Comanche chief was blasted from his saddle.[13]

The remaining Comanches hauled clear, not even pausing to carry off their own dead and wounded. One ranger was dead, and at least four others lay wounded. In return, Hays estimated that his men and their .36-caliber Colts had killed at least twenty Indians and wounded as many as thirty others. The Texans camped on the battlefield that night, tending to their wounded. Before the rangers could head out for San Antonio the next day, four Comanches appeared near camp. They appeared to be searching for some of their own men. Hays instantly ordered Lieutenant McCulloch and five rangers in pursuit. The chase carried on for a mile; three-quarters of the Comanches perished in the fight.

Captain Hays returned to San Antonio on June 15 to tend to his wounded and execute the will of Ranger Peter Fohr. His men had killed twenty-three men in two days of fighting and had seriously wounded about thirty more. "The Indians made a magnificent fight under the circumstances," Hays reported. They had underestimated the power of a lethal new frontier weapon—the Colt five-shooter.

The rules of the game had changed in Texas. Frontier warfare would never be the same.

CAPTAIN HAYS'S BIG FIGHT on Walker's Creek received plenty of notice in Texas. The June 29, 1844, issue of the *Houston Morning Star* ran a long account of the battle. Ranger Sam Walker later reflected: "Up to this time, these daring Indians had always supposed themselves superior to us, man to man, on horse. The result of this engagement was such as to intimidate them and enable us to treat with them."[14]

Jack Hays remained in San Antonio for several weeks of July 1844, bedridden with illness that had overtaken his body. Years of hard living on the unforgiving frontier had finally caught up with him. He eventually regained full health, but he allowed his company mates to handle much of the ranging duties during that time. Their most serious encounter came on August 12, when a four-man patrol sent to check on Mexican cavalrymen rounding up horses between the Nueces and the Rio Grande was attacked by about two dozen Indians.

Rangers James Dunn and John Carolin escaped the ambush in their camp, but were separated from Rufe Perry and Kit Acklin in the process. Acklin struggled back into San Antonio a week later, having survived on only beans and prairie prickly pear apples. Perry stumbled back on foot in much worse condition. He believed he had caused great injury with his Colt pistol, but he was barely clinging to life. He had been shot through the belly and had had another bullet glance off his temple. An arrow had pierced his left shoulder while a third lodged in his jawbone. Rufe Perry would spend two years recovering from his wounds before he was well enough to saddle up again.[15]

By that time, the Republic of Texas had become the state of Texas. Dr. Anson Jones, the last president of the republic, had favored Texas to remain independent rather than being annexed by the United States. Thousands of U.S. troops had poured into Texas during 1845 as tensions with Mexico once again escalated toward a war. Major Jack Hays had become the chosen leader of a battalion of rangers charged with scouting and reporting for the U.S. Army while keeping Indian resistance in check. By the summer of 1846, the First Regiment of Mounted Riflemen was formed for duty in the Mexican War. The recovered Rufe Perry would see his share of service in one of the Texas volunteer companies.

The Texas Mounted Riflemen, sworn into federal service, were headed by the one man who had seen Texas through its most trying years—Colonel Jack Hays. The punishing summer sun warmed their faces as Hays, Sam Walker, Mike Chevallie, Ben McCulloch, and their fellow rangers rode south toward Monterrey to take part in a new siege.

A new chapter in the history of Texas and its men had begun. Its pages would be filled with tales of familiar characters who had ably served since the dawn of the former republic's first rising.

EPILOGUE

JACK HAYS AND HIS Texas Rangers changed the nature of frontier warfare. His 1844 Walker's Creek battle with Yellow Wolf's Comanches was later depicted as an engraving on the cylinder of about one hundred presentation model pistols produced by Samuel Colt's company in 1847. Colt called his new .44-caliber, six-shot revolver the Walker Colt in honor of Ranger Sam Walker, who was killed during the Mexican War that year.[1]

Colonel Hays and his Texas Mounted Riflemen gained a national reputation during the Mexican War. The much fabled frontiersman married his sweetheart, Susan Calvert, in 1847 and raised six children. Hays later pioneered trails through the Southwest to California, where he became a prominent citizen and was elected sheriff of San Francisco County in 1850. John Coffee Hays died in 1883 and is honored as the namesake of Hays County, Texas.

Numerous other Texas counties—such as Burleson, Caldwell, Coleman, Crockett, Dawson, Deaf Smith, Eastland, Erath, Fannin, Gillespie, Hockley, Houston, Karnes, Kimble (Kimbell), Lamar, McCulloch, Milam, Robertson, Rusk, Sherman, Travis, Walker, and Williamson—are named after heroes of the rising republic years.

Sidney Sherman, one of the most brazen leaders of the Battle of San Jacinto, died at home in Galveston—a short distance from the battlefield—in 1873. His commander in chief, Sam Houston, served as a U.S. senator after Texas became a state and his name was even mentioned as a possible presidential candidate. He returned as governor of Texas in 1859 but was removed from office when he refused to take the oath of office to the newly formed Confederate States of America. He died of pneumonia at the age of seventy in 1863 in his Steamboat House in Huntsville, Texas—where the world's tallest American hero statue, a sixty-seven-foot-tall granite, concrete, and steel frame rendition of the Raven, stands near the city in his honor.

Santa Anna, Houston's chief antagonist during the revolution, was president of Mexico five times. He was ultimately banished by the country's liberals in 1855, and he spent years living in exile in Cuba, the Dominican Republic, and Nassau in the Bahamas writing his memoirs. In 1874 Santa Anna was finally allowed to return to Mexico City, where he lived in obscurity until his death in 1876.

Emily West, the fabled "Yellow Rose of Texas," was eager to return to New York after the Texas Revolution but her papers showing her freedom had been lost on the San Jacinto battlefield. Major Isaac Moreland, commanding the local garrison at Galveston, vouched for Miss Emily in her application passport and she made her way back to New York in March 1837.

David Burnet, the ad interim president of the Republic of Texas during the San Jacinto campaign, remained a bitter opponent of Sam Houston. He died penniless in Galveston in 1870 and was buried by friends. Former president Mirabeau Lamar led mounted volunteers during the Mexican War and served in the Second Legislature of the state of Texas. Anson Jones, the final president of the republic, became a prosperous planter and established the first Masonic lodge in Texas at Brazoria. He was bitterly disappointed when his hopes of being appointed to the U.S. Senate in 1846 were dashed by the election of Sam Houston and Thomas Rusk in his place. He eventually sold his vast plantation for a quarter of its value and traveled to Houston in January 1858 in deep depression. Jones sequestered himself there in the Old Capitol Hotel for four nights before putting a pistol to his head on the morning of January 10.

THE PASSAGE OF THE Republic of Texas and the commencement of the twenty-eighth state of the Union was witnessed by many who had participated in the rebellious uprising that helped birth the Lone Star State.

The climatic moment was centered around an aged wooden flagpole. It stood near the capital building in Austin, with the defiant red, white, and blue Texas banner snapping in the breeze from its peak as a crowd gathered on February 19, 1846. They were there to witness the end of the proud republic and the inauguration of the first governor of the new state of Texas, James Pinckney Henderson.

Judge Robert Baylor and outgoing president Anson Jones delivered addresses to the crowd of legislators. Members of the House and Senate were seated in chairs removed from their chambers and placed on the east side of the capital building. Many of those partaking in the proceedings had sacrificed their own bodies and families during the prior decade of battles with foreign armies, the U.S. government, and marauding bands of Indians. There was former president Sam Houston, whose left leg still bore the scars of San Jacinto. There was Congressman William Sadler, the former ranger captain whose first wife and child had been slain by Indians. Ed Burleson, whose own brother had had his heart removed by Comanches in 1839, had seen more than his fair share of fights in both legislative chambers and on the embattled frontiers. Benjamin McCulloch—an artilleryman at San Jacinto, a ranger under Jack Hays in the Mexican War, and veteran of numerous expeditions—had served his republic in noble fashion. Three-Legged Willie Williamson, the peg-legged lawyer who once commanded one of the first Texas Ranger battalions, was also on hand for the passage.[2]

Emotions ran high as the Texas colors were lowered. A fresh new pennant boasting the U.S. stars and bars was readied. "The final act in this great drama is now performed," Anson Jones said in concluding his speech. "The Republic of Texas is no more."

Jones then lowered the Lone Star Flag from its pole as a brass cannon on President Hill boomed a salute to the newest American state. Jones delivered the proud flag into the waiting arms of the general who had achieved the greatest victory in the history of Texas—Sam Houston.

ACKNOWLEDGMENTS

I AM INDEBTED TO many people who helped make this book possible. Some of them have assisted both in recent months and during my previous years of researching Texas Rangers and San Jacinto campaign material.

Lisa Struthers, director of the San Jacinto Museum of History's Albert and Ethel Herzstein Library, has helped me sift through countless files of battle participants to unearth rare gems of personal accounts. For *Texas Rising*, she was vital once again by quickly stepping in to help to secure quality illustrations. Dr. Stephen L. Hardin kindly shared artwork produced by Gary Zaboly in Steve's critically acclaimed military history of the Texas Revolution, *Texian Iliad*. Dr. Gregg Dimmick, who has allowed me to participate in some of his state-authorized archaeological surveys with metal detectors on and near the battleground in past years, shared testimony from Mexican soldiers that he has mined from the archives and translated.

Other research assistance and permission for the use of illustrations came from a variety of sources. Nick Springer helped take this work to a new level with his quality cartography. From the Texas Ranger Hall of Fame and Museum in Waco, I am grateful for the help from Byron Johnson, executive director; Christina Stopka, deputy director and head of the Armstrong Texas Ranger Research Center; and Shelly Crittendon, collections manager.

William Adams kindly granted permission for the use of his copyrighted 1978 painting by Lee Herring, *Delaying Action: The Battle of Plum Creek*. Frank Horlock and Texas artist Donald Yena of San Antonio were generous enough to allow the use Don's paintings of the Goliad Massacre and the 1839 Battle of the Neches. My thanks also go out to: Donaly Brice and John Anderson of the Texas Archives, and to Linda Peterson and Steven Williams of the Center for American History, The University of Austin at Texas. Donaly in particular has assisted me for many years in my exploration of Republic of Texas audited military claims, pension papers, army papers, and ranger muster rolls.

From HarperCollins, I am grateful for Nick Amphlett for his assistance on the artwork, to Kaitlyn Kennedy for her tireless work on the publicity end, to Andrea Molitor for the quality layouts, and to Tom Pitoniak for top-notch copyediting. Executive editor Peter Hubbard served as my key liaison between his teams and the key advisors from A+E Networks—Kate Winn and Kim Gilmore—to keep the project moving swiftly along. My agent, Jim Donovan, served as my guide, friend, and editorial sounding board throughout the process.

Finally, thanks go to my wife and kids for enduring the late hours I kept in order to maintain deadlines that would coincide with the History Channel series. My daughter Emily lent her musical aptitude to help me comprehend the musical qualities of the Mexican *degüello* music. Fortunately, my family understands my passion for Texas history and my desire to pay tribute to our revolutionary forefathers, who helped the Lone Star State rise from the seeds of rebellion.

NOTES

1. RANGER LIFE

1. Jo Ella Powell Exley, *Frontier Blood: The Saga of the Parker Family* (College Station: Texas A&M University Press, 2001), 42–44.
2. Lucy A. Erath, "Memoirs of Major George Bernard Erath," *Southwestern Historical Quarterly* 26, no. 3 (January 1923): 207–8.
3. Ibid., 209–17.
4. Ibid., 218–26.
5. Ibid., 227–28.
6. "Robert Morris Coleman, Texas Patriot," article on Ancestry.com, via http:// freepages.genealogy.rootsweb.ancestry.com/~mobjackbaycolemans/g05robt morris.htm, accessed September 1, 2014.
7. John H. Jenkins and Kenneth Kesselus, *Edward Burleson: Texas Frontier Leader* (Austin, Tex: Jenkins Publishing Co., 1990), 29; Malcolm D. McLean, *Papers Concerning Robertson's Colony in Texas* (Arlington, Tex: The UTA Press, 1983), X:43.
8. John Henry Brown, *Indian Wars and Pioneers of Texas* (1880; repr., Austin, Tex: State House Press, 1988), 26; McLean, *Papers*, X:43–44; John Holland Jenkins, *Recollections of Early Texas. The Memoirs of John Holland Jenkins* (Austin, Tex.: University of Texas Press, 1958), 239–40.
9. Jenkins, *Burleson*, 29–30; James T. DeShields, *Border Wars of Texas* (1912; repr., Austin, Tex.: State House Press, 1993), 99–100.
10. Jenkins, *Burleson*, 29–30; Jenkins, *Recollections*, 21–22; McLean, *Papers*, X:43.
11. Jenkins, *Burleson*, 30–31; McLean, *Papers*, X:44; Erath, "Memoirs," 228.
12. Jenkins, *Recollections*, 23; Coleman to Henry Rueg, July 20, 1835, in McLean, *Papers*, X:47, 465.
13. Erath, "Memoirs," 228–29.
14. Jenkins, *Recollections*, 24–26.
15. Moses S. Hornsby audited claims of the Republic of Texas, Texas State Library, R47, F51; Jenkins, *Recollections*, 25–26.

2. SEEDS OF REBELLION

1. James Donovan, *The Blood of Heroes: The 13-Day Struggle for the Alamo and the Sacrifice That Forged a Nation* (New York: Little, Brown and Company, 2012), 25–26.
2. Christopher Long, "Old Three Hundred," Handbook of Texas Online, http://www.tshaonline.org/handbook/online/articles/umo01, accessed September 0, 2014. Uploaded on June 15, 2010. Published by the Texas State Historical Association.
3. Noah Smithwick, *The Evolution of a State/Recollections of Old Texas Days* (Austin, Tex.: University of Texas Press, 1983), 1.
4. Robert M. Utley, *Lone Star Justice: The First Century of the Texas Rangers* (New York: Oxford University Press, 2002), 14.
5. Eugene C. Barker, *Austin Papers* (Austin, Tex.: University of Texas Press, 1926), I:650–51; Robert Kuykendall to Luciano Garcia, July 12, 1823, Bexar Archives; Allen G. Hatley, *The Indian Wars in Stephen F. Austin's Texas Colony, 1822–1835* (Austin, Tex.: Eakin Press, 2001), 7–9.
6. Hatley, *The Indian Wars*, 11–12.
7. Ibid., 13–15; Utley, *Lone Star Justice*, 15.
8. John Wesley Wilbarger, *Indian Depredations in Texas* (1889; repr., Austin, Tex.: State House Press, 1985), 204–5; Frederick Wilkins, *The Legend Begins: The Texas Rangers, 1823–1845* (Austin, Tex.: State House Press, 1996), 6.
9. Hatley, *The Indian Wars*, 14.
10. A. J. Sowell, *Rangers and Pioneers of Texas* (1884; repr., Austin, Tex.: State House Press, 1991), 25; Walter Prescott Webb, *The Texas Rangers: A Century of Frontier Defense* (Austin, Tex.: University of Texas Press, 1991), 21.
11. Donovan, *The Blood of Heroes*, 15–20.
12. Ibid., 21.
13. Stephen L. Hardin, *Texian Iliad. A Military History of the Texas Revolution* (Austin, Tex.: University of Texas Press, 1994), 97; Donovan, *The Blood of Heroes*, 37–38.
14. Paul D. Lack, *The Texas Revolutionary Experience. A Political and Social History, 1835–1836* (College Station: Texas A&M University Press, 1992), 33; Donovan, *The Blood of Heroes*, 39–40.

3. "COME AND TAKE IT"

1. Donovan, *The Blood of Heroes*, 57.
2. Hardin, *Texian Illiad*, 7.
3. Ibid., 8–12.
4. Donovan, *The Blood of Heroes*, 59–60.
5. The New Handbook of Texas, "Goliad Campaign of 1835," 3:209–214; Hardin, *Texian Iliad*, 14.
6. Hardin, *Texian Iliad*, 26–27.
7. Smithwick, *Evolution of a State*, 70–73.

8. Hardin, *Texian Iliad*, 27; Pleasant M. Bull PD, R 141, F 233. Bull joined the volunteer army of Texas on October 7, 1835.

9. Jesus de la Teja (editor), *A Revolution Remembered: The Memoirs and Selected Correspondence of Juan N. Seguín* (Austin, Tex.: State House Press, 1991), 78, 134.

10. William R. Williamson, "Bowie, James," Handbook of Texas Online, http://www.tshaonline.org/handbook/online/articles/fbo45, accessed September 5, 2014. Uploaded on June 12, 2010.

11. Donovan, *The Blood of Heroes*, 43–50.

4. "THE DAY WAS SOON OURS"

1. John J. Linn, *Reminiscences of Fifty Yeras in Texas* (New York: D&J Sadlier & Co., 1883), 112–13; Exley, *Frontier Blood*, 46.

2. McLean, *Papers*, X:47.

3. Brown, *Indian Wars*, 26; McLean, *Papers*, X:43–44.

4. Hardin, *Texian Iliad*, 28–29.

5. De la Teja, *A Revolution Remembered*, 78; Hardin, *Texian Iliad*, 30.

6. Smithwick, *Evolution of a State*, 77.

7. Hardin, *Texian Iliad*, 32.

8. Smithwick, *Evolution of a State*, 80; De la Teja, *A Revolution Remembered*, 78.

9. Hardin, *Texian Iliad*, 41–42.

10. Ingram to Royall in John Holland Jenkins, *Papers of the Texas Revolution, 1835–1836* (Austin, Tex.: Presidial Press, 1973), II:#1040.

11. Hardin, *Texian Iliad*, 43–44.

12. Keith Guthrie, "Lipantitlan, Battle of," Handbook of Texas Online, http://www.tshaonline.org/handbook/online/articles/qfl03, accessed September 6, 2014. Uploaded on June 15, 2010.

13. Turner to Dimitt, November 30, 1835, in Jenkins, *Papers*, III:51.

5. THE RAVEN

1. Evidence of the use of the name Fort Sterling prior to the Battle of San Jacinto can be seen in some of the correspondence from Silas Parker to R. R. Royall of November 2, 1835, and Parker to the Council, December 17, 1835.

2. Joseph A. Parker AC, R 80, F 529–30; Evan W. Faulkenberry PP, R 214, F 604–5.

3. Daniel B. Friar AC, R 33, F 487–91.

4. DeShields, *Border Wars of Texas*, 118–23.

5. Silas Parker to Council, November 2, 1835, in Jenkins, *Papers,* II:303.

6. McLean, *Papers Concerning Robertson's Colony in Texas*, XII:32; (Karl) Hans Peter Marius Nielsen Gammell, *The Laws of Texas, 1822–1897* (Austin, Tex.: The Gammell Book Company, 1898), I:525–27.

7. Gammell, *The Laws of Texas*, I:928–34.

8. James L. Haley, *Sam Houston* (Norman: University of Oklahoma Press, 2002), 14–15.

9. Marshall DeBruhl, *Sword of San Jacinto: A Life of Sam Houston* (New York: Random House, 1993), 98.
10. Haley, *Sam Houston*, 65–75.
11. Donovan, *The Blood of Heroes*, 70–71.
12. Herbert Gambrell, *Anson Jones: The Last President of Texas* (Austin, Tex.: 1947; repr., Austin: University of Texas Press, 1988), 53.
13. Hardin, *Texian Iliad*, 58.
14. Jenkins, *Papers*, II:287–88.
15. Ibid., II:322.
16. Ibid., Travis to Austin, II:442–43.
17. Smither to Austin, November 4, 1835, Barker, *Austin Papers*, III:236–38; Hardin, *Texian Iliad*, 59–60.
18. Hardin, *Texian Iliad*, 61.
19. Cleburne Huston, *Deaf Smith: Incredible Texas Spy* (Waco, Tex.: Texian Press, 1973), 1–2.
20. Hardin, *Texian Iliad*, 61–63.
21. Gammell, *The Laws of Texas*, I:925–26; Hardin, *Texian Iliad*, 58–59.
22. Gammell, *The Laws of Texas*, I:538–39, 924–25.
23. Ibid., II:601.
24. Daniel B. Friar AC, R 33, F 491; Stephen Jett PD, R 164, F 536–40; Calvin B. Emmons AC, R 29, F 440–45.
25. Hardin, *Texian Iliad*, 64–65.
26. Robert Hancock Hunter, *Narrative of Robert Hancock Hunter* (1936; repr., Austin, Tex.: Encino Press, 1966), 25.
27. Hardin, *Texian Iliad*, 66.
28. Morris to Houston, November 29, 1835, Jenkins, *Papers,* III:31–32; Maverick diary, December 4, 1835.
29. Hardin, *Texian Iliad*, 64.
30. Donovan, *The Blood of Heroes*, 79.
31. Henderson Yoakum, *History of Texas From Its First Settlement in 1865 to its Annexation to the United States in 1846* (1855; repr., Austin, Tex.: Steck Company, 1935), II:198–201.
32. Donovan, *The Blood of Heroes*, 84–86.
33. Hardin, *Texian Iliad*, 88–90.
34. Ibid., 90–91.
35. Herman Ehrenberg, *With Milam and Fannin. Adventures of a German Boy in Texas' Revolution* (Austin, Tex.: Pemberton Press, 1968), 95–99; Donovan, *The Blood of Heroes*, 91–92.

6. REVOLUTIONARY RANGERS

1. Joseph A. Parker AC, R 80, F 529–30.
2. Jenkins, *Papers*, III:258–60.
3. Ibid., III:230; Joseph A. Parker AC, R 80, F 529–30.
4. James W. Parker AC, R 80, F 512; Loreno D. Nixon AC, R 78, F 128.
5. Edna McDonald Wylie, "The Fort Houston Settlement" (Houston, Tex.: Thesis in collection of Houston Public Library's Clayton Genealogy Branch,

August 1958), 7–9; Hulen M. Greenwood, *Garrison Greenwood: Ancestors and Descendants* (Houston, Tex.: Privately published, 1986), 57–61.

6. Mirabeau B. Lamar, "Journal of My Travels" (Woodson Research Center, Fondren Library, Rice University); Stephen L. Moore, *Taming Texas. Captain William T. Sadler's Lone Star Service* (Austin, Tex.: State House Press, 2000), 7–24.

7. Daniel B. Friar AC, R 33, F 447–91; Stephen L. Moore, *Savage Frontier: Rangers, Riflemen and Indian Wars in Texas. Vol. II: 1838–1839* (Denton: University of North Texas Press, 2006), 67–69.

8. McLean, *Papers*, XIII:38–40, 509; DeShields, *Border Wars*, 126; *Muster Rolls of the Texas Revolution* (Austin, Tex.: Daughters of the Republic of Texas, 1986), 128–29.

9. Smithwick, *The Evolution of a State*, 82.

10. DeShields, *Border Wars*, 167–68; Brown, *Indian Wars*, 89.

11. Smithwick, *Evolution of a State*, 83.

12. Brown, *Indian Wars*, 89–90.

13. Smithwick, *Evolution of a State*, 85–86.

14. Brown, *Indian Wars*, 90; DeShields, *Border Wars*, 171; Jenkins, *Recollections*, 33, 241; Smithwick, *Evolution of a State*, 86–87.

15. Brown, *Indian Wars*, 90.

7. "YOU MAY ALL GO TO HELL AND I WILL GO TO TEXAS"

1. Hardin, *Texian Iliad*, 98.

2. Donovan, *The Blood of Heroes*, 126–29.

3. Ibid., 131–32.

4. Hardin, *Texian Iliad*, 103; Donovan, *The Blood of Heroes*, 132–40.

5. José Enrique de la Peña, *With Santa Anna in Texas. A Personal Narrative of the Revolution* (College Station: Texas A&M University Press, 1975), 10–11.

6. Richard G. Santos, *Santa Anna's Campaign Against Texas, 1835–1836* (Austin, Tex.: Texian Press, 1968), 11.

7. Donovan, *The Blood of Heroes*, 98–99.

8. Hardin, *Texian Iliad*, 106–7.

9. Ibid., 109–10.

10. Bowie to Henry Smith, February 2, 1836, in Jenkins, *Papers*, IV:236–38; Jameson to Houston, January 18, 1836, in Jenkins, *Papers*, IV:58–61.

11. Jenkins, *Papers*, IV:185; Hardin, *Texian Iliad*, 117.

12. Michael A. Lofaro, "CROCKETT, DAVID," Handbook of Texas Online, http://www.tshaonline.org/handbook/online/articles/fcr24, accessed September 11, 2014. Uploaded on June 12, 2010.

13. Hardin, *Texian Iliad*, 118–19; Donovan, *The Blood of Heroes*, 160–61.

14. Hardin, *Texian Iliad*, 119.

15. McLean, *Papers*, XIII:53–54, 338; DeShields, *Border Wars*, 144–45.

16. Jenkins, *Papers*, IV:249–50.

17. William C. Binkley, *Correspondence of the Texan Revolution* (New York: Appleton-Century, 1936), I:409.

18. Vicente Filisola, *Memoirs for the History of the War in Texas* (Austin, Tex.: Eakin Press, 1985), 157; De la Peña, *With Santa Anna in Texas*, 26–27.
19. Hardin, *Texian Iliad*, 120–21.
20. Donovan, *The Blood of Heroes*, 173–74.

8. "I SHALL NEVER SURRENDER OR RETREAT"

1. Donovan, *The Blood of Heroes*, 181–82.
2. Ibid., 191–93.
3. Travis to Ponton, February 23, 1836, in Jenkins, *Papers*, IV:420.
4. Donovan, *The Blood of Heroes*, 196–97.
5. Hardin, *Texian Iliad*, 127.
6. Mary Whatley Clarke, *Chief Bowles and the Texas Cherokees* (Norman: University of Oklahoma Press, 1971), 62–63; Stephen L. Moore, *Last Stand of the Texas Cherokees* (Garland, Tex.: RAM Books, 2009), 41.
7. Travis to Public, February 24, 1836, in Jenkins, *Papers*, 423.
8. Donovan, *The Blood of Heroes*, 216–17.
9. Ibid., 218–219; Frank X. Tolbert, *The Day of San Jacinto* (New York: McGraw-Hill Book Co., 1959), 17–18; Walter Lord, *A Time to Stand: The Epic of the Alamo as a Great National Experience* (New York: Harper & Row, 1961), 119.
10. Travis to Houston, February 25, 1836, in Jenkins, *Papers*, IV:433.
11. Todd Hansen (editor), *The Alamo Reader* (Mechanicsburg, PA: Stackpole Books, 2003), 199–200; Donovan, *The Blood of Heroes*, 219–20.
12. Hansen, ed., *The Alamo Reader: A Study in History*, 236–38. The letter from Travis, with appeals written on it by Albert Martin and Smither, is in the possession of the Texas State Archives.
13. Williamson to Tumlinson, in Binkley, *Official Correspondence of the Texan Revolution*, II:453–54; McLean, *Papers*, XIII:75.
14. "A Critical Study of the Siege of the Alamo," *Southwestern Historical Quarterly* 37, no. 4 (April 1934): 305–7; Lord, *A Time to Stand*, 125–27.
15. Fannin to Robinson, February 26, 1836, Jenkins, *Papers*, IV:455–56.
16. Carlos Eduardo Castañeda (translator), *The Mexican Side of the Texan Revolution, 1836* (Dallas: P. L. Turner Company, 1971), Urrea's "Diary of the Military Operations," 215.
17. Hardin, *Texian Iliad*, 158–59.
18. Ibid., 160–61.
19. Travis to Convention, March 3, 1836, in Jenkins, *Papers*, IV:502–4.
20. DeBruhl, *Sword of San Jacinto*, 182–83.
21. McLean, *Papers*, IX:378–81, XII:60–61, 93–96, XIII:487–89; William C. Weatherred AC, R 111, F 217.
22. Hardin, *Texian Iliad*, 136.
23. Donovan, *The Blood of Heroes*, 241–43; 1870s interview with Susanna (Dickinson) Hannig, Hansen, *The Alamo Reader*, 45.
24. Hansen, *The Alamo Reader*, 247–93; Lord, *A Time to Stand*, 201–4; Donovan, *The Blood of Heroes*, 270–72.

25. Donovan, *The Blood of Heroes*, 272.
26. De la Peña, *With Santa Anna in Texas*, 44; Filisola, *History of the War in Texas*, II:176–77.
27. Hardin, *Texian Iliad*, 138.

9. THE FALL OF THE ALAMO

1. Hardin, *Texian Iliad*, 139.
2. Francisco Becerra (as told to John S. Ford), *A Mexican Sergeant's Recollections of the Alamo & San Jacinto* (Austin, Tex.: Jenkins Publishing Company, 1980), 24–25; De la Peña, *With Santa Anna in Texas*, 47.
3. Hardin, *Texian Iliad*, 147.
4. Madame Candelaria interview in *San Antonio Light*, February 19, 1899; Donovan, *The Blood of Heroes*, 278, 442. Many historians do not subscribe to the belief of *degüello* music being played at the Alamo. The first to publish such an account was Reuben M. Potter in his 1878 article, "The Fall of the Alamo," contained in *Magazine of American History*, 2:1–21.
5. J. M. Morphis, *History of Texas, From its Discovery and Settlement* (Ann Arbor: Scholarly Publishing Office, University of Michigan Library, 2006), 174–77.
6. Sowell, *Rangers and Pioneers*, 138–39.
7. Donovan, *The Blood of Heroes*, 287–88; Hardin, *Texian Iliad*, 148.
8. Donovan, *The Blood of Heroes*, 292–93.
9. Hardin, *Texian Iliad*, 148. Donovan, in the *Blood of Heroes,* pp. 446–53, makes a strong case that there is insufficient evidence to support the belief that David Crockett was among the five executed.
10. Hardin, *Texian Iliad*, 155.
11. Ibid., 155; Donovan, *The Blood of Heroes*, 294.
12. Lord, *A Time to Stand*, 207–8.
13. Ibid., 177–80; Donovan, *The Blood of Heroes*, 300–301.
14. [Robert M. Coleman], *Houston Displayed, or Who Won the Battle of San Jacinto? By a Farmer in the Army* (Austin, Tex.: The Brick Row Book Shop, 1964) 9; Marquis James, *The Raven: A Biography of Sam Houston* (Austin, Tex.: University of Texas Press, 1988), 189–90.
15. Jose Antonio Menchaca, "The Memoirs of Captain Menchaca, 1807–1836," Contained in Jose Antonio Menchaca Reminiscences, 1807–1836, Briscoe Center for American History, The University of Texas at Austin, Section I:1–7.
16. De la Teja, *A Revolution Remembered,* 79, 107; Menchaca, "Memoirs," I:7–8.
17. 1844 letter, Baker to Houston, published in Eugene C. Barker, "The San Jacinto Campaign," *Quarterly of the Texas State Historical Association* 4, no. 4 (April 1901): 274.
18. C. Richard King, *James Clinton Neill: The Shadow Commander of the Alamo* (Austin, Tex.: Eakin Press, 2002), 100–101; Wallace O. Chariton, *Exploring the Alamo Legends* (Plano, Tex.: Republic of Texas Press, 1992), 100; De la Teja, *A Revolution Remembered*, 107.

19. De la Peña, *With Santa Anna in Texas*, 65; Filisola, *Memoirs*, II:205–8, 149–52.
20. James, *The Raven*, 190–91; Jenkins, *Papers*, 5:69.
21. Jenkins, *Recollections*, 36–37.
22. Chariton, *Exploring the Alamo Legends*, 65–68; Jenkins, *Papers*, 5:48–53; De la Teja, *A Revolution Remembered*, 107.
23. Huston, *Deaf Smith: Incredible Texas Spy*, 53; Jenkins, *Recollections*, 37–38; John Milton Swisher, *The Swisher Memoirs* (San Antonio, Tex.: Sigmund Press, 1932), 30–31.
24. Henry Stuart Foote, *Texas and the Texans* (Philadelphia: Thomas, Cowperthwait & Co., 1841), 268; Horace Eggleston biographical sketch, Louis Wiltz Kemp Papers, The San Jacinto Museum of History, La Porte, Texas.
25. Jenkins, *Recollections*, 40.
26. Billingsley to *Galveston News*, published Saturday, September 19, 1857; Swisher, *The Swisher Memoirs*, 31–32.
27. Swisher, *The Swisher Memoirs*, 32.

10. FANNIN'S BATTLE AT COLETO CREEK

1. Jenkins, *Papers*, 5:51–53; Sowell, *Texas Indian Fighters*, 10; Sons of Dewitt Colony, Texas, http://www.tamu.edu/faculty/ccbn/dewitt/andrew3.htm, accessed November 1, 2014.
2. Hardin, *Texian Iliad*, 164.
3. Charles H. Ayers, "Lewis Ayers," *Quarterly of the Texas State Historical Association* 9 (April 1906).
4. Harbert Davenport and Craig H. Roell, "Goliad Campaign of 1836," Handbook of Texas Online, http://www.tshaonline.org/handbook/online/articles/qdg02, accessed September 15, 2014. Uploaded on June 15, 2010.
5. Hardin, *Texian Iliad*, 166–67.
6. Foote, *Texas and the Texans*, II:245.
7. Hardin, *Texian Iliad*, 168–69; Shain to father, June 25, 1836, Kemp Papers.
8. Hardin, *Texian Iliad*, 171–72.
9. Kuykendall, "Recollections of the Campaign," in Barker, "The San Jacinto Campaign," 296; Jenkins, *Papers*, 5:77–78; Forbes v. Labadie, R. B. Blake compilation, II:35.
10. De la Peña, *With Santa Anna in Texas*, 66.
11. *The New Handbook of Texas*, 2:402; Tolbert, *The Day of San Jacinto*, 41–43.
12. Jenkins, *Papers*, 5:150.
13. Foote, *Texas and the Texans*, 269–70; Jenkins, *Papers*, 5:152.
14. Kuykendall, "Recollections of the Campaign," in Barker, "The San Jacinto Campaign," 297; Jenkins, *Papers*, 5:152.
15. *Austin's Old Three Hundred. The First Anglo Colony in Texas* (Austin, Tex.: Eakin Press, 1999), 48–49.
16. Filisola, *Memoirs*, II:210–11.
17. William Physick Zuber, *My Eighty Years in Texas* (Austin, Tex.: University of Texas Press, 1971), 56–58.

18. Kuykendall, "Recollections," in Eugene C. Barker, "The San Jacinto Campaign," *Quarterly of the Texas State Historical Association* 4, no. 4 (April 1901): 298.

19. Hunter, *Narrative*, 11; Benjamin Fort Smith biographical sketch, Kemp Papers.

20. Foote, *Texas and the Texans*, 273; N. D. Labadie, "San Jacinto Campaign," 1859 *Texas Almanac*, 43; Robert J. Calder, "Recollections of the Texas Campaign of 1836," 1861 *Texas Almanac*, 63.

11. "DAMNED ANXIOUS TO FIGHT"

1. Jenkins, *Papers*, 5:167.

2. Ibid., 5:168–70.

3. Baker to Houston in 1844, in Barker, "The San Jacinto Campaign," 277; 1860 *Texas Alamanac*, 57–58.

4. De la Peña, *With Santa Anna in Texas*, 66, 80; Zuber, *My Eighty Years in Texas*, 61; C. Edwards Lester, *The Life of Sam Houston* (Biographical Center for Research, 2009), 102.

5. Barker, "The San Jacinto Campaign," 245.

6. Daniel Shipman, *Frontier Life: 58 Years in Texas* (1879, repr., Pasadena, Tex.: The Abbotsford Publishing Co., 1965), 126–28.

7. 1860 *Texas Almanac*, 57; Swisher, *The Swisher Memoirs*, 33–34.

8. William T. Sadler PP, R 237, F 95; Daniel Parker Jr. PP, R 232, F 300; Zuber, *My Eighty Years in Texas*, 62–63.

9. Paul C. Boethel, *Colonel Amasa Turner: The Gentleman from Lavaca and Other Captains at San Jacinto* (Austin, Tex.: Van Boeckmann-Jones, 1963), 21–22; Ellis Benson biographical sketch, Kemp Papers.

10. John Forbes biographical sketch, Kemp Papers; Stephen L. Moore, *Eighteen Minutes: The Battle of San Jacinto and the Texas Independence Campaign* (Dallas: Republic of Texas Press, 2004), 120–24.

11. Calder, "Recollections of the Texas Campaign of 1836," 63.

12. Harbert Davenport and Craig H. Roell, "Goliad Massacre," Handbook of Texas Online, http://www.tshaonline.org/handbook/online/articles/qeg02, accessed September 17, 2014; Craig H. Roell, "Morgan, Abel," Handbook of Texas Online, http://www.tshaonline.org/handbook/online/articles/fmo47, accessed November 03, 2014. Uploaded on June 15, 2010.

13. Keith Guthrie, *Raw Frontier: Armed Conflict Along the Texas Coastal Ben, Volume One* (Austin, Tex.: Eakin Press, 1998), 81–82; Shain to father, June 25, 1836, Kemp Papers.

14. Guthrie, *Raw Frontier,* 78–83; John C. Duval, *Early Times in Texas* (Lincoln: University of Nebraska Press, 1986), 89–99.

15. Lester Hamilton, *Goliad Survivor* (San Antonio, Tex.: The Naylor Company, 1971), 3–9; Jenkins, *Papers*, 5:367–68.

16. Spohn account, published in a Pennsylvania newspaper on August 9, 1836, and reprinted in the *New York Evening Star.*

17. Kathryn Stoner O'Connor, *Presidio La Bahía*, 1721–1846 (Austin, Tex.: Eakin Press, 2001), 142–43; Hardin, *Texian Iliad*, 173–74.

18. Jenkins, *Papers*, 5:209.
19. Haley, *Sam Houston*, 130.
20. Baker letter to Houston of 1844, published in Barker, "The San Jacinto Campaign," 279.
21. Hunter, *Narrative*, 13; James W. Pohl, *The Battle of San Jacinto* (Texas State Historical Association, 1989), 12.
22. Foote, *Texas and the Texans*, 283; Isaac Lafayette Hill biographical sketch, Kemp Papers; Baker 1844 letter, in Barker, "The San Jacinto Campaign," 279; Yoakum, *History of Texas*, II:268.
23. Labadie, "San Jacinto Campaign," 44–45.
24. Jenkins, *Papers*, 5:234–35.
25. Huston, *Deaf Smith*, 15.
26. Kuykendall, "Recollections," in Barker, "The San Jacinto Campaign," 301; Jenkins, *Papers*, 5:287.
27. Zuber, *My Eighty Years in Texas*, 67; Jenkins, *Papers*, 5:253–55, 286.
28. Jenkins, *Papers*, 5:286–87; Labadie, "San Jacinto Campaign," 44; Donald Jackson, *Voyages of the Steamboat Yellow Stone* (New York: Ticknor & Fields, 1985), 124–27.
29. Gambrell, *Anson Jones*, 64.
30. Jenkins, *Papers,* 5:245; Thomas F. Corry biographical sketch, Kemp Papers; *The Handbook of Texas*, II:812–13.
31. Jenkins, *Papers*, 5:297–300.
32. DeBruhl, *The Sword of San Jacinto*, 197; Haley, *Sam Houston*, 135.
33. Swisher, *The Swisher Memoirs*, 36; Hunter, *Narrative*, 13; Calder, "Recollections of the Texas Campaign of 1836," 64.
34. Jenkins, *Papers,* 5:321.
35. Filisola, *Memoirs*, II:205–10; De la Peña, *With Santa Anna in Texas*, 96; Pohl, *The Battle of San Jacinto*, 11.
36. Ann Fears Crawford (editor), *The Eagle. The Autobiography of Santa Anna* (Austin, Tex.: State House Press, 1988), 52.

12. THE FORK IN THE ROAD

1. Paul D. Lack, *The Diary of William Fairfax Gray. From Virginia to Texas, 1835–1837* (Dallas: SMU, 1987), 144; 1860 *Texas Almanac*, 59; Pohl, *The Battle of San Jacinto*, 13.
2. Jenkins, *Papers*, 5:313, 320.
3. Erath, "Memoirs," 255.
4. Swisher, *The Swisher Memoirs*, 35–36.
5. Sparks, "Recollections," *Quarterly of the Texas State Historical Association* 12 (July 1908): 66–67.
6. Jenkins, *Papers*, 5:343, 349.
7. Filisola, *Memoirs*, II:220; Isaac Lafayette Hill biographical sketch, Kemp Papers; Jenkins, *Papers*, 5:407.
8. Hill biographical sketch, Kemp Papers; Jenkins, *Papers*, 5:369; Filisola, *Memoirs*, II:221.
9. Jenkins, *Papers*, 5:360–61, 382.

10. Jenkins, *Papers*, 5:404; Filisola, *Memoirs*, II:221.
11. Jenkins, *Papers*, 5:415, 417; 1860 *Texas Almanac*, 60.
12. Jenkins, *Papers*, 5:428, 406–8; Haley, *Sam Houston*, 137.
13. Charles Shain account in June 30, 1836, *Louisville Journal;* Shain biographical sketch, Kemp Papers; Labadie, "San Jacinto Campaign," 45.
14. Jenkins, *Papers*, 5:444–45.
15. Houston biographical sketch, Kemp Papers.
16. Gambrell, *Anson Jones*, 65.
17. Jack C. Ramsay, Jr., *Thunder Beyond the Brazos: Mirabeau B. Lamar* (Austin, Tex.: Eakin Press, 1985), 1–2; Pohl, *The Battle of San Jacinto*, 17; Tolbert, *The Day of San Jacinto*, 86.
18. Samuel E. Asbury (editor), "The Private Journal of Juan Nepomuceno Almonte," *Southwestern Historical Quarterly* XLVIII, no. 1 (July 1944) 32; Hardin, *Texian Iliad*, 187.
19. Delgado, "Mexican Account of the Battle of San Jacinto," 613.
20. Jenkins, *Papers*, 5:461–62.
21. De la Peña, *With Santa Anna in Texas*, 105–6; Jackson, *Voyages of the Steamboat Yellow Stone*, 131–33.
22. Filisola, *Memoirs*, II:221–22.
23. Jenkins, *Papers*, 5:468–70.
24. Baker letter to Houston of 1844, in Barker, "The San Jacinto Campaign," 281.
25. Jenkins, *Papers*, 5:474–75; Haley, *Sam Houston*, 138.
26. Houston biographical sketch, Kemp Papers.
27. [Coleman], *Houston Displayed*, 17.
28. Filisola, *Memoirs*, II:212.
29. Billingsley to *Galveston News*, September 19, 1857, in Billingsley biographical sketch, Kemp Papers.
30. 1860 *Texas Almanac*, 61–62; Calder, "Recollections of the Texas Campaign," 64.
31. Hunter, *Narrative*, 13–14.
32. James Washington Winters, "An Account of the Battle of San Jacinto," *Southwest Historical Quarterly* 6 (October 1902): 140.

13. "DARING CHIVALRY": THE FIRST DUEL

1. Tolbert, *The Day of San Jacinto*, 71–73.
2. Dr. George M. Patrick letter, printed in the August 25, 1841, issue of the *Telegraph and Texas Register;* Pohl, *The Battle of San Jacinto*, 26.
3. Delgado, "Mexican Account of the Battle of San Jacinto," 614; De la Peña, *With Santa Anna in Texas*, 114.
4. Filisola, *Memoirs*, II:222.
5. Tolbert, *The Day of San Jacinto*, 73–75; Delgado, "Mexican Account of the Battle of San Jacinto," 615.
6. "West, Emily D.," Handbook of Texas Online, http://www.tshaonline.org/handbook/online/articles/fwe41, accessed October 12, 2014.
7. Martha Anne Turner, *The Yellow Rose of Texas. Her Saga and Her Song.*

With the Santa Anna Legend (Austin, Tex.: Shoal Creek Publishers, Inc., 1976), 9–10; Tolbert, *The Day of San Jacinto*, 76–78; Filisola, *Memoirs*, II:223.

8. Huston, *Deaf Smith*, 68–69.
9. Bryan to Sherman, July 2, 1859, in Sidney Sherman and Mirabeau Buonaparte Lamar, Jesse Billingsley, et al., "Defence of Gen. Sidney Sherman Against the Charges Made by Gen. Sam Houston, in his Speech Delivered in the United States Senate, February 28th, 1859," (1859, repr., Houston, Tex.: Smallwood, Dealy & Baker, 1885) 29; Menchaca, "Memoirs," II:2; Tolbert, *The Day of San Jacinto*, 94–96; William C. Swearingen biographical sketch, Kemp Papers.
10. Moore, *Eighteen Minutes*, 244–46.
11. Zuber, *My Eighty Years in Texas*, 85–86; Menchaca, "Memoirs," II:3–4.
12. Haley, *Sam Houston*, 148; "Juan N. Seguin," Tejano Association for Historical Preservation, Lorenzo de Zavala Chapter, "El Filosofo" newsletter, October 2002.
13. Winters, "An Account of the Battle of San Jacinto," 141; Labadie, "San Jacinto Campaign," 50; Erath, "Memoirs," 265.
14. Alphonso Steele, *Biography of Private Alphonso Steele (Deceased). Last Survivor of the Battle of San Jacinto* (Privately published pamphlet, 1909), 4.
15. Hardin, *Texian Iliad*, 201.
16. Jenkins, *Papers,* 5:513; Labadie, "San Jacinto Campaign," 51.
17. Delgado, "Mexican Account of the Battle of San Jacinto," 615; Filisola, *Memoirs*, II:223; Castaneda, *The Mexican Side of the Texas Revolution*, 112–13.
18. Pohl, *The Battle of San Jacinto*, 21; Labadie, "San Jacinto Campaign," 49; William C. Swearingen biographical sketch, Kemp Papers.
19. Erath, "Memoirs," 257.
20. Labadie, "San Jacinto Campaign," 49; Forbes v. Labadie, R. B. Blake compilation, II:14.
21. Labadie, "San Jacinto Campaign," 49–50.
22. Pohl, *The Battle of San Jacinto*, 28.
23. Benjamin Cromwell Franklin, "The Battle of San Jacinto. By One Who Fought in It." *Little's Living Age*, September 7, 1844, 259–65. This article was written anonymously by Franklin in 1837 and reprinted in 1844. See Moore, *Eighteen Minutes*, 481, for more on Franklin being the author.
24. Frank W. Johnson, *A History of Texas and Texans* (Chicago: The American Historical Society, 1916), I:268–74; [Coleman], *Houston Displayed*, 21; Labadie, "San Jacinto Campaign," 49–50; Steele, *Biography of Private Alfonso Steele*, 4.
25. Delgado, "Mexican Account of the Battle of San Jacinto," 615; Tolbert, *The Day of San Jacinto*, 113.
26. Labadie, "San Jacinto Campaign," 51; Bryan to Sherman, July 2, 1859, in Sherman, "Defence," 30; Hardin, *Texian Iliad*, 202. Many accounts of San Jacinto incorrectly state that the Mexican cannon fired first on April 20,

but the Golden Standard artillery piece had not yet even been advanced
onto the field at this point.
27. Delgado, "Mexican Account of the Battle of San Jacinto," 615.
28. Bryan to Sherman, July 6, 1859, in Sherman, "Defence," 36; Menchaca, "Memoirs," II:6; Labadie, "San Jacinto Campaign," 51–52.
29. Thomas C. Utley biographical sketch, Kemp Papers.
30. Erath, "Memoirs," 258.
31. Delgado, "Mexican Account of the Battle of San Jacinto," 616.
32. Sherman, "Defence," 4; Foote, *Texas and the Texans*, II:298.
33. Foote, *Texas and the Texans*, II:298–303.
34. Delgado, "Mexican Account of the Battle of San Jacinto," 617.
35. Walter Paye Lane, *The Adventures and Recollections of General Walter P. Lane* (Austin, Tex.: Pemberton Press, 1970), 12.
36. Foote, *Texas and the Texans*, II:301–2.
37. Labadie, "San Jacinto Campaign," 52–53.
38. Lane, *The Adventures and Recollections of General Walter P. Lane*, 12–16.
39. Hockley in Foote, *Texas and the Texans*, II:303.
40. Foote, *Texas and the Texans*, II:300–2; Calder, "Recollections," 65; Billingsley to *Galveston News*, September 19, 1857, Billingsley biographical sketch, Kemp Papers.
41. Delgado, "Mexican Account of the Battle of San Jacinto," 617; Houston's Official Report to Burnet, April 25, 1836.
42. Heard to Sherman, June 15, 1859, in Sherman, "Defence," 10.
43. Billingsley to *Galveston News*, September 19, 1857, Billingsley biographical sketch, Kemp Papers.
44. Erath, "Memoirs," 259.

14. SLAUGHTER AT SAN JACINTO
1. Hardin, *Texian Iliad*, 206; Tolbert, *The Day of San Jacinto*, 124; James, *The Raven*, 206.
2. [Coleman], *Houston Displayed*, 24; Filisola, *Memoirs*, II:223–24.
3. Delgado, "Mexican Account of the Battle of San Jacinto," 617.
4. Huston, *Deaf Smith*, 77.
5. Filisola, *Memoirs*, II:224; Maillard, *The History of the Republic of Texas* (1842), 107, Battle of San Jacinto Notebook, McArdle Papers.
6. James, *The Raven*, 190; Sam Houston biographical sketch, Kemp Papers; [Coleman], *Houston Displayed*, 25.
7. Labadie, "San Jacinto Campaign," 53; Sam Houston biographical sketch, Kemp Papers; 1860 *Texas Almanac*, 65.
8. Sherman to Billingsley letter, 1859, Jesse Billingsley biographical sketch in Kemp Papers.
9. Samuel Houston biographical sketch, Kemp Papers; Forbes v. Labadie, R. B. Blake compilation, II:30; Y. P. Alsbury, "Burning of Vince's Bridge," 1861 *Texas Almanac*, 55–58; [Coleman], *Houston Displayed*, 25; Labadie, "San Jacinto Campaign," 53.
10. Alsbury, "Burning of Vince's Bridge," 57.

11. Declarations of Corporal Juan Reyes and Private Toribio Reyes, 1836 depositions in Archivo General de Mexico, Center for American History, courtesy of Dr. Gregg Dimmick.
12. Erath, "Memoirs," 260.
13. Calder, "Recollections of the Texas Campaign of 1836," 65; Erath, "Memoirs," 260; Tolbert, *The Day of San Jacinto*, 135.
14. Erath, "Memoirs," 263. See Moore, *Eighteen Minutes*, 294–97, 435–58, for the numbers and rosters of the Texans.
15. Houston and Lamar biographical sketches, Kemp Papers; Lamar to Sherman, September 24, 1857, from Sherman, "Defence," 3.
16. Shain letter of June 25, 1836, Kemp Papers.
17. Bob Tutt, "New Twists Discovered in Saga of 'Yellow Rose of Texas,' " *Port Arthur News*, March 13, 1997, 4B; Tolbert, *The Day of San Jacinto*, 144. Stephen Hardigan, in his *Texian Iliad*, page 286, insists that there "is not a scintilla of primary evidence to support the oft-repeated myth that Santa Anna was engaged in a tryst with mulatto slave girl Emily Morgan."
18. James M. Hill to McArdle, October 20, 1895, Battle of San Jacinto Notebook, McArdle Notebooks.
19. "Recollections of S. F. Sparks, 70–71."
20. Houston biographical sketch, Kemp Papers; Andrew Jackson Houston, *Texas Independence* (Houston: Anson Jones Press, 1938), 229; Tolbert, *The Day of San Jacinto*, 143.
21. Erath, "Memoirs," 263–66.
22. John W. Hassell biographical sketch, Kemp Papers; Turner, *The Yellow Rose of Texas*, 25; Calder, "Recollections," 66.
23. Filisola, *Memoirs*, II:227; Declarations of Corporal Juan Reyes and Private Toribio Reyes, courtesy of Dr. Gregg Dimmick.
24. Filisola, *Memoirs*, II:225; Foote, Texas and the Texans, II:309; Lane, *The Adventures and Recollections of General Walter P. Lane*, 14.
25. Foote, *Texas and the Texans*, II:310–11; Huston, *Deaf Smith*, 88.
26. Rodriquez, "Memoirs of Early Texas"; Foote, *Texas and the Texans*, 310.
27. Hassell and Lonis biographical sketches, Kemp Papers.
28. Stevenson letter of April 23, 1836, Kemp Papers; Shain letter, June 25, 1836, Kemp Papers.
29. Delgado, "Mexican Account of the Battle of San Jacinto," 618; Filisola, *Memoirs*, II:225; Labadie, "San Jacinto Campaign," 58.
30. Houston, *Texas Independence*, 229; Stevenson letter, April 23, 1836, Kemp Papers; Labadie, "San Jacinto Campaign," 55; Babineck, Mark, "Houston's 1853 Letter Proves Historians Wrong," *Houston Chronicle*, April 21, 2002, 40A. William Huddle's famous 1886 San Jacinto painting incorrectly shows Sam Houston with a bandaged right leg. Houston wrote to his wife in 1853 complaining about the left leg, which had been wounded at San Jacinto. Houston's son later wrote that his father had been hit in the left ankle.
31. Calder, "Recollections of the Texas Campaign of 1836," 69.
32. Lane, *The Adventures and Recollections of General Walter P. Lane*,

14–15; Deposition of Grenadier Bernardino Santa Cruz, translated by Dr. Gregg Dimmick; Denham letter, May 3, 1836, Kemp Papers; Winters, "An Account of the Battle of San Jacinto," 142–43.

33. Tolbert, *The Day of San Jacinto*, 152–53.
34. Labadie, "The San Jacinto Campaign," 54–55; Forbes v. Labadie, R. B. Blake compilation, II:2–3, 10–11, 95.
35. Forbes v. Labadie, R. B. Blake compilation, I:43–45, II:2–3, 10–11, 52–53, 56–57, 21–22, 137.
36. Taylor, "Pursuit of Santa Anna," 1868 *Texas Almanac*, 537–40; Lapham letter of May 17, 1836, Kemp Papers; Young Perry Alsbury biographical sketch, Kemp Papers.
37. William S. Taylor to William C. Crane, March 8, 1866, McArdle Notebooks; Calder, "Recollections of the Texas Campaign of 1836," 67.
38. Labadie, "The San Jacinto Campaign," 55; Tolbert, *The Day of San Jacinto*, 156; Winters, "An Account of the Battle of San Jacinto," 142–143.
39. Turner account from Barker, "The San Jacinto Campaign," 341–42; Tolbert, *The Day of San Jacinto*, 159–60.
40. Jenkins, *Papers*, 6:12–13.
41. Swearingen biographical sketch, Kemp Papers.
42. James Tarlton letter, April 22, 1836, Kemp Papers. His letter was published in the June 3, 1836, edition of Cincinnati's *Daily Commercial Republican and Commercial Register*.

15. TEXAS RISING

1. Erath, "Memoirs," 267–68.
2. Hardaway biographical sketch, Kemp Papers.
3. 1859 *Texas Almanac*, 166; James Austin Sylvester letter published in *Telegraph and Texas Register*, August 2, 1836.
4. Winters, "An Account of the Battle of San Jacinto, 143; Sparks, "Recollections," 72; Bostick, "Reminiscences," 95; Moore, *Taming Texas,* 73. The Sadler story was related to the author by his grandmother, Evaline Kolb Moore, and her cousin, former Texas land commissioner Jerry Sadler, in 1980.
5. Yoakum, *History of Texas*, II:258–59; Tolbert, *The Day of San Jacinto*, 179.
6. [Coleman], *Houston Displayed*, 30; Foote, *Texas and the Texans*, II:312–13; Yoakum, *History of Texas*, II:258–59.
7. Tolbert, *The Day of San Jacinto*, 181; Filisola, *Memoirs*, II:235–36; Jenkins, *Papers*, 6:15–16.
8. John J. Linn, *Reminiscences of Fifty Years in Texas* (New York: D&J Sadlier & Co., 1883), 264.
9. Forbes v. Labadie, R. B. Blake compilation, II:119, 28–30; Delgado, "Mexican Account of the Battle of San Jacinto," 623.
10. Filisola, *Memoirs*, II:244–245; Tolbert, *The Day of San Jacinto*, 226–27.
11. Hockley biographical sketch, Kemp Papers; Crawford, *The Eagle*, 57–58; Will Fowler, *Santa Anna of Mexico* (Lincoln, NE: University of Nebraska Press, 2007), 183.

16. NEW CHALLENGES FOR A NEW NATION

1. Binkley, *Official Correspondence of the Texan Revolution*, II:879; Francis M. Doyle Audited Claims.
2. Jenkins, *Recollections*, 45–46; Wilbarger, *Indian Depredations*, 255–57.
3. Rachel (Parker) Plummer, *Narrative of the Capture and Subsequent Sufferings of Mrs. Rachel Parker* (Houston, 1839), 5–7.
4. Exley, *Frontier Blood*, 41, 54–55.
5. Brown, *Indian Wars*, 40–43; Exley, *Frontier Blood*, 103–4, 114–15.
6. Dr. Dan. B. Wimberly, "Daniel Parker: Pioneer Preacher and Political Leader" (diss., Texas Tech University, May 1995), 239, 274–75.
7. Jenkins, *Papers*, VI:392; McLean, *Papers*, XIV:423.
8. Jenkins, *Papers*, VI:410.
9. Yoakum, *History of Texas*, 300; Jenkins, *Papers*: VII:135–36.
10. Cox, *Texas Ranger Tales II*, 4–12.
11. Yoakum, 1855 *History of Texas*, II:181–82; Mike Cox, *Texas Ranger Tales II* (Plano, Tex.: Republic of Texas Press, 1999), 4–12.
12. Jenkins, *Papers*, VII:197–99.
13. Joseph M. Nance, *After San Jacinto: The Texas-Mexican Frontier, 1836–1841* (Austin, Tex.: University of Texas Press, 1963), 17–18.
14. "Biography of Cicero Rufus Perry, 1822–1898," Special collections of the Daughters of the Republic of Texas Library, San Antonio, Texas; Jenkins, *Recollections*, 192–96.
15. Moore, *Savage Frontier*, II:174; Nance, *After San Jacinto*, 46–47, 20–21.
16. Jenkins, *Papers*, 8:214–16; McLean, *Papers*, XV:133–35; Smithwick, *The Evolution of a State*, 108.
17. Erath, "Memoirs," 273.
18. Jenkins, *Papers*, 9:360–61, 370–71, 483; Abram Anglin AC, R 3, F 133; Gerald Swetnam Pierce, *Texas Under Arms. The Camps, Posts, Forts, and Military Towns of the Republic of Texas* (Austin, Tex.: Encino Press, 1969), 162–63.
19. Williams, *Writings of Sam Houston*, I:497; Pierce, *Texas Under Arms*, 72–73.
20. Fisher to Jewell, February 13, 1837, Army Correspondence, Box 1214–16, Texas State Library and Archives Commission; Williams, *Writings of Sam Houston*, II:232–35.
21. McLean, *Papers*, XV:65; Gammell, *Laws of Texas*, I:1113–16.
22. Gammell, *Laws of Texas*, I:1134.
23. Nance, *After San Jacinto*, 29–31; Henry W. Karnes AC, R 55, F 505–9; Huston, *Deaf Smith*, 112–13; Charles P. Roland, *Albert Sidney Johnston: Soldier of Three Republics* (Austin: University of Texas Press, 1964), 66; Pierce, *Texas Under Arms*, 123.
24. McLean, *Papers*, XV:42, 51–58, 231; George B. Erath AC, R 29, F 617; Erath, "Memoirs," 274; Smithwick, *Evolution*, 113.
25. Smithwick, *The Evolution of a State*, 113; McLean, *Papers*, XV:468; *Telegraph and Texas Register*, July 8, 1837.
26. Erath, "Memoirs," 275–78.

27. Smithwick, *The Evolution of a State*, 112–13.
28. Huston, *Deaf Smith*, 113.
29. John C. Caperton, "Sketch of Col. John C. Hays, The Texas Rangers, Incidents in Texas and Mexico, Etc. from Materials Furnished by Col. Hays and Major John Caperton," (1879, typescript copy, James T. DeShields Papers, Center for American History, University of Texas at Austin); James Kimmins Greer, *Texas Ranger: Jack Hays in the Frontier Southwest* (College Station: Texas A&M University Press, 1993), 15–17.
30. Greer, *Texas Ranger*, 20–21. Texas researcher Jody Edward Ginn points out that the actual arrival date of Jack Hays in Texas is questionable. Texas General Land Office returns show Hays as arriving "early in 1838" versus the 1836 given by Greer and others.
31. Francis W. White AC, R 113, F 476; Huston, *Deaf Smith*, 112–14.
32. Captain Erastus Smith report to Secretary of War W. S. Fisher, March 27, 1837, published in the April 11, 1837, edition of the *Telegraph and Texas Register;* Huston, *Deaf Smith*, 115–16; Nance, *After San Jacinto*, 34.
33. Huston, *Deaf Smith*, 116–18.
34. James Matthew Jett biographical sketch, Kemp Papers; Nance, *After San Jacinto*, 37.
35. Greer, *Texas Ranger*, 24–25; Juan N. Seguin, AC, R 93, F402–7.
36. Smithwick, *Evolution*, 132; DeShields, *Indian Wars*, 194; McLean, *Papers*, XV:516–17; Erath to Lamar in Gulick, *Lamar Papers*, IV:32; Sowell, *Texas Indian Fighters*, 299.
37. Nance, *After San Jacinto*, 38–40.
38. Gammell, *The Laws of Texas*, I:427–28.
39. William M. Eastland AC, R 28, F 255–59; Noah Smithwick, R 98, F 482; Smithwick, *The Evolution of a State*, 151.
40. Greer, *Texas Ranger*, 27–28.
41. DeShields, *Border Wars of Texas*, 221; Greer, *Texas Ranger*, 29.
42. DeShields, *Border Wars*, 221–23; McLean, *Papers*, 16:538–40.
43. DeShields, *Border Wars*, 224; McLean, *Papers*, 16:447–49, 541–43; *Texas Indian Papers*, I:50–52.
44. Brown, *Indian Wars*, 50–51; Greer, *Texas Ranger*, 28; Charles A. Gulick, Winnie Allen, Katherine Elliott, and Harriet Smither, *The Papers of Mirabeau Buonaparte Lamar* (1922, repr., Austin, Tex.: Pemberton Press, 1968), IV:230.

17. LAMAR'S CHEROKEE WAR OF EXTINCTION

1. Nance, *After San Jacinto*, 117–20; Gary Clayton Anderson, *The Conquest of Texas: Ethnic Cleansing in the Promised Land* (Norman: University of Oklahoma Press, 2005), 158–64; *Telegraph and Texas Register*, August 25, 1838.
2. Nance, *After San Jacinto*, 120; John Salmon Ford, *Rip Ford's Texas* (Austin, Tex.: University of Austin Press, 1994), 35–36; Mary Whatley Clarke, *Thomas J. Rusk: Soldier, Statesman, Jurist* (Austin, Tex.: Jenkins Publishing Company, 1971), 110–11.

3. Lacy narrative in W. G. Robertson, *The Lone Star State* (Privately published, 1893), 238–39; Moore, *Savage Frontier*, II:19–36.
4. McLean, *Papers*, 16:587–92; Gerald Swetnam Pierce, *The Army of the Republic of Texas, 1836–1845* (University of Mississippi, dissertation, 1964), 137–38.
5. McLean, *Papers*, 16:260–61; Wylie, "The Fort Houston Settlement," 128, 41.
6. *Cherokee County History* (Crockett, Tex.: Cherokee County Historical Commission and the Publications Development Co. of Texas, 1986); Albert Woldert, "The Last of the Cherokees in Texas," *Chronicles of Oklahoma* 1, no. 3 (June 1923): 179–226; McLean, *Papers*, 16:260–62.
7. Harry McCorry Henderson, "The Surveyors' Fight," *Southwestern Historical Quarterly* 56 (July 1952), 26–29; Walter P. Lane account in DeShields, *Border Wars*, 226.
8. Jimmy L Bryan, Jr., "More Disastrous Than All: The Surveyors' Fight, 1838," *East Texas Historical Journal* 38, no. 1 (2000): 3–14; Henderson, "The Surveyors' Fight," 31–35; DeShields, *Border Wars*, 227.
9. McLean, *Papers*, 16:628–30; Brown, *Indian Wars*, 56.
10. Lois Blount, "A Brief Study of Thomas J. Rusk Based on His Letters to His Brother, David, 1835–1856," *Southwestern Historical Quarterly* XXXIV (April 1931): 279–80.
11. Rusk letter in *Telegraph and Texas Register*, November 3, 1838; *Lamar Papers*, II:266.
12. Judge Andrew J. Fowler, "The Edens Massacre," Historical Sketch of Anderson County notebook, Palestine Library; McLeod account in Gulick, *Lamar Papers*, II:266; McLean, *Papers*, 16:625.
13. Moore, *Taming Texas*, 131–40; Edens Family Association, *The Edens Adventure: A Brief History of the Edens Family in America* (Privately published, 1992), 32–41; Gulick, *Lamar Papers*, II:263–65.
14. DeShields, *Border Wars*, 243–44; Benjamin Franklin Cage biographical sketch, Kemp Papers; Miles Squier Bennett diary, Center for American History, University of Texas at Austin.
15. Wilbarger, *Indian Depredations*, 1–4; Gulick, *Lamar Papers*, II:303–7.
16. Rusk to Douglass, November 21, 1838, Douglass Papers, James Harper Starr Papers, Center for American History, University of Texas at Austin; Gulick, *Lamar Papers*, II:294–99, 302, 308–9; McLean, *Papers*, 16:187–88.
17. McLeod and Rusk to Lamar in Gulick, *Lamar Papers*, II:405–6; *Journals of the Fourth Congress, Republic of Texas*, Vol. 3: Reports and Relief Laws, 89.
18. Gammell, *The Laws of Texas*, II:15–20.
19. DeShields, *Border Wars*, 251; General Morehouse to Major Jones, January 21, 1839, Adjutant General's Papers, Texas State Archives.
20. DeShields, *Border Wars*, 254–55; Wilbarger, *Indian Depredations*, 362–63; Dudley G. Wooten (editor), *A Comprehensive History of Texas, 1685 to 1897* (Dallas: William G. Scharff, 1898), I:750–51.
21. DeShields, *Border Wars*, 255–58; Gulick, *Lamar Papers*, IV:30.
22. Gulick, *Lamar Papers*, II:420.

23. Gulick, *Lamar Papers*, II:464–65; Sadler's original letter is housed in the Texas State Archives.

24. Smithwick, *The Evolution of a State*, 155–57; Jenkins, *Recollections of Early Texas*, 183–86; "Biography of Cicero Rufus Perry," 5–6; "Capt. J. H. Moore's report of a battle with the Comanches, on the 15th of February 1839," *Journals of the Fourth Congress*, III:108–10; Brown, *Indian Wars*, 75.

25. Jenkins and Kesselus, *Edward Burleson*, 181; Colonel Burleson's report in *Journals of the Fourth Congress*, III:112–13; Brown, *Indian Wars*, 61; Jenkins, *Recollections*, 56–57; Sowell, *Rangers*, 55–56.

26. Wilbarger, *Indian Depredations*, 148–49; Jenkins, *Recollections*, 58; Sowell, *Early Settlers and Indian Fighters of Southwest Texas*, 1–17; Sowell, *Rangers*, 56–57.

27. Burleson report, 112; Wilbarger, *Indian Depredations*, 149–50; Sowell, *Texas Indian Fighters*, 17; Jenkins, *Recollections*, 248, 268–69.

28. Jenkins, *Burleson*, 186; Nance, *After San Jacinto*, 90–91.

29. Nance, *After San Jacinto*, 123.

30. Ibid., 123–27; Jenkins, *Recollections*, 84–85.

31. Brown, *Indian Wars*, 64; Nance, *After San Jacinto*, 128–29; Catherine W. McDowell (editor), *Now You Hear My Horn. The Journal of James Wilson Nichols, 1820–1887* (Austin, Tex.: University of Texas Press, 1961), 34–36; Sowell, *Texas Indian Fighters*, 417–25.

32. Burleson report, May 22, 1839, in *Journals of the Fourth Congress*, III:113–14; Wilbarger, *Indian Depredations*, 158–63; Nance, *After San Jacinto*, 132–34.

33. Thomas Clarence Richardson, *East Texas: Its History and Its Makers* (New York: Lewis Historical Publishing, 1940), I:116.

34. Dianna Everett, *The Texas Cherokees: A People Between Two Fires, 1819–1840* (Norman: University of Oklahoma Press, 1990), 51, 102–3; *Journals of the Fourth Congress of the Republic of Texas*, III:77; Woldert, "The Last of the Cherokees," 197–98; Gulick, Lamar Papers, II:590–94; Dorman Winfrey and James M. Day, *The Texas Indian Papers, 1825–1843* (Austin, Tex.: Austin Printing Company, 1911), II:61–66.

35. John H. Reagan, *The Memoirs of John H. Reagan* (Austin, Tex.: The Pemberton Press, 1968), 30.

36. Brookshire report, May 31, 1839, in *Journals of the Fourth Congress of the Republic of Texas*, III:110–11; Brown, *Indian Wars*, 70–72; DeShields, *Border Wars*, 260–62; William H. Weaver PD, R 195, F 70.

37. C. W. Webber, *Tales of the Southern Border* (Philadelphia: J.B. Lippincott & Co., 1856), 54–55.

38. Miles Squier Bennett diary, Valentine Bennett scrapbook, Center for American History, University of Texas at Austin; De la Teja, *A Revolution Remembered*, 184–86; Rena Maverick Green (editor), *Memoirs of Mary A. Maverick* (1921, repr., Lincoln: University of Nebraska Press, 1989), 23–24.

39. Clarke, *Thomas J. Rusk*, 127.

40. Everett, *The Texas Cherokees*, 105.

41. Clarke, *Thomas J. Rusk*, 129–30; Everett, *The Texas Cherokees*, 105–6.
42. John H. Reagan, "Expulsion of the Cherokees from East Texas," *Quarterly of the Texas State Historical Association* I (1897), 43.
43. Douglass to Johnson, July 16, 1839, in Gulick, *Lamar Papers*, III:45–46; Ben H. Procter, *The Life of John H. Reagan* (Austin, Tex.: University of Texas Press, 1962), 24–25.
44. Hart to Starr, July 24, 1839, in Starr Papers, Center for American History, University of Texas at Austin.
45. Crane family history courtesy of John Crane's great-great-grandson, Don Crane. He cites an account of the Battle Creek written by John S. Cadell on September 20, 1929.
46. Peter Rodden to David Rodden, October 26, 1839, Starr Papers; Moore, *Last Stand of the Texas Cherokees*, 139–41.
47. Reagan, *Memoirs*, 34.
48. Brown, *Indian Wars*, 68; Moore, *Taming Texas*, 191–92; Reagan, *Memoirs*, 46.
49. Everett, *The Texas Cherokees*, 108.
50. Clarke, *Chief Bowles and the Texas Cherokees*, 111.
51. Clarke, *Thomas J. Rusk*, 135–36.
52. *Journals of the Fourth Congress*, III:88–91; Johnston to Lamar, December 12, 1839, Army Papers, 1837–1839 Correspondence, Texas State Archives.
53. Gerald S. Pierce, "Burleson's Northwestern Campaign," *Texas Military Monthly* 6, no. 3 (Fall 1967): 195; Jenkins, *Burleson*, 216.
54. Burleson report of December 26, 1839, in *Appendix to the Journals of the House of Representatives: Fifth Congress*, Document C, 132.
55. Captain Howard's report of "Engagement with Indians," in *Appendix to the Journals of the House of Representatives, Fifth Congress*, 125–26.
56. McLean, *Papers*, 16:300.
57. J. W. Benedict, "Diary of a Campaign Against the Comanches," *Southwestern Historical Quarterly* 32 (April 1929): 300–10; John James PD, R 164, F 355–57.
58. Hays to Lamar in Gulick, *Lamar Papers*, IV:231–32; Greer, *Texas Ranger* 36.
59. Benedict, "Diary," 309; *Telegraph and Texas Register*, December 11, 1839.

18. WAR WITH THE COMANCHES

1. W. W. Newcomb Jr., *The Indians of Texas: From Prehistoric to Modern Times* (Austin, Tex.: University of Texas Press, 1961), 155–60; Anderson, *The Conquest of Texas*, 20–24; Pekka Hämäläinen, *The Comanche Empire* (New Haven: Yale University Press, 2008), 102.
2. *Journals of the House of Representatives of the Republic of Texas: Fifth Congress, Appendix*, 133.
3. Green, *Memoirs of Mary A. Maverick*, 25, 38.
4. McLeod to Lamar, in *Appendix to the Journals of the House of Representatives: Fifth Congress,* 136–39; Brown, *Indian Wars*, 77–78; Paul N.

Spellman, *Forgotten Texas Leader: Hugh McLeod and the Texan Santa Fe Expedition* (College Station: Texas A&M University Press, 1999), 46–50; DeShields, *Border Wars*, 288–94.

5. Charles M. Robinson III, *The Men Who Wear the Star: The Story of the Texas Rangers* (New York: Random House, 2000), 61–62; Webb, *The Texas Rangers*, 84–85; Wilkins, *The Legend Begins*, 65–66; Thomas W. Knowles, *They Rode for the Lone Star: The Saga of the Texas Rangers. The Birth of Texas—The Civil War* (Dallas: Taylor Publishing Company, 1999), 97.

6. Green, *Memoirs of Mary A. Maverick*, 36; Wilkins, *The Legend Begins*, 79–80; Brown, *History of Texas*, II:177; DeShields, *Border Wars of Texas*, 293–94.

7. Howard to Fisher, April 6, 1840, in Ford, "Memoirs," II:227–29.

8. Donaly E. Brice, *The Great Comanche Raid: Boldest Indian Attack of the Texas Republic* (Austin, Tex.: Eakin Press, 1988), 25–26; Green, *Memoirs of Mary A. Maverick*, 31.

9. Brice, *The Great Comanche Raid*, 28; Anderson, *The Conquest of Texas*, 185–87.

10. Brown, *Indian Wars*, 79; Jenkins, *Recollections*, 62.

11. *Telegraph and Texas Register*, September 9, 1840; Brown, *Indian Wars*, 79; Brice, *The Great Comanche Raid*, 29.

12. Brice, *The Great Comanche Raid*, 30–31; Linn, *Reminiscences of Fifty Years in Texas*, 338–39; Brown, *Indian Wars*, 79–80; McDowell, *Now You Hear My Horn*, 56–57.

13. *Telegraph and Texas Register*, September 2, 1840; Brice, *The Great Comanche Raid*, 32, 99; Linn, *Reminiscences*, 341.

14. Brown, *Indian Wars*, 80; Miller to *Austin City Gazette*, August 17, 1840; *Telegraph and Texas Register*, September 9, 1840.

15. Victor M. Rose, *The Life and Services of Gen. Ben McCulloch* (1888, repr., Austin, Tex.: The Steck Company), 56.

16. Jenkins, *Burleson*, 248–49.

17. McDowell, *Now Your Hear My Horn*, 59.

18. Ibid., 72–74; Brazos (pseudo.), *The Life of Robert Hall* (Austin: Ben C. Jones and Company, Printers, 1898), 53; Jenkins, *Recollections*, 64–65.

19. McDowell, *Now You Hear My Horn*, 61; Greer, *Texas Ranger*, 40; Z. N. Morrell, *Flowers and Fruit in the Wilderness* (St. Louis: Commercial Printing Company, 1872), 65–66; Paul C. Boethel, *A History of Lavaca County* (Austin, Tex.: Von Boeckmann-Jones, 1959).

20. John Harvey biographical sketch, Kemp Papers; Jenkins, *Burleson*, 258.

21. John H. Moore report in *Austin City Gazette*, November 11, 1840; Webb, *The Texas Rangers*, 45; Robinson, *The Men Who Wear the Star*, 59; Wilkins, *The Legend Begins*, 86–87; Pierce, *Army*, 199–200; Brown, *Indian Wars*, 83.

22. Brown, *Indian Wars*, 83–84; Anderson, *The Conquest of Texas*, 190–91; *Telegraph and Texas Register*, September 3, 1840, and November 18, 1840, 2; Brice, *The Great Comanche Raid*, 62–63.

23. Pierce, *Army*, 201; Brice, *The Great Comanche Raid*, 56–57.

19. CAPTAIN DEVIL JACK

1. Pierce, *Army*, 204–7; McLean, *Papers*, XVIII:146; Nance, *After San Jacinto*, 97; McLeod to Archer, December 17, 1840, in *Journals of the House of Representatives: Fifth Congress, Appendix*, 376.
2. Gammell, *Laws of Texas*, II:475–76; Nance, *After San Jacinto*, 399.
3. Greer, *Texas Ranger*, 37–40; Caperton, "Sketch of Colonel John C. Hays," 8–9.
4. Caperton, "Sketch of Colonel John C. Hays," 9–10; Webb, *The Texas Rangers*, 85.
5. Hays to Lamar in Gulick, *Lamar Papers*, IV:232.
6. Nance, *After San Jacinto*, 402–3.
7. Ibid., 408–10; *Journals of the Sixth Congress, Republic of Texas*, III:411–12.
8. Hays to Lamar in Gulick, *Lamar Papers*, IV:232; Buquor, "An Episode of 1841," from *Floresville Chronicle*, in Ford, "Memoirs," 243–47.
9. Hays to Lamar in Gulick, *Lamar Papers*, IV:233.
10. Moore, *Savage Frontier*, III:234, 274.
11. Green, *Memoirs of Mary A. Maverick*, 49–50.
12. Caperton, "Sketch of Col. John C. Hays," 16; Hays battle report in *Journals of the Sixth Congress Republic of Texas*, III:422; Hays to Lamar in Gulick, *Lamar Papers*, IV:234.
13. *Journals of the Sixth Congress, Republic of Texas*, III:423–24; Caperton, "Sketch of Col. John C. Hays," 18.
14. Gulick, *Lamar Papers*, IV:235; Caperton, "Sketch of Col. John C. Hays," 20–21.
15. *Journals of the Sixth Congress, Republic of Texas*, III:424; Hays to Lamar in Gulick, *Lamar Papers*, IV:235. Other details of the Llano battle can be found in Caperton, "Sketch," 16, although this early Hays historian mixes details of Hays's June 29 and July 24 Comanche fights.
16. John C. Hays AC, R 160, F 378–493; Greer, *Texas Ranger*, 51–52.
17. Robinson, *The Men Who Wear the Star*, 66–67; Wilkins, *The Legend Begins*, 203–4; Caperton, "Sketch of Col. John C. Hays," 30–31; Samuel C. Reid, *The Scouting Expeditions of McCulloch's Texas Rangers* (Philadelphia: G. B. Zieber and Company, 1847), 111–12; Sowell, *Early Settlers and Indian Fighters of Southwest Texas*, 334–35; Greer, *Texas Ranger*, 52. For a detailed examination of the Enchanted Rock battle, see Moore, *Savage Frontier*, IV:342–48.
18. Reid, *McCulloch's Texas Rangers*, 111–12.
19. Nance, *After San Jacinto*, 480; Pierce, *Texas Under Arms*, 11; Robinson, *The Men Who Wear the Star*, 66.
20. Greer, *Texas Ranger*, 60–61.
21. Joseph M. Nance, *Attack and Counter-Attack: The Texas-Mexican Frontier, 1842* (Austin, Tex.: University of Texas Press, 1964), 15–17; Brown, *History of Texas*, II:212; Greer, *Texas Ranger*, 63.
22. Nance, *Attack and Counter-Attack*, 26–29; Brown, *History of Texas*, II:213–14.

23. Jenkins, *Recollections*, 220; John Twohig PE, R 242, F 648.
24. De la Teja, *A Revolution Remembered*, 44–45.
25. Nance, *Attack and Counter-Attack*, 111–12; Moore, *Savage Frontier*, IV: 21–25.
26. McDowell, *Now You Hear My Horn*, 76.
27. Accounts of the so-called Bandera Pass battle of the Jack Hays rangers on the Guadalupe vary widely. For varying version of it, see Sowell, *Early Settlers and Indian Fighters of Southwest Texas*, 22–23, 317–19, 809–10; Creed Taylor, "Jack Hays Fight on the Guadalupe"; and McDowell, *Now You Hear My Horn*, 76–78. For an analysis of this battle from these sources and Texas Archives documents, see Moore, *Savage Frontier*, IV:33–39.
28. McDowell, *Now You Hear My Horn*, 123.
29. Nance, *Attack and Counter-Attack*, 280–81.
30. Brian DeLay, *War of a Thousand Deserts: Indian Raids and the U.S.-Mexican War* (New Haven: Yale University Press, 2008), 45, 20, 48, 79–83; Hämäläinen, *The Comanche Empire*, 196, 210, 216.
31. Nance, *Attack and Counter-Attack*, 300–4.
32. Moore, *Savage Frontier*, IV:75–81.
33. Morrell, *Flowers and Fruits in the Wilderness*, 92.
34. Nance, *Attack and Counter-Attack*, 389–93.
35. Ibid., 394–95; McDowell, *Now You Hear My Horn*, 111.
36. Wilkins, *The Legend Begins*, 141; Morell, *Fruits and Flowers in the Wilderness*, 95.
37. Wilkins, *The Legend Begins*, 146; Brown, *The History of Texas*, II:233.
38. Nance, *Attack and Counter-Attack*, 481–84.
39. Sam W. Haynes, *Soldiers of Misfortune: The Somervell and Mier Expeditions* (Austin: University of Texas Press, 1990), 52–54; Nance, *Attack and Counterattack*, 503–15.
40. Nance, *Attack and Counter-Attack*, 553–57; Wilkins, *The Legend Begins*, 154.
41. Greer, *Texas Ranger*, 88–89.
42. Haynes, *Soldiers of Misfortune*, 119–25.

20. TRIUMPH AT WALKER'S CREEK

1. Gammell, *The Laws of Texas*, II:846–48, 865; Wilkins, *The Legend Begins*, 163–64.
2. Greer, *Texas Ranger*, 90; Wilkins, *The Legend Begins*, 168; Rufus Perry letter, Center for American History.
3. Mike Cox, *The Texas Rangers: Wearing the Cinco Peso, 1821–1900* (New York: Forge, 2008), 89.
4. Caperton, "Sketch of Colonel John C. Hays," 34–35, 42.
5. Hays to George Washington Hill, November 12, 1843, Texas State Archives.
6. Greer, *Texas Ranger*, 93.
7. Gammell, *The Laws of Texas*, II:943–44.
8. Greer, *Texas Ranger*, 104–5.

9. Wilkins, *The Legend Begins*, 177.
10. Hays report to Secretary of War George W. Hill, June 16, 1844, contained in *Journals of the House of Representatives of the Ninth Congress of the Republic of Texas*, 32–33.
11. Anderson, *The Conquest of Texas*, 206; Wilkins, *The Legend Begins*, 178; Cox, *The Texas Rangers*, 90–91; Hays report.
12. Greer, *Texas Ranger*, 98; Hays report; Sowell, *Texas Indian Fighters*, 809; Wilkins, *The Legend Begins*, 179–80.
13. Hays report; Caperton, "Sketch of Colonel John C. Hays," 22; Knowles, *They Rode for the Lone Star*, 100; Wilkins, *The Legend Begins*, 180.
14. Cox, *The Texas Rangers*, 92.
15. Perry, "Memoir of Capt'n C. R. Perry," typescript in possession of the Daughters of Republic Library; Cox, *The Texas Rangers*, 95.

EPILOGUE

1. Moore, *Savage Frontier*, IV:152.
2. Gambrell, *Anson Jones*, 418–19; Haley, *Sam Houston*, 294.

BIBLIOGRAPHY

DOCUMENTS, MANUSCRIPTS AND COLLECTIONS

Aldrich, Armistead Albert. Papers. Center for American History, University of Texas, Austin.

Appendix to the Journals of the House of Representatives: Fifth Congress. Printed at the Gazette Office for the Republic of Texas, Austin, 1841.

Army Papers, Republic of Texas. Archives and Library Division, Texas State Library in Austin, Texas.

Bennett, Miles Squier. Diary from Valentine Bennett Scrapbook, The Center for American History, University of Texas at Austin.

"Biography of Cicero Rufus Perry, 1822–1898. Captain, Texas Rangers." Special collections of Daughters of the Republic of Texas Library, San Antonio, Tex.

Caperton, John C. "Sketch of Colonel John C. Hays, The Texas Rangers, Incidents in Texas and Mexico, Etc. from Materials furnished by Col. Hays and Major John Caperton." Typescript version. Original prepared in 1879. Original copy in the Bancroft Library at the University of California at Berkley. Typescript copy part of James T. DeShields Papers, Center for American History, University of Texas at Austin.

"Declaration of Corporal Juan Reyes." Archivo General de Mexico—Guerra, Frac I, Leg 2, Mil. Texas, 1836, The University of Texas, Center for American History. T976.405, Book 335, 13–19. Translated version courtesy of Dr. Gregg Dimmick. Gregg also provided copies of his English translations for Toribio Reyes and Bernardino Santa Cruz (Book 335, 20–24.)

Douglass, Kelsey Harris. Douglass Papers, James Harper Starr Papers, Center for American History, The University of Texas at Austin.

Edens, Dr. Frank N. Unpublished research on Daniel Parker family.

Forbes v. Labadie libel suit. Transcripts of veteran depositions prepared by Robert Bruce Blake, East Texas Research Center at Stephen F. Austin State University's Steen Library.

General Land Office of Texas: records and papers collection.

Hunter, Mary Kate. Unpublished Papers of, located in Carnegie Library in Palestine, Texas. Miss Hunter was a school teacher who collected statements

Bibliography

in the early 1900s from many of the county's earliest citizens. Some of her collected works are referenced, including, Judge A. J. Fowler's "The Edens' Massacre" and "Historic Sketches of Anderson County."

Journals of the Fourth Congress of the Republic of Texas. Austin, Tex: Von Boeckmann-Jones Co. Printers, 1930.

Journals of the House of Representatives of the Republic of Texas: Fifth Congress, Appendix. Austin: Gazette Office, 1841.

Journals of the Sixth Congress, Republic of Texas. Austin: np, 1842.

Journals of the House of Represenatatives of the Ninth Congress of the Republic of Texas. Washington, TX: Miller & Cushney, 1845.

Kemp, Louis Wiltz. Kemp Papers (including biographical sketches of the San Jacinto veterans). The San Jacinto Museum of History. La Porte, Texas.

Lamar, Mirabeau B. "Journals of My Travels." Woodson Research Center, Fondren Library, Rice University.

McArdle, Henry Arthur. The Battle of San Jacinto. The McArdle Notebooks. Archives and Information Services Division, Texas State Library and Archives Commission.

Menchaca, Jose Antonio. "The Memoirs of Captain Menchaca, 1807–1836." Contained in Jose Antonio Menchaca Reminiscences, 1807–1836, Briscoe Center for American History, The University of Texas at Austin.

Muster Rolls of the Texas Army and the Texas Militia, courtesy of the Texas State Archives. See individual chapter footnotes and appendices for those referenced.

Nicholson, James. Papers. Center for American History, University of Texas, Austin.

"Report of K. H. Douglass of the Campaign Against the Cherokees," August 1839. Courtesy of Donaly E. Brice, Texas State Library and Archives Commission.

Republic Claims Papers, 1835–1846 (microfilmed). Texas State Library and Archives Commission, Austin.

Rusk, Thomas Jefferson. Original Papers of. East Texas Research Center in Stephen F. Austin State University Library, Nacogdoches.

Sadler, Robert H. "Notes Relative to the Edens Massacre." Written on January 1, 1971. "Facts related to Robert H. Sadler by Lula Sadler Davis of Grapeland, Texas, widow of John A. Davis." Courtesy of Howard C. Sadler collection.

Sadler, William Turner. Texas Pension Papers and Audited Military Claims. Provided courtesy of Howard C. Sadler. Also referenced: William Turner Sadler land documents provided by the General Land Office of Texas.

Sherman, Sidney, and Mirabeau Buonaparte Lamar, Jesse Billingsley, et al. *Defence of Gen. Sidney Sherman Against the Charges Made by Gen. Sam Houston, in His Speech Delivered in the United States Senate, February 28th, 1859.* Galveston: Printed at the "News" Book and Job Office, 1859; reprint, Houston: Smallwood, Dealy & Baker, 1885; copied by George L. Crocket in January 1934. George Louis Crocket Papers, East Texas Research Center, Steen Library, Stephen F. Austin State University. (Crocket changed the original spelling of "Defence" to "Defense" in his typescript.)

368

Starr, James Harper. Papers. Center for American History, University of Texas, Austin. Includes papers of Brigadier General Kelsey H. Douglass.

Uniform of the Army of the Republic of Texas. Prescribed and published by order of the President.

Wimberly, Dan B. "Daniel Parker: Pioneer Preacher and Political Leader." History dissertation submitted to the Graduate Faculty of Texas Tech University in May 1995. Courtesy of Dr. Frank N. Edens.

Wylie, Edna McDonald. "The Fort Houston Settlement." A Thesis from August 1958 in the collections of the Houston Public Library's Clayton Genealogy Branch.

ARTICLES, INTERNET

Alsbury, Y. P. "Burning of Vince's Bridge." Letter of Young Perry Alsbury written January 14, 1858, and published in 1861 *Texas Almanac.*

Asbury, Samuel E. (Editor). "The Private Journal of Juan Nepomuceno Almonte." *Southwestern Historical Quarterly,* Vol. XLVIII, No. 1 (July 1944).

Ayers, Charles H. "Lewis Ayers," *Quarterly of the Texas State Historical Association* 9 (April 1906).

Babineck, Mark, "Houston's 1853 Letter Proves Historians Wrong," *Houston Chronicle,* April 21, 2002, 40A.

Barker, Eugene C. (editor). "Journal of the Permanent Council." *The Quarterly of the Texas State Historical Association.* Vol. 7 (1904).

Barker, Eugene C. "The San Jacinto Campaign," *The Quarterly of the Texas State Historical Association.* Vol 4, No. 4 (April 1901), 274.

Benedict, J. W. "Diary of a Campaign against the Comanches." *Southwestern Historical Quarterly.* Vol. 32 (April 1929) 300–10.

Blount, Lois. "A Brief Study of Thomas J. Rusk Based on His Letters to His Brother, David, 1835–1856." *Southwestern Historical Quarterly,* XXXIV (April 1931).

Brown, Jennifer. "Their Spirits Still Live On Battleground: "Indian Group Buys East Texas Site of Famed Battle of Neches." *Tyler Morning Telegraph,* (December 14, 1997).

Bryan, Jimmy L. Jr. "More Disastrous Than All: The Surveyors' Fight, 1838." *The East Texas Historical Journal* 38, No. 1 (2000):3–14.

Calder, R. J. "Recollections of the Texas Campaign of 1836." 1861 *Texas Almanac,* 62–70.

Chriesman, Horatio. "Reminiscences of Horatio Chriesman." *The Quarterly of the Texas State Historical Association.* Vol. 6 (1903).

"Robert Morris Coleman, Texas Patriot," article on Ancestry.com, accessed http://freepages.genealogy.rootsweb.ancestry.com/~mobjackbaycolemans/g05robtmorris.htm on September 1, 2014.

"A Critical Study of the Siege of the Alamo," *Southwestern Historical Quarterly,* Vol. 37, No. 4 (April 1934).

Crosby, David F. "Texas Rangers in The Battle of Brushy Creek." *Wild West,* Vol. 10, No. 2, (August 1997): 60–64, 89–90.

Delgado, Col. Pedro. "Mexican Account of the Battle of San Jacinto." Published in 1870 *Texas Almanac* and in Day, James M. (Compiler). *The Texas Almanac 1857–1873. A Compendium of Texas History.* Waco, TX: Texian Press, 1967.

Erath, Lucy A. "Memoirs of Major George Bernard Erath."*Southwestern Historical Quarterly,* Vol. 26, no. 3 (January 1923): 207–233; Vol. 26, no. 4 (April 1923): 255–280; Vol. 27, no. 1 (July 1923): 27–51; Vol. 27, no. 2 (October 1923): 140–163.

Franklin, Benjamin Cromwell, "The Battle of San Jacinto. By One Who Fought in It." *Little's Living Age,* September 7, 1844, 259–265. This article was written anonymously by Franklin in 1837 and reprinted in 1844.

Fuquay, John W. "The Smith Family." *Tyler Today* (Summer 1996), 24–26. Courtesy of the Smith County Historical Society.

Handbook of Texas Online.

Henderson, Harry McCorry. "The Surveyors' Fight."*Southwestern Historical Quarterly,* Vol. 56 (July 1952), 25–35.

Hiatt, James. "James Parker's Quest." *Wild West,* Vol. 3, No. 3 (October 1990): 10, 16, 62–63.

Johnson, Norman K. "Chief Bowl's Last Charge." *Wild West,* Vol. 2, No. 2 (August 1989), 12–16, 62–66.

Jones, Ernest. "Captain W. T. Sadler Helped Create County."*Palestine Herald-Press,* (February 5, 1969): 10.

"Juan N. Seguin," Tejano Association for Historical Preservation, Lorenzo de Zavala Chapter, "El Filosofo" newsletter, October 2002.

Labadie, N. D. "San Jacinto Campaign." 1859 *Texas Almanac,* 40–64.

Long, Christopher, "Old Three Hundred," Handbook of Texas Online (http://www.tshaonline.org/handbook/online/articles/umo01), accessed September 02, 2014. Uploaded on June 15, 2010. Published by the Texas State Historical Association.

Looscan, Adele B. "Capt. Joseph Daniels." *Texas Historical Association Quarterly,* Vol. V, No. 1 (1901–1902), 19–21.

Mann, William L. "James O. Rice, Hero of the Battle on the San Gabriels. *Southwestern Historical Quarterly,* Vol. 55 (July 1951) 30–42.

Pierce, Gerald S. "Burleson's Northwestern Campaign." *Texas Military Monthly.* Fall 1967, Vol. 6, No. 3: 191–201.

Potter, Rebuen M. "The Fall of the Alamo." *Magazine of American History,* 1878, 2: 1–21.

Reagan, John H. "Expulsion of the Cherokees from East Texas." *Quarterly of the Texas State Historical Association,* Vol. I (1897), 38–46.

"The Records of an Early Texas Baptist Church." *The Quarterly of the Texas State Historical Association.* Volume I (1833–1847) of the church's history is published in the Vol. XI, No. 2 issue of October 1907 and Volume II (1847–1869) is published in Vol. XII, No. 1 of July 1908.

"Sadler Descendant of County Pioneer." *Palestine Herald-Press,* (January 10, 1975).

Sparks, S. F. "Recollections of S. F. Sparks." *Quarterly of the Texas State Historical Association.* XII: No. 1 (July 1908).

Telegraph and Texas Register. See source notes from individual chapters for dates between 1836 and 1839 copied from microfilm in the Texas Room of the Houston Public Library.

Tutt, Bob. "New Twists Discovered in Saga of 'Yellow Rose of Texas,'" *Port Arthur News,* March 13, 1997, 4B.

Uniform of the Army of the Republic of Texas. Prescribed and published by order of the President.

Wilcox, S. S. "Laredo During the Texas Republic." *Southwestern Historical Quarterly,* Vol. 42, No. 2 (1939), 83–107.

Winfrey, Dorman. "Chief Bowles of the Texas Cherokee." *Chronicles of Oklahoma* 32 (Spring 1954): 29–41.

Winters, James Washington. "An Account of the Battle of San Jacinto." *Southwestern Historical Quarterly,* Vol. 6 (October 1902), 139–140.

Woldert, Albert, M.D. "The Last of the Cherokees in Texas, and the Life and Death of Chief Bowles." *Chronicles of Oklahoma,* Issued by The Oklahoma Historical Society in Oklahoma City, Okla., Volume I, Number 3, (June 1923): 179–226. Copy provided by the Texas State Archives, which included supplemental notes made by Woldert after the original publication of this article.

Yates, Becky. "Historical Date Line: Edens-Madden Massacre." *The East Texas Roundup,* Crockett, Texas, (December 17, 1970): 6. Courtesy of Howard C. Sadler.

BOOKS

Aldrich, Armistead Albert. *History of Houston County, Together with Biograhical Sketches of Many Pioneers*. San Antonio, Tex: The Naylor Co., 1943.

Anderson, Gary Clayton. *The Conquest of Texas: Ethnic Cleansing in the Promised Land*. Norman: University of Oklahoma Press, 2005.

Aubrey, Betty Dooley and Claude Dooley. *Why Stop? A Guide to Texas Historical Roadside Markers*. Houston, Tex: Lone Star Books, Fourth Edition, 1999. Reprint, 1978.

Austin's Old Three Hundred. The First Anglo Colony in Texas. Austin: Eakin Press, 1999.

Barker, Eugene C. *The Life of Stephen F. Austin: Founder of Texas, 1793–1836*. Austin: University of Texas Press, 1985.

———. *Austin Papers*. Austin: The University of Texas, 1926.

Bate, W. N. *General Sidney Sherman: Texas Soldier, Statesman and Builder*. Waco, Tex: Texian Press, 1974.

Becerra, Francisco (as told to John S. Ford in 1875). *A Mexican Sergeant's Recollections of the Alamo & San Jacinto*. Austin: Jenkins Publishing Company, 1980.

Binkley, William C. *Official Correspondence of the Texas Revolution*. New York: Appleton-Century, 1936.

Biographical Directory of the Texan Conventions and Congresses, 1832–1845. Austin, Tex: Book Exchange, 1941.

Biographical Gazetteer of Texas. Austin, Tex: W. M. Morrison Books, 1987.

Bibliography

Boethel, Paul C. Colonel Amasa Turner. *The Gentleman from Lavaca and Other Captains at San Jacinto.* Austin: Van Boeckmann-Jones, 1963.

———. *A History of Lavaca County.* Austin: Von Boeckmann-Jones, 1959.

Brice, Donaly E. *The Great Comanche Raid: Boldest Indian Attack of the Texas Republic.* Austin, Tex: Eakin Press, 1987.

Brown, Gary. *The New Orleans Greys. Volunteers in the Texas Revolution.* Plano, Tex: Republic of Texas Press, 1999.

Brown, John Henry. *Indian Wars and Pioneers of Texas.* 1880. Reprint. Austin, Tex: State House Press, 1988.

Carter, W. A. *History of Fannin County, Texas.* Bonham, Tex: Bonham News, 1885. Reprint. Honey Grove, Tex: Fannin County Historical Society, 1975.

Castañeda, Carlos Eduardo (translator). *The Mexican Side of the Texan Revolution (1836). By the Chief Mexican Participants.* (Recollections of General Antonio Lopez de Santa Anna, Secretary Ramon Martinez Caro, General Vicente Filisola, General Jose Urrea, and General Jose Maria Tornel.) Dallas, TX: P. L. Turner Company, 1971.

Chariton, Wallace O. *Exploring the Alamo Legends.* Plano, Tex: Republic of Texas Press, 1992.

Cherokee County History. First Edition, 1986. Crockett, Tex: Published by the Cherokee County Historical Commission and the Publications Development Co. of Texas.

Clark, Sara. *The Capitols of Texas: A Visual History.* Austin, Tex: Encino Press, 1975.

Clarke, Mary Whatley. *Chief Bowles and the Texas Cherokees.* Civilization of the American Indian Series, No. 113. Norman, Okla.: University of Oklahoma Press, 1971.

———. *Thomas J. Rusk: Soldier, Statesman, Jurist.* Austin, Tex: Jenkins Publishing Company, 1971.

[Coleman, Robert Morris.] *Houston Displayed, or Who Won the Battle of San Jacinto? By a Farmer in the Army* (anonymously published). Austin: The Brick Row Book Shop, 1964.

Connor, Seymour V., et. al. *Capitols of Texas.* Waco, Tex: Texian Press, 1970.

Cox, Mike. *Texas Ranger Tales II.* Plano, Tex: Republic of Texas Press, 1999.

———. *The Texas Rangers: Wearing the Cinco Peso, 1821–1900.* New York: Forge, 2008.

Crawford, Ann Fears (editor). *The Eagle. The Autobiography of Santa Anna.* Austin: State House Press, 1988.

Day, James M. *Post Office Papers of the Republic of Texas, 1836–1839.* Austin: Texas State Library, 1966.

———.(Compiler). *The Texas Alamanac 1857–1873. A Compendium of Texas History.* Waco, Tex: Texian Press, 1967.

De Bruhl, Marshall. *Sword of San Jacinto: A Life of Sam Houston.* New York: Random House, 1993.

Delay, Brian. *War of a Thousand Deserts: Indian Raids and the U.S.-Mexican War.* New Haven: Yale University Press, 2008.

DeShields, James T. *Border Wars of Texas*. 1912. Reprint. Austin:State House Press, 1993.

———. *Tall Men with Long Rifles*. San Antonio, Tex: Naylor Company, 1935.

Dixon, Sam Houston and Louis Wiltz Kemp. *The Heroes of San Jacinto*. Houston, Tex: The Anson Jones Press, 1932.

Donovan, James. *The Blood of Heroes: The 13-Day Struggle for the Alamo and the Sacrifice That Forged a Nation*. New York: Little, Brown and Company, 2012.

Duval, John C. Edited by Mabel Major and Rebecca W. Smith. *Early Times in Texas*. Lincoln: University of Nebraska Press, 1986.

The Edens Adventure: A Brief History of the Edens Family in America. Published by the Edens Family Association, 1992.

Ehrenberg, Herman. *With Milam and Fannin. Adventures of a German Boy in Texas' Revolution*. Austin: Pemberton Press, 1968

Erath, George Bernard as dictated to Lucy A. Erath. *The Memoirs of Major George B. Erath, 1813–1891*. Austin, Tex: Texas State Historical Society, 1923. Reprinted by The Heritage Society of Waco in 1956.

Ericson, Carolyn Reeves. *Nacogdoches-Gateway to Texas. A Biographical Directory, Vol. I*. Nacogdoches, Tex: Ericson Books, 1977.

Everett, Dianna. *The Texas Cherokees: A People Between Two Fires, 1819–1840*. Norman: University of Oklahoma Press, 1990.

Exley, Jo Ella Powell. *Frontier Blood: The Saga of the Parker Family*. College Station: Texas A&M University Press, 2001.

Fehrenbach, T. R. *Lone Star: A History of Texas and the Texans*. Reprint. New York: American Legacy Press, 1983.

Filisola, Vicente. *Memoirs for the History of the War in Texas*. Austin: Eakin Press, 1985.

Foote, Henry Stuart. *Texas and the Texans*. 2 volumes. Philadelphia: Thomas, Cowperthwait & Co., 1841.

Ford, John Salmon, edited by Stephen B. Oates. *Rip Ford's Texas*. Austin: University of Texas Press, 1994.

Fowler, Will. *Santa Anna of Mexico*, The University of Nebraska Press, 2007.

Gambrell, Herbert. *Anson Jones: The Last President of Texas*. Austin: University of Texas Press, 1988 reprint. 1947. Reprint.

Gammell, (Karl) Hans Peter Marius Nielsen. *The Laws of Texas, 1822–1897*. Ten volumes. Austin, Tex: The Gammel Book Company, 1898.

Gonzales County History. Published by Gonzales County Historical Commission and Curtis Media Corp., 1986.

Green, Rena Maverick (editor). *Memoirs of Mary A. Maverick*. 1921. Reprint, Lincoln: University of Nebraska Press, 1989.

Greenwood, Hulen M. *Garrison Greenwood: Ancestors and Descendants*. Privately published by author in Houston, Tex: 1986.

Greer, James Kimmins. *Texas Ranger: Jack Hays in the Frontier Southwest*. College Station, TX: Texas A&M University Press, 1993. This book was originally published by E.P. Dutton and Company, Inc. as *Colonel Jack Hays: Texas Frontier Leader and California Builder* in 1952.

Groneman, Bill. *Alamo Defenders. A Genealogy: The People and Their Words.* Austin, TX: Eakin Press, 1990.

———. *Battlefields of Texas.* Plano: Republic of Texas Press, 1998.

Gulick, Charles A. Jr., Winnie Allen, Katherine Elliott, and Harriet Smither. *The Papers of Mirabeau Buonaparte Lamar,* 6 Volumes, 1922. Reprint. Austin, Tex: Pemberton Press, 1968.

Guthrie, Keith. *Raw Frontier. Armed Conflict Along the Texas Coastal Bend, Volume One.* Austin: Eakin Press, 1998.

Haley, James L. *Sam Houston.* Norman: University of Oklahoma Press, 2002.

Hämäläinen, Pekka. *The Comanche Empire.* New Haven, CT: Yale University Press, 2009.

Hamilton, Lester. *Goliad Survivor.* San Antonio, TX: The Naylor Company, 1971.

Hansen, Todd (Editor). *The Alamo Reader.* Mechanicsburg, PA: Stackpole Books, 2003.

Hardin, Stephen L. *Texian Iliad. A Military History of the Texas Revolution.* Austin: University of Texas Press, 1994. Reprint, 1999.

Hatley, Allen G. *The Indian Wars in Stephen F. Austin's Texas Colony, 1822–1835.* Austin: Eakin Press, 2001.

Haynes, Sam W. *Soldiers of Misfortune: The Somervell and Mier Expeditions.* Austin: University of Texas Press, 1990.

History of Houston County: 1687–1979. Compiled and edited by the History Book Committee of Houston County Historical Commission of Crockett, Texas. Tulsa, Okla.: Heritage Publishing Company, 1979.

Hohes, Pauline Buck. *A Centennial History of Anderson County, Texas.* San Antonio, Tex: Naylor, 1936.

Houston, Andrew Jackson. *Texas Independence.* Houston: Anson Jones Press, 1938.

Hunter, Robert Hancock. *Narrative of Robert Hancock Hunter.* 1936. Reprint, Austin: Encino Press, 1966.

Huston, Cleburne. *Deaf Smith: Incredible Texas Spy.* Waco, Tex: Texian Press, 1973.

———. *Towering Texan: A Biography of Thomas J. Rusk.* Waco, Tex: Texian Press, 1971.

Jackson, Donald. *Voyages of the Steamboat Yellow Stone.* New York: Ticknor & Fields, 1985.

James, Marquis. *The Raven: A Biography of Sam Houston.* Austin: University of Texas Press, 1988.

Jenkins, John H. and Kenneth Kesselus. *Edward Burleson: Texas Frontier Leader.* Austin, Tex: Jenkins Publishing Co., 1990.

Jenkins, John Holland. *Papers of the Texas Revolution 1835–1836.* Ten Volumes. Austin, Tex: Presidial Press, 1973.

———. *Recollections of Early Texas. The Memoirs of John Holland Jenkins.* Edited by John Holmes Jenkins III. Austin: University of Texas Press, 1958. Reprint. 1995.

Johnson, Frank W. *A History of Texas and Texans.* Edited by Eugene C. Barker. Chicago: The American Historical Society, 1916.

King, C. Richard. *James Clinton Neill. The Shadow Commander of the Alamo*. Austin: Eakin Press, 2002.

Knowles, Thomas W. *They Rode for the Lone Star. The Saga of the Texas Rangers. The Birth of Texas-The Civil War*. Dallas, Tex: Taylor Publishing Company, 1999.

Koury, Michael J. *Arms For Texas: A Study of the Weapons of the Republic of Texas*. Fort Collins, Colo.: The Old Army Press, 1973.

Lack, Paul. *The Diary of William Fairfax Gray. From Virginia to Texas, 1835–1837*. Dallas: SMU, 1987.

Lack, Paul D. *The Texas Revolutionary Experience. A Political and Social History, 1835–1836*. College Station: Texas A&M University Press, 1992.

Ladd, Kevin. *Gone to Texas: Genealogical Abstracts from The Telegraph and Texas Register 1835–1841*. Bowie, MD: Heritage Books, 1994.

Lane, Walter Paye. *The Adventures and Recollections of General Walter P. Lane*. Austin, Tex: Pemberton Press, 1970.

Lester, C. Edwards. *The Life of Sam Houston*. Biographical Center for Research, 2009.

Linn, John J. *Reminiscences of Fifty Years in Texas*. New York: D&J Sadlier & Co., 1883.

Lord, Walter. *A Time To Stand: The Epic of the Alamo as a Great National Experience*. New York: Harper & Row Publishers, 1961.

Maillard, N. Doran. *The History of the Republic of Texas: From the Discovery of the Country to the Present Time, and the Cause of Her Separation from the Republic of Mexico*. London: Smith, Elder, 1842.

McDowell, Catherine W. (ed.). *Now You Hear My Horn. The Journal of James Wilson Nichols, 1820–1887*. Austin: University of Texas Press, 1961.

McLean, Malcolm D. *Papers Concerning Robertson's Colony in Texas*. Published by the University of Texas at Arlington. Arlington, Tex: The UTA Press.

Moore, Stephen L. *Eighteen Minutes: The Battle of San Jacinto and the Texas Independence Campaign*. Dallas: Republic of Texas Press (an imprint of Rowman & Littlefield Publishing Group), 2004.

———. *Taming Texas. Captain William T. Sadler's Lone Star Service*. Austin, Tex: State House Press, 2000.

———. *Last Stand of the Texas Cherokees. Chief Bowles and the 1839 Cherokee War in Texas*. Garland, TX: RAM Books, 2009.

———. *Savage Frontier: Rangers, Riflemen and Indian Wars in Texas. Vol. I. 1835–1837*. Denton: University of North Texas Press, 2002.

———. *Savage Frontier: Rangers, Riflemen and Indian Wars in Texas. Vol. II. 1838–1839*. Denton: University of North Texas Press, 2006.

———. *Savage Frontier: Rangers, Riflemen and Indian Wars in Texas. Vol. III. 1840–1841*. Denton: University of North Texas Press, 2007.

———. *Savage Frontier: Rangers, Riflemen and Indian Wars in Texas. Vol. IV. 1842–1845*. Denton: University of North Texas Press, 2010.

Morphis, J. M. *History of Texas, From its Discovery and Settlement*. Ann Arbor: Scholarly Publishing Office, University of Michigan Library, 2006.

Morrell, Z. N. *Flowers and Fruits in the Wilderness.* 1872. Reprint, St. Louis: Commercial Printing Company, undated third edition.

Muster Rolls of the Texas Revolution. Austin: Daughters of the Republic of Texas, 1986.

Nance, Joseph M. *After San Jacinto: The Texas-Mexican Frontier, 1836–1841.* Austin: University of Texas Press, 1963.

———. *Attack and Counter-Attack: The Texas-Mexican Frontier, 1842.* Austin: University of Texas Press, 1964.

Nevin, David. *The Texans (The Old West Series).* Alexandria, Va: Editors of Time-Life Books, 1975. Reprint. 1980.

The New Handbook of Texas. Austin: The Texas State Historical Association, 1996, Six Volumes.

Newcomb, W. W. Jr. *The Indians of Texas: From Prehistoric to Modern Times.* Austin, Tex: University of Texas Press, 1961.

Neyland, James. *Palestine (Texas): A History.* Palestine, Tex: Empress Books.

O'Connor, Kathryn Stoner. *Presidio La Bahía 1721–1846.* Austin: Eakin Press, 2001.

Peña, José Enrique de la. *With Santa Anna in Texas. A Personal Narrative of the Revolution.* College Station: Texas A&M University Press, 1975. Reprint, 1999.

Pierce, Gerald Swetnam. *The Army of the Republic of Texas, 1836–1845.* Dissertation from the University of Mississippi, copyright 1964, on file in the Texas Room of the Houston Public Library.

———. *Texas Under Arms. The Camps, Posts, Forts, and Military Towns of the Republic of Texas.* Austin, Tex: Encino Press, 1969.

Pioneer Families of Anderson County Prior to 1900. Palestine, Tex: Anderson County Genealogical Society, 1984.

Plummer, Rachel (Parker). *Narrative of the Capture and Subsequent Sufferings of Mrs. Rachel Plummer.* Houston, Tex: 1839.

Pohl, James W. *The Battle of San Jacinto.* Texas State Historical Association, 1989.

Powell, Mrs. Doris Daniel. *The Genealogy of Hugh Alva Menefee Jr.* Cleburne, Tex: Privately published, 1972.

Procter, Ben H. *The Life of John H. Reagan.* Austin, Tex: The University of Texas Press, 1962.

Purcell, Robert Allen. *The History of the Texas Militia.* Austin: University of Texas Press, 1981.

Ramsay, Jack C. Jr. *Thunder Beyond the Brazos: Mirabeau B. Lamar.* Austin, Tex: Eakin Press, 1985.

Ray, Worth S. *Austin Colony Pioneers. Including History of Bastrop, Fayette, Austin, Grimes, Montgomery and Washington Counties, Texas.* Austin, Tex: Jenkins Publishing Company, 1970.

Reagan, John H. *The Memoirs of John H. Reagan.* Edited by John F. Jenkins. Austin, Tex: The Pemberton Press, 1968.

Reid, Samuel C. *The Scouting Expeditions of McCulloch's Texas Rangers.* Philadelphia: G. B. Zieber and Company, 1847.

Bibliography

Republic of Texas Pension Application Abstracts. Published by the Austin Genealogical Society. Austin, Tex: Morgan Printing and Publishing, 1987.

Richardson, Rupert N. *Texas, The Lone Star State*. New York: Prentice-Hall, 1943.

Richardson, Thomas Clarence. *East Texas: Its History and Its Makers*. New York: Lewis Historical Publishing, 1940.

Roberts, Madge Thornall (Editor). *The Personal Correspondence of Sam Houston. Volume I: 1839–1845*. Denton: University of North Texas Press, 1996.

Robertson, W. G. *The Lone Star State*. Privately published: 1893.

Robinson, Charles M. III. *The Men Who Wear the Star. The Story of the Texas Rangers*. New York: Random House, 2000.

Robinson, Duncan W. *Judge Robert McAlpin Williamson. Texas' Three-Legged Willie*. Austin: Texas State Historical Society, 1948.

Rodríguez, Rodríguez. *Rodríguez Memoirs of Early Texas*. Forgotten Books: 2012.

Roland, Charles P. *Albert Sidney Johnston: Soldier of Three Republics*. Austin: University of Texas Press, 1964.

Rose, Victor M. *The Life and Services of Gen. Ben McCulloch*. Philadelphia: Pictorial Bureau of the Press, 1888. Facsimile reproduction. Austin: The Steck Company.

Santos, Richard G. *Santa Anna's Campaign Against Texas, 1835–1836*. Austin: Texian Press, 1968.

Scott, Zelma. *History of Coryell County*. Austin: Texas State Historical Society, 1965.

Shipman, Daniel. *Frontier Life. 58 Years in Texas*. 1879. Reprint, Pasadena, Texas: The Abbotsford Publishing Co., 1965.

Smither, Harriet (Editor). *The Papers of Mirabeau Buonaparte Lamar*. Austin: Von Boeckmann-Jones Co., 1922.

Smithwick, Noah. *The Evolution of a State/Recollections of Old Texas Days*. Austin: University of Texas Press, 1983.

Sowell, A. J. *Texas Indian Fighters. Early Settlers and Indian Fighters of Southwest Texas*. 1900. Reprint. Austin, Tex: State House Press, 1986.

———. *Rangers and Pioneers of Texas*. 1884. Reprint. Austin, Tex: State House Press, 1991.

Spellman, Charles E. *The Texas House of Representatives: A Pictorial Roster, 1846–1992*.

Spellman, Paul N. *Forgotten Texas Leader: Hugh McLeod and the Texan Santa Fe Expedition*. College Station: Texas A&M University Press, 1999.

Steele, Alfonso. *Biography of Private Alfonso Steele (Deceased). Last Survivor of the Battle of San Jacinto*. Privately published pamphlet, 1909.

Stroud, Harry A. *Conquest of the Prairies*. Waco: Texian Press, 1968.

Swisher, John Milton. Edited by Rena Maverick Green. *The Swisher Memoirs*. San Antonio: Sigmund Press, 1932.

Teja, Jesus F. de la (Editor). *A Revolution Remembered. The?Memoirs and Selected Correspondence of Juan N. Seguin*. Austin, Tex: State House Press, 1991.

Thompson, Karen R. (Editor). *Defenders of the Republic of Texas.* Austin, Tex: Daughters of the Republic of Texas via Laurel House Press, 1989.

Tolbert, Frank X. *The Day of San Jacinto.* New York: McGraw-Hill Book Co., 1959.

Turner, Martha Anne. *The Yellow Rose of Texas. Her Saga and Her Song. With the Santa Anna Legend.* Austin: Shoal Creek Publishers, Inc., 1976.

Tyler, George W. *The History of Bell County.* San Antonio, Tex: The Naylor Company, 1936.

Utley, Robert M. *Lone Star Justice: The First Century of the Texas Rangers.* New York: Oxford University Press, 2002.

Wallace, Ernest, David M. Vigness and George B. Ward. *Documents of Texas History.* Austin, Tex: State House Press, 1994.

Webb, Walter Prescott (Editor-in-Chief). *The Handbook of Texas: A Dictionary of Essential Information* (Three Volumes). Austin: The Texas State Historical Association, 1952.

Webber, C. W. *Tales of the Southern Border.* Philadelphia: J. B. Lippincott & Co., 1856.

———. *The Texas Rangers: A Century of Frontier Defense.* Austin: University of Texas Press, 1991.

White, Gifford. *1830 Citizens of Texas: A Census of 6,500 Pre-Revolutionary Texians.* Austin, Tex: Eakin Press, 1983.

———. *1840 Census of Texas.* Austin, Tex: The Pemberton Press, 1966.

———. *1840 Citizens of Texas Land Grants.* Austin, Tex: 1988.

Wilbarger, John Wesley. *Indian Depredations in Texas.* 1889. Reprint. Austin, Tex: State?House Press, 1985.

Wilkins, Frederick. *The Legend Begins: The Texas Rangers, 1823–1845.* Austin, Tex: State House Press, 1996.

Williams, Amelia W. and Eugene C. Barker. *Writings of Sam Houston.* Austin: The University of Texas Press, 1938–43.

Winchester, Robert Glenn. *James Pickney Henderson: Texas' First Governor.* San Antonio, Tex: The Naylor Company, 1971.

Winfrey, Dorman, and James M. Day. *The Texas Indian Papers, 1825–1843.* Four volumes. Austin, Tex: Austin Printing Co., 1911.

Wooten, Dudley G., ed. *A Comprehensive History of Texas, 1685 to 1897.* 2 vols. Dallas: William G. Scharff, 1898.

Yoakum, Henderson. *History of Texas From its First Settlement in 1685 to its Annexation to the United States in 1846.* Two volumes. New York: Redfield Publishers, 1855. Reprint. Austin, Tex: Steck Company, 1935.

Zuber, William Physick. *My Eighty Years in Texas.* Austin: University of Texas Press, 1971.

INDEX

Acklin, Christopher Black "Kit," 330, 331, 335
Adams, John Quincy, 21
Adams, Thomas Jefferson, 154
Aguirre, Miguel, 199
Alabama, 9, 11, 28, 177, 329
Alabama Indians, 103, 279
Alamo, the, 1, 4, 63, 72–75, 89–94, 99–112, 115–18, 119–33, 143, 189–90, 195, 212, 219, 224–26, 230
Alavez, Francita, 155
Alexander, Amos R., 12–14
Allen, James Lemuel, 116–17
Alley, John, 38
Alley, Thomas, 71
Almonte, Juan Nepomuceno, 116, 176, 180, 183–85, 220, 226, 229
Alsbury, Perry, 208
Amador, Juan, 121
Amat, Augustin, 164
Anadarko Indians, 264–65
Anahuac, Tex., 27–29, 39, 51
Andrade, Juan, 88
Andrews, Micah, 126, 269–70, 301
Andrews, Richard, 50–51, 126
Angelina River, 256
Archer, Branch Tanner, 58, 61, 303
Arenal, Ignacio, 199, 215
Arista, Mariano, 313
Arkansas River, 294
Arnold, Hayden, 212
Arnold, Hendrick, 71, 209
Arrington, William, 67, 76, 95

Augustine, Hugh, 280
Austin, Maria, 22
Austin, Moses, 21–22, 169
Austin, Stephen Fuller, 19, 22, 26–28, 31–32, 38–45, 48–52, 61–65, 149, 160
Austin, Tex., 283, 303, 312, 326, 339
Austin, William T., 64, 71–72
Ayers, Lewis T., 136

Bachiller, Miguel, 186–87
Baker, Moseley, 127–28, 159, 170–71, 175–78, 208–11, 251
Barbier, Gabriel, 20
Barbier, Madame, 20
Barcena, Andrew, 129
Barnett, George Washington, 7, 10, 14–16
Barragán, Marcos, 191–92
Barrera, Mechora Iniega, 106
Barron, Thomas Hudson, 115
Bastrop, Baron de, 22
Bastrop (Mina), Tex., 11–14, 17, 35, 76, 96, 108–9, 143, 232, 243, 267
Bateman, William W., 34
Batres, José, 218
Baugh, John, 118–20
Baylor, John Walker, 154
Baylor, Robert, 339
Bayne, Griffin, 114–15, 231, 235–37
Beason, Benjamin, 148
Becerra, Francisco, 120
Becknell, William, 312

Bee, Barnard, 253
Bee, Hamilton P., 299
Belcher, Isham G., 7
Bell, Josiah, 24
Ben (slave of Almonte), 131
  see also Almonte, Juan
  Nepomuceno
Benavides, Plácido, 41, 72, 111
Bennett, Joseph, 147, 170–71, 206–8,
  250
Bennett, Valentine, 49
Benton, Jesse, 114–15, 231
Bergara, Anselmo, 129
Béxar, Tex., 21, 36–40, 48, 52, 61,
  64–65, 68, 71, 74–75, 84–91,
  95–103, 109, 113–15, 130–31,
  305, 313, 319, 320, 327
Bigfoot, Chief, 314
Big Mush, Chief, 103, 256, 271, 276,
  280
Billingsley, Jesse, 126, 132, 167, 180,
  202–3, 213, 223, 268–69
Biloxi Indians, 103, 256, 269, 279
Bird, John, 132, 159, 272–73, 319
Blair, Samuel, 106
Blakely, Ed, 213
Blue Wing, 312
Bogart, Samuel, 323, 324
Bonham, James Butler, 113, 122
Booker, Fee C., 244
Booker, Shields, 192
Boom, Garrett E., 154
Borden, Gail, Jr., 45, 48, 179
Boren, Joseph, 264
Bostick, Sion, 225
Bourland, James G., 307
Bowie, James, 42–44, 48–51, 60–62,
  65, 68–70, 90–92, 99–100,
  104–7, 112, 116, 122, 126, 276
Bowie, Rezin, 43
Bowie, Ursula Veramendi, 43
Bowles, Chief, 91, 103–4, 256–57,
  263, 271, 275–81
Bowles, John, 277, 282–83
  see also Chief Bowles
Bowyer, John M., 250
Box, James, 260
Bracken, William, 53
Bradburn, John (Juan) Davis,
  27–28

Bradshaw, James, 259, 260
Bravo, Calixto, 306, 307, 314
Brazoria, Tex., 32, 46, 176, 338–39
Brazos River, 9–10, 14, 45–47, 55,
  113, 144, 151–53, 159, 166–75,
  238, 240, 251, 264, 284, 303
Breece, Thomas H., 63, 72
Brenan, William, 172
Bricker, John, 170
Bringas, Juan, 185, 198
Briscoe, Andrew, 29, 48–51, 62, 67,
  142, 199, 210
Brookshire, Nathan, 273
Brown, John Henry, 299
Brown, Robert, 107
Brown, Ruben R., 111
Brown, Squire, 259
Bryan, Elizabeth, 295
Bryan, Moses Austin, 149, 160, 169,
  186–87, 190, 226
Bryant, Benjamin Franklin, 161,
  264–65
Buck, Spy, 276
Buckman, Oliver, 17
Buffalo Hump, Chief, 273, 295–97,
  319
Bull, Pleasant M., 40
Buquor, Pasqual Leo, 305, 306
Burleson, Edward, 12–13, 17, 35, 58,
  62–65, 68, 71, 74–75, 126, 170,
  208, 211–16, 223, 238–40, 251,
  265, 268–71, 275–79, 282–84,
  289, 296–99, 302, 312, 339
Burleson, Jacob, 267–68
Burleson, Susan, 296
Burnam, Jesse, 141
Burnet, David Gouverneur, 142, 166,
  169, 172–73, 176, 179, 183–84,
  229, 237, 263, 275–76, 280,
  305, 338
Burnet, Hannah Este, 183
Burton, Isaac Watts, 67, 76, 95, 143,
  188, 235–39, 259, 266, 275–76

Caddell, John S., 278
Caddo Indians, 12–14, 79, 103,
  232–33, 237–39, 258, 262–64,
  271–72, 279, 307
Cage, Benjamin Franklin, 254, 261
Cage, Robert, 246

Calder, Robert, 153–54, 163, 180, 202, 208–10, 217
Caldwell, Mathew, 95, 269, 283, 291, 297–99
Caldwell, Paint, 320, 321, 322
California, 337
Callahan, James, 314
Calvert, Jeremiah H., 329
Calvert, Susan, 329, 337
Camino Real, 87, 97, 106
Campbell, David, 265
Canales, Antonio, 303, 318
Canalizo, Valentin, 269–70
Canoma, Chief, 12–13
Carey, William, 73, 89, 106
Caro, Ramón, 4, 123, 175, 220, 224–27
Carolin, John, 333, 335
Carpenter, John W., 259
Carrasco, José María, 315
Carson, Samuel P., 142, 176–77, 180
Carter, James, 277–79
Casa Blanca, 41
Castaneda, Francisco, 34–36
Castillo y Iberri, José María, 184
Castner, Isaac, 245
Castrillón, Manuel Fernández, 85, 106, 123, 179, 185, 205, 211, 214–15
Castro, Chief, 252–53, 266, 283
Céspedes, Manuel, 214–15
Chance, Joseph Bell, 144, 188
Chapman, George W., 56
Cherokee Indians, 13–15, 58–60, 91, 103, 114, 257–58, 262–63, 271, 276–84, 307, 312
Chevallie, Mike, 305–8, 314–15, 328–30, 336
Childress, George C., 114
Choctaw Indians, 279
Clapp, Elisha, 241
Clendenin, Adam, 302
Coahuila y Tejas, 6–7, 30, 97
Coe, Philip Haddox, 10–11, 14–17, 126
Coffee's Fort, 303
Coleman, Alexander, 331
Coleman, Caroline, 11
Coleman, Elizabeth Bounds, 11–12, 267

Coleman, Robert Morris, 8, 11–18, 35, 47–49, 67, 125, 178–79, 194–95, 201, 204, 240–45, 252, 267
Coleman's Fort, *see* Fort Houston
Coleto Creek, 134, 137–38, 154, 157
Collinsworth, David M., 52
Collinsworth, George Morse, 37–38, 52, 67
Colorado River, 10–12, 25–26, 47, 58, 95, 127, 140–47, 165, 238–40, 245, 249, 252, 267, 270, 282
Colt, Samuel, 291, 337
Columbus, Tex., 35
Comanche Indians, 24, 79, 108, 232–34, 245, 249, 253–54, 261, 264–68, 272–74, 284–87, 288–301, 304, 308–18, 327, 331–34, 337–39
Condelle, Nicolas, 74
Conner, Henry C., 281
Cooke, William Gordon, 71, 125, 289–90, 302–5
Corpus Christi, Tex., 303
Corry, Thomas, 193, 219
Cos, Martín Perfecto de, 36–38, 41, 49–52, 61–65, 68–70, 73–74, 84–85, 89, 103, 119, 175, 184, 187, 191, 205–6, 209–11, 214, 221, 224, 227
Costley, Michael, 241–42
Coushatta Indians, 103, 279
Cowpens, S.C., 39
Coy, Antonio, 314
Crane, John, 72–73, 278
Creek Indians, 15, 59, 78, 92
Crockett, Davy, 92–94, 99, 102, 106–7, 112, 115–17, 121–23
Crosby, Nancy Darst, 295
Cruz, Antonio, 107, 127
Cummings, Rebecca, 28
Cummins, Moses, 13
Curtis, Jim, 218
Córdova, Vicente, 255–57, 268–71, 320

Daniels, Williamson, 133
Darst, Jacob, 295
Davis, Alligator, 328

Davis, George Washington, 34, 58, 231
Dawson, Nicholas Mosby, 248–49, 300, 320
Day, James Milford, 269
Delaware Indians, 103, 276, 279
Delgado, Pedro, 175, 185, 191, 199, 202, 205, 217, 228
Denham, Lieutenant, 218
Denton, John B., 307, 308
Despallier, Charles, 107
DeWitt, Green, 33
DeWitt, Naomi, 35
Dick (former New Orleans slave), 204
Dickinson, Almeron, 34, 71, 106–8, 115, 122, 132
Dickinson, Angelina, 115–17, 122–24, 131
Dickinson, Susannah, 115–17, 122–24, 131
Dimitt, Philip, 38, 51–52, 89, 99
Dixon, Joe, 218
Donoho, Charles, 173, 177
Douglass, Kelsey H., 251, 256, 277–82
Díaz, Martias, 305
Dunn, James, 314–17, 335
Dunnington, William, 290
Duque, Francisco, 88, 119–21
Durán, Guadalupe Ruiz, 64
Durst, James H., 262
Durst, John, 256
Duval, Burr H., 104, 138
Duval, John C., 156
Dyer, John H., 251, 262

Eastland, William, 250, 252, 266
Edens, John, 260
Edwards, Haden Harrison, 72
Egg, Chief, 283
Eggleston, Horace, 132
Ehrenberg, Herman, 75
Ellison, James, 315
English, John, 71–73
Erath, George Bernard, 5–10, 13–17, 167, 189, 192, 198, 203, 208–9, 213, 223–24, 240, 243–45
Erath, Jacob, 9, 15
Erskine, Andrew, 333

Essomanny, Chief, 253
Essowakkenny, Chief, 253, 254
Evan, William G., 272
Ewing, Alexander Wray, 162, 221, 228

Falls of the Brazos, 12–13, 56, 79, 94, 284
Fannin, James, Sr., 48–51
Fannin, James Walker, 48, 65, 90–91, 102–4, 107, 110–13, 116, 129, 134–41, 150–51, 154, 157, 167
Fannin, Minerva Fort, 48
Faulkenberry, David, 56, 95
Fentress, James, 269
Fields, Fox, 277
Filisola, Vicente, 85, 117, 128, 146, 164, 175–76, 187, 214, 227, 255, 269
Fisher, William S., 153, 247, 265, 289–92, 324
Fitzgerald, Archibald, 314
Flaco, Chief, 253, 266, 308–10
Flores, Manuel, 216, 268–71
Flores, Martin, 147
Flores, Salvador, 41, 127, 308
Floyd, Dolphin, 108
Fohr, Peter, 334
Foley, Tucker, 294
Forbes, John, 93, 103–4, 152–53, 193, 219, 226
Fort Bend, 166–67, 171–76, 272
Fort Colorado, *see* Fort Houston
Fort Defiance, 110, 134–37, 140, 154–57
Fort Duty, 259
Fort Fisher, 250
Fort Gibson, 234
Fort Houston, 78, 143, 147, 234–35, 240–44, 252, 257–60
Fort Jesup, 177
Fort Lipantitlán, 51–54, 111, 318
Fort Milam, 79, 250
Fort Parker, 7–8, 10–11, 14, 46–47, 55–57, 76–77, 231–34, 238, 258, 285
Fort St. Louis, 20
Fort Smith, 250, 272–74
Fort Sterling, *see* Fort Parker

Fort Velasco, 175
Fort Viesca, *see* Fort Milam
France, 19–21
Franklin, Benjamin Cromwell, 194
Franks, Louis B., 71, 94–95, 143, 274
Frazier, Stephen, 57
Friar, Daniel Boone, 47, 56, 67, 79, 95, 231, 304, 314
Frio River, 274, 308–9
Frost, Robert B., 232
Frost, Samuel, 14, 232
Fuqua, Galba, 109, 122

Gaines, Edmund Pendleton, 177
Galveston, Tex., 169, 178–79, 227–29, 236, 265, 337–38
Gaona, Antonio, 88, 106, 128, 164, 175, 227
Garay, Francisco, 155
García, Ignacio, 305, 306
García, Marcellino, 53
Garner, John T., 163–64
Garrett, Jacob, 47
Garza, Felix de la, 73
Garza, Padre, 62
Gaston, Johnnie, 109
Gholson, Albert, 265
Gibson, Arch, 322
Gillaspie, James, 188
Gillespie, Ad, 333–34
Goheen, Michael R., 10, 17, 49
Goliad, Tex., 1, 4, 21, 24, 37–38, 51–54, 70, 84, 90, 97, 102–4, 107–9, 117, 128–30, 134–37, 140–41, 150–51, 154–55, 158, 164, 167, 189, 212, 224–26, 314
Gonzales, José María, 285–86
Gonzales, Tex., 33–40, 58, 63, 70, 76, 84, 95, 101–2, 107–9, 124–29, 135, 141, 186, 243, 294
González, Eulogio, 128
Grant, James, 71, 74, 89–91, 104, 111
Great Britain, 1
Green, Thomas Jefferson, 325
Greenwood, Garrison, 47, 77–79, 231
Groce, Jared Ellison, 159, 169
Groce, Leonard, 162, 173

Groce's Landing, Tex., 159–61, 167, 170
Guadalajara, Mexico, 215
Guadalupe River, 33–36, 130–32, 158, 235, 240, 261, 269, 292, 316–17, 327
Guerrero, Mexico, 85, 88, 324

Haddin, William, 156, 167
Haggard, Howell, 232
Haggard, Squire, 241–42
Halderman, Jesse, 14
Hall, James, 260
Hall, Robert, 297
Hamilton, Isaac D., 156
Handy, Robert Eden, 130–31, 145
Harbert, Nat, 306, 314
Hardaway, Samuel, 224
Hardeman, Bailey, 142
Hardeman, Thomas Monroe, 296
Hardin, Ennes, 56, 67
Harris, Ben, 124
Harris, Chief, 277
Harrisburg, Tex., 169–73, 176–81, 184–89, 231
Harrison, William Henry, 146
Hart, William, 278, 281
Harvey, John, 299
Hassell, John, 214–16
Hays, Elizabeth Cage, 254
Hays, Jack, 246–49, 252–54, 261, 274–75, 285–87, 292, 298–99, 304–37, 340
Hays, John Coffee, 246, 303, 337
Hazen, Nat, 172
Head, James A., 77
Heard, William, 181, 202
Hemphill, John, 291
Henderson, James Pinckney, 339
Henderson, William Fenner, 258
Herrera, Captain, 121
Highsmith, Ben, 134
Hill, Isaac, 170
Hill, William Warner, 7, 126, 238–39, 340
Hillhouse, Eli, 55–56, 77
Hockley, George, 125, 145, 160–63, 178, 181, 198, 201, 210, 226, 229, 253
Holland, Benjamin, 156

Holland, Tapley, 116
Holsinger, Juan José, 136
Hood, Joseph L., 47, 261
Hornsby, Moses Smith, 17
Hornsby, Reuben, 232
Horseshoe Bend, 59, 146, 159
Horton, Albert C., 136–40, 154
Horton, Alexander, 125
Houston, Andy, 239
Houston, Diana Roger Gentry, 60
Houston, Sam, 2, 58–61, 65, 68,
  78, 89–94, 103–4, 107, 114–15,
  125, 129–34, 140–54, 158–82,
  185–213, 216–17, 220–21,
  224–28, 235, 238, 240–48,
  251–53, 256–57, 262–63,
  280–81, 312, 316–18, 323,
  326–30, 338–40
Houston, Tex., 47, 78, 254, 265,
  318
Howard, George T., 278, 284,
  290–92, 328
Huerta, Carolino, 157
Hunter, Robert Hancock, 68–70,
  163, 182
Hunter, William L., 157
Huntsman, Adam, 92
Huntsville, Tex., 338
Huston, Felix, 249, 298–300

Ioni Indians, 14, 103, 256, 258, 264,
  279
Indians, 7–12, 18–19, 43, 339; *see
  also specific tribal groups*
Isomania, Chief, 287, 292

Jack, Patrick, 27–28
Jack, William H., 68–70
Jackson, Andrew, 59–60, 92,
  146–48, 159, 229, 246, 263
Jameson, Benjamin, 89, 98, 105,
  115
Jaques, Mrs. William B., 328
Jarvis, Pen, 50
Jenkins, John, 129–33, 298
Jett, James Matthew "Matt," 304,
  313–14, 327, 330
Jett, Stephen, 304, 314, 320, 327
Jett, William, 327, 330
Jewell, George Washington, 241–42

Joe (slave of Travis), 98, 120,
  124–25, 131
  see also Travis, William Barret
Johnson, Frank, 28–29, 64, 70, 73,
  89–90, 104, 110–11
Johnson, John B., 102, 109
Johnston, Albert Sidney, 243,
  248–49, 253, 271, 275–77,
  280–82, 289
Jones, Anson, 61, 151, 162, 174, 312,
  335, 338–40
Jones, David, 172
Jones, William Jefferson, 264, 270
José María, Chief, 264–65, 284

Karankawa Indians, 20, 23–26
Karnes, Henry, 50, 68, 73, 130–32,
  141, 144–47, 186–87, 192,
  199–201, 205–7, 210, 219, 224,
  243, 246, 249–54, 264, 268–70,
  274–75, 284–89, 293, 303–4
Kellogg, Elizabeth, 234
Kemp, Thomas, 172
Kent, Andrew, 108
Kent, David Boyd, 134
Kentucky, 11, 93, 127, 148, 172, 202,
  212, 222
Kerr, James, 52, 67
Kerr, Peter, 151
Key, Chief, 276
Kichai Indians, *see* Caddo Indians
Kickapoo Indians, 56–57, 103,
  258–60, 271–72, 279
Killough, Isaac, 257
Kimbell, George C., 108–9, 112, 132
Kimbro, William, 161, 181
King, Amon B., 135
Kiowa Indians, 294, 331
Kuykendall, Robert, 25–27

Labadie, Nicholas, 161, 172, 193,
  200, 218–19
La Bahía del Espiritu Santo, *see*
  Goliad, Tex.
Lafitte, Jean, 42
La Grange, Tex., 10–13, 266
Lamar, Mirabeau Buonaparte, 2, 78,
  174, 199–202, 210, 228, 257,
  262–68, 271, 274–75, 280–84,
  289, 302, 308, 312, 338

Lampasas River, 283
Landrum, Willis, 275, 277
Lane, Walter, 200–201, 218, 258
Laredo, Mexico, 85–86, 90, 247,
    304–5, 323–24
La Salle, René-Robert Cavelier, Sieur
    de, 20
Leclerc, Frédéric, 254
Lee, James, 333
Lemsky, Frederick, 147
Leon River, 57
Lewellen, Captain, 73
Lewis, Mark B., 270, 275
Linn, John, 52
Linney, Chief, 261, 276
Lipan Indians, 252, 253, 308–10
Little River, 56, 240, 244, 250, 272
Llano River, 287, 309, 330
Lockhart, Andy, 327
Lockhart, Byrd, 95, 108, 289
Lockhart, John W., 330
Lockhart, Matilda, 261, 289–90, 327
Logan, William, 160
Lonis, George Washington, 216
Louisiana, 20–22, 42–43, 87, 153,
    176–77, 243, 262
Luckie, Sam, 321, 327
Luelmo, Santiago, 204
Lynch, Joseph P., 126
Lynch's Ferry, 187, 191–94

Mabbitt, Leonard, 257
McAllister, John, 159
McCarley, Samuel, 180
McCormick, Arthur, 192
McCormick, Margaret ("Peggy"),
    191–92, 204, 211, 227–28
McCoy, Jesse, 33–34, 108
McCulloch, Ben, 294–96, 321,
    328–31, 334–36, 340
McCulloch, Henry, 297–99, 321
McCulloch, Samuel, 37
McDonald, John, 313
McDonald, William, 72
McFall, Samuel, 12, 15–16
McGregor, John, 112
McLean, Ephraim Walton, 316
McLeod, Hugh, 252, 256–61, 275,
    280–82, 289–91
McNutt, Robert, 127, 188–89

Magill, William, 17
Mann, Pamelia, 181–82
Mare, Achelle, 213
Marlin, John, 13, 264
Martin, Albert, 34–35, 105, 108–9,
    112
Martin, Wyly, 146, 159, 166, 173,
    177–78
Matagorda, Tex., 37–39, 46
Matamoros, Mexico, 44, 75, 89–90,
    94–95, 111, 155, 176, 255,
    268–70
Mataquo Indians, 279
Mathews, William A., 95
Maverick, Mary Ann, 275, 289, 308
Maverick, Samuel, 62, 70–71
Mayfield, James S., 275–77, 322
Medina River, 97, 247, 254, 274,
    321–23, 328
Memphis, Tenn., 92–93
Menard, Peter J., 47
Menchaca, José Antonio "Tony,"
    126–27, 150, 187–90, 319
Menefee, Laban, 285
Mercer, Eli, 181
Mexico, 1, 6, 19, 22, 30–31
    see also specific cities
Mexico City, 20–22, 84–87, 325,
    338
Mier y Terán, Manuel de, 27
Milam, Benjamin Rush, 37, 40,
    70–74, 79
Milam, Tex., 95, 114, 243
Miles, Alfred H., 251
Miles, Ed, 213
Millard, Henry, 170, 206, 216
Millen, Bill, 221
Miller, Joseph, 308
Miller, Thomas R., 109
Miller, Washington, 296
Mina (Bastrop), Tex., 11–14, 17, 35,
    76, 96, 108–9, 143, 232, 243,
    267
Miracle, Julian Pedro, 255–57
Mission Aguayo, 49
Mission Capistrano, 49
Mission Concepción, 49, 63, 316
Mission Espada, 48–49
Mission River, 135
Mission Rosario, 135

Mission San José y San Miguel de
Aguayo, 292
Mississippi, 20, 37, 177, 246
Mississippi River, 20, 42, 93, 162,
263
Miñon, José Vicente, 101, 106
Monclova, Mexico, 87, 96
Monroe, Daniel, 250
Monterrey, Mexico, 336
Moore, John Henry, 10, 12–17,
35–36, 126, 142–44, 266, 284,
300, 322
Moore, Thomas, 214
Moore, William H., 266
Moore's Fort, 10–12
Morales, Juan, 119–21, 128
Moreland, Isaac, 160, 196–97, 200,
338
Morgan, Abel, 155
Morgan, George, 264
Morgan, James, 183–85, 195, 211,
227
Morgan's Point, 183–85
Morrell, Zachariah, 322
Morris, Robert, 70–71
Morrison, Moses, 25–26
Mottley, Junius William, 212–13
Muestyah, Chief, 254
Muguara, Chief, 254, 290–92
Murchison, John, 260
Murphree, David, 145, 216
Murphy, Daniel, 157–58, 172

Nacogdoches, Tex., 20–21, 28,
43–46, 57, 78, 93, 178, 181, 189,
234, 237, 247, 255–56, 260–62,
276
Nacogdoches Indians, 20, 27
Napoleon, Bonaparte, 21
Nash, James, 215
Natchitoches, La., 177
Navarro, José Antonio, 114
Navarro de Alsbury, Juana, 124
Navasota River, 8, 15
Navidad River, 141, 145
Neches River, 47, 77, 259, 277–81
Neill, James Clinton, 15, 35, 72,
89–92, 99, 128–30, 177,
196–98
Neill, John C., 284–85

New Orleans, La., 9, 22, 75, 153,
228, 247
New Washington, Tex., 68, 179–80,
183–85, 191–92, 211
New York, 338
Nichols, Jim, 297–98, 316–18
Nixon, Sarah Parker, 232
Nueces River, 52–53, 239, 243, 263,
270, 303–4, 314, 327, 335

Ogden, Duncan Campbell, 314
Oklahoma, 303
Oolooteka, Chief, 59–60
O'Riley, James, 53
Owen, Clark L., 296
Ownby, James P., 270, 275

Panther, Captain, 262
Parker, Ben, 232–35
Parker, Cynthia Ann, 8, 234
Parker, Daniel, Jr., 78
Parker, Daniel, Sr., 45–47, 235
Parker, Dickerson, 78
Parker, Isaac, 235
Parker, James, Sr., 7
Parker, James Wilson, Jr., 8, 46–47,
55–57, 77, 231–35
Parker, John, Jr., 234
Parker, John, Sr., 8, 233
Parker, Joseph Allen, 56, 76–77, 95
Parker, Lucy, 234
Parker, Orlena, 8
Parker, Sally White, 233
Parker, Silas, Sr., 7, 14
Parker, Silas Mercer, Jr., 8, 47–48,
55–57, 67, 76–79, 231–35
Parker's Fort, *see* Fort Parker
Parmer, Martin, 46
Patton, William H., 71, 93, 147
Peacock, John W., 72–74
Pedernales River, 286, 310, 330–31
Peggy's Lake, 194, 198, 217–19
Perry, Cicero Rufus, 239
Perry, Daniel, 68
Perry, James Franklin, 64–65
Perry, James Hazard, 151, 171
Perry, Rufe, 327, 330, 335–36
Petty, George M., 143–44
Peña, José Enrique de la, 88, 96–97,
116–17, 121–23, 176

Pérez, Antonio, 303–9
Pia Kusa, Chief, 319
Piava, Chief, 292–93
Piedras, José de las, 28
Placido, Chief, 253, 283, 297
Plummer, James Pratt, 233–34
Plummer, Luther Thomas Martin, 7
Plummer, Rachel Parker, 233–34
Poe, George, 196–97
Ponton, Andrew, 34, 101
Ponton, Joel, 294
Porter, John W., 9–10
Portilla, José Nicolás de la, 155–58
Potsanaquahip, Chief, *see* Buffalo
   Hump, Chief
Potter, Robert, 125, 142, 166,
   171–72
Powell, Elizabeth, 171
Power, James, 52
Price, John T., 303–4
Putman, Elizabeth, 261, 292–93
Putman, James, 261
Putman, Juda, 261
Putman, Rhoda, 261

Quanah Parker, Chief, 234
Quapaw Indians, 103, 279
Quinoñes, Agatón, 305, 327–28

Rabb, Thomas J., 127, 300
Ramírez y Sesma, Joaquín, 85–88,
   97, 101, 116, 122, 128, 141,
   145–48, 169–71, 175
Reagan, John Henninger, 271, 281
Redd, William, 292
Red River, 93, 231, 251, 257,
   262–63, 275, 302, 305
Refugio, Tex., 52, 91, 104, 135–36,
   235, 314, 329
Reyes, Juan, 208, 214
Reynolds, Dave, 269
Rice, Christopher Columbus, 162
Rice, James, 270
Riley, James, 79
Riley, Thomas, 79
Rio Grande River, 20, 74, 85, 88, 90,
   97–99, 239, 303, 306–7, 314–15,
   322–24, 335
Robbins, Jack, 220
Robbins, Thomas, 188

Roberts, Abraham, 178
Robertson, Joseph, 267
Robertson, Sterling, 11, 55, 114,
   235–37, 242–44
Robertson's Colony, 7, 10, 14, 56, 76,
   79, 94, 115, 143, 188
Robinett, James W., 273
Robinson, Andrew, 25
Robinson, James W., 58, 90, 94–95,
   110
Robison, Joel, 225
Robless, Alexander, 244
Rodden, Peter, 279
Rodriguez, Don Nicolás, 52–54
Rogers, James, 267–68
Rogers, John, 60
Rohrer, Conrad, 180–82
Roman, Richard, 153, 163
Romero, José María, 119
Rose, Louis, 116
Ross, John E., 161, 173, 176
Royall, Richardson, 46
Ruiz, Francisco, 114
Rusk, Thomas Jefferson, 142, 150,
   160, 166–70, 173–74, 180–81,
   190–92, 199–201, 210–13, 221,
   226–28, 235–38, 251, 255–61,
   275–79, 339

Sabine River, 76, 143, 177, 251
Sadler, William Turner, 78, 143, 147,
   188, 215, 225, 241, 259–61,
   266, 281, 339
Salado River, 124–25, 315, 327
Saltillo, Mexico, 86–88, 325
San Antonio, Tex., 1, 22–26, 37–40,
   44, 48, 63–65, 68, 73–74,
   89–91, 94, 98, 109, 112–13,
   124, 143, 164, 239, 243, 247–49,
   253–54, 270, 274–75, 285–92,
   303–20, 323–26, 329–30,
   334–35
San Antonio de Béxar, *see* Béxar,
   Tex.
San Antonio River, 20, 24, 49,
   110, 137, 156, 246, 286, 293,
   315
San Augustine, Tex., 93, 237,
   256
San Bernard River, 147, 154, 171

San Felipe, Tex., 12, 28–29, 35, 45, 52, 57–58, 61–62, 76–79, 89–90, 94, 108–9, 128, 132, 159, 164–66, 227

San Gabriel River, 67, 79, 238, 266, 270, 283

San Jacinto, Tex., 204, 217, 222–24, 227–31, 238–41, 248, 251, 264, 277, 280, 313, 316, 337–40

San Jacinto River, 4, 142, 191, 194

San Luis, Mexico, 85, 106

San Luis Potosí, 38

San Marcos River, 58, 302

San Patricio, Tex., 52–54, 104, 111, 243

San Saba River, 43, 266, 286

Santa Anna, Antonio López de, 1–4, 30–31, 36, 41, 44, 48, 75, 84–88, 97, 101, 105–8, 113, 117–20, 123–26, 141, 155, 158, 164–65, 169–71, 175, 179, 184–87, 191–207, 211, 214–17, 220, 224–31, 235, 251, 277, 319, 325, 338

Santa Cruz, Bernardino, 218

Sánchez-Navarro, José Juan, 73–74, 123

Scales, Abraham, 163

Scott, Winfield, 66

Scurry, Richardson A., 125

Seale, Eli, 77

Secrest, Washington, 145

Seguín, Erasmo, 41

Seguín, Juan Nepomuceno, 2, 41, 49–51, 63, 75, 99, 107, 126–28, 187–88, 209, 215, 243, 247, 274, 308, 316

Seguin, Tex., 329

Seguín María Gertrudis Flores de Abrego, 307–8

Seminole Indians, 15, 78

Sewell, Marcus, 108

Shackelford, Jack, 137, 154

Shain, Charles, 138–40, 155–58, 172, 216

Sharp, John, 145

Shawnee Indians, 103, 261–62, 271, 276, 279–80, 284, 312

Shelby, Tex., 243

Sherman, Sidney, 2–3, 127, 130, 146–54, 170, 174, 180, 187–92, 197–202, 206, 208–12, 215, 220–21, 228, 337

Shipman, Daniel, 152

Shoshone Indians, 331

Simmons, William, 223

Simpson, Bill, 170

Slein, John, 308–9

Smith, Benjamin Fort, 38, 148, 151, 172

Smith, Bob, 281

Smith, Erastus "Deaf," 2, 63–64, 68, 71–72, 130–31, 141, 145–47, 160–61, 186, 199, 205–9, 213, 215, 219–20, 227, 243, 246–48, 304

Smith, Gertrudes, 130

Smith, Henry, 58, 89–91, 94, 99, 103, 142–44

Smith, James, 241

Smith, John W., 71, 100–102, 109, 112

Smith, Leander, 162, 169, 173

Smith, Lupe, 130, 248

Smith, Mack, 172

Smith, Simona, 130

Smith, Susan, 130

Smith, Travis, 130

Smith, William H., 128–29, 141, 186, 199, 207, 210, 243–45, 249

Smith, William P., 35

Smither, Launcelot, 35, 63, 101, 107–8

Smithwick, Noah, 39, 50–51, 244–45, 252, 266–67

Smothers, John, 299

Snively, Jacob, 259–60, 266

Somervell, Alexander, 170, 190, 323–24

Sowell, Andrew, 39, 132

Spain, 6, 19–22, 30

Sparks, Stephen Franklin, 1–3, 212, 225

Splane, Peyton R., 141

Spohn, Joseph H., 157

Stafford, William, 179

Stevenson, Robert, 216

Stroud, Ethan A., 265

Sublett, Philip, 64–65
Sutherland, George, 52
Sutherland, John, 100–102
Swearingen, William, 187, 218
Swisher, James G., 72, 131
Swisher, John, 152, 163, 168
Sylvester, James, 224–25

Tahocullake Indians, 103, 279
Tallapoosa River, 59
Tampico, Mexico, 30, 36
Tarlton, James, 125, 152
Tarrant, Edward H., 262, 307, 314
Tawakoni Indians, 14, 23, 26, 47, 258
Taylor, Creed, 50
Taylor, Joseph, 56–57
Taylor, Nancy, 57
Taylor, William, 219
Teal, Henry, 147, 170
Tenaha, Tex., 46
Tennessee, 7, 59–60, 78, 92–94, 102, 144, 169, 177, 241, 246
Tenorio, Antonio, 29
Tenoxtitlan, 9–10
Thomas, Alexander, 9
Thomas, David, 142, 173, 178
Thompson, William, 141
Tinsley, James W., 243
Tipp, Peter, 278
Tolsa, Eugenio, 88, 128, 141, 151
Toluca, Mexico, 215
Tonkawa Indians, 23, 253, 266, 307–8
Townsend, Stephen, 95–96, 143, 147, 188
Trask, Olwyn, 200–202
Travis, William Barret, 27–29, 39, 51, 62, 91, 98–120, 226
Trespalacios, José Félix, 24–25
Trimble, Robert C., 252
Trinity River, 15–17, 47, 55, 77–78, 178, 235, 241–42, 251, 268, 285, 302
Trueheart, John, 309
Tumlinson, John, Sr., 24–26
Tumlinson, John Jackson, Jr., 26, 67, 76, 95, 108, 143, 188, 218, 231, 284, 294–96
Tumlinson, Joseph, 26

Turner, Amasa, 153, 163, 170, 181, 199, 206, 210, 221

Ugartechea, Domingo de, 34, 50, 68, 70, 73
Untanguous Indians, 103
Urban, Joseph, 46
Urrea, José, 97, 110–11, 128, 135, 138–41, 155, 176, 227
Urriza, Fernando, 196–99
Usher, Patrick, 190
Utley, Thomas C., 198

Vanbenthuysen, A. B., 250, 251
Vansickle, Elias, 257
Vásquez, Rafael, 303, 314–16
Vázquez de Coronado, Francisco, 19
Velasco, Tex., 9, 28, 49, 140, 153, 236, 244
Veracruz, Mexico, 30–31
Veramendi, Don Juan Martín de, 43
Victoria, Tex., 130, 134, 138–40, 164, 295, 314
Viesca, Tex., 14, 46, 56
Villaneuva, Andrea Castañón, 121
Villareal, Enrique, 303
Vince, William, 184
Violet, John, 258

Waco Indians, 16–17, 23, 26, 47, 258
Walker, Samuel Hamilton, 330, 333–37
Wallace, Joseph Washington Elliott, 35
Wallace, William Alexander Anderson, 314, 319, 325
Walters, Baley, 271, 275
Ward, Thomas W., 71
Ward, William, 135, 140
Ware, William, 146
Warnell, Henry, 124
Washington, D.C., 229
Washington, George, 100
Washington, Tex., 14, 35, 114–15, 160, 329
Webber, Charles Wilkins, 274
Webster, Booker, 293
Wells, Lysander, 199–201, 206, 243, 253, 291
West, Emily D., 185–86, 211, 338

Westover, Ira J., 52–54
Wharton, John Austin, 66, 151, 209, 218, 221
Wharton, William Harris, 58
Wheelock, E. L. Ripley, 231
Wichita Indians, 327
Wilkinson, Curtis A., 56
Williams, Ezekiel, 35
Williams, John, 157–58, 232
Williams, Samuel May, 154, 158
Williamson, Robert Mcalpin (Three-Legged Willie), 10–11, 14, 17, 28–29, 67, 76–79, 95–96, 108, 143–44, 181, 188, 231, 340
Wilson, James, 152
Wilson, William C., 114, 231
Wilson, William F., 285
Winkler, William, 272
Winters, James, 218, 225
Wolfenberger, Samuel, 245
Woll, Adrian, 319–23

Wood, William, 209, 212
Woodlief, Devereaux Jerome, 200, 264, 271, 275–77
Wren, Nicholas, 249
Wright, Felix G., 161
Wright, Norris, 42

Yegua River, 239
Yellow Wolf, Chief, 316, 317, 331, 332, 333, 334, 337
York, John, 71–73, 160
Young, John, 314
Ysleta Mission, 19–20
Yucatán, Mexico, 30

Zacatecas, Mexico, 30–31, 84–85
Zavala, Lorenzo de, 142, 174–76, 179, 185–87, 202, 224, 227
Zuber, William Physick, 147, 151, 188
Zumwalt, Adam, 33, 294–96